Race, Ideology, and the Decline of Caribbean Marxism

UNIVERSITY PRESS OF FLORIDA

Florida A&M University, Tallahassee
Florida Atlantic University, Boca Raton
Florida Gulf Coast University, Ft. Myers
Florida International University, Miami
Florida State University, Tallahassee
New College of Florida, Sarasota
University of Central Florida, Orlando
University of Florida, Gainesville
University of North Florida, Jacksonville
University of South Florida, Tampa
University of West Florida, Pensacola

Race, Ideology, and the Decline of Caribbean Marxism

Anthony P. Maingot

University Press of Florida

Gainesville / Tallahassee / Tampa / Boca Raton

Pensacola / Orlando / Miami / Jacksonville / Ft. Myers / Sarasota

LIBRARY OF CONGRESS CATALOGING-IN-PUBLICATION DATA

Maingot, Anthony P., author.

Race, ideology, and the decline of Caribbean Marxism / Anthony P. Maingot.

pages cm

Includes bibliographical references and index.

ISBN 978-0-8130-6106-1

1. Philosophy, Marxist—Caribbean Area. 2. Communism—Caribbean Area.
3. Socialism—Caribbean Area. 4. Race relations. 5. Blacks—Caribbean Area—
History. 6. Caribbean Area—Race relations. 7. Caribbean Area—Social conditions.
8. Caribbean Area—History. I. Title.

HX151.A6M35 2015

335.43'4—dc23   2015013774

The University Press of Florida is the scholarly publishing agency for the State
University System of Florida, comprising Florida A&M University, Florida Atlantic
University, Florida Gulf Coast University, Florida International University, Florida
State University, New College of Florida, University of
Central Florida, University of Florida, University of North Florida, University
of South Florida, and University of West Florida.

UNIVERSITY PRESS OF FLORIDA

15 Northwest 15th Street
Gainesville, FL 32611-2079
http://www.upf.com

To Consuelo, my eternal Bidi

Contents

Illustrations

Figures

Maps

Tables

Acknowledgments

It was impossible for me not to have a life-long interest in studying the Caribbean. My birth in Trinidad to a French Creole father and Costa Rican mother, studies in Trinidad and Costa Rica, and high school in Curaçao, introduced me to most of the languages and cultures of the region. At the University of Florida (Gainesville) I was fortunate to have Raymond Crist lecture on the region and Lyle McAlister emphasize the necessity of an interdisciplinary approach to area studies. At the Institute of Caribbean Studies of the University of Puerto Rico, I was enriched by the lectures of Gordon K. Lewis, Harry Hoetink, and Thomas Mathews. At Yale University Richard McGee Morse and Wendell Bell were more than mentors, they were good and constructive colleagues.

In Trinidad once again, I was honored by Prime Minister Eric Williams' invitation to serve on the Constitution Reform Commission. For three years I absorbed extraordinary wisdom and knowledge on comparative politics and the role of constitutions in democracies from two of the best, Sir Hugh Wooding and Chief Justice Telford Georges. Also on the Commission was Dr. Selwyn Ryan, prolific scholar and true friend during difficult political times. At the Institute of International Relations I had, as director, Leslie Manigat whose knowledge of Haitian and Caribbean politics was unparalleled. There, I also benefitted from the intellectual companionship of Anthony (Peter) Gonzales, David Nicholls, and Henry Gill whose premature passing left a big gap in the West Indian understanding of Latin America.

Finally, for the thirty-five years preceding my retirement in 2004, I shared the excitement of contributing to the birth and development of Florida International University in Miami. My collegial relationships with James A. Mau, Ralph Clem, Mark B. Rosenberg, John Stack, and Lisandro Pérez made the task all the more pleasurable and rewarding.

This book owes much to all my travels and all my professors and colleagues over these years. I can only hope that I have lived up to their teachings and love of the Caribbean.

Prologue

The Modern-Conservative Society Framework

My 1982 inaugural address as president of the Caribbean Studies Association cost me the friendship of a number of my academic associates and left me with a reputation of being a "conservative," perhaps even one of those despised "reactionaries."[1] I understand even better now what Robert Nisbet said decades ago: in the social sciences, to be labeled a conservative is "more often to be damned than to be praised."[2] This was a time when most Caribbean intellectuals were what Edward Shils called "radical progressives," people who discard the received past in favor of the "here and now." "Change," said Shils, "has become coterminous with progress, innovation with improvement."[3] I quickly learned that one of the major impediments to the objective study of tradition and conservatism is precisely the fear of being "labeled" a reactionary.

But my theoretical argument on that occasion was not ideological. I was not confessing to being a conservative, much less asking my colleagues to become "conservatives" or, God forbid, "reactionaries." I was arguing in favor of doing what most classical sociologists had done: study traditional (conservative) society in order to understand better how modernity was changing it and in turn, how tradition was affecting modernity. In other words, I was asking them to read their Edmund Burke along with their Karl Marx and their Alexis Tocqueville along with their Vladimir Lenin. I was trying to convince them that Karl Mannheim (the father of the sociology of knowledge) was correct when he argued that patterns of conservative thought, far from becoming superfluous through modernization, tend to survive and adapt themselves to each state of social development and continue to have real social bases. As such, conservative thought is functional and useful as a guide to social action.[4] Understanding this helps us understand that, as Robert Nisbet argues, there is a paradox in sociology which calls for as broad and flexible a conceptual framework as possible. That paradox, he explains, results from the fact that while classical sociological theory is squarely in the "mainstream of modernism," its essential concepts and implicit perspectives "place it much closer, generally speaking, to philosophical conservatism."[5]

Family, authority, tradition, the sacred, all components of Gemeinschaft or community, are primary conservative preoccupations and also the central concerns of the classics, Durkheim, Weber, Tönnies, and Simmel. They were all concerned in one fashion or another with analyzing what secular or liberal or modern trends were doing to communities everywhere. Whether we use the term *liberal* or *modern, traditional* or *conservative*, there can be no excuse for not studying that paradoxical ongoing interaction between the conservative and the modern in social change. If, as John Stuart Mill advises, the best way to understand the soundness of an argument is to present a counterargument, this book is my counterargument to decades of studies describing Caribbean societies as somehow radical and even revolutionary in ideological orientation.

This is made all the more necessary because of an evident incongruity in the reaction of so many of my colleagues: the fact that by 1982 it was already clear that so much of what was being discarded or ignored about the past had proven to work relatively well, and so many of the new social experiments were sputtering and in some cases even regressing. There was the case of Cuba, heroic and under siege by the United States for sure, but hardly a successful model that could or indeed should be replicated. There was Suriname under the thuggish regime of Desi Bouterse, Guyana regressing under the corrupt regime of Forbes Burnham, the Grenada revolution already showing the schisms so typical of Marxist-Leninist parties, and sadly there was the collapse of Michael Manley's democratic socialist program in Jamaica. Above and beyond all this were the Caribbean people who—when given the freedom—were voting at the ballot box or voting with their feet heading north and telling multiple pollsters just how dissatisfied they were with many such "progressive" experiments.

In other words, much of the Caribbean was adopting a posture Michael Oakeshott termed "skeptical conservatism," a peculiar mixture of political conservatism and radical individualism and skepticism. Oakeshott would have understood what was occurring in the region because he believed that one of the characteristics of the conservative disposition or temperament is an understanding that not all innovations are improvements and that to innovate without improving is indeed folly. To Oakeshott's assertion that the innovations which will receive freely given support, and thus have a chance of succeeding, will be those which do the least harm to valued traditions. The skeptical conservative, he said, "will be suspicious of proposals for change in excess of what the situation calls for, or rulers who demand extraordinary powers in order to make great changes and whose utterances are tied to generalities like 'the public good' or 'social justice.'"[6] In 1982, and even more so three decades later, Oakeshott's rationalism and clarity of thought ring true. This study aims to document the contemporary relevance and plausibility of his thinking by unraveling the conservative foundations of many Caribbean historians and thinkers regarding race, ideology, geopolitics, and social movements in the region.

Before plunging further into a theoretical discussion of the concept of modern-conservative societies, however, it is necessary to articulate and justify a geographical generalization I used then and use here which also came in for heavy criticism: my use of a geopolitical definition of the Greater Caribbean. This includes all the islands as well as the circum-Caribbean countries. How could I justify defining as the Caribbean an area so complex and then advance the very broad generalization that they share in one way or another a "modern-conservative" political culture?

First, it should be clear that I was not the first to define the region in that fashion. Several of the historians dealt with in chapters 1, 2, and 3 approach the region's history from this perspective. In the purely academic area, Richard M. Morse used a similar geopolitical definition in a brilliant essay that should be better known, as did David Ronfeldt in a more policy-oriented but equally incisive treatise.[7] That said, I was asked why I was ignoring the position of one of the foremost students of the region, Sidney Mintz. Mintz had argued in a highly influential essay, "The Caribbean as a Socio-Cultural Area," that the Caribbean as a bloc of nations does not warrant being considered a "culture area," if by "culture" we mean a common body of historical tradition. He prefers, he said, the concept of "societal area," because its component societies "probably share many more social-structural features than they do cultural features."[8]

Clearly, the debate between those emphasizing culture and those focusing on social structure will not be settled here. Students should be aware that that debate has a distinguished scholarly pedigree in Caribbean studies. The point is, rather, that as with any other geographical region (Africa, Latin

America, Asia), where each unit deserves to be studied individually, there is also value in an understanding of the broader continuities and similarities. Even Mintz's concept of societal area suits our purposes well, since he speaks of a "special distinctiveness" of the Caribbean area, their "demonstrably parallel historical experiences during more than four centuries of powerful (though intermittent and whimsical) European influence."[9] It was Melville Herskovits who reminded us that the concept of culture area is a theoretical construct that does not denote a self-conscious grouping but is rather a way of focusing on the "broad lines of similarities and differences between cultures, not on the details seen by those who are too close to a culture. It has the sweep of the mural, not the delicacy of the miniature."[10] This book aims to demonstrate that in the Caribbean, these continuities and similarities result from a blending of modern and conservative features in the composition of major institutions as well as in social and behavioral dynamics.

An ideologically driven predisposition to erase a past no longer in favor might be psychologically pleasing but does not change the persistence of certain conservative foundations in social change. This then is the challenge of this book—how to present a single empirically valid coherent image of a region as complex as the Greater Caribbean and how to demonstrate that there is indeed a shared political culture in which conservative and traditional and modern traits coexist. Clearly these concepts have to be operationalized and conceptualized much more thoroughly.

Like all concepts or heuristic devices in the social sciences, the concept of modern-conservative societies which guides the discussions in this book is used to explain complex social structures and processes. We are not talking about uniformly traditional societies: those relatively static, passive, and acquiescent societies generally resistant to change.[11] Modern-conservative societies are not only capable of social change; they are often prone to dramatic calls for and engagement in radical, even violent, social movements for change. The empirical questions are: what triggers such desires for change, and what tend to be their initial manifest goals? The working hypothesis of this book is that the most common trigger is of a conservative nature: a grinding sense of moral indignation brought about by perceptions of widespread discrimination, corruption, and abuse of power. This is especially the case when economic conditions deteriorate, leading to perceptions of relative deprivation. This approach to understanding social and political dynamics in the modern-conservative society derives largely from the thinking of two men generally regarded as paragons of true conservatism: Edmund Burke and Alexis Tocqueville. True conservatism is not to be confused with the pseudo-philosophies undergirding many of the right-wing movements in the United States and Europe for the past few decades.

Any student of modern (or liberal) conservative leadership has to begin by revisiting the position of the undisputed "father" of modern British and American conservatism, Edmund Burke (1730–97). Burke, says the dean of U.S. conservative thinkers, Russell Kirk, is not only still relevant but continues to be "the touchstone" of American conservative political thought.[12] Keep in mind that this Irish-English political philosopher and statesman's vehement opposition to the French Revolution led even such luminaries as Thomas Jefferson and Thomas Paine to consider him a "reactionary." Remember also that Karl Marx once described him as "that celebrated sophist and sycophant" who had sold out to the American colonial rebels.[13] But Burke was not easily pigeonholed, as we will see throughout this book, but especially in chapter 2 where the Fabian thinker Gordon K. Lewis repeatedly praised his humane stances.

The point is that Burke was no ideologue; he could, and did, distinguish between one "revolution" and another and between different stages or circumstances of a revolutionary process. Even in that great counterrevolutionary tract, *Reflections on the Revolution in France* (1790), Burke refused to be ideologically fixed and dogmatic, asserting that he could not stand forward and give praise or blame to anything which related to human actions and human concerns "on a simple view of the object." "Circumstances," he maintained, "give in reality to every political principle its distinguishing colour and distinguishing effect. The circumstances are what render every civil and political scheme beneficial or noxious to mankind."[14] That is the basis on which he judged that the American rebels were no threat to Britain, while the French in their Jacobin stage were.

To apply Burke to the present situation in Cuba, for instance, one must ask whether his position vis-á-vis the early "Jacobin" Cuba, which was executing opponents after summary trials and openly exporting revolution to other countries, would be the same toward a Cuba in a different phase, a more Gironde-like Cuba that is exporting doctors, teachers, and athletic coaches. The answer has to be that Burke's attitude and the policies advocated would probably have recognized the differences between the two phases. The basis of this conclusion is the well-established fact that Burke in his assessment

of circumstances understood the importance of nationalism in social movements. In fact, he can legitimately be called the father of the anthropological
interpretation of nationalism.[15] He spoke of the national spirit and character of a people who had to be understood and respected, and because of
that, specific policies had to be designed in accordance with the "unique
dispositions" of that people. Burke had a profound respect for the right of
any society to dispose of its own future, so much so that when the Genoese
sold Corsica to the French, he lamented that a nation had been disposed of
"without its consent, like the trees on an estate." Along with his insistence on
what is today called sovereign consent, Burke opposed (except in the case of
Jacobin France) the use of force and coercion. These were seldom a solution
to governance since, as Burke insisted, a country is not governed if it has to
be repeatedly reconquered. This held especially in the relations between the
strong and the weak, which was the case of England's relationships with Ireland, India, and the American colonies and in colonialism generally. Surely
his original minority status as an Irish Roman Catholic had something to do
with his advocacy for the weak, which, for instance, explains his passionate
defense of the Jews of St. Eustatius, who were brutally mistreated by Adm.
George Rodney in 1781.[16] On a more general level, it was his profound understanding that colonial situations in themselves tend to engender rebellions.
This led him to argue that if the powerful colonial power could not make
the rebellious colonists accept the forms and modes it wished to impose on
them, it was incumbent on the colonial power to change its policies. This is
so, said Burke, because "if such a [colonial] government as this is universally
discontented, no troops under Heaven [will] bring them to obedience."[17]

The fundamental lesson is that Burke was especially adamant that policymakers understand the character of the colonists and the spirit that drove
them. Referring to the American rebels, he repeatedly warned that coercion
would make them recalcitrant, not submissive. This sociological reality
had direct relevance to policy: the "Mother Country's" policies toward the
American rebelliousness could go in one of three directions:

(1) It could seek to do what Burke felt impossible: change the nature of
    the American character and spirit.
(2) It could do what Burke believed irrational and unjust: label the
    American spirit "criminal" and persecute and prosecute it, that is,
    bring it to heel.

(3) It could do what Burke believed reasonable and ultimately more productive: admit to the relative permanence of an American character and spirit and come to terms with it. In other words, come to terms with American rebellious nationalism.[18]

When challenged in Parliament to say what the nature of the government for the rebellious Americans should be, he answered: "If you mean to please any people, you must give them the boon which they ask; not what you may think better for them."[19]

Lest there be some confusion, it should be understood that Burke's American writings were not revolutionary. They were, as Conor Cruise O'Brien has noted, "an attempt to prevent the development and exacerbation of a revolutionary situation." This was the proper stance of one who understood and respected traditions, even colonial traditions, but who also understood nationalism and self-determination as the pivots of many a colonial rebellion.[20] How different from the ontologically fixed positions of both Marx and Engels, who welcomed English and French colonialism because it meant the transfer of a culture of technology that would shake India and Algeria out of their "undignified, stagnatory, and vegetative life."[21]

All this points to one of the paradoxes of the history of American foreign policy addressed in this book: the Americans, whom Burke so adamantly defended in their right to self-determination, seem never to have learned the lessons and precepts he set forth. More often than not, their international behavior has been characterized by attempts to "change the nature and character" of those they deal with, especially those less powerful. This, as we shall see, has been the case with Cuba and Puerto Rico as well as a distressingly consistent pattern in the Caribbean.[22]

Alexis Tocqueville is an equally clear example of a thinker and actor in whom the liberal, the modern, and the conservative coalesce. His personal associations were with the liberal reformists of his time, serving in an influential role in the Constituent Assembly in France following the revolutions of 1848. There was no thought or illusion in Tocqueville about the revival of an authoritarian monarchical past. For him democracy is one of the irresistible, irreversible movements of history. Yet the special cast of his consideration and criticism of democracy is emphatically conservative.[23]

Tocqueville pleases conservatives when he warns against big government and favors voluntary associations; he pleases liberals when he warns against the materialism of capitalism and the industrial elites it spawns. He pleases conservatives when he praises the role of religion in American society; he pleases liberals when he argues for the strict separation of church and state. The point is that Tocqueville, like Burke, was a pragmatic conservative, not an ideologue or moralist. Even his statement that "whenever a nation destroys its aristocracy, it almost automatically tends toward centralization of power" can be submitted to empirical verification.[24] Unlike the reactionaries or the ideologically entrenched who adhere steadily to a given line regardless, Tocqueville asked sociological questions. Why was it that France, where the aristocracy had been losing political and economic power for a century, had a destructive revolution, while England, where an unscathed aristocracy retained its wealth and status and evolved to manage the best farming in Europe and allowed the advancement of modernity all around, had no such revolutionary upheaval? We will see examples of this paradox in some of the Caribbean cases in this book and quite certainly in the concluding chapter on Barbados.

But it was arguably in the area of slavery and race that Tocqueville's sociological frame of mind revealed itself and is most relevant to Caribbean history. He clearly regarded slavery as one of the greatest calamities in the world but understood that there was a difference between slavery in antiquity and in the America through which he traveled. That difference was "race ... united with the physical and permanent fact of color."[25] Anticipating Frantz Fanon by over a century, Tocqueville noted that even after Emancipation, the emancipated would have three prejudices to contend with: first, the prejudice of the former masters; second, the prejudice of race; and third, the prejudice of color. All, in his opinion, were "irreconcilable differences." In his classic *Democracy in America,* Tocqueville was very pessimistic as to the outcome of this tragedy. He was terrified, he wrote, of the "inevitability" of "horrible civil wars."[26]

> If liberty be refused to the Negroes of the South, they will in the end forcibly seize it for themselves; if it be given, they will before long abuse it.[27]

The student necessarily has to ask what examples Tocqueville might have had in mind of ex-slaves abusing their freedom. We get something of a clue that he had Haiti in mind from his assertion that it was in the West Indies that his vision of the future of race relations turned very dark. He wrote that "in the West Indies islands the white race is destined to be subdued, and upon the continent the blacks."[28] A clash between white and black is inevitable, and that fact "perpetually haunts the imagination of the Americans, like a painful dream." I analyze the probable origins of this painful dream in chapter 5.

Oakeshott understood the thinking of Burke and Tocqueville. He speaks of the man or woman of "conservative temperament" who draws three "conclusions" by which to guide his views and actions. First, all innovation (modernization) involves losses and gains. He/she is skeptical and wishes to be persuaded that the scale will tip toward the benefits. Providing proof that the innovation will be beneficial rests with the would-be innovator, and it is to him or her to whom the bill should be passed if the promised benefits do not materialize. Second, the conservative individual tends to believe that innovations which are closer to public wishes, and thus the least imposed, will be the ones least likely to end in losses. Third, he or she believes that innovations which are made to correct defects and identifiable social ills are preferable to innovations founded on promises based on utopian-like visions of perfection. "The man of conservative temperament," said Oakeshott, "believes that a known good is not likely to be surrendered for an unknown better."[29] He understands that the utopian best is the enemy of the existing good. Consequently, he and she prefer a slower pace of change which allows for observation and periodic evaluation. This translates into the Caribbean-wide demand for periodic elections.

How then to interpret either of the only two authentically revolutionary movements in the Caribbean, the Haitian and the Cuban? The first answer the student using a modern-conservative society approach will give is that one has to study revolutions not just in the revolutionary moments but over the *longe durée*. This is French Africanist Georges Balandier's position when he speaks of the "dialectic of traditionalism and revolution." During the early stages of the revolution, the charismatic leadership promises improvements by creating "myths with ideological implications." People are persuaded by the myths, not the ideology. Once in power, that leadership creates "ideology with mythical implications." That ideology calls for revolutionary stability, that is, to "stay as they are." In other words, they become ultraconservative in nature.[30] Stagnation, however, sets the dialectic in motion again, and demands for change led by organic intellectuals challenge the status quo. The unfolding of this dialectic in Cuba is fully discussed in chapter 9.

These illustrations have introduced us to some of the characteristics of the modern-conservative society. But what about the "modern" dimension of the concept? To some, such as the relatively radical sociologist C. Wright Mills, there are only two kinds of conservatives, both steadfast defenders of exploitative capitalism: the "economically practical" and the "sophisticated conservatives." The former are in full support of all the reactionary forces that believe that capitalism is the utopia; the latter are more sophisticated and use liberal symbols to dissimilate their conservative purposes.[31] Clearly, the more ideologically driven Mills ignores the fundamental insight of Oakeshott: "it is not at all inconsistent to be conservative in respect to government and radical in respect of almost every other activity."[32] It is this flexibility which allows us to understand the modern dimension in S. N. Eisenstadt's concept of "traditional modernity."

To Eisenstadt, modernity means, first, flexibility, society's ability to continually adjust to changing problems and demands. Second, it means social mobilization and general participation in social changes, that is, urbanization and a prominent role for the mass media and communication systems. Third, despite forms of protest and incidental eruptions, societal changes continue. Eisenstadt notes that often populism may be associated with conservative tendencies.[33] He cites as examples politicians such as Gandhi, Sun Yet-sen, Mossadeq, Nkrumah, and Sukarno who represented "revivalist populism," which in Eisenstadt's view represented "traditional modernity."[34] Fourth, modernity tends to characterize societies where the secondary and tertiary (especially services) economic functions overshadow the primary (extractive) occupation. A Caribbean very much dependent on tourism and financial services certainly fits Eisenstadt's definition of being modern.

Eisenstadt explains why it is wrong to think that intellectuals are necessarily opponents of tradition. First, the ideological bias which maintains that those that hold roles with conservative perspectives (viz. religious leaders) are rarely regarded as intellectuals. Important also is a social status bias: the refusal to acknowledge the roles that "secondary" or "minor" intellectuals (viz. school leaders, preachers, social workers, and journalists) play in the broad process of construction and transmission of the more enduring elements of tradition.[35] These are certainly important caveats for a Caribbean where "intellectuals" are perceived to be limited to either university graduates or at least highly intelligent graduates of first-rate secondary schools.

C.L.R. James, as we shall see, fits the latter; the former form the group that Lloyd Best used to call practitioners of "doctor politics."

We conclude this theoretical prologue by once again outlining the basic structure of our conceptual framework of the modern-conservative society. It should at the outset be understood that to speak of "structures" does not imply anything static. It merely means that certain underlying factors or interrelationships are more durable, more tenacious and retentive, than many of the immediate and observable manifestations of those relationships suggest. Such ideas or concepts as family, tradition, community, history, life, being, and identity are central to this conservative view of life especially in ex-colonial, multiethnic, and highly stratified societies. In such societies, as Harry Hoetink very clearly points out (see chapter 3), not everything about the past is treasured and consciously retained. But neither is everything cherry-picked to suit a contemporary, here-and-now, ideological agenda of leaders bent on creating the myth of a revolutionary Caribbean. Even among such leaders and thinkers (analyzed in chapter 1), however, we will show how strong residual traditional, even conservative, strains make an occasional but critical appearance.

Precisely because our definition of the Greater Caribbean includes Latin American societies, methodological completeness compels us to cross geopolitical areas to look at the same phenomenon in Latin America. It was the distinguished Latin Americanist Kalman H. Silvert who, at least to my knowledge, first used the term "modern traditionalists."[36] He was referring to the strong retention of conservative traditions by a middle class striving to be modern while dragging along traits and attitudes of the conservative societies they wish to leave behind. Silvert was describing a fairly widespread understanding of the continued conservatism in Latin American societies. Writing on Brazil, Charles Wagley said: "The middle class is, in a sense, the most conservative social segment of their society. Because they are insecure in their position, they make a point of preserving most of the old Latin American values and traditional patterns of behavior."[37]

Similarly Richard Adams describes how upwardly mobile sectors, with their own value systems, "manifest some parallel structural features" with the sector they are leaving behind as well as taking on the values of the traditional upper cultural sector.[38] Truly comparative approaches compel us to go even further afield to explore parallel theories developed in other area studies. So, for example, Rupert Emerson describes how both Gandhi and Nehru had political styles that were "inextricably intermixed" with their social, religious, and ethical outlooks. This provided "a vital link between the modernist and the traditional approaches.[39] Surely a similar description could fit both Burke and Tocqueville.

Finally, a note on understanding the sociological fallacy of certain ideo-logically driven objections to conservative thoughts that strike contempo-raries as obnoxious. In my conclusion I hypothesize that as distasteful as the prejudice-ridden social structure of colonial Barbados seems today, it performed a longer-term function. As contemptible as social prejudice is, according to Burke, it plays a vital latent social and historical function: it contributes to holding society together, "providing a kind of emotional ce-ment for beliefs and habits." Disturbing on its face certainly, but in this Burke was articulating a principle similar to that later adopted by Émile Durkheim when he argued that crime was a "normal fact." According to Durkheim, "it might be regrettable but it was inevitable . . . indispensable to the normal evolution of morality and law." Burke was no more in favor of prejudice than Durkheim was of criminality.[40] Understanding the role of latent functions is part of the contemporary sociological enterprise.[41]

In other words, Caribbean societies are not akin to those societies where conservatism and tradition exercise a strong restraining force on change. Georges Balandier noted such stagnation in Central Africa and attributed it to inertia and fear of fundamental change. Once transported to the New World, however, many of these stationary African traditions, including the role of drumming and dance, become "storehouses" of cultural forms which had, and still have, significant positive functions in the New World. As George Balandier notes, "Voodoo and the Candomblé still serve as a reposi-tory of tradition for those utterly deprived peoples. In such cases, conserva-tism is far from being sterile."[42] It is no longer possible to continue ignoring the dynamics of modern-conservative societies, of the continued influence of traditional values, no matter how distasteful that might seem to scholars socialized in the literature of a supposedly inherent revolutionary nature of Caribbean societies.

1

Eric Williams vs. Juan Bosch

On Caribbean Historical Fundamentals

It was arguably pure coincidence that in 1970 two of the Caribbean's most popular politicians should publish books carrying the same titles—Trinidadian Eric Williams's *From Columbus to Castro: The History of the Caribbean, 1492–1969*, and Dominican Republic's Juan Bosch's *De Cristóbal Colón a Fidel Castro*. Williams was by then prime minister of independent Trinidad and Tobago, and Bosch was in exile in Paris, years after having been overthrown by a military coup d'état in 1963. They wrote quite different books, but by doing it at all, they negated Fritz Stern's belief that "the role that ideology plays in our century, history tended to play in the last century."[1] No, written history continued to play a fundamental role in the twentieth century, whether written from the left, center, or right of the political spectrum. As such, the roles of Williams and Bosch as historian-politicians have to be analyzed from historiographical and sociological perspectives. Both contributed to the sociological and historical interpretation of origins and social change in the Caribbean, especially Bosch's version, which had five Dominican, two Spanish, and two Cuban editions.

From a functional point of view, the careers of both men demonstrate that the sociological roles of history and ideology continue to be valid and useful. Popular history and ideology respond to similar social and economic needs and serve similar functions. Historical models—usually in the form of analogies—tend to function in the decision-making process just as ideology does. As historians and as politicians, Williams and Bosch operated in a *trialectical* fashion: the past as interpreted, the present as perceived, and a desired (or feared) future interacting with each other in their studies. Generally speaking, this trialectical process operates in everyday contexts but tends to be especially compelling when the historian is also an active politician writing during a period of rapid ideological change, as Arthur Schlesinger Jr. points out. Schlesinger confesses to not being sure whether historical interpretations are the sources of policy decisions or merely post facto vindications of such decisions.[2] Yet he maintains that all decisions of public policy involve historical judgment, and assumptions concerning future developments are derived from an interpretation of the past and arguments by analogy. These assumptions and analogies can remain unstated, but often they are made explicit and appear to transcend ideological differences, driven by what Schlesinger calls "the bewitchment of analogy."[3]

While logicians readily agree that analogies are central to human thinking, they also recognize the danger of false analogies of a historical nature, fallacies which often follow the clichés that "history teaches."[4] Both Bosch and Williams believed that through their writings they were part of fundamental nation-building—that they were influencing both decision makers and public opinion. This was no mere illusion. F. A. Hayek goes so far as to say that historians are more influential than political theorists who launch new ideas because the historian is "at least one step nearer to direct power over public opinion than is the theorist."[5] It is evident that the use of historical models and analogies is increasing rather than decreasing in the twentieth century. This might explain the numerous autobiographies-cum-histories we will encounter in this book. The functions of such personal testimonies seem to place them in the same category as ideology or belief systems.[6]

Nowhere is this use of history more evident than in revolutionary or post-colonial periods, periods in which, virtually by definition, much of the past as remembered is perceived in terms of exploitation and injustice. It appears that a conception of the past (especially a colonial past) as repugnant is in many ways a necessary precondition for radical social change. "Despoiled . . . of his history, he is a stranger to himself," writes an African historian speaking for considerable sectors of the nonwestern world and not a few "minorities" in the western world.[7] This view explains the high priority the nationalist policymakers give to elevating their version of history to a place of honor; they rewrite history as a means of restoring their own and their nation's self-respect.[8]

The Trinidadian Eric Williams and the Dominican Juan Bosch differed in ideology and political paths. Their historiography reflected these differences. Their differences reflect and express the great variety of cultures and world-views that is the Caribbean. They had two features in common, however: they believed they were writing the history of the entire region, and they interpreted and wrote history as part of a wider political activism. What is attempted here is not a critique of their activism or what it aspired to achieve; it is a critical look at the trialectical interaction between their perceptions of their present reality, their aspirations for the future, and their interpretations of the past and how these changed over time. The analysis of this political historiography demonstrates that the "use" of history in social movements serves two functions: it provides powerful myths for the movement, and it provides historical analogies to assist in decision making. Being instrumental, the historical interpretation often changed as the politics required different decisions.

Any analysis of Williams's distinguished career as historian and politician has to begin by citing his PhD thesis at Oxford, finally published in the United States in 1944. His determination to make his historical studies and excellent written products count politically was made evident in his autobiography. "Trinidad in 1911," Williams wrote, "would move in only one direction—forward."[9] But why 1911 when the island was a tightly controlled Crown colony with few signs of liberalization by the Colonial Office? The autobiography contains no clues, but a contextual reading will show that, in addition to being the year of his birth, 1911 marked, in his opinion, a national as well as a personal beginning. The baby of 1911 would move on to be an Island Scholar, an Oxford PhD, a university professor, and finally the political leader of Trinidad and Tobago for twenty-four years. He never appeared to have lost his egocentric view of his status and role, for his was an "inward hunger." He was "determined," he told us, "to prove that, like Dante's Ulysses, I

> Could conquer the inward hunger that I had
> To master earth's experience, and to attain
> Knowledge of man's mind, both good and bad."[10]

Eric Williams's autobiography recalls W. Somerset Maugham's warning about all autobiographies: "No one can tell the whole truth about himself." By contrast, it is a telling fact that Juan Bosch never wrote an autobiography; his life's trajectory has to be gleaned from his many writings.

From the perspective of the political use and influence of Williams's writings, however, it is best to deal with his writing once he returned to Trinidad and entered politics. On the very day of the formal launching of Williams's political party, the People's National Movement (PNM), Williams launched the Party newspaper. Issue no. 1 carried an editorial by Williams. "The first need," he advised, "is education." This was a theme he would carry forward with the metaphor "Your country's future is in your school bag." Immediately upon that came the need "to stimulate and promote the growing feeling of nationalism which the PNM symbolizes and which it has made respectable." Williams clearly understood that his party was perceived as the party of black Trinidadians, so he took pains in his editorial to warn that "divisions in a cosmopolitan society such as ours are suicidal. . . . To knock opponents on the head invites retaliation; to suppress minorities endangers democracy." Noting that while the society was composed of various racial stocks and diverse religions, "they all mess out of the same pot."[11]

To a large extent, Williams avoided the theme of race as he prepared his formal campaign. Of the seventeen major speeches he delivered in 1955 and 1956, fifteen dealt with economic and political development; only two dealt directly with race. On July 29, 1955, he spoke in the mixed black-Indian town of San Juan on "The Need for Racial Understanding." On August 16, 1955, when he spoke of "The Historical Background of Race Relations in the Caribbean" to a mostly black, urban Port-of-Spain audience, his tone was somewhat different but still largely conciliatory. Despite Williams's arguments that racial divisions would be ruinous for the island, those divisions had long existed, and an Indo-Trinidadian party, the Democratic Labour Party (DLP), was launched to challenge the PNM. As the twin islands approached independence, Williams, then premier, appeared to be ratcheting up the belief that Afro-Trinidadian culture represented the true national essence of the nation. It came to a head on March 22, 1961, when he delivered the speech that would establish the theme of his campaigning and, indeed, that of the island's political history: the "Massa Day Done" address.

Of all the speeches given by Williams, this one delivered in what was already known as the "University of Woodford Square" on March 22, 1961, is arguably the most memorable. It certainly is the most cited and quoted. In fact, the concept "Massa Day Done" has become an integral part of Trinidadian (and to a certain extent West Indian) political parlance. Thus Woodford Square became the people's "university," and Williams was its vice chancellor and key professor. The speech was a response to an editorial in the *Trinidad Guardian* praising the entry into politics of a white creole, Sir Gerald Wight. Wight had entered into the Indo-Trinidadian DLP, potentially the most formidable opponent of Williams's PNM. Although the speech was openly partisan, it was neither demagogic nor a simple knee-jerk response. It was a well-thought-out argument about the persistence of the "plantation mentality." Williams had spent three and a half months preparing what he fully intended to be a "watershed" statement about race, ethnicity, social class, and—fundamentally in Fanonian terms—colonial collective psychology in the transition to nationhood. The speech helped Williams achieve his political and pedagogical goals by rallying his Afro-Trinidadian party loyalists.

The opposition DLP (in a full-page ad) called on Williams to withdraw the "wicked and race-baiting statement 'Massa Day Done'" and to offer an unqualified apology for introducing it into the campaign. Williams refused to withdraw what he called "a historical analysis which is the product of more than twenty years of assiduous research," and he accused the DLP of being "the stooge of the Massas who still exist in our society."[12] They were a "pack of benighted idiots and obscurantists." *Massa*, he said, was not a racial term; it was the symbol of an age gone by—rule by the mostly absentee plantation owners. He mentioned many a white, both foreign and local, who opposed the Massa syndrome, but then insisted that whites were an "aristocracy of the skin."

The speech set the stage for the sale on the day of Independence (for 1 TT$1) of Williams's book on *The History of the People of Trinidad and Tobago*. Local historian Keith O. Lawrence described the book as representing an imperfect marriage between the historian and the politician with the result that "the nationalist politician has from time to time led the historian to swerve dangerously." Future generations, said Lawrence, will need books "written as histories, not as nationalist manifestoes."[13] This was a professional historian's review. The book sold by the thousands in quickly constructed kiosks around the country. Evidently taken with the public's hunger for popular history, Williams then wrote *British Historians and the West Indies*. This, he states, was written from a very "personal" point of view to show his development into "a rebel against the British historical tradition which Oxford has done so much to develop."[14] He wanted to liberate himself from "the inferior status to which these [British] writings sought to condemn" him and his fellow West Indians.

These hastily written books, but especially the one on British historians, led to a devastating review by one of the ablest West Indian historians at the time, Elsa V. Goveia, originally from Guyana but teaching in Jamaica at the time. Her critical essay "New Shibboleths for Old" declared Williams's work on British historians "disappointing and even somewhat irresponsible." She went further, noting that Williams did not seem to be reading the many excellent books written by the faculty at the University College of the West Indies on that topic: "the intellectual isolation which has plagued him since he was a rebellious undergraduate at Oxford continues to make itself felt in his work, and he still writes like a man who finds himself the only voice crying out in the wilderness of an alien and hostile historical tradition."[15] She then called on Williams to do the kind of historical work she knew he was capable of. Before he tried to do just that in *From Columbus to Castro*, Williams published his autobiography, *Inward Hunger*, a long memoir of his birth in Trinidad, education at Oxford, and entry into Trinidad politics. The response to this autobiography ranged from mild approval to indifference. No such indifference followed *From Columbus to Castro*, which appeared a year later. The academic response was mostly critical.

Perhaps the sharpest broadside came from Gordon Rohlehr, a Guyanese professor of literature at the University of the West Indies in Trinidad.[16] Rohlehr's lengthy critique certainly deserves to be read in its entirety, since it covers virtually all of Williams's writings. For our purposes of comparison with Bosch's *De Cristóbal Colón a Fidel Castro*, however, Rohlehr's key criticisms can be summarized as follows: First, he noted Williams's "fantastic claims" that his book was the "true" history of four hundred years of Caribbean history. Second, he scolded Williams for his criticism of local and West Indian historians and their "inadequate" contributions to their own history. Rohlehr found rather that Williams had totally ignored their works. Third, it was strange that although Williams claimed to have spent eighteen years preparing it, the book drew extensively from his previous work, *Capitalism and Slavery*. Fourth, the book lacked documentation. It contained so few reference notes that "the worth of the book is immediately in question." This meant that it could not be used as a reference text.[17] "Lack of references must therefore be cited as a grievous flaw." Fifth, and critically, the whole work was informed by a "simple fatalism," which sounds familiar since it is essentially in the style of Trinidad novelist V. S. Naipaul, the so-called Mohun Biswas Syndrome. Rohlehr described this syndrome as absurdity leading to rebellion, which in turn "is reinitiated into fresh absurdity."[18]

This is what brought Rohlehr to his central criticism. "The difference between Naipaul and Dr. Williams," he said, "is that the former uses irony to probe and analyze the pain of his own loss, cultural orphanage, forced ambivalence and futility, while the latter exploits irony as a means of reassuring himself of his own moral and intellectual superiority."[19] As specifically accurate and telling as all these critiques of Williams's writings were, most seem to miss the fact that Williams did have a historian-politician's grand vision of Caribbean history with a comparative reach. After all, the real purpose of his writing history was to advance that grand vision and his political career.

A basic principle of the Eric Williams treatise was to reveal how and why a given political or constitutional act in the Caribbean hardly ever had its expected social and economic complement. Leaving aside any Marxist ontology he might have had but never alluded to, Williams believed that there was more paradox than predictability in Caribbean history, and he wrote without a trace of irony. To win a military battle in the Caribbean was rarely to win the social war. For example, the passing of slavery in Haiti and then in the West Indies meant the dawn of a new era of slavery in Brazil and Cuba. Metropolitan interests were hardly affected by abolition in the British West Indies: England adopted a free trade policy in 1852 to so become the largest single market for slave-produced sugar. That meant that the free labor-produced sugar of the Caribbean could not compete. In the same way, the decline of the slave-worked sugar economies of Haiti and the British West Indies signaled a new era of sugar *latifundismo* in the Caribbean, the beginning of the industrialization of the colonial crop worked now by either indentured foreign labor or domestic *peones*.

Continuing his theme of irony and paradox, Williams shows how watersheds for one island rarely meant the same for the rest of the islands. Somehow historical lessons, no matter how heroic, were lost as each Caribbean people seemed determined to go through the same process. Characterized by different colonial structures but competing for the same metropolitan markets, there developed a "beggar thy neighbor" syndrome: the problems and travails of one meant the profit of the other. According to Williams it was so in the past, it was so in his day; witness, he said, the redistribution of the American sugar quota following the cutting off of the Cuban share! Williams's study honestly faces this fundamental economic issue of the Caribbean, and his candidness is chillingly stark. Commenting on René Dumont's suggestion that Cuba should diversify its economy and seek a broader market in the Caribbean area, Williams does not beat around the bush: "But Trinidad and Tobago, producing sugar, ammonia, petroleum, garments, condensed milk, and other products complementing Cuba's could hardly be expected to surrender its independent development of its own economy in order to be a dumping ground for Cuba's products and allow Castro to be the sugar bowl of the Caribbean."[20] The vision of a Cuba capable of producing ten million tons of sugar annually is not one that Caribbean leaders relished or, frankly, one that their island economies could long withstand.

Williams's projection is more complex and forms the most complete discussion of possible Caribbean futures at that time. It is in the last two chapters on "Castroism" and "The Future of the Caribbean" that Williams, the scholar, complements Williams, the statesman. Three competing models are discussed: the Puerto Rican type of industrialization for the U.S. market, the Cuban model, and the Trinidad and Tobago model, "a path less revolutionary and more gradualistic, and less totalitarian and more democratic than the Cuban path, but more autonomous and ultimately self-reliant than the Puerto Rican one."[21] Clearly there were to be no more Cuban or Puerto Rican models in Williams's historical projections.

Williams projects his "Trinidad" model only for the Commonwealth Caribbean, noting that it is not possible to sketch at this time what the relationship will be with the rest of the area. But what about the rest of the area then? Williams's analysis loses some of its sharp focus on this score. On the one hand, he asserts that future Caribbean integration will require looser ties between France and its *departments* in the Caribbean; on the other, he visualizes "true" integration without Puerto Rico, which he sees irremediably (a fait accompli he calls it) moving toward closer ties with the United States. Not that Williams seems happy over this. "Economic growth has been achieved (in Puerto Rico), but national identity lost," he notes, asking rhetorically, "What shall it profit a country if it gain the whole world and lose its own soul?" As we shall see in chapter 3, whatever "soul" means sociologically, Puerto Rico does not seem to have lost it.

It is clear that if Williams judges the Cuban model to have resulted in totalitarianism and advocates steps to prevent its exportation, and he also opts the Puerto Rican model out of the Caribbean, one is left only with the Trinidad and Tobago development model as a viable alternative. Unfortunately, nowhere does he submit that model to the kind of scrutiny given to the Cuban case. At no time could one predict, for instance, the April 1970 Black Power uprising in Trinidad from Williams's study, for while he is cautious, he nevertheless gives the impression that his program is viable and working. But the facts speak differently and bring 1970 into focus. For instance, the

Industrial Development Corporation (IDC), the entity which carried the burden of the Island's development program, simply was not meeting the needs of the island. In 1966 there were 79 enterprises assisted by the IDC; these enterprises gave jobs to 1,758 persons; unemployment stood at 48,700, and there were 8,000 young people leaving school that year. After 1966 things deteriorated further. Unemployment in 1970 was considerably higher than the 15 percent cited by Williams, and corruption in higher circles (including cabinet members) had tended to demoralize lower echelons of the civil service. In short, the development program Williams projected was not one which Caribbean scholars interested in a new approach to the area's future could readily accept. It was not one, indeed, that was sufficiently justified by the very historical analysis of colonialism which Williams had so masterfully presented in the first half of the book.

On a more general plane, Williams argues that the burden of future integration depended on a "psychological revolution" taking place in each island; this would lead to economic independence and from that independence "the development of a cultural identity will involve them in even closer ties one with another—at economic and at other levels."[22] This was putting the cart before the horse. Strongly developed cultural identities in the midst of colonial social structures and neocolonial economic and market situations was, of course, a tragic possibility, as much of tribal Africa demonstrated at the time. Since Williams was on record as opposing this, it is unfortunate that the very "model" he projected, the so-called Trinidad and Tobago development model, had by 1970 not resulted in anything even approximating what his history established as a reality.

This was the broad sweep of Caribbean economic history presented by Williams. It differed fundamentally from Bosch's version. If the "Castro" cut-off point for both studies implies a sort of Caribbean domino theory—that events in Cuba will eventually materialize elsewhere—the very historical treatments of both authors show that to be a myth. The international demonstration effect of social acts is a double-edged sword, as Che Guevara noted in 1961. The Cuban Revolution, like the Haitian Revolution before it, provided hope and stimulus to some and a lesson in prevention to others. Revolution in the Caribbean and in Latin America had, in fact, been made more difficult. There was no spontaneous revolutionary collective inclination evident in the Caribbean. Race, not revolutionary ideology, was the trigger for broader Caribbean social movements; ideology tended to motivate a few pockets of radical intellectuals. Be that as it may, both Williams and Bosch aspired to final liberation, that is, the matching of economic to political independence. It is difficult, however, to see any concrete similarities beyond that in what these authors project for the future.

It is evident that Juan Bosch's view of the Caribbean differs radically from that of Eric Williams. Bosch sees the Caribbean as a major imperial frontier, and he sets out to describe the European events that have a direct bearing on conditions and events in the frontier area. He writes from a Spanish point of view justified, as he tells us, because this was a Spanish frontier which others were determined to rip apart and conquer. Over half the book is spent on the period up to the Peace of Paris (1763). All major imperial military campaigns are described in detail, complemented by very insightful treatments of "internal" violence against the imperialists by Indians, black slaves, and later, free men. In essence, Bosch writes in a very Latin American tradition which in British Caribbean scholarly circles is no longer acceptable—the colonial Caribbean is seen exclusively as an extension of European military history.

Juan Bosch implicitly projects a future of struggles along an imperial frontier similar to those of the past four centuries. To him, the 1961 Bay of Pigs invasion of Cuba symbolized the first major victory against the American "frontier." But, aside from the constant allusions to the desirability and promised benefits of socialism, there are no other indications in Bosch as to the kind of program or form those battles would or should take. Bosch, surprisingly, makes no contribution to the so direly needed discussion of the reconciliation of racial and ethnic movements and "identities" in the broader social trends in the area. His Sorelian[23] concern with violence never reaches the level of theoretical sophistication of a Frantz Fanon, a Caribbean scholar who—as we shall see—saw in violence the necessary "cleansing" process to psychological decolonization. Bosch, in fact, does not even mention Fanon, since to him racial violence was a natural result of class warfare and therefore required no further theoretical introspection.

Williams, by contrast, spends little time on European political and military history and provides few or no details of filibuster and buccaneer life. He is more interested in demonstrating how, by the seventeenth century, the Caribbean Sea had become "virtually a Dutch canal" with all its economic implications.[24] While Bosch is still describing the doings of corsairs, buccaneers, and pirates, Williams tells us that Jean Baptiste Colbert, French secretary of the navy, had become "the architect and symbol of the seventeenth-century colonial system."[25] It is not surprising that Colbert is not mentioned even in passing by Bosch. Similarly, Bosch notes that the Spanish-American War of 1898 signaled the entry of the United States into the Caribbean as an "empire." Williams's analysis of the Yankee trading circles illustrates how the American New Englanders had already entrenched themselves economically in the area by the second half of the seventeenth century. To Williams, American economic interests in the Caribbean predate their military and political designs on it by over two centuries. As a general principle, Williams's economic frontier consistently anticipates Bosch's military-political one.

Williams does not waste much time in getting to the point regarding Caribbean "internal" history. By page 25 Williams brings Caribbean history into focus by noting the main features already present in 1520: subsidies from and protection by the state, concentration of ownership, all productive activity for export, and an abandonment of the domestic market. The central concern has already become the question of ensuring a stable market, for example. We have the paradox, therefore, that while Bosch's intent throughout is revolutionary, his approach and method are traditional. On the other hand, in his successful attempt at producing a major historical work, Williams's intent is traditional; his method and approach are radical, similar, in fact, to the approach of his *Capitalism and Slavery* (1944), one of the most influential pieces of scholarship in Caribbean history.

It is because Bosch has the most pronounced (though implicit) revolutionary thrust in his history writing and later in his politics that one does well to probe into the intellectual structure of his arguments. And there are weaknesses. Bosch has a way of describing the behavior of various actors and sectors in an excessively mechanistic fashion: all petit bourgeois members behave the way petit bourgeois are supposed to behave; all upper-class members behave as their class is supposed to behave; the success or failure of any movement is nearly always attributed to the particular class origins of its leaders; all leaders who spring from the people fight for the people, while all those who spring from the bourgeoisie or aristocracy have ulterior motives when they take up the cause of the people. This deterministic unicausal focus leads Bosch to the creation of a few new myths. The bloodthirsty José Boves, formidable leader of the Royalist cavalry in the Venezuelan Wars of Independence, becomes a new hero on the grounds that his followers were the rural mulatto and mestizo *llaneros*. Simón Bolívar's motives, on the other hand, are suspect: true popular leadership could not come from a member of the *mantuano* upper class to which Bolívar belonged. Nowhere does Bosch tell us that Boves's real name was José Tomás Bobes y de la Iglesia, that he was a white Asturian of considerable education and some economic status, or that he first favored independence before he took up the Royalist cause—or rather the cause of pillage and sadistic cruelty, becoming a veritable "monster of cruelty," as the Spanish historian Salvador de Madariaga and many others called him.[26] It is purely political-ideological sentiments which lead Bosch to include him in the pantheon of popular Caribbean heroes that justly includes the likes of César Agusto Sandino, José Martí, and Toussaint L'Ouverture.

First let us look at the question of outright barbarism: the case of the *caudillo* Boves in particular, since the issue reappears in our discussion of Bolívar's call for a *guerra a muerte!* There is no need to engage in an argument concerning the historical relativity of the terms *cruelty* and *barbarism*, because all sides in the Venezuelan civil war were cruel and because the standard ethical-cultural judgments on "cruel" behavior had not shifted that much over the period under discussion here. Note the following three cases taken from the many recorded by Venezuelan historians. (1) The entire populations of the towns of San Joaquín and Santa Ana were ordered put to the knife by Boves after they had surrendered. (2) The wives, mothers, and daughters of captured officers in Valencia were made to dance to whiplashes while their husbands were being decapitated; in Barcelona the same scene took place, but with an added touch: an orchestra of creole musicians were decapitated one by one each half hour; the last remaining violinist was forced to play while the women were raped and decapitated. (3) Men, women, and children were herded before the altar of the local church, where they were raped and disemboweled.

Boves's penchant for ritualistic and sadistic killing was clearly psychopathological. Captured officers were known to be put in local bull rings with bull horns stuck to their foreheads and made to play bull while the *picadores* stabbed at them. Since Bosch in 1970 elevates Boves to the status of hero of the masses, let it be said that the three cases cited here are taken from Bosch's own earlier history written in 1966, *Bolívar y la guerra social*.[27] In this book, arguably one of Bosch's most solid historical works, he does not minimize the importance of Boves in the *guerra social* of 1812–14, but he retains in 1966 a balanced analysis when evaluating the personal roles and merits of Boves and Bolívar that is lost in his *De Cristóbal Colón a Fidel Castro*.

In 1966 Bosch argued that Boves's idea was simply to destroy the *criollo* whites and that "equality was not sought by means of the creation of a State which would guarantee it and maintain it through the authority of law; it was sought through the destruction of the *mantuano* class."[28] The *guerra social* of Venezuela from 1812 to 1814 was, according to Bosch in 1966, destructive, not creative. Only Bolívar tried to find a constructive way out. Bosch very carefully noted that being white and upper class himself, Bolívar could not offer the colored masses the same immediate gratifications Boves did. He did, however, offer them something that in the long run would have been more revolutionary, because it attacked the structural rather than the super-structural aspects of social action: the nationalization of all property. Bosch noted that in declaring on January 25, 1814, that all property belongs to the state, Bolívar had established his reformist credentials. "A more revolution-ary and equalizing piece of legislation could not be given. Not even Lenin, upon taking power a hundred years later, dared declare that all property be-longs to the State."[29] Because the masses were not in a position to appreciate the depth of the measure, but the remaining *mantuanos* and other property owners were and naturally resented it, Bolívar was left without support in 1814, the fateful year of defeat that Venezuelan history calls the Año Terrible, the end of the First Republic.

All this was magisterially researched by Germán Carrera Damas, the dean of Venezuelan social historians. It is surprising, therefore, that Bosch, the historian in 1966, never mentions Carrera Damas's work in his 1970 *From Columbus to Castro* where the new assessment of Boves as popular hero ap-pears. Carrera Damas had been engaged in a massive historiographical study of the literature on Boves. His study, "Sobre el significado socio-económico de la acción histórica de Boves," specifically dealt with the new interpreta-tion that Boves was the initiator of the struggle for land and that he was an "agrarian reformer."[30] So important were Carrera Damas's findings that in a subsequent work, *Historiografía marxista venezolana*, he does a methodolog-ical essay on the analysis of sources and he repeats his fundamental conclu-sion on the myth of Boves as a reformer: the study showed that the version of Boves the reformist leader "was not based on respectable foundations." Boves, rather, appeared as an *administrador de secuestros*—confiscating prop-erty not for his followers but for the *Real Hacienda*, the king of Spain. "In this manner, utilizing the known documentation, it was not possible to state that Boves turned out to be a distributor of land, or a 'redistributor' of property; instead, that same documentation authorizes us to believe that Boves was an orthodox *administrador de secuestros*, and so we concluded."[31] Carrera Damas also approvingly published the new findings of Julio Febres Cordero, who concluded that Boves "did not have, nor could he have had, agrarian concerns, since his role was reduced to being a simple guarantor of the properties and possessions of the Crown."[32] These and similar new findings were published in the preface to the second edition in 1968.

The crucial question is: If Bosch had dealt with Boves and Bolívar in a new and balanced way in 1966, why did he change his interpretation radically in 1970? Did he discover new sources? What other historical figures came in for a reinterpretation in 1970? Again, in 1970 there was a shift in Bosch's position on Haitian history. He shifts his interpretation of the two men: the black ex-slave Henri Christophe, king of the northern part of Haiti, who maintained the large *latifundia* with its harsh labor routine and discipline, became Bosch's new hero, and Alexandre Pétion, prominent member of the *mulâtre* class and president of the republican south, who carried out one of the most radical land reforms in recorded history to that time, was portrayed as reactionary. But, once again, while Bosch debunked the theory of Pétion's land reform in 1970, in 1966 he had a different version of that piece of Haitian history:

> Henri Christophe I and Alexandre Pétion used the lands of the nation in quite different ways. The King (Christophe) returned to the *latifundia colonial*, for the benefit of himself and that of the nobility he had created, and with the *latifundia* he resuscitated slavery in fact, if not in law. The logical result of the *latifundista* monarchy had to be, and it was, a political tyranny based on an army which the King maintained recruited from peasants without land. Pétion, on the other hand, distributed among the peasants of the south the lands of the State, and frequently he himself did the distributing. With a population of frugal life, in which all the adults had been born slaves or at best black and ex-slave freedmen, the agrarian republic of Pétion lived in a simple and peaceful sort of patriarchal democracy, equally nationalistic as calm. . . . In 1816 Haiti in the south was happy but poor; it would never again be the splendid land of other times; Haiti in the north was a tyranny of horrors.[33]

Which was the accurate version, Bosch in 1966 or Bosch in 1970? The work of Haitian Leslie Manigat corroborates Bosch's 1966 position, but Bosch does not mention Manigat's work in his 1970 book. In his meticulous study *La politique agraire du gouvernement d'Alexandre Pétion, 1807–1818*, Manigat is under no illusions as to why Pétion proceeded in the fashion he did, but he does conclude that Pétion's policies represented a "decisive epoch" in Haitian history: "The moment it represents is, thus, a key moment in the evolution of Haiti's agrarian sector, a moment of property divisions which stamped its imprint on the rural face of the country."[34]

It might be worth mentioning what the historical results have been. A large-scale study of Haitian lower-class peasantry by Carline J. Legerman discovered in the south "a relatively stable core population who had been cultivating its own lands since the time of Independence if not before."[35] Housing, family life, and other sociocultural aspects in the south compared most favorably vis-à-vis the other areas studied where large-scale production, absentee landlordism, wage labor, and sharecropping predominated.

As far as it can be documented, Bosch's 1966 version of Pétion and Christophe stands in the literature, not his dramatic reinterpretation of 1970. Similarly, Bosch's 1970 idea that the Haitian Revolution embodied every idea Marx ever had of revolution is surprising. Bosch notes that this is limited to the struggle stage, since afterwards the Haitian Revolution would be something other than Marxist, "but up to the moment of gaining power any student of Marx can find all the ideals of Marx converted into actions."[36] One wonders why Marx, who knew the history of the French Revolution well and should certainly have known about the Haitian Revolution, never mentioned Haiti in any of his major works. Naturally, once accepting this interpretation of things, it is only logical to extend the analogy one step further, and indeed, Bosch does not make us wait long. One hundred and sixty years later, he notes that what had happened in Haiti would be repeated in Cuba, and it would not be a fortuitous repetition. "The Cuban Revolution of Fidel Castro would historically be a daughter of the Haitian Revolution."[37] Unfortunately, Bosch's treatment of the Cuban Revolution is limited to an analysis of the 1961 Bay of Pigs invasion and combat. The statement thus must be judged on exterior evidence or deduced from Bosch's central thesis of the struggles on the frontier.

This is where Bosch the historian becomes Bosch the politician. The Caribbean, he says, is a unit shaped by imperialism. "Logically," he concludes, "no country of the Caribbean can be seen isolated from the rest."[38] From this historical analysis he concludes that the only way to confront this imperialism throughout the Caribbean is with revolution. But does Bosch's thesis of the imperial frontier provide a sufficient and necessary explanation of the revolutions of the Caribbean—*even as described by Bosch himself*? The answer is no. Let us cite but one case, the history of Cuba during the nineteenth century, which he describes as unique.

> No country in the Caribbean has had an historical process similar to that of Cuba. The wars in Haiti were provoked directly by the French Revolution; the wars in Venezuela and Nueva Granada by the Napoleonic intervention in Spain; the independence in Central America was a by-product of the wars in Venezuela, Nueva Granada and Mexico; all the events which resulted from the French Revolution influenced the birth of the Dominican Republic. But the case of Cuba was and has continued to be different. . . . Cuba became the source of its own historical acts, something singular in the Caribbean.[39]

Why should Fidel Castro's revolution be a daughter of the Haitian Revolution when Cuba's history of struggles up to then responded to internal socioeconomic contradictions? Part of the explanation lies in a methodological confusion throughout the structure of the 1970 book. Because Bosch attempts to provide a Marxist interpretation of events while leaving out "internal" history, the results of his study are blurry. With the exception of the analysis of Cuba, there is little effort at social history.

First, there is Bosch's statement that "this book is designed to be exclusively an account of the imperial aggressions produced in the Caribbean."[40] Thus in describing the Haitian Revolution he notes that the phenomenon of the social displacement of one group in Haiti "corresponds to what we can call the private history of Haiti: and therefore had no place in the book."[41] Similarly, in his discussion of the Wars of Independence of Nueva Granada, Bosch suddenly stops to announce that "in any case given the fact that these struggles were internal there is no place in this book to describe them."[42] *Historia privada* and *luchas internas* have no place in Bosch's work. The problem is that nowhere is the reader told where "internal history" ends and "imperial history" begins. The two are very difficult to separate. Fortunately, not only does Bosch depart from this methodological stricture, but the best parts of the book are precisely those where he does depart from his stated aim, as, for example, in the description of the internal social-structural conditions which were conducive to Cuba's revolutions during the nineteenth century.

There is, therefore, an intrinsic weakness to Bosch's definition of "imperialism." The military conquest and aggression aspects of imperialism are only the tip of the iceberg. The real form embodies the enduring "internal" consequences of that structure which Eric Williams described: distorted colonial economies, ethnic groups divided against each other, intellectuals with metropolitan views and ambitions, societies which in the end are tossed into the trash bins of history once their usefulness to the metropolis has come to an end. And imperialism came under many different forms and guises. Bosch's overriding anti-Americanism often distorts his view of that fact. Spain, he asserts, was not an imperial power, since it did not have the one social ingredient necessary for such a role: a national bourgeoisie. Time and again he repeats this assertion without ever fully explaining why a national bourgeoisie is essential for imperial colonization. It brings to mind the nineteenth- and twentieth-century role of Portugal in Africa. Can anyone claim that that was not an imperial colonization? Yet few would claim that Portugal's weak and underdeveloped national bourgeoisie was the crucial factor in that imperialist venture. Portuguese imperialism, like Spanish imperialism before it, was a state-administered enterprise which responded to the interests of the social and economic elites who ran that country.

Surely Bosch must have understood that if one concludes, as he does, that the history of decolonization and liberation in the Caribbean in the past as in the present and future has been, is, and will be achieved only through revolutionary violence, something more than an analysis of battles and conflicts on an imperial frontier is necessary. A sound historical understanding of the elements and sources of the antithetical forces in each island and in the area as a whole is indispensable. Following that, a thorough analysis of the motives behind the revolutionary movement is in order. Are they driven by an ideological belief in social revolution or by the moral indignation which drives modern-conservative societies against tyranny and corruption? Only then can one project revolutionary action, violent or nonviolent.

Bosch's 1970 book contributed to the theory that the Caribbean is a revolutionary frontier. Yet, in analyzing Juan Bosch's total body of historiography, one can only conclude that he was a historian and politician in ideological transition and that "revolution" came late in the process. If one examines his works from, let us say, *Cuba la isla fascinante* (1955, finished in 1952) to *De Cristóbal Colón a Fidel Castro* (1970) one finds an increasing shift to the left in ideology. This shift is irreproachable. What is subject to reproach is that there is no parallel methodological shift. In fact, there is not even a consistent methodology. Bosch moves from an economic interpretation of social change to a psychologistic interpretation, to a psychoanalytic interpretation, and then to even a mystical interpretation. This last can be found, for example, in his study *Trujillo: Causas de una tiranía sin ejemplo* (1959)—in which the trauma of hurricanes determines Trujillo's psyche.

The fact is that Bosch was caught up in the wave of radicalism of the area, but lacking a consistent Marxist methodology he reverted to the traditional search for heroes who are seen to embody not only the dynamics of the historical period under study but who also can be held up as paragons of radical virtue, as reference points for contemporary believers. There is nothing intrinsically wrong in the use of particular men to illustrate social forces which were embodied in their leadership. But to elevate them to revolutionary "event-making" men on the basis of their skin color or the intensity of their class hatreds is categorically un-Marxian and unrevolutionary. In fact, it comes close to what Lenin termed "revolutionary phrasemongering."

There are certain similarities between how Juan Bosch ended his writing career and the way Eric Williams ended his. Bosch, who spent his political career combatting communism, writes a last book that is a manual on how a Leninist party should be structured. Williams's last publication was a compilation of his many speeches, an autobiographical look at his twenty-eight years in power, *Forged from the Love of Liberty*. It could be considered a companion volume to his 1969 book, *Inward Hunger: The Education of a Prime Minister*. In the epilogue Williams legates a bitter final word that is worth analyzing in depth for reasons other than the search for what Selwyn Ryan calls the psychopathological in Williams's personality. It is the clearest testament to the decline of the early and original ideas and ideals with which Williams—through the PNM—launched Trinidad into party politics, independence, and nationhood. It is Williams's version of Simón Bolívar's plaint that to make a revolution in the Americas is to "plow the sea." With a stream-of-consciousness style, Williams legated a document steeped in cynicism and invective—an outpouring of resentment and frustration, pettiness, and pique so palpable in its anguished and tortured nature as to appear nearly paranoid. The scholar whose celebrated historical materialist interpretations of capitalism and slavery never once quoted Marx, Engels, or other early historical materialists now quotes Lenin to describe Latin America as financially and diplomatically dependent. The

Caribbean, that area which he laid so many claims to understanding and explaining sympathetically, is nothing more than "an appendage of metropolitan economics, pandering to metropolitan vices and contemporary deviants."[43] The Puerto Rico he once so admired is now "a farce," Cuba and Jamaica are "mere dependencies," and even the Caribbean Sea is becoming "as polluted as the Mediterranean." The Caribbean Group for Cooperation and Economic Development, "originally a Trinidad and Tobago proposal," is now "a high-falutin title . . . much ado about nothing."[44] CARICOM? That too "is on its last legs."[45] The north-south dialogue for which he originally traveled around the world? A "total waste of time." The man who spent his political career calling for "discipline and production" now was lambasting the island's private sector, borrowing from Vidia Naipaul to jeer: "What will our capitalist mimic men do now?"[46]

In other words, in the analysis in this chapter one finds the early Williams and the later Williams, and as with any leader whose career spans such a length of time, it is difficult to conclude which is the "real" man. This is where the epilogue will tip the scales toward a particular unflattering historical interpretation of Williams.

This last evaluation is not made lightly, because the evidence of Williams's persistent sense of persecution and fear of victimization was beginning to appear. The first to write of it publicly was Dr. Winston Mahabir, a minister in the first preindependence cabinet, who relates the prime minister's constant fears of plotting by his ministers, Muslims, and even at one point a "Chinese coalition."[47] Next, physician Patrick Solomon was close to Williams from the very beginning, holding down cabinet and diplomatic posts until 1977 when he "could no longer continue to serve a prime minister whose petty spite and personal animosities were placed before the national interests."[48] Trinidad political scientist Selwyn Ryan described the fear that the whole cabinet had of their leader.[49] Ryan later published what can be considered the definitive biography of Eric Williams, including what might be a final judgment on the peculiar circumstances of Williams's death, which suggest an "altruistic suicide."[50] That said, Ryan concludes that Williams "left Trinidad and Tobago better than he found it in 1956." Added to the legacy of his considerable scholarship, this meant that "on balance . . . his performance was worthy of History's applause." Beyond all that, his centrist political and economic model, though not his party, has survived to this day.

While certainly not Marxist in any sophisticated way, Bosch's later writings do reflect a dramatic shift in his historiography. As such, Bosch's conversion to Marxism—though apparently not totally to its Leninist variety—came late. In his 1964 book, *Crisis de la Democracia de América en la República Dominicana*, written in exile in Puerto Rico, he shows himself highly offended when a Jesuit priest calls him a Communist, saying that the democratic revolution cannot be Communist. He describes the Communists in the Dominican Republic and Cuba as opportunistically taking advantage of the struggles against dictatorship and injustice.[51] As radical as it was, no one could consider Bosch's 1970 *De Cristóbal Colón a Fidel Castro* (written while in exile in Paris) a Marxist treatise in the way Eric Williams's 1944 book *Capitalism and Slavery* was. One of the earliest signals that he had turned into a radical socialist with strong anti-American sentiments came in his 1967 *El Pentagonismo: sustituto del Imperialismo*.[52] The United States, he argued, was "the World's champion of greed and the defender of the *status quo*."

Two years later, Bosch traveled to North Korea, China, Vietnam, and Cambodia. He was, he said, "seeking the truth."[53] In a most uncritical fashion, he says that he found what he was looking for: everywhere abundance and happiness. North Korea's Kim El Sung was a national hero who defeated the "oligarchical front," while South Korea was the instrument of "Yankee imperialism."[54] Even China's Cultural Revolution was a "voluntary, popular movement." Such was his socialist epiphany that even the brutal dictator Nicolae Ceaușescu of Romania was worthy and a victim of Yankee lies.[55] In 1983 Bosch published *Democracia, capitalismo y liberación nacional*, a selection of his essays that had appeared in his new political party's newspaper between 1978 and 1979. Significant essays reprinted here are taken straight out of his 1970 *De Cristóbal Colón a Fidel Castro*.[56] By then the conversion was quite thorough: the 1983 book is full of quotes from Marx, Engels, and Lenin.

In his final writings Bosch began to use the language of the "laws of the dialectic" and said that his party, the Partido de la Liberación Dominicana (PLD), had been following Lenin's principles of party organization and his principle of "better fewer but better." In many ways one can trace the decline of the PLD to this new structure of "cadres" and the idea that the party—as distinct from his old party, the PRD—was neither populist nor simply reformist but Leninist. Predictably, there soon developed the typical factional disputes with each accusing the other of "ideological deviations."[57] The results of the 1982 elections were devastating: Jorge Blanco's PRD—839,092, Joaquín Balaguer's Reformistas—702,483, and Juan Bosch's PLD—179,847. Again, in 1986 in a treatise on the petit bourgeoisie, Bosch argued that to understand Dominican history one has to understand class conflict as described by Marx in his *Class Wars in France, 1848–1850*.[58] By then the politician had completely overwhelmed the historian. There was absolutely no analytical caution or methodological self-consciousness in the use of the historical analogy—France in 1850 and the present Caribbean. As far as Bosch's "final hurrah," it was paradoxical to an extreme. His candidate for the 1996 elections was an erstwhile radical young man, Leonel Fernández, born in the Dominican Republic but raised in the Bronx, New York. However, to gain that victory over the favorite, José Francisco Peña-Gómez of the PRD, Bosch had to make a deal with his former sworn enemy, Joaquín Balaguer, the openly anti-Afro and certainly anti-Haitian politician. Balaguer did not wish to support his own vice president, Jacinto Peynado, and certainly not the black Peña-Gómez. It is with Balaguer's support that Leonel Fernández of the PLD became president. Bosch had spent a major part of his life organizing expeditions against Trujillo (whom Balaguer served so loyally) and other Caribbean dictators and a major part of his life writing about a "revolutionary" path for his country. In 1996 he made a deal that not only left all his theories as mere dreams but elected a man who had no interest in revolution. With that, Bosch's decades of radical political history condemning the neoliberal programs of both the PRD and Balaguer remained purely for the history books. Fernández just continued the policies of Balaguer, which were little different from the conservative measures that Peña-Gómez was recommending.[59]

This was the debate on paper between what were arguably the most popular historians of the Caribbean. Their writings illustrate how the decades dominated by interest in the Cuban Revolution (and by extension the Haitian Revolution) caused them, albeit mostly Bosch, to shift historical interpretations. Both contributed to the myth of the region's revolutionary proclivities and also to the idea that only total independence engenders a true national identity. And yet, in the final analysis, their political activities shifted to an accommodation to the majoritarian conservative nature of their respective societies.

Finally, because Bosch was widely accepted as a Caribbean historian, it is important to note his peculiar views on the non-Hispanic Caribbean, a

Table 1. Caribbean territories by size, population, and income

Territory	Area (km^2)	Population (1,000)		GDP (per capita)	
		1998	2011	1998	2010
Independent states					
Cuba	114,500	11,000	11,000	—	4,541
Dominican Republic	49,000	7,600	10,000	1,799	4,390
Haiti	28,000	7,000	10,000	208	660
Jamaica	11,000	2,500	2,700	1,559	4,870
Trinidad and Tobago	5,000	1,290	1,300	4,618	16,540
Bahamas	13,900	272	347	12,944	21,021
Barbados	430	261	276	7,894	12,178
St. Lucia	620	153	174	3,907	5,530
St. Vincent/Grenadines	390	127	101	2,635	5,140
Grenada	340	108	108	3,347	5,710
Antigua/Barbuda	440	92	91	8,559	13,620
Dominica	750	96	72	3,310	4,250
St. Kitts/Nevis	270	48	50	6,716	10,960
Mainland					
Guyana	215,000	760	750	825	1,420
Suriname	163,000	457	524	710	4,990
Belize	23,000	211	345	2,725	3,820
European departments/territories					
Guadeloupe (France)	1,710	413	420	12,287	22,000
Martinique (France)	1,100	371	400	14,524	26,000
French Guiana (France)	90,000	135	237	13,044	21,000
Land Curaçao (Neth.)	444	—	143	—	21,000
Bonaire (Neth.)	294	—	17	—	—
Sint Maarten (Neth.)	34	—	41	—	—
St. Martin (France)	53	—	37	—	16,000
Aruba (Neth.)	90	77	101	16,186	23,000
Cayman Islands (UK)	264	33	54	23,966	47,000
British Virgin Islands (UK)	150	17	28	14,010	43,366
Turks & Caicos (UK)	417	14	45	7,061	17,200
Montserrat (UK)	102	11	5.2	3,846	8,500
Anguilla (UK)	90	10	14	6,937	8,800
Puerto Rico (USA)	8,900	3,700	4,000	9,815	27,588
U.S. Virgin Islands (USA)	347	104	109	12,038	—
Bermuda (UK)	21	—	65	70,300	97,000
Sint Eustatius (Neth.)	21	—	35	—	—
Saba (Neth.)	13	—	1.8	—	—

Sources: CARICOM, http://www.caricom.org; World Bank, High-Income Economies, http://www.data.worldbank.org; World Bank, World Development Indicators, http://www.worldbank.org/country.

part of the region he never dealt with even in his *De Cristóbal Colón a Fidel Castro*. His views are, to say the least, fundamentally flawed. The English-speaking states are, he says, "anomalous" states that are partly responsible for "the modern erosion of true statehood." Barbados "is treated as if it were an independent country" when in fact the queen of England is its head of state. Similarly, Jamaica, Trinidad and Tobago, and the others are all "anomalous," since they make final judicial appeals to Britain's Privy Council.[60] Sad, indeed, that such a popular Hispanic Caribbeanist author had such erroneous views.

2

Eric Williams vs. Frank Tannenbaum

On Slave Laws, Slavery Systems, and Subsequent Race Relations

What might be considered the first truly Pan-Caribbean conference was held in Puerto Rico in December 1956. The sponsor was the American Association for the Advancement of Science, and the organizer was Vera Rubin, then a research associate at the New York–based Institute for the Study of Man in the Tropics. Virtually everyone who was anyone in the field was there, as is evident in the table of contents of the publication that resulted from the conference.

Table 2. Contents of *Caribbean Studies: A Symposium*, 1956

Source: Vera Rubin, ed., *Caribbean Studies: A Symposium* (Seattle: University of Washington Press, 1960).

At the time the University of the West Indies was still the University College of the West Indies, and the University of Puerto Rico had not yet established its Institute of Caribbean Studies. Since up to that date there were only three independent countries in the insular Caribbean (Cuba, Haiti, and the Dominican Republic), it can be said that Caribbean studies emerged before final Caribbean decolonization and, as such, provided the future leaders of many of these countries with an admirable body of scholarship from which to draw. Their interest in issues of race and class were very much present already.

Judging from the proceedings,[1] most of the conference was conducted with the customary academic propriety, certainly tame compared with future Caribbean conferences described in the prologue. Be that as it may, this conference did witness, and the proceedings did record, a monumental debate—indeed, confrontation—on a sensitive topic, comparative slavery, between two distinguished scholars from very different backgrounds: Eric Williams and Frank Tannenbaum. Williams, at the time, was chief minister in pre-independent Trinidad and Tobago. His book *Capitalism and Slavery*, based on his dissertation at Oxford, published in 1944, was by 1956 a recognized classic. In addition, he was editor of the *Caribbean Historical Review* published in Trinidad. Williams had every professional and intellectual right to be at this conference.

But why was Frank Tannenbaum there? Tannenbaum had published on the Latin American labor movement (1921) and a "Whither Latin America?" article very much in vogue at the time. Undoubtedly, however, his most prodigious work was on Mexico, including *The Mexican Agrarian Revolution* (1928) and *Peace by Revolution* (1933). He would much later return to Mexico with *The Struggle for Peace and Bread* (1950).

In addition, Tannenbaum already had a reputation as a major liberal thinker. In academic year 1938–39, he participated with three other professors in the first seminar at Columbia University. Its theme was the history of slavery in the western world. It was the ideal setting for a man of Tannenbaum's background, ideology, and temperament: interdisciplinary and instructed by an ongoing concern for contemporary events. Not surprisingly, given what was occurring in Germany and Italy, the concern was with questions of freedom, liberty, justice, law, and morality. The central question was also its operating hypothesis: even under the most difficult circumstances, whenever man was defined as a moral being, freedom was eventually achieved. Proof certain of this, according to Tannenbaum, was to be found in the comparative study of slavery. Where the slave was governed by a system of laws that accepted him as a moral being, slavery was abolished peacefully and congenial race relations followed. Where the slave was regarded as chattel and denied any moral status, a harsh system of race relations (even revolution) endured after emancipation.

This became Frank Tannenbaum's firm position, and he presented it to the academic and general public in his inimitable way: a small book written in his unadorned but impactful style. *Slave and Citizen: The Negro in the Americas* appeared in 1946 and immediately became required reading for students in history and all the other social sciences. Although there was already a substantial literature on the slave trade, it is not too daring an assertion to claim that it was Tannenbaum's little book which shocked whole generations of American readers, previously ignorant or in denial, into confronting the slave trade, one of the greatest acts of barbarity in which virtually every European nation as well as Islam had participated.

In his first and only book on the topic of slavery and race relations, Tannenbaum maintained that it was Spanish law and tradition, transferred to the New World, which governed the nature of slavery in the Spanish colonies. His argument that there was a big difference between Spanish and Anglo-Saxon law and tradition was based on several historical facts. First, there was a long history of dealing with slavery in Spain, but slavery was relatively new in England. The laws of each country reflected this fact. In Spain, said Tannenbaum, it was the tradition of the Justinian Code, elaborated into the Ley de Siete Partidas (1263–65), that governed. More than just codes of law such as are found in English Common Law, these were codes detailing what moral behavior was. Tannenbaum then described at length how these codes defined the equality of all men in the eyes of God. It is an interesting fact that Tannenbaum was advancing this argument well before Lewis Hanke had published his groundbreaking studies on Bartolomé de las Casas and the Spanish search for justice in the Americas.[2] In his famous debates with Sepulveda, Las Casas established that the Indians were *persona*, that is, they had souls and as such could not be enslaved. The Africans had not yet been brought as slaves to the New World. Second, Tannenbaum argued that slavery in the Spanish world "had become a matter of financial competence on the part of the slave." This allowed the slave with income to buy his freedom (manumission). Later, even the title of whiteness (*que se tenga por blanco*) could be purchased. Based on these findings Tannenbaum compared the Latin American system with its "expansive," "pliable," and "malleable" characteristics to that of the English and American systems where the slave was simple property or chattel and "the Negro was considered a slave by nature."[3]

Clearly it was this "Tannenbaum Thesis" which Williams had in mind when he opened his presentation to the conference with the oratorical directness that was his style in academia and in politics. His argument was predictably opposed to that of Tannenbaum.

> The attempt has been made to explain . . . divergences [in race relations] as a difference between the Latin tradition and the Anglo-Saxon. . . . This is far too simple. The explanation is rather to be sought in the nature of property in these different countries at different periods.

Williams proceeded to give a lesson in the comparative historical method worthy of an Émile Durkheim:

> The distinction in race or colour was only the superficial visible symbol of a distinction which in reality was based on the ownership of property. . . . This general truth, which many writers have refused to recognize, can be illustrated for our present purpose in two ways. The first is in the treatment of the slaves, one of the principal forms of property at different periods in the history of the Caribbean. For example, the brutality of the plantation system in Saint Domingue in 1789 was in striking contrast to the relative benevolence of the relations between master and slave at the same time in Trinidad. To give another example, the slave code of Cuba in 1789 was a vastly different thing, so far as its practical operation was concerned, from the slave code of Cuba in 1840.

Williams explained that Cuba and Trinidad in 1789 were for the most part subsistence economies, which, he adds with evident sarcasm, could tolerate the sort of paternal slavery and benevolent despotism "that one finds eulogized in the works of Hesiod and the sophistry of Aristotle."

It was Tannenbaum's turn. He was accepting none of it and stated his objections to the Williams presentation in no uncertain terms:

> My differences with Dr. Williams are many—not with his stated political objectives and purposes, but with his underlying theory of history

and with his implied concepts of the nature of society and the social process. There is an implicit indifference to tradition, custom and *mores* and a sort of denial of the place of customary law and the role of religious belief in the way men deal with one another that I find difficult to adjust to the things I know. . . . Dr. Williams talks the language of the French Philosophes and of the Enlightenment, a language widely respected and, in its time, of enormous impact on what men thought right policy and good works. But to me this language is like a thorn in the flesh, for it caricatures the nature of man and falsifies and distorts the character of human institutions. Institutions, that is the slow accretions of customary ways that become traditions and law, community and society, whether as church or guild or even family, or anything that stands in the way of the individual's isolated relation to the State seems to this view to be iniquitous and a conspiracy.

Calling Williams's interpretation a case of "economic determinism," Tannenbaum brought home his main critique of it, citing the fact that "a theory can never be true." It can be a lot of interesting and pleasing things, but "truth is not one of them."

The debate which followed was not published, so we leave it there for others to unravel the "truth" or falsity in the debate over the Hispanic vs. Anglo-Saxon world of slavery. Franklin Knight and Rebecca Scott have done revealing follow-up analyses on the subject. Knight reopens the debate in his introduction to the new edition of Tannenbaum's *Slave and Citizen*. There he outlines the two major schools of thought on the treatment of slaves. The Tannenbaum thesis "gained wide currency and refinement" from later writers such as Gilberto Freyre, Stanley Elkins, Herbert Klein, and Harry Hoetink, he writes. But Knight has already opined, in his very thorough case study of slave society in Cuba, that "Tannenbaum's valiant argument does not stand up to comparative inquiry."[4]

Knight points to Marvin Harris as a close follower of the Williams thesis. Knight is not satisfied that the "truth" lies there, since the relationship between capitalism and slavery is far more complicated than either Williams or Harris suggested. In this, Knight finds support in the work of David Brion Davis, who, he says, made the most cogent appreciation of this point. "We should greatly oversimplify the problem," says Davis, "if we were to see too close a correlation between economic profit and social values, or to con-

clude that antislavery attitudes were a direct response to economic change."
It is this less than definite statement about the debate that Knight finds most
pertinent to his Cuban case study. The reason is stated in stark terms in his
book on Cuban slavery: "By 1850 the Cuban sugar industry was the most
advanced the world had ever experienced. Why then did abolition of slavery
[1886] take so long?"[5]

The answer he gives covers much history: the Ten-Year War in Cuba
(1868–78), political upheavals in Spain, and a series of technological changes
such as the steam engine railroads and new developments in sugar engineer-
ing and chemistry. After a thorough review of all these factors, he does seem
to lean toward the Williams thesis when he concludes with a veiled critique
of the Tannenbaum thesis and a plea for case studies: "It is knowledge of the
society as a whole with its economic ramifications, rather than of narrower
segments of legal and cultural heritage, which will lead to a better understanding of conditions during and after slavery."[6]

Knight laid down a challenge to many in the fields of race and ethnic relations, which invariably base their theories on the comparative analysis of
slave and plantation regimes. One who took up this challenge was Rebecca J.
Scott.[7] In a study grounded in both good social science conceptualizing and
deft use of primary sources, Scott critiques the Williams materialist explanation without adopting the Tannenbaum thesis. In her frankly revisionist
approach, she blames both "theories" for focusing only on slavery and never
on the slave as a rational actor. The latter were neither mere instruments of
production nor mindless followers of cultural, legal, and religious systems.
They were, says Scott, individuals who made choices. Rather than being passive witnesses to the collapse of a system, they adapted and made choices
in response to options available in the society. This is where differences in
the particular legal and religious systems allowed for different access and
outcomes. The historical materialist explanation and its extension into a
Marxian ontology, argues Scott, is inadequate to explain the complexities of
emancipation in Cuba. The resilience of the system and the dynamic initiatives and counter initiatives of the various actors all belie an explanation of
mechanistically driven doom. Demonstrating that the slaves were not passive but had options open to them, Scott has the burden of proving that these
actors understood the existence of these options and actually attempted to
achieve them despite all odds. She elegantly describes this process as "the
dialectic of striving and constraint."[8] By showing their continued initia-

tives—both collective and individual—Scott reintroduces the role of values and the spirit of freedom to the study of emancipation. At no point does she deal with the opportunities and options available to slaves as hypothetical situations; they are demonstrated as historical facts, individually documented and explained through a skillful use of statistics, group histories, and biographical data taken from plantation or court records.

By introducing the actions of slaves in the political system, Scott reformulates the research questions by expanding the parameters of the problem. She begins by emphasizing that abolition in Cuba took place in quite a different political context than it did, for instance, in the West Indies or in the United States. The British emancipation act, says David Brion Davis, was a model of decisive action, an "act of the nation not of its rulers."[9] Cuba was also a colony, but unlike the British government in 1833 or the U.S. government in 1864, the Spanish metropolitan government was not at all of one mind on emancipation. Its main goal was to preserve the colonial link. The difference in political context became crucial as Spain tried to reconcile three often contradictory goals. First, it strove to protect its revenues from Cuba by guaranteeing enough labor to the expanding Cuban plantation decades after the end of the international slave trade. Second, it tried to safeguard the colonial tie by placating and making concessions to a politically aroused and militarily important population of color. Finally, it made mighty efforts not to alienate the planter class who generated the revenues, which in the final analysis could be done only by allowing the planter class to control their workforce and therefore upholding slavery.

Spain attempted this balancing act in an international context antagonistic to slavery, first by British actions after 1834 and then after 1865 by its newly slave-free neighbor, the United States. Using an implicit model of behavior that conceptualizes groups and individuals consciously engaged in a means-goals process, Scott describes the range of existing group agendas that overlapped or intersected according to perceived strategic needs. All parties—whether slave, freedman, planter, or Spanish government—showed will and purpose, which kept the process dynamic as they adjusted and shifted agendas and tactics.

The analysis introduces the reader to issues long left out of studies of emancipation: the persistence and functional importance of family ties among the slaves; the persistence of prized values such as friendship and loyalty toward the enslaved, especially on the part of those who gained their freedom; and the capacity of illiterate Africans to understand and use the law, manipulate the state, and rely on friendly allies of all types.

Those laboring in the rich field of comparative slavery and plantation systems might not applaud Scott's strong caveat against facile generalization and thus easy comparisons, since she specifically rules out the complete comparability of her particular study. Indeed, her detailed descriptions of the differences between, for instance, Matanzas, an archetypical province of large plantations, and a province such as Santiago de Cuba, where by 1878 "the rigid patterns of a slaveholding society were to a large extent broken," make generalization even about Cuba dangerous.[10] Social scientists will have to join this methodological fray, especially those who still cling to that popular theory about the Caribbean plantation society that I discuss in chapter 6. Despite this caveat, Scott does not reject comparative studies. In a fine essay in the *Journal of History* she calls for a possible comparative analysis of emancipation and of postemancipation societies. "Comparison," she says, "has . . . functions beyond that of affording the historian the nearest approximation to a controlled experiment."[11] On that score, it is good to emphasize that as distinct from the British Caribbean where emancipation was celebrated everywhere on the same date (1834), this was not the case in Latin America. Each country had its own political and economic reasons to accelerate but mostly to delay emancipation: in Central America, 1824; Mexico, 1829; Colombia, 1851; Venezuela, 1854; Peru, 1855; Uruguay, 1853; Argentina, 1864; Cuba, 1886; and Brazil, 1888.

In order to achieve a holistic view and avoid the reductionism of focusing strictly on the period of emancipation, the reorganization of labor, or the transition of the free labor plantation into the global market, she proposes a framework that incorporates all three phases. It is important that she chose studies by three Caribbean historians who came close to meeting this standard: the Guyanese Walter Rodney, the Jamaican Douglas Hall, and the Cuban Raúl Cepero Bonilla.[12] All three describe the emancipated slaves (freedmen) engaged in an ongoing process of negotiation, bitter and asymmetrical but nevertheless proactive—and because of that, the Caribbean showed a variety of postemancipation forms. In British Guiana (today's Guyana) and Trinidad, the entry of indentured Indian labor and the limited farmland sustained by dikes and canals pushed the former slaves into urban work, leaving plantation work to the Indians. In Jamaica, as Hall explains, things were different: a vibrant sector of small farmers came about. In none of these cases were the ex-slaves passive. As Rodney explains, the sense of injustice led to the watershed riots of 1905 in Guyana and to the Morant Bay Rebellion in 1865 in Jamaica. Subsequent to this, the British colonial authorities set up a Lands Department in 1867 and expanded state title to Crown lands. As Erna Brodber notes, "In this way government and private sales produced a class of small landowning blacks, so nationally recognized by the turn of the century that the administration gave them a special name: the 'small settler.'"[13] Similarly, the British response to the West Indies riots of 1937 was an even more extended land settlement program.

Where the freemen did not fare at all well was in Cuba. After the freed slaves joined the struggle for independence, they found recent Spanish and Canary Islanders occupying the available land and serving the large estates as *colonos*. In addition, the Cuban freedman, not dissimilar from the cases of Guyana and Trinidad, had to face the competition from low wage Jamaicans and even lower wage Haitian *braceros*. Like all black freemen, what Cubans desired most was to own land. Alejandro de la Fuente cites an American observer in the early twentieth century who said, "The Cuban negro has a marked trait in the instinct of land ownership."[14] This desire was true of all Cubans, but it was a particularly difficult goal for Afro-Cubans. In 1899, blacks controlled 25 percent of the farms on the island as owners or renters, but in Oriente they controlled 43 percent. Afro-Cubans controlled 48 percent of the land devoted to rice production in the province, 59 percent of coffee, 61 percent of cocoa, and 61 percent of *malanga*. Especially in Oriente, there was a good chance that each acre acquired by foreign investors and devoted to sugar production represented an acre lost to Afro-Cubans' subsistence and independent farming. Some of the southeastern municipalities in which the process of land dispossession was more intense were also those with the island's highest proportion of Afro-Cubans. Sugar expansion took place in the northern area of Oriente as well, but population densities were significantly lower there. The long-term effects of this process of land displacement can be summarized in just a few words: the proletarianization of the Afro-Cuban peasantry, particularly in the east. Between 1899 and 1931 blacks' control over land decreased 50 percent in terms of the number of farms and the total farmland (table 3). By 1931 Afro-Cubans represented approximately 28 percent of the total population but controlled only 8.5 percent of the farmland in the country. No wonder Ramiro Guerra stated in 1929 that blacks had been the first victims of sugar *latifundia*. While the causes of the ferocious race

Table 3. Percentage of distribution and landownership by race, 1899–1931

Category	Number of farms		Total farmland	
	1899	1931	1899	1931
Whites	75.3	88.4	84.0	91.5
Owners	24.0	37.1	33.3	45.6
Renters	51.3	51.4	50.7	45.9
Blacks	24.7	11.6	16.0	8.5
Owners	5.3	5.1	3.7	4.4
Renters	19.4	6.5	12.3	4.1

Sources: U.S. War Department, Report 1899, 555; Cuba, Censo 1931, table 37.
Note: The category "blacks" includes mulattos.

war of 1909 were many, there can be little doubt that land hunger and land displacement joined with general racial discrimination to agitate and then ignite the black insurrection. And to bring the story forward, blacks have not fared well in terms of landownership under the Cuban Revolution. A University of Havana survey found that by 1992, whites represented 98 percent of private farmers and 95 percent of cooperative agricultural members.[15]

In the case of Puerto Rican ex-slaves—much fewer in number than in Cuba—the situation was not much better. While the sugar industry had mobility of capital as well as expertise,[16] the *jibaro* would not be liberated from his miserable living conditions until liberal New Dealers such as Rexford Tugwell joined forces with the reformist Luís Muñoz Marín.

It might be too much to claim that the pioneering works of Eric Williams and Frank Tannenbaum initiated the field, but it is evident that each in his own way enriched studies in the areas of comparative slavery and comparative race relations. A truly solid scholarship is now available to the student wishing to pursue further studies, especially if they are case studies. That said, one senses that the central point of what became known as the "Tannenbaum thesis," the "malleability" and "pliability" of Latin American race relations as distinct from the harsher Anglo-Saxon modes, is still the dominant interpretation. Tannenbaum repeats the comparison in his 1966 book, *Ten Keys to Latin America*, one of the most influential books ever written on Latin America: "The difference between the basic conditions of social equality and opportunity in the United States and Latin America is broad and deep—and not really changeable for a long time to come."[17]

The debate around that point has to be revisited lest we leave standing a great myth: that Latin American (including Brazilian) race relations are much more cordial than those in the United States. They were not during the colonial period, the postcolonial period, or today. Three brief case studies (herein called "exhibits") will illustrate the nature of Latin American race relations.

The first "exhibit" deals with the nature of race relations in eighteenth-century Spanish America. Racial distinctions and grading were an integral part of the Spanish mentality. They had been the basis of the discrimination and social distance established between *gente decente* (decent people), on the one hand, and Jews and Moors, on the other. In similar fashion it was used in the New World to put Indians, Africans, and their mixed-blood progeny in a subordinate position. As Stanley and Barbara Stein have argued, it was not just that Spain legated a stratified social structure; that existed everywhere. Rather, they say:

> The tragedy of the colonial heritage was a social structure further stratified by color and physiognomy—by what anthropologists call phenotype. . . . As North America has come to perceive, a society may perpetuate social inequalities far more effectively when the maldistribution of income is buttressed by phenotype.[18]

Eventually the system of stratification extended, with different degrees of prejudice, to everyone born in the colonies—the *criollos*. Suspicions of being tainted with "impure blood" could be overcome only through *pruebas de limpieza de sangre*—proofs of purity of the blood—that were "minutely examined, without any possibility of trickery."[19] The Inquisition was charged with enforcing that law and set of conventions. Certainly there was some "passing," as there is even in the most rigid caste system, but it was the exception. Franklin Knight discovered in nineteenth-century Cuba a large number of applications for royal permission to breach the color barrier so as to enter universities, professions, or the all-white bureaucracy. He does not indicate the rate of approvals, but does explain that "there must have been tens of thousands whose obvious handicap of skin color or lack of the socially valuable *limpieza de sangre* completely deterred [them] from any attempt to break out of their artificially narrowed worlds."[20] There was, says Knight, a built-in inequality in the system upheld by all whites in the Spanish overseas colonies.

Contrary to the belief that Africans were brought to the New World only after the plantations and mines had modernized, the fact is that African slaves were present since early times. Table 4 shows the number of slaves known to be introduced between 1604 and 1625. The combination of official discriminatory legislation combined with the ongoing reality of race mixing had become so complex that by 1735 two Spanish engineers, Jorge Juan and Antonio Ulloa, discovered a bewildering array of "castes" or "tribes" in Cartagena de Indias, Lima, Panama, and Santo Domingo. They began with simple descriptive categories—*mestizo, mulato,* and *sambo*—followed by categories indicating biological proportions. An individual with one-third African blood was known as a *tercerón; cuarterón* indicated one-fourth African blood; *quinterón,* one-fifth; and *octarón,* one-eighth. Following such finely calibrated categories were descriptive ones such as *tente al aire* (mixture of *cuarterón* and a *mulato*). The term *salto atrás* (literally, a "jump back") was reserved for anyone suspected of even the minutest degree of mixing, the so-called "one-drop" rule.

The two Spaniards were struck by the punctiliousness of the social etiquette surrounding interpersonal relations and of the *fueros* (legal privileges as well as deference) due each: "Every person is so jealous of the order of their tribe or caste, that if, through inadvertence, you call them by a degree lower than what they actually are, they are highly offended, never suffering themselves to be deprived of so valuable a gift of fortune." The struggle was always to be or approximate being white, especially among those whose mixture was not apparent. Race was supreme, for "the conceit of being white alleviates the pressure of every other calamity."[21]

The second "exhibit" dealt with an event that took place on the island of Trinidad, conquered and wrested from Spain by the British in 1797. The

Table 4. African slaves brought to Spanish America, 1604–25

To Veracruz, Mexico	29,785
To Cartagena, Colombia	35,311
To Havana, Cuba	980
To Santo Domingo	1,788
To Puerto Rico	1,114
To Venezuela	1,096
To Santa Marta, Colombia	800

Source: Enriqueta Vila Vilar, *Hispano-américa y el comercio de esclavos* (Seville: Escuela de Estudios Hispanoamericanos, 1977), 204.

1806 torture of a mulatto girl accused of theft by the military governor, Col. Thomas Picton, caused a public and political ruckus in England. Picton was found guilty under British law prohibiting torture but was, upon appeal to the Privy Council, found not guilty under the laws of Spain, which under the 1797 Articles of Capitulation were still governing the island. It had been found, says J. N. Brierley, that Picton's actions had been in accordance with the laws of Castile, which were very much different from British law.[22]

The moral of this vignette is that the English moved to reform and ameliorate slave laws at the beginning of the nineteenth century, but it would take another seven decades for the Spaniards and eight for the Portuguese to do the same. Contrary to Tannenbaum's thesis regarding Spanish law, they were in fact very harsh on nonwhites.

The third "exhibit" illustrates much of the type of race relations that we will encounter in chapter 4. It deals with the execution of a black Venezuelan colonel of Bolívar's army, Leonardo Infante. This execution had dire consequences for the future relations between Venezuela and Colombia. Here we deal only with the reasons given for executing him.[23] Colombian historian José Manuel Groot began his analysis of the case by noting that Vice President Santander's honor had been injured in public by some of Infante's jokes about effete lawyers and poets who did no fighting. It should be noted that Bolívar himself often made reference to this stereotype of the Colombian Bogotá elite as being effete civilians. Infante only repeated a widely held prejudice, except in a cruder form. Groot then describes what followed:

> [His neighbors] were afraid of him because he was a complete plainsman (*era todo un llanero*) and plainsmen have obnoxious games (*chanzas pesadas*); to which was added his imposing presence. He was a Negro of the purest type, a plainsman from Maturín [Venezuela], a fierce cavalryman (*de lanza brava*), robust, well shaped. . . . He always wore his uniform with its silver epaulettes and high ribboned hat [although he was not a drunkard nor did he ever misbehave with anyone]. Even so, with these manners of a plainsman he bothered those of the neighborhood, and even those whom he knew regarded him with hostility, *because a plainsman in a society of educated people* (gentes cultas) *is like a bulldog which enters a hall wagging its tail and even though its owner says that it does not bite, they all look at it with hostility and want it thrown out.*[24]

A more appropriate metaphor to describe the clashing styles would be difficult to find. Even one as sympathetic to Infante as the priest who heard his last confession describes the officer in essentially negative terms:

> Although Colonel Infante was a pure Negro and was not known to have any political education, even so he was a Roman and Apostolic Catholic; and even though he could not express himself except in harsh and barbaric terms, one cannot deny that he had great talent.[25]

Infante, on his way to the gallows, is reported to have looked up at the Congress building and several civilian representatives and exclaimed, "I am the one who put you in those positions!" Again, before dying he shouted to the assembled troops, "This is the payment I am given. . . . I am the first, but others will follow me."[26]

Evaluations of social honor and styles of life have traditionally played an important role in the stratification of Spanish and Latin American society. The concepts of *hidalguía* (literally "proper to the son of somebody") and *pundonor* ("point of honor") perhaps embody the multiple facets of the phenomenon. Related to this concept of honor is that of *decoro*, which is more than the literal translation of "decorum." It implies dignity and honor, keeping up the necessary appearances and behavior of one's status, and thus adherence to the conventional rules that embody a status group's style of life. *Hidalguía, pundonor,* and *decoro* all convey the importance of an honorable mode of comportment and presentation of self in the evaluation of status. This form of analysis has a long basis in classical sociological theory. Max Weber speaks of social esteem, social honor, status honor, and prestige in portraying a social structure based on status groups; these are the critical factors that create the social distance between groups and generally color their relationships. "In context," says Weber, "status honor is normally expressed by the fact that above all else a specific *style of life* can be expected from all those who wish to belong to the circle."[27]

The status group institutionalizes its style of life and conserves it through shared conventions and also by the fact that those who defy those conventions, such as by engaging in dishonorable occupations, can suffer a status disqualification. Considerations of racial purity, family connections, and education were all part of the constellation of attributes of status in Spanish America. It is good to remember, however, that behind these very real albeit often intangible and subjective social factors, there was, of course, the stark reality of economic power. This power provided the opportunities and wherewithal of a given style of life. Weber was emphatic on this point. "Stratification by status," he maintained, "goes hand in hand with a monopolization of ideal and material goods and opportunities."

What the "exhibits" point to is a stratification system so rigid that it is best considered caste-like. The problem with the Tannenbaum thesis is the problem of all general studies based mostly on legal dispositions in Spanish-American relations. They are too far removed from the local communities where issues of social mobility play themselves out. Notice how C. H. Haring argues that since 1503 "Castilian law" allowed any subject above the rank of peasant to erect his property into a *mayorazgo* or entail, "and thus acquire the privileges of *hidalguía* with the title of *don*."[28] This might be what the law provided; what occurred at the local level where everyone knew who was who proved a different story. In the early 1960s, a group of U.S. and Colombian sociologists studied social mobility in Cereté, Colombia, an area of prosperous coffee *latifundias*. A group of fast-rising landowners made claims to being part of the "upper class." This was blocked by the traditional upper-class members who were the ones establishing the criteria of mobility: "racial purity, family lineage, education, social club membership, and economic position." The aspiring nouveau riche were not admitted to the traditional circle.[29]

Any concluding thoughts on the Williams vs. Tannenbaum debate would not be complete without some personal testimonials based on my own travels and research. I have recently visited and looked informally at Afro-Latin American communities in Nicaragua, Costa Rica, Ecuador, and Colombia. What is immediately apparent is that the blacks in all these countries are clearly discriminated against in residence, jobs, and social relations, yet their situations are different in important ways. Neither Tannenbaum nor Williams seems to have adequately explained these differences.

Nicaragua, May 12–13, 2014

In Nicaragua, "Afro-descendientes" have lived mostly on what has generally been called the Miskito (Mosquito) Coast on the Atlantic, especially in the city of Bluefields. They had their own kingdom there, recognized by Great

Britain. It was a safe haven for escaped slaves from all points. There is enormous pride in their past, a significant part of their identity of being *muy diferentes* from what they call *los del Pacífico*. The authoritarian and harsh efforts of the Sandinistas to "integrate" the Miskitos into the nation of Nicaragua and their courageous resistance tell us a lot about their distinct identity.[30] The region is officially called the Región Autónoma Atlántico Sur. Bluefields is its capital. Historically isolated from the dominant Spanish-speaking and Catholic mestizos, these English (in its *kriol* version) speakers are mostly of Jamaican and Miskito Indian descent and Protestant, originally mostly of the Moravian Church. In the 1960s many moved to Managua for work and for the higher education not available on the coast. Another migratory wave took place in the late 1970s and early 1980s, escaping from being drafted by either the "Contras" or the Sandinista army.

According to the special report of *La Prensa*, March 21, 2014, Nicaragua counts 22,890 Afro-descendientes, 18,890 known as Kriols (Creoles), and 4,000 Garifunas, the mixture of Carib Indians from Dominica and black slaves.[31] In Managua, Afro-descendientes live in specific neighborhoods and are not much in evidence in central Managua.[32] The largest concentration is found in Bello Horizonte, which is popularly known as "Negrorizonte." There the atmosphere is pure *costeño*. *Kriol* English, creole foods, and Jamaican reggae and Trinidadian soca music seem to pulsate from every one of the humble but clean and welcoming abodes. One walks the narrow streets safely while taking in the familiar music and wafting scents of the ever-present *patis*. The latter, of Jamaican origin, is now, by the way, fully a part of the Nicaraguan and Costa Rican repasts.

In Managua, according to anthropologist María Dolores Alvarez, Nicaraguan mestizos discriminated against the blacks; they saw them, she says, "as slaves." Blacks, however, appear to reverse the stereotypes and take great pride in openly identifying themselves as "black people." This is a case where black Nicaraguans, even after partly assimilating to the Spanish language and mestizo culture of the majority, live voluntarily in black neighborhoods where they speak Kriol at home, attend their own Baptist churches, and enjoy their creole food and West Indian music. Nicaraguan Afro-descendientes are proud of their distinct culture and origins, facts reinforced by visits to and arrivals from La Mosquitia. One leaves Nicaragua with the distinct impression that blacks there march to their own drummer, increasingly integrated but hardly fully assimilated into the culture of los del Pacifico. This could be a form of cultural disassociation found elsewhere in the Caribbean, and this might explain the absence of resentment and conflict in their daily relations.

Costa Rica, May 6–11, 2014

The Ticos of Costa Rica consider themselves the most "European" of Central Americans. This auto-description is only partly true. As the data presented by Duncan and Meléndez indicate, there was considerable Indian admixture over two centuries, leaving an essentially mestizo population.[33] They calculate the mestizo population in 1824 at 73 percent. Two informed scholars estimate that at most 6 to 9 percent of the population had no mixed blood.[34] Small Spanish settlements moved to the Meseta Central and planted cacao and coffee. Because there were few Indians and no mines to exploit, Costa Rican farmers tended to take care of their small *fincas* themselves. Blacks, mostly from Jamaica, were brought in the 1880s to build railroads and work on the banana plantations along the Atlantic coast. Marcus Garvey had been a time-keeper on the plantations in 1909. He returned to visit twice after achieving prominence. It is estimated that at emancipation in 1824, no more than 100 slaves were freed. The 1950 census was the last one to enumerate by race: 15,118 blacks, 92 percent of whom resided in Limón.[35]

Around 1948 white Costa Ricans began to migrate to Limón, and the displacement of blacks from their small plots accelerated. The government of León Cortés passed laws that defined the black as *extranjero*.[36] And the town of Turrialba on the Atlantic side was an informal but widely recognized township that adhered to the dividing line between the white highlands and the black Atlantic coast. Molina and Palmer speak of a "racist anxiety" about the breaching of this line.[37] The anger and resentment of the Costa Rican blacks are evident in the many novels of Quince Duncan, a Costa Rican of West Indian descent. In his 1973 novel, *Los cuatro espejos,* the black protagonist feels inadequate because he has been a failure in sports, music, and artisanal work. Not only is he a mere anthropologist but "he could never overcome being identified as a Limonense."[38] Note the distinction between Costa Ricans and the blacks in the prologue to Duncan's 1971 novel, *Hombres curtidos:* "The Negro, men with skin like cured leather of the Atlantic Coast, conceal a drama which we the Costa Ricans still do not understand."[39] The fact that these blacks from Limón have been in the country for three generations appears to make little difference. As Duncan and Meléndez put it, "No son costarricenses, no son jamaicanos. . . . Vegetan en un país que de pronto se vuelve hostil, restringiéndolos[40] [They are not Costa Ricans, they are not Jamaicans. . . . They vegetate in a country which can suddenly turn hostile, resisting them]. Despite the removal of laws restricting the movement of blacks from Limón, after the victory of José Figueres's revolutionary campaign in 1948, Costa Rican blacks continued marginalized and spatially segregated. In 1967 Michael David Olsin published *The Negro in Costa Rica*, which argued that "the Negros, living in the lowlands [Limón], are still viewed by most Costa Ricans as foreigners."[41]

Not surprisingly, the two themes of the sparse literature on the blacks in Costa Rica repeat two ideas: the miseries of their life on the banana plantations and on railroad construction, and the painful efforts to integrate into the national society and culture.[42] It was not until Carlos Luís Fallás published his novel *Mamíta Yunai* in 1941 that the Costa Rican public was introduced to the black workers and inhabitants of their Atlantic coast. The novel was summed up as "una narración directa y cruda de una Realidad brutal e inhumana que persiste, a pesar de calculadas apariencias."[43]

Ecuador, February 26–28, 2014

Anthropologist Jean Muteba Rahier describes race relations in Esmeraldas, a major oil exporting port of Ecuador where blacks and mulattos are 70 percent of the population but are not part of the elites. This, let it be said, is one of the country's major oil transshipment ports. A visit to the vast, technically advanced oil shipment installations did not reveal much of an Afro-Ecuadorean presence. Nor were they evident in other middle-class circles, as Rahier tells it: "Esmeraldian elites reproduce the national ideology of mestizaje . . . and apply a racist reading of the map. . . . The northern sector of the province, usually referred to as *El Norte*, . . . is seen as a place of backwardness because it is the place of the *negros azules*, the "blue blacks," so called for the darkness of their skins . . . people without 'culture.'" Among those who left their fully Afro-Ecuadorean villages to try and integrate into mestizo society, Rahier notes, there is a strong tendency to accommodate to mestizo-white society through skin whitening (*blan-queamiento*), "a dominant theme of the social fabric of life."[44]

Elites are white-mestizo from Quito or even Colombia. On a visit to the Museo de Esmeraldas, I did not see a single exhibit on Afro-Esmeraldeños. It was dedicated to the pre-Columbian Indian cultures. Similarly, the catalogue of the museum was dedicated to pre-Columbian cultures with exactly one and a half pages on "El poblamiento afro-esmeraldeño." The most celebrated black personality of Esmeraldas was Petita Palma, prominent promoter of black music and dance. I was surprised by the fact that her poem "Ser negro no es afrenta" was promoted as an exclamation of pride, since I saw it as abjectly apologetic.

> Ser negro no es afrenta [To be black is not an affront]
> ni es color que quita forma [nor is it a color that takes away good taste]
> porque el zapatito negro [because the little black shoe]
> Le luce a la mejor dama.[45] [looks nice on the most distinguished lady]

Similarly, Julio Estupiñan Tello's claim that despite the "inclemencias y pretensiones centenarias" [centenarian inclements and pretentions] *and* "superadas las deprimente condiciones materiales y socio-políticas que le agobian," [having overcome the depressing material and political conditions which oppress him] Esmeraldan blacks will achieve "un vigoroso florecimiento."[46] No such "thriving" was evident in the way they live. Not a single taxi driver (all mestizos) would take me into the black ghetto that sits on the coast, below the city proper. They all expressed great fear of the blacks. It should not be surprising that Lonely Planet's guide to Ecuador warns the traveler that "Esmeraldas is considered one of Ecuador's most dangerous major cities . . . an unappealing destination . . . [a] notorious reputation . . . avoid arriving after dark."[47] The history of police abuse and harassment of blacks in Ecuador's largest city and major modern trading port, Guayaquil, is dramatically portrayed in a documentary, *Los Afroecuatorianos*, produced by the Museo y Centro Cultural de Esmeraldas (February 2014). There is evident racial labeling and profiling of blacks as potential criminals or at least deviants. Despite the evidence, the documentary ends by promoting the country as a multiethnic society. Multiethnic it might be, but equitable or hospitable to its black population it is not—except, of course, to its football players, 90 percent of whom are black, a situation that is repeated in many other Latin American countries.

Colombia, May 19–20, 2014

Beyond the observations about Colombian elite attitudes toward blacks described above, it is important to relate some on-site participant observations. Afro-Colombians reside on both the Atlantic and Pacific coasts. They represent 25 percent of the country's population. Visits to Atlantic cities such as Barranquilla, Santa Marta, and especially Cartagena reveal a well-integrated and assimilated Afro community. Such is not the case on the Pacific side in the state of Valle. There, in Buenaventura, which is 90 percent black and is the port that handles 50 percent of the country's trade, these Afro-descendientes live with the most miserable conditions and under constant threat by criminal gangs. In 2007, a *New York Times* correspondent called it the country's "deadliest urban center," showing the highest murder and kidnapping rates.[48] Attitudes of those brought in from Bogotá or Cali reveal very strong prejudices and stereotypes. The *Times* article cites the commander of the military garrison remarking: "It's as if we have a little Haiti within Colombia. It feels like another country." Showing the same disdain for his charges, the Bogotá police chief said: "These vagabonds are good only for drinking, dancing, and killing." Needless to say, Buenaventura was one city I did not visit, but analyzed from the city of Cali, capital of the state of Valle. The opinions even of Caleño blacks are anything but charitable toward Esmeraldas. The Esmeraldeños are blamed for giving all blacks a "bad reputation," a porter at the hotel told me. Others see the situation as a reflection of Colombian racism generally, a racism that is occasionally seen in sports events in which blacks participate.[49] But Esmeraldas is a distinct case. As the country's respected journalist Daniel Samper Pizano put it: "Difícilmente se encuentra en América Latina (incluyendo a México y las favelas brasileñas) una situación más atroz que la que vive Buenaventura"[50] [It is hard to find in Latin America (including in Mexico and in the Brazilian *favelas*) a worse situation than the one found in Buenaventura]. In 2009, Colombia's Corte Constitucional declared Buenaventura "a national shame . . . an emblematic case of violation of the human rights of the Afro-Colombian population." With the Colombian economy accelerating, with more and more trade with Asia passing through Buenaventura, why aren't the region's black populations participating in this progress? Neither secular nor religious laws and precepts nor the availability of modern enterprises seem to make any difference to the outright racism shown the citizens of Buenaventura.

Throughout this book we will confront the reality of varieties of race relations that in no way conform to either the Tannenbaum or the Williams theses. It brings to mind Rebecca Scott's caveats about generalizations based on facile comparisons. Just as she found important differences between race relations in Matanzas and Santiago, Cuba, so we found profound differences between race relations in Cartagena and Buenaventura, Nicaragua's city of Bluefields and Ecuador's Esmeraldas, just as one would find between Boston and Montgomery, Alabama. Generalizing about Latin American race relations makes no more sense than generalizing about North American race relations.

3

Arturo Morales Carrión vs. Gordon K. Lewis

On United States Colonialism in Puerto Rico

Arturo Morales Carrión (henceforth Morales) belonged to what in Puerto Rico is known as "La Generación del 40," the group that emerged in the 1940s to change many aspects of their island, considered "colonial" in all its pernicious dimensions. Their leader was undoubtedly Luís Muñoz Marín, and Morales was their historian. They were determined to reverse many stereotypes about the Puerto Rican society and put their island on the varied ethnic and cultural map of the Caribbean. Their target audience was invariably where the power lay: the United States. In Morales's words, their efforts were meant to ensure that "Puerto Rico is no longer a Caribbean Madagascar waiting to be discovered by American curiosity or scholarship."[1]

Perhaps even more urgent than this identification as a Caribbean people was the question of their own identity, a question that had absorbed the thoughts of a previous generation. As Eugenio Fernández Méndez noted, the great query of the "agonized men" (*hombres agónicos*) of a previous generation—the Generation of 1930—was "What are we? . . . How are we? . . . Where are we going?"[2] The answers given by the Generation of 1930 were pessimistic to the point of revealing traces of cultural intellectual defeatism.

Arguably the most influential exponent and, in a way, gestator of this collective anomie was Antonio S. Pedreira. Pedreira traced the "crisis" of identity to the dramatic transition from a virtually stagnant Spanish colonialism to an American colonialism bursting with capitalist energy and geopolitical self-assurance. Pedreira knew the United States, having lectured at Columbia University and the Brookings Institution before returning to his island in 1927. As chair of the already prestigious Department of Hispanic Studies of the University of Puerto Rico and founder and director of the University's Social Research Center, Pedreira's voice carried authority and circulated widely through his regular column in the newspaper *El Mundo* and his literary magazine, *Índice*. It was his 1934 book, *Insularismo: ensayos de interpretación puertorriqueña*, however, which made him the voice and guide of the Generation of 1930. To Pedreira, Puerto Rico was a vessel adrift (*una nave al garete*) even as he recognized the great material achievements under U.S. colonialism. Never denying the economic achievements of American rule, he insisted on talking about culture, and there he found *una desgracia colectiva*, a situation which was an *incubadora de incertidumbres*. Pedreira was an elitist in the mold of José Ortega y Gasset and José Ingenieros, and he believed that public education democratized the culture, but in doing so it cultivated mediocrity, which in turn led to the withdrawal of "superior men" from the public arena. His elitism is evident in his admiration for Ortega y Gasset: "Si Ortega y Gasset fuera puertorriqueño, hubiese escrito su libro sobre *La Rebelión de las Masas*, veinte años atrás."[3]

To Pedreira, the Puerto Rican Afro-Caribbean poet Luís Pales Matos described the island's confusion and disorder with the "hurtful" phrase "Puerto Rico *burundanga*." His list of ills resulting from American utilitarianism and materialism is long, beginning with his claim that the Puerto Rican "soul" had been reduced in size, a process he termed *enchiqueramiento* [shrinking]: "La vida se nos corrompe dentro de un sórdido utilitarismo, y la cultura ha perdido sus mejores categorías por la plebeya depauperación intelectual a que la ha sometido la vulgaridad del presente."[4] This was the widely accepted claim of a generation suffering from collective anomie which Morales and the Generation of 1940 confronted and wished to overcome. Morales was singularly well prepared to argue against such defeatist positions and thereby contribute to the goal of moral and spiritual renewal articulated by Luís Muñoz Marín and the Generation of 1940.

Born in Havana, Cuba, in 1913 to Puerto Rican parents, Morales arrived in Puerto Rico at age six and pursued his primary, secondary, and university studies there. He graduated from the University of Puerto Rico (UPR) in Río Piedras in 1935, after spending his summers in special studies at Columbia University and the University of San Marcos, Lima, Peru. Morales was rightfully proud of the liberal cosmopolitanism of the UPR. This pride was shared with another member of the Generation of 1940, Jaime Benítez: "At the University, students could read John Dewey. . . . Keep abreast of the U.S. social sciences; come into contact with . . . Miguel Unamuno and Ortega y Gasset . . . read the deeds of the Mexican Revolution and meet one of its intellectual mentors, José Vasconcelos."[5]

Among those younger ones who knew Morales well was the historian Luís E. Agrait Betancourt. He analyzed Morales's participation in the celebrated seminar on Latin American politics that Frank Tannenbaum offered at Columbia University. Agrait noted that while Morales's intellectual and ideological formation was essentially complete by the time he joined the seminar, "no one could avoid being influenced by Frank Tannenbaum." That influence was a left-leaning liberalism very much in tune with the Fabian-like social democratic philosophy promoted by Muñoz Marín and that was then competing for political space against more conservative traditional forces in Puerto Rico.[6]

Driven by an increasing interest in Latin America, Morales earned a master's in history and Latin American studies at the University of Texas, Austin, in 1936. His mentor there was Herbert Bolton, whose emphasis on the much-ignored "borderlands" of the United States introduced the Puerto Rican student to the Spanish and Mexican settlements before Manifest Destiny occupied them. As we will see, the idea of an imperial frontier (not dissimilar in some ways from that of the early Bosch) became an integral part of Morales's scholarship on Puerto Rico and the Caribbean.

His first job was in the cultural section of the U.S. Department of State from 1940 to 1944. He returned to his native island and established the Centro de Investigaciones Históricas, and in 1945 he was appointed chair of the University of Puerto Rico's Department of History. His formal education ended in 1950 with a PhD in history and international relations from Columbia University. His dissertation, published in 1952 as *Puerto Rico and the Non-Hispanic Caribbean: A Study in the Decline of Spanish Exclusivism,* was a critique of the many followers of Antonio Pedreira's *Insularismo,*[7] which had dominated Puerto Rican history and philosophy. Contrary to Pedreira's thesis that Puerto Rico had existed in isolation from the rest of the region, a Spanish backwater, which explained its consequent cultural trauma at the American conquest, Morales cited economic and demographic data pointing to an open economy in constant growth. He demonstrated that the island was in regular contact with its English, Danish, Dutch, and French neighbors and that the Puerto Rican islands of Culebra and Vieques were veritable bridges to the Virgin Islands and the Eastern Caribbean. Morales described this openness as follows:

> From 1528 to 1625 . . . the social history of Puerto Rico was linked to
> the international chaos which existed in the Caribbean. . . . After 1528,
> Puerto Rico was turned into an attractive zone for successive genera-
> tions of French, English, and Dutch corsairs.[8]

Additionally, because the island escaped from the straitjacket of the slave-
based plantation society, its society was better geared to leveling processes
that were brought on by the integration of the rural area with San Juan, the
walled city (*ciudad amurallada*). This openness, said Morales, had political
implications for the future development plans of the Generation of 1940.

> In this sense, the pre-1898 period is no mere prologue; it is rather the
> key to understanding the roots of the folk culture, the attachment to
> the Spanish language, the origins of an ethnically mixed society, the
> literary and artistic expressions, and the modalities of thought and feel-
> ing that, in spite of many dramatic social changes, are at the bottom of
> the Puerto Rican personality.[9]

Morales set out to educate Puerto Ricans, and it would not be an overreach
to say that, at the time, nowhere else in the Greater Caribbean was there a
more intellectually vibrant set of revisionist history lectures given than those
that Morales gave at the University of Puerto Rico. Similarly, the only Caribbean scholar who could compare with Morales's breadth of scholarship and
comparative knowledge of the region was Eric Williams. Both were using
their talents and pens in the service of political and cultural projects: autonomy—not yet "independence"—within their respective colonial systems.

Aside from refocusing the island's history for his students, Morales had
another goal: that of bringing the island to the attention of U.S. decision
makers. This explains why when President John F. Kennedy and his key advisors Arthur Schlesinger Jr. and Richard Goodwin invited him to be part
of a Latin America study and action group, Morales jumped at the offer. He
was fully prepared for the task of collaborating with diplomats Adolf Berle
and Lincoln Gordon and academics Robert Alexander and Arthur Whita-
ker. Driven by the fear of the spread of Cuban revolutionary ideology, their
mission was to create the counterweight. The Alliance for Progress was the
result, and their test-by-fire was the historic meeting of the Organization of
American States in Montevideo, Uruguay, in August 1961. This meeting fol-

lowed on the heels of the ill-conceived and ultimately disastrous Bay of Pigs invasion of Cuba and the exchange of Cuban prisoners for U.S. goods. It was in Montevideo that Fidel Castro and Che Guevara launched pointed attacks on American imperialism. It was journalist Georgie Anne Geyer who put it most precisely: Kennedy, leader of the powerful United States, and Castro, leader of the small and powerless island nation of Cuba, "were now competitors for what was, in effect, the soul of the developing world. The Alliance for Progress was Kennedy's pledge not only to defeat poverty in Latin America but even more so to defeat his nemesis, Fidel Castro."[10] The Generation of 1940 chose its side and with that they began the promotion of the "Puerto Rican model" as an alternative to the Cuban model. Morales was again well placed to serve his island and his party, which was extending its role more and more into the international arena. The "timidity" and "insularism" of the Generation of 1930 was nowhere in evidence. These Puerto Ricans were as brash as the "mainlanders" they had to deal with.

Later, as deputy assistant secretary of state for Latin American affairs, Morales managed the fallout from the demise of the Trujillo dictatorship as well as the overthrow of the elected government of Juan Bosch. After a stint as assistant to the secretary general of the Organization of American States from 1964 to 1968, Morales returned as president to his beloved UPR (1973–77). He continued to be active through the Fundación Puertorriqueña de las Humanidades and in Luís Muñoz Marín's Partido Popular. He never stopped writing history, including publishing his truly excellent study of the rise and fall of the slave trade in Puerto Rico, *Auge y decadencia de la trata negra en Puerto Rico, 1820–1860*.

Determined not to get involved in ongoing disputes à la Williams vs. Tannenbaum on the slavery system and contemporary race relations, his goal in that book was to convey the history of how the slave trade forced Puerto Rico onto the Caribbean. Keeping a strictly professional stance, he argued— as did Eric Williams—that only research in the original documents of various imperial centers "can lead to a comparative understanding of the slave trade and its impact on Caribbean history."[11] He focused especially on one of the key factors he found in his own research in all the imperial archives, something I will return to in chapter 4: the decisive role of the fear of Haiti in perpetuating colonial rule and delaying the abolition of slavery. This is how Morales sums up the nineteenth century in Puerto Rico:

> Los gobernantes españoles en las islas desconfían de ingleses, fran-
> ceses y norteamericanos, mientras les embarga la ansiedad que despi-
> erta en las clases dominantes el recuerdo de Haití y el espectro de un
> abolicionismo que traiga como secuela la guerra de castas y el fin del
> predominio blanco[12] [The Spanish governors mistrust Englishmen,
> Frenchmen, and North Americans; meanwhile, they are overcome
> with the anxiety which the memory of Haiti instills in the ruling
> classes and the specter of an abolition which will have as outcome a
> war of castes and the end of White predominance].

Describing a weak imperial Spain's determination to hold on especially to plantation-rich Cuba, Morales writes of the numerous and relatively poor peasants of Puerto Rico scraping an existence by smuggling.[13] Spain was sell- ing its slaves to Cuba and Brazil and always fearful of Haiti: "¡Haití, siempre Haití, como el fantasma del Caribe!"[14]

The landing of U.S. troops in Puerto Rico was an offshoot of the U.S. in- tervention in Cuba. With Puerto Rico, as distinct from Cuba, the United States occupied a country with a majority of subsistence agriculturalists and a miniscule urban population. It was a colony with no say in its own affairs. In 1880, Spain reduced the number of eligible electors to 2,004 (out of a popu- lation of 373,640) in order to favor the small, pro-Spanish white elite. Was it any surprise, Morales asked, that most of the liberal elite rejoiced at the arrival of the Americans?[15]

Alas, they were rebuffed in their hopes and expectations. What the Puerto Ricans received from the United States was the status of a possession juridi- cally defined as an "Unincorporated Territory" in which racism was the ally of colonialism. Even the "progressive" Teddy Roosevelt could not interpret its people as anything better than "pathetic and childlike."[16] "Puerto Rico," Morales noted, "was not to be a happy, prosperous island, well-taught and well-behaved, but a poor house . . . a 'stricken land.'"[17] He was never under any illusions about the generosity of what he called "the American theory of colonial tutelage,"[18] which included the view that Puerto Ricans were not yet ready for self-government and that there had to be congressional supremacy over the island. "The Jeffersonian philosophy of government by consent," he concluded, "was conveniently shelved."[19] Nor did he have any illusions that Puerto Ricans were a rebellious people. Throughout his historical research, Morales claimed that he never found any evidence that Puerto Ricans, as distinct from the Cubans, were a people prone to rebellion. He studied the multiple interpretations surrounding the nationalist and revolutionary movement led by Pedro Albizu Campos in the 1930s and 1940s and found it out of step with broader Puerto Rican culture and politics. While Albizu claimed to speak for the whole island and boasted that he had an "army of patriots" of 5,000 men, his Nationalist Party received only 5,257 votes of the 383,722 cast in the 1932 elections. Facing such a popular rejection, Albizu abandoned electoral politics and depended thereafter nearly completely on a small but close-knit and ideologically committed group of black-shirted Nationalists.

The second of Morales's goals was to support Muñoz and the Popular Party's efforts to counter two aspects of the U.S.–Puerto Rico relationship: the negative U.S. image of Puerto Ricans and the constraints on Puerto Rican autonomous actions imposed by the colonial compact. As far as negative American views, Morales noted that even the radical New Dealer, Rexford Guy Tugwell, later governor of the island, could not dissimulate his initial disdain for his country's new charges, as he told his friend Henry Wallace:

> I rather dislike to think that our falling fertility must be supplemented by these people. But that will probably happen. Our control of the tropics seems to me certain to increase immigration from here and the next wave of the lowly . . . succeeding the Irish, Italians, and Slavs . . . will be these mulatto, Indian, Spanish people from the south of us. They make poor material for social organization but you are going to have to reckon with them.[20]

Despite such evident ethnic biases, Tugwell would later become a progressive governor and a major contributor to Puerto Rican autonomy and economic growth. With the New Deal in full swing in the United States, with World War II looming and Puerto Rico strategically placed in the defense of the Panama Canal scheme, it was time to send a reformer to the island. In addition, by sending Rexford Tugwell, the Roosevelt administration was casting the man known for "Tugwellian socialism." Like so many others, the situation in the island dismayed him. As he said in his 1947 book, *The Stricken Land: The Story of Puerto Rico*, he was "shocked, as all Northerners are at the squalor in which the island workers live." The situation, Tugwell said, was "ripe for class warfare." Given this, and given his own social democratic inclinations, Tugwell did not hold his tongue:

That is what colonialism was and did: it distorted all ordinary processes of the mind, made beggars of honest men, sycophants of cynics, American-haters of those who ought to have been working beside us for world betterment—and would if we had encouraged them.

Tugwell analyzed the economic situation and found it exploitative. The colony sold its raw products (sugar and coffee) cheaply and bought at the same price the imported goods sold in the Metropolis. The products all had to be carried on American bottoms, meaning a colonial system such as was found in the British colonial system of the seventeenth and eighteenth centuries. Tugwell concluded:

Puerto Rico was just as badly off. And relief was something which the Congress made Puerto Rico beg for, hard, and in the most revolting ways, as a beggar does on a church step, filthy hat in hand, exhibiting sores, calling and grimacing in exaggerated humility. And this last was the real crime of America in the Caribbean, making Puerto Ricans something less than the men they were born to be.[21]

Morales understood Tugwell and argued that before a more productive bargaining posture vis-à-vis the U.S. Congress could be gained, Puerto Ricans had to make themselves and their culture better understood. As he noted in the introduction to his *Puerto Rico: A Political and Cultural History*:

A prime consideration of this book is to establish a more balanced perspective of what Puerto Rico constitutes as a people, a cultural nationality, of a distinctive Caribbean entity. It is not a book written by Puerto Ricans for Puerto Ricans, but by Puerto Ricans who wish to bring their outlooks and scholarship to the attention of the reader in the United States.

He fully understood the need to repeatedly engage the American Congress and people in the debate about Puerto Rico's future. His many speeches on this score reveal his persistence on this point.[22] It is not a stretch to argue that Morales, through his solid professional history writing, helped mightily to lay the intellectual basis of the Estado Libre Asociado, the new Commonwealth status of Puerto Rico. He argued persuasively that a people with the strength and conviction of their identity, even if not an independent nation, could enter into a political compact with the colonial power, pushing continually for greater autonomy. He did for historical foundations what another member of the Generation of 1940, Ricardo Alegría, was doing for cultural identity as director of the Institute of Puerto Rican Culture and what Jaime Benítez did for academia as president of the University of Puerto Rico. They all contributed to the great transformational leap forward led by Muñoz. Tugwell would later change—at least publicly—his opinion of Puerto Ricans, and as governor he actively promoted the leadership and plans of Muñoz and his fellow Populares.

The island that these progressive Puerto Ricans inherited in 1940 began to transform and was sold to the world as a new model of development. Nationalism would be subordinated to what they called the "new patriotism": a new era of the *nación pueblo*—the "people-nation"—rather than the nation-state that was the goal of the majority of those engaged elsewhere in the decolonization process. Muñoz would elaborate greatly on this idea and win successive elections over the years. There certainly were many very vocal critics of this singular and innovative model, but the most articulate opponent turned out to be a Welsh professor at UPR, Gordon K. Lewis.

Born in Wales, educated at Oxford, and having entered Harvard University's graduate school, Lewis decided to go to Puerto Rico in 1951. It was an exciting time and a rare opportunity for a political scientist. In Puerto Rico he was assigned as an assistant to one of America's most prestigious political scientists, Harvard's Carl Friedrich, hired as a special consultant to the Constituent Assembly established by the government of that island. In the Caribbean, in the early 1950s, this was the place to be. And indeed many of the most innovative social scientists were there, including Rupert Emerson, Kingsley Davis, Julian Steward, Clarence Senior, J. Mayone Stycos, Henry Wells, Pedro Muñoz Amato, C. Wright Mills, John Kenneth Galbraith, and somewhat later, Richard M. Morse and Sidney Mintz. What was occurring in Puerto Rico radiated out to every corner of the Caribbean and to U.S. academics. What excitement for a young Welshman whose master's thesis had dealt with the Christian Socialist movement in nineteenth-century England. Additionally, it was important that Lewis's pre-Caribbean writings provided the outlines of a distinct ideological orientation not too dissimilar from that of the New Dealers, all in a way social democrats and liberals were giving shape to a new Puerto Rico and, unwittingly and secondarily, to a new Caribbean. Lewis entered a Puerto Rico and Caribbean in political and constitutional ferment and, although mostly new to him, took it on with a brio and panache that immediately drew the attention of Puerto Rican and regional intellectuals and statesmen.

His first foray into wider Caribbean studies came via an invitation from Eric Williams, the premier of not-yet-independent Trinidad and Tobago (TT), to study the wider implications of Puerto Rico's association with the United States. There was a very specific reason behind Williams's commission. The West Indies Federation, a mere infant of three years, was in danger of collapse. Important sectors in Jamaica, led by Alexander Bustamante and his Jamaica Labour Party, wanted out. Norman Manley, in a desperate attempt to salvage that which West Indians had talked about since time immemorial, proposed an association of Jamaica in a confederate relationship to the Federal Centre. This explains Premier Williams's mandate to Lewis with the key research question: Did the Puerto Rico–U.S. relationship provide a model relevant to the Jamaican proposal and other cases? With that, Lewis entered into the ongoing debates over Puerto Rican and Caribbean constitutional development. Lewis's eventual answer to the Williams query was unequivocal: Puerto Rico could not serve as a model for any emerging society, because it was "an aberration inspired by circumstances of a peculiar rather than a universal significance."[23] Beyond the general conclusion, Lewis made wider and, for Puerto Rico, deeper assertions of a political nature. "In terms of constitutional status," he declared, "Puerto Rico became a curious hybrid which had disastrous consequences for the development of local freedom and self-government."[24] With this conclusion, Lewis showed that he had already decided that the creation of Muñoz, Morales, and others of the Generation of 1940 was not to his liking. And so, by the late 1950s, Lewis was ready to seek a publisher for a major book on Puerto Rico and the Caribbean. But which publisher? With the Cold War in full swing, with McCarthyism a not too distant memory, with the Caribbean already the arena of two Cold War confrontations (British Guiana in 1952 and Guatemala, 1954), and with the Cuban Revolution already showing signs of bubbling over, finding a university press publisher for a radical book was not easy. Lewis, who had already published in the socialist-oriented journal *Monthly Review*, turned to them, and they took a gamble on his manuscript. They bet well. The now celebrated *Puerto Rico: Freedom and Power in the Caribbean* (1963) put that press on the map and the Puerto Rican debate back on the front burner, with Lewis as an articulate opponent of the Puerto Rican model.

The book's impact was enormous. It established Lewis as a maximum authority not only on Puerto Rican politics but on constitution and political system building in the Caribbean. Though hardly the hero of the piece, Lewis had to have been impressed with the intellectual freedom on the island when Governor Luís Muñoz Marín made the book the topic of a special cabinet meeting and then invited Lewis for a private discussion of its thesis.[25] One of the cabinet members present was Morales, who, again demonstrating the liberal creed of the Generation of 1940, was most generous in his praise. After reading the veritable trashing of the Commonwealth project, he wrote, "Lewis believes in style, in wit, in urbanity. His is a scholarly, sophisticated exposition [because of] his sense of fairness . . . one is impressed above all, by his humanism, more than by his opinions."[26]

Lewis's *Puerto Rico: Freedom and Power in the Caribbean* is an in-depth attempt to show the political, social, cultural, and even psychological dimensions of American imperialism; not the heavy-handed Belgian Congo type of imperialism, mind you, but rather the various processes whereby the United States was "tying Puerto Ricans by chains of silk to the American power." He adopted Kwame Nkrumah's term *neocolonialism*. But he was not content to write about Puerto Rico as a case study in U.S. federalism, no matter how outstanding that case study was. He gave it a Caribbean context and projected Puerto Rico as a "prototype" of a new type of colonial relationship between developed and underdeveloped countries which, in his opinion, could only end up badly.

It is an exhaustive, though never exhausting, book, angry but never virulent, with occasional streaks of mean-spiritedness, but with much wider swatches of generosity and bonhomie. It is also, however, not lacking in explanatory contradictions. He repeatedly introduces the reader to the island's "uniqueness." Very much in keeping with the conclusions of Morales's historiography, Lewis argued that Puerto Rico was never a real sugar/slave colony under Spanish rule, and its experience with American rule was sui generis.[27] That was not the total extent of Lewis's agreement with the Morales historical findings. Yet it is primarily on this idea of the island's uniqueness that Lewis repeatedly speaks of what can only be called the Puerto Rican "national character." Widely considered an elusive concept in the social sciences, Lewis delves into what he terms the Puerto Rican "fundamental nature" with gusto. The result is truly a mixed and often contradictory characterization. In keeping with some of the seminal literature on the Puerto Rican of the Generation of 1930, Lewis finds the Puerto Rican "passive," "docile," and "lacking in civic spirit," driven by a "guilt complex," even suffering from a certain "paranoiac anxiety." In short, he says with regret, Puerto Ricans are not revolutionaries; they are fundamentally legal-minded negotiators and reformists. This explains what he calls "the almost pathological preoccupation" of the island's politicians with legal and constitutional issues.[28] With this, Lewis revived the Antonio Pedreira intellectual confrontation with the Morales version of an island open to the world of ideas and ready to innovate.

How then have these "docile" Puerto Ricans handled U.S. imperialism? Here Lewis's harsh judgment of the Puerto Ricans goes into full retreat. Not only does he soften his words but he paints a picture of a wonderfully complex people, negotiating a fate that they never invited and against which they had only intellectual and moral arrows in their national quiver with which to fight. "Docility," he then said, can be seen as a good sense of timing and proportion, "insularity" as the "picaresque" (one of Lewis's favorite words) predisposition of the *jibaro* (peasant) raised to understand the art of the possible. On this, Lewis is as one with Morales. This was, to be sure, one side of the coin; the other was the nature of the U.S. occupation. Lewis repeatedly maintained that U.S. imperialism was hardly of the European type. There was no colonial tradition in the United States. Indeed, U.S. territorial expansion into the Caribbean represented what he terms a "national aberration" that resulted in "an American Imperial Dilemma."[29] The management of Empire by a democracy, says Lewis, is a contradiction in terms.[30] Since there was no brutal repression, rather much more of what Rexford Tugwell called "imperial neglect,"[31] why would one expect an à la Haiti, Vietnam, Algeria, or other such violent reaction to colonial rule?

Nowhere is Morales's work mentioned—except for a brief note on his stint at the U.S. Department of State—but his ideas were. He was logically included in Lewis's position that Muñoz and the extraordinary group of the Generación del 40 had developed a theory of consent based on universal democratic freedoms. This much he was ready to concede, given that the model was based on the "most persuasive Burkean empiricism."[32] He also conceded that the component concepts of "potential creativity" and of "unfolding liberalization" are, in Lewis's own words, "a plausible enough thesis."[33] To Lewis this was all good and fair, . . . as far as it went. Alas, it did not go far enough. Decolonization required much more than the merely plausible. It required leaders and parties driven by solid ideological commitments. And in Puerto Rico Lewis claims that he found none. What he found, rather, was "the astonishing ability" of Puerto Ricans to bypass uncomfortable truths—"a penchant for constitutionalist utopia-mongering."[34] Puerto Rico, he emphasized, is "a jungle of juridical legerdemain," and even worse it has a tendency toward "constitutionalist mumbo-jumbo."[35] As far as the Commonwealth theory of a new U.S.–Puerto Rico compact, Lewis calls forth Herbert Spencer's remark about a beautiful theory murdered by a gang of brutal facts.

What are these "facts?" It is hard to conclude that these facts are fundamentally of a material nature, since the book details the impressive gains achieved under Muñoz's Operation Bootstrap. At least in fiscal and economic terms, said Lewis, the territory achieved what can truly be called a "privileged status."[36] He was not off the mark. In 1979, under Puerto Rican urging, President Jimmy Carter ordered a full study of the Puerto Rican economy and its links to the U.S. market.[37] Lewis would not have quibbled with that study's largely positive economic findings. Puerto Rico in the 1970s, as already noted, was no longer a "stricken land." The answers to the island's underdevelopment had to be two. First, create the conditions that would bring capital and investments to industrialize. In other words, use W. Arthur Lewis's idea of bringing industry to where you had surplus labor to create an export-led development program. Second, since this was not enough, encourage migration to the United States.

The economic gains and changes of what became known as Operation Bootstrap were very real. The human welfare gains between 1940 and 1980 were impressive. Life expectancy went from 46 to 74 years. Literacy among those 10 years and older went from 68.5 to 91.3 percent; teachers per 1,000 students went from 6.3 to 30.6; motor vehicles went from 27 to 1,035; electricity consumption (1,000 KWH) went from 423 in 1950 to 11,121. The economy grew significantly.

- Gross domestic product increased from $572 million in 1947 to $9,717 million in 1977. In real terms (1954 dollars) it increased by 565 percent over the period.
- Gross product (equivalent to GNP in U.S. national account terms) grew from $612 million in 1947 to $7,914 million in 1977. In real terms, it increased by 410 percent.
- GNP per capita rose from $154 in 1940 to $2,391 in 1977. It increased in real terms by 197 percent from 1950 to 1973, after which

it declined slightly, falling from $1,186 to $1,086 in 1977. This in-crease is all the more remarkable when it is considered that pop-ulation rose from 2,200,000 in 1950 to 2,912,000 in 1973 and to 3,267,000 in 1977.

- Employment increased from 536,000 in 1947 to 775,000 in 1974.
- The per capita income went from $296 in 1950 to $2,422 in 1976.

So, if not economic failure, what was Lewis's persistent gripe? After all, Puerto Rico had already been cleared of being a "colony" by the United Na-tions, which removed it in 1953 from the list of non-self-governing territories by a vote of 26–16. With the Soviet Union and Cuba repeatedly raising the issue of the island's colonial status, new votes were taken, and again Puerto Rico was voted a "self-governing territory" in 1971 by 57–26 and in 1982 by a vote of 70–30. This vote was crucial in allowing Muñoz to operate as a mem-ber of the international community, arguing as he always had against tyran-nies generally and the various ones in the Caribbean at the time.[38] Many of the democrats exiled by their dictators chose Puerto Rico as their tempo-rary home. Muñoz was so committed to his democratic allies that when Juan Bosch was overthrown in 1962, he sent an airplane from the island's agricul-ture department to bring Bosch from Martinique to Puerto Rico, where he then taught at the University of Puerto Rico.

Muñoz and those of the Generation of 1940 were going against Third World ideological currents. The general tone was set by Kwame Nkrumah, who argued, "Seek ye first the political Kingdom and all things else shall be added unto you" and that "we prefer self-government with danger than servitude in tranquility."[39] According to Rupert Emerson, Puerto Rico had avoided ethno-nationalism and was the only case to choose a path between colonialism and independence.[40] To its great credit, it had chosen that path democratically in a plebiscite in which 375,594 voted in favor and 82,777 against. Even so, not everyone was persuaded that the island was decolo-nized, and certainly Lewis was not. He provided an interpretation of the island's "colonial" status, which contrasted sharply with that of Morales.

Turning once more to harsh condemnatory language, Lewis said that his objection was to what he called the "running sore of American overlord-ship."[41] It had to do with psychology, not material things. American rule, he says, echoing Pedreira, has created a "deep psychological wound" in the Puerto Rican human nature. This was not an alienation from the fruits of their labor but alienation from what he considers the true "natural state": being sovereign and independent. These are "the only appropriate prescriptions" that would cure the anomie, the collective malaise. In a most un-Marxist fashion, Lewis's arguments remain at the superstructural level: only an independent political status could restore "moral integrity," overcome the "servile mentality," and ultimately reestablish the "natural bond" of Puerto Rico with the Caribbean. The Muñoz-Morales agenda could never overcome Puerto Rico's unnatural state. But how was Puerto Rico to achieve what was being prescribed? Again, in most un-Marxian terms, Lewis argued that it would take not just a Puerto Rican *prise de conscience* but an American generosity of spirit. It is an American "moral obligation" that should lead them to launch Puerto Rican independence with a Marshall Plan, even economic "reparations."[42] Independence, he says, would be nothing more than a test of Washington's "statesmanship."[43] But what is to be done with the people's repeated electoral rejection of the independence option? Again Lewis leans on the moral argument: lack of electoral support is not a measure of "moral worth."[44] Puerto Ricans have to reach higher than they have so far. How high? That answer would come later in another book, *Notes on the Puerto Rican Revolution: An Essay on American Dominance and Caribbean Persistence,* published in 1974, in which he argues that the only way out is a revolution.

If one follows both the Burkean idea of trusteeship and the Lockean idea of the natural rights doctrine of government by the consent of the people, as do the innovative ideas of Muñoz and Morales about the situation of Puerto Rico (and for that matter the Dutch and French West Indies), why would anyone consider the Puerto Rican situation, as Lewis says, "perverse"? Did not the people of these islands repeatedly have the opportunity to freely decide their future in what Burke calls a "trusteeship of liberty"? This can only be called "perverse" if you agree with Lewis that political independence and national sovereignty respond to something akin to a natural law that ranks higher than mere plebiscitarian liberty. Clearly, Lewis's thinking had radicalized. By 1983, Lewis had come to have the highest compliments for revolutionary leaders such as the Haitian Jean-Jacques Dessalines and the Dominican Gregorio Luperón, whose actions sought "to hold intact the national patrimony." Similarly, the most celebrated Cuban leaders were those whose nationalism was geared toward the island's absolute independence and sovereignty. It is evident, however, that the emphasis on national state sovereignty separate from the wishes of the people is neither Burkean nor

Lockean. It could be classical Marxism only if one believes that the millions of people in Puerto Rico, Martinique, Curaçao, and so forth are all suffering from some form of national, political false consciousness, hardly a tenable thesis post-Perestroika and Glasnost. Equally untenable is Lewis's thesis that it will be in what he calls "the more radical" post-1959 Cuban literature that the Caribbean will find true "psychological decolonization." Of course, Lewis's life scholarship ended with his death in 1987, before the collapse of the Soviet system and, with it, the end of the extraordinarily generous Soviet subsidies provided Cuba.

Beyond ideology, it is quite apparent that Lewis's many references to the Cuban Revolution were driven by his incurably romantic heart. This is so when he calls on Puerto Ricans to combat their "cult of the automobile" and replace it with "the mass use of the bicycle."[45] Equally peculiar is his claim that one of the results of being "under the U.S. flag" is that it prevents Puerto Ricans from adopting "the Russian method" of controlling urban population growth by restraining migration from the countryside, which the Cuban regime had also tried.[46] Cubans ride bicycles out of necessity, not choice, and no Puerto Rican government would dare prohibit the movement of people into the city, whether it be San Juan or New York City. These are the advantages that Lewis himself admits are "not lightly abandoned" and that go a long way in explaining what he calls the "almost paranoiac Puerto Rican anxiety" over a possible break with the United States.[47]

The 1970s might be called the revolutionary phase of Lewis's anti-imperialism. Other than being radical, it is not at all clear, however, just what his intellectual and ideological inclinations were at that point. To judge from his early published work, he was in the mold of the more radical Fabian, non-Marxist socialists who were interested in the Colonial Question and in promoting radical, not revolutionary, change in those areas. On the other hand, later he would confess to having been a Marxist since secondary school days.

A newly available transcript of Lewis's presentation to the essentially Marxist-oriented Centro de Estudios de la Realidad Puertorriqueña (CEREP) in 1983 reveals him saying:

Yo soy marxista desde mi juventud intelectual. Yo aprendí el marxismo por primera vez cuando fui un joven estudiante en una escuela pública en Gales. . . . Yo entre como miembro del Left Book Club en la era de los 30 en Inglaterra, bajo la influencia de un miembro de la facultad de la escuela, un hombre de Yorkshire radical marxista[48] [I have been a Marxist since my young intelectual days. . . . I became a member of the Left Book Club in England during the 1930s, influenced by a faculty member of the school, a radical Marxist from Yorkshire].

He had already revealed in 1978 that he had been strongly influenced by two Marxist teachers in his public school in Wales. But what is revealed in the CEREP tapes goes well beyond being influenced. After arguing that the Marxist analysis of class conflict is the correct approach to an understanding of history, Lewis makes a surprising claim that he was a member of the Welsh Communist Party International Brigade, which fought in the Spanish Civil War in 1938. This is difficult to verify, and the chronology does not support the claim. He then concludes, "Es muy obvio que yo personalmente soy marxista desde la experiencia, desde el pensamiento por toda mi vida física e intelectual" [It is obvious that I am personally a Marxist from experience, during my whole physical and intellectual life].

All that can be documented concerning Lewis's Marxist past is that in May 1961 Gordon K. Lewis was one of several prominent Marxist scholars (some of the others being Paul Baran, William Appleman Williams, Herbert Aptheker, and Bernice Shoul) who received money from the Fund for Social Analysis, an American Marxist think tank dedicated to researching social problems. The inevitable, because logical, question is whether Lewis was a *Marxist* rather than the *Marxian* that he has traditionally been held out to be. Were his Marxist stances Marxian, that is, merely the occasional politically correct attitude to take in radical milieus that abounded in the 1970s in Puerto Rican and Caribbean intellectual circles? Had he been caught up in the renovated interest in revolutionary violence that made an appearance among *independentista* circles in the 1970s?

Part of Lewis's new interest was a revisionist approach to the one leader who openly advocated the armed struggle approach to Puerto Rican independence, Pedro Albizu Campos. As already noted, Albizu's poor showing in the 1932 elections led him to abandon electoral politics and advocate direct action. His followers, called Nacionalistas, claiming a sovereign right to fight for independence by any means, engaged in a series of violent acts. In 1937 they assassinated Police Chief Francis Riggs, in 1950 they attempted to assassinate President Harry Truman, and in 1954 they shot several members of Congress from the public gallery. Albizu was convicted and jailed, but the Nacionalistas never abdicated the right to violent action, often citing the Irish Sinn Fein as a model.[49]

Gordon K. Lewis's changing attitude toward the use of violence was hardly hidden. In 1963 he condemned the Riggs murder because it was "so untypical, in its stark brutality, of a society remarkable for the comparative absence of serious violence in its public life."[50] He knew where to lay the blame: "Behind [these] ugly episodes there lay the resurgence of the Creole Fascist-Nationalist movement led by the fanatical genius of Pedro Albizu Campos." He described the Nationalists as "sterile in theory" and suffering from "political megalomania" and "perverted idealism." Lewis went further: "As with their European counterparts, there was the same mask of hate, the same hostile and psychotic nationalism; what was distinctive was that the Puerto Rican crypto-fascism took on the same guise, in addition, of an exaggerated pride in things Spanish."[51]

By 1974, however, Lewis had despaired of what he called "the legislative-constitutional road, in colonial conditions." It was, he said, "a dead-end . . . neither the best nor, indeed, the only road to the socialist republic."[52] *Notes on the Puerto Rican Revolution* appeared the same year the Partido Socialista Puertorriqueño (PSP) presented its new program, which called for independence, nationalization, "and the right to resort to revolutionary violence."[53] Indeed, they now proclaimed that any electoral participation on their part would be modeled on the approach Lenin recommended: voting, but engaging in armed struggle as necessary, since it was the "indispensable requisite" to achieve what they called the República Democrática de los Trabajadores.[54] They summed up their program by saying: "La totalidad del proceso se recoge en la severa sentencia albizista: 'Pueblo definido por las armas es pueblo respetable e indestructible'"[55] [The totality of the process is summed up by the severe Albizu maxim: a society that is defined by the force of arms is a respected and indestructible society].

It is difficult to believe that Lewis used Marxism either opportunistically or, as do so many in the Caribbean, as a unidimensional radical critique of the status quo. His training in classical and radical theory was too profound for such ideological posturing and radical bravado. Students have to assume that his ideas on social change had to have an internal logic and consistency in the interpretation of historical causality. Lewis had many facets, not many faces. That being the case, the new revelations compel us to reevaluate assertions such as the following made on page 269 of *Notes on the Puerto Rican*

Revolution: "There is, finally the disillusionment with the old style politics of court action, peaceful demonstration, and political activism; these have now to be replaced with open armed self-defense." He now supported "revolutionary spontaneity" à la Rosa Luxemburg and advocated the "demolition," the "thorough destruction" of the bourgeois society.[56] He was also ready to admit that American imperialists were incapable of understanding nationalism such as that of Albizu Campos.[57] This is so, he argued, because American capitalism was in its aggressive "imperialist phase." The latter, of course, is Lenin's adaptation of Hobson's theory of imperialism, and Lewis cites it without presenting even minimal evidence that significant numbers of Puerto Ricans were responding to any such "phase." On its face, it was a radical challenge to the historical interpretations of Puerto Rican preference for more conservative, peaceful change being advanced by Muñoz, Morales, and his disciples.

All these revelations and the rereading of much of his work put in stark relief one of the great paradoxes of this complex man: rather than a consistently Marxian analysis, he repeatedly shows a propensity to lean on Edmund Burke and English moderate socialism (Fabianism), not merely at different junctures but consistently, indeed, even when explaining phenomena already outlined in Marxian terms.

In pursuing the consistency of Lewis's anti-traditionalism and even revolutionary inclinations, we have to ask why it is Edmund Burke, whom Lewis calls "the great figure," that he cites most frequently. Understand, however, that it was invariably Burke the anti-imperialist and supporter of colonial liberation. This was only logical because, in a way, all of Lewis's works are attacks on imperialism and colonialism in all its forms. Anti-imperialism, he once admitted, came as easily to him as did British socialist tradition and English progressive thought, which, he noted, was "influenced as much by Burke as by Marx." Marx certainly had an impact on key Fabians, especially through the influence of the London School of Economics where Harold Laski and the Marxist Ralph Miliband taught for decades. Laski had great respect for Marx's writings but lamented the "canons of orthodoxy" which Lenin and then Stalin laid on them. Lenin, said Laski, was an "intellectual heretic."[58] But again the paradox: why was it invariably in Burkean not Marxian terms that Lewis phrased his anti-colonialism? His lifelong opposition to the Puerto Rican Estado Libre Asociado, for instance, was more than once phrased with this quotation from Burke on colonial bondage:

> This servitude, which makes men subject to a state without being citizens, may be more or less tolerable from many circumstances, but these circumstances, more or less favorable, do not alter the nature of the thing. The mildness by which absolute masters exercise their dominion leaves them masters still.

Even in a rare visit with the Rastafarian leadership in Jamaica, Lewis indicated that he believed Burke had helped him understand the righteousness of their demands. "For, as Edmund Burke remarked, every people must have some compensation for its slavery."[59] Yet one must again be reminded that Burke believed in traditionalism, in the accumulation and testing of experience over generations, and he spoke of the advantages of the "collected reason of ages" as distinct from the radical rationalism of revolutionaries.

There was no doubting Burke's anti-imperialism and humanism, however. The natural rights of men—all men, regardless of ethnicity or station—he said, were sacred. "God forbid," he said, "it should be bruited from Perking to Paris, that the laws of England are for the rich and the powerful; but to the poor, the miserable, and the defenceless, they offer no recourse at all." As he said in his opening speech at the impeachment of Warren Hastings:

> The laws of morality are the same everywhere, and . . . there is no action which would pass for an act of extortion, of peculation, of bribery, and of oppression in England, that is not an act of extortion, of peculation, of bribery and oppression in Europe, Asia, Africa, and all the world over.

In the face of such Burkean humanism one has to wonder what Lewis made of the cold—even callous—"scientific" nature of Marx's analysis in his chapter in *Capital* on the value of labor power.

Noting that slave labor should not be considered unpaid labor because "the property-relation conceals the labour of the slave for himself," he adds the following footnote:

> The "Morning Star," a London free-trade organ, naïf to silliness, protested again and again during the American civil war, with all the moral indignation of which man is capable, that the negro in the "Confederate States" worked absolutely for nothing. It should have compared the daily cost of such a negro with that of the free workman in the East end of London.[60]

Is the moral issue of slavery, of human bondage, to be subordinated to the comparative costs of maintaining a slave as distinct from a *free* workman? It can make sense only in a general scheme in which "superstructural" factors are, if not irrelevant, at least quite secondary. The point is that while Lewis was convinced by the broader Marxian theory of social change, his analysis in and of the Caribbean kept bringing him back to superstructural—especially moral—factors. Again, the differences between Marx and Burke on this score are revealing and, arguably, even explanatory of some of the paradoxes in Lewis's analyses of the region.

Even more important than the differences between Burke and Marx and Engels over questions of race and ethnicity is another major paradox in Lewis's theory of social change. Contrary to Marxian theory, which interpreted the colonization by a "higher" economic order as the necessary precondition to the creation of a working class as the only route to socialism, Lewis's basic theoretical argument is premised on the idea that socialism in Puerto Rico and the Caribbean can be achieved only after political independence, that is, after a break with American imperialism. "The cardinal fact to be considered," he says, "is the American connection."[61] No need to belabor the point that in Marxist theory it is precisely that "connection" which is the necessary historical antecedent to socialism.

How then does one interpret Lewis's declarations of a Marxist orientation and his paradoxical preference for the type of humanity-centered anti-imperialism professed by Burke? Certainly this is a complex historiographical inquiry but one which calls out for at least a hypothetical answer. Such a hypothesis has to place Lewis in the context of the general climate and attitudes toward Marxist thought (and especially communism) in the England where his philosophy of history was forged.

Lewis's flirtation with violent revolution was brought to dramatic closure by the self-destruction of the Grenada Revolution of 1979–83, discussed in chapter 9. Lewis began his own treatment of that case, which he called a "Caribbean tragedy," in his last book, *Grenada: The Jewel Despoiled*. This brought him closer to the Morales point of view about the need for democratic politics than he had ever been. The Caribbean left "without apology" should learn from the mistakes of Grenada. What was that lesson? That modern socialism, in the Caribbean as elsewhere, "is historically the child of the European rationalist tradition, obligated to search for the universal laws that govern human behavior."[62]

It is a fact that Lewis returned to his more moderate social democratic positions, which were not dissimilar in fact to those of Morales and the Generation of 1940. That said, as distinct from the conclusion of Morales and the Populares, Lewis's fundamental understanding of Puerto Rico's colonial economic dependence was later vindicated. His warning that as admirable and perhaps inimitable as Muñoz, Morales, and the Generation of 1940's event-making leadership was, it is good to understand the favorable national and international environment which contributed to Muñoz's success and which, let it be said, was not to be repeated, at least not in similar form. This has led to two types of critiques of this legacy. First, that Operation Bootstrap perverted the nature of the island's economy. As can be seen in table 5, by 1976, agriculture was providing a mere 5 percent of total net income. As a consequence, the second critique was that Puerto Ricans developed a high dependency on imported food.

The result of this dependency was that Puerto Ricans had self-sufficiency in none of the food products they consumed. Lewis would describe this with the quip about the island's export economy: "They don't consume what they produce and they don't produce what they consume." According to the island's Department of Agriculture, local production as a percentage of total consumption was in steep decline between 1961 and 1975. There was no self-sufficiency in any of the staples consumed.[63]

As Lewis predicted, Puerto Ricans had become consumers at the level of New Yorkers. Consumption expenditures were $236 million in 1940, in 1969

Table 5. Changes in the importance of Puerto Rican economic sectors, 1940, 1950, and 1976

Sector	Net income (%)			Employment (%)		
	1940	1950	1976	1940	1950	1976
Agriculture	31	24	5	43	36	7
Manufacturing	12	14	31	10	9	19
Commerce	12	17	18	10	15	20
Construction	1	4	6	3	5	7
Government	8	11	22	2	8	22
Services	9	7	13	14	13	17

Source: Puerto Rico Planning Board, in U.S. Department of Commerce, Economic Study of Puerto Rico (Washington, D.C., 1979), 2:293.

they became $3,189 million, and in 1972 they rose to $4,457 million. How ·
could they sustain that level when the deficit in the balance of trade that was
$105 million in 1950 had reached $5,097 million by 1984?[64] The answer had to
be transfers from the federal government. This was no different, then, from
what occurs in virtually all the remaining European dependent territories
and the French DOMs. The figures are impressive. For the period 1970–77,
federal disbursements grew by 270 percent from $839 million to $3,108 million, representing 30 percent of Puerto Rico's GNP in 1977. Subsequent
scholars would point out that a significant part of these large increases had
to do with the inclusion in 1975 of the federal food stamp program. The heavy
criticism from these later, and credible, sources tended to indicate that Lewis
was on to something significant which Morales and others had overlooked.

Arguably the first to do a full-scale study of the effects of the food stamps
that were going to more than half of the Puerto Rican population was Richard Weisskoff. His argument was that of all the transfers from the United
States to Puerto Rico, food stamps were the most pernicious because it affected the wage structure, spending patterns, and, perhaps fundamentally,
attitudes. Weisskoff is critical of the whole "surplus labor" model on which
Operation Bootstrap was built:

> Tax-exempt factories and the food stamps are symmetric. The first is
> a subsidy to some of the nation's largest corporations. The second is a
> subsidy to America's poorest people. The island economy, from private
> enterprise to private citizen, survives on grants from the U.S. taxpayer
> to everyone's long-run detriment. To give *more* of both tax credits and
> food stamps will accelerate the crisis.[65]

Weisskoff's serious analytical and policy-oriented effort is undermined by its
strident political tone. Reminiscent of Lewis's own polemics, twice Weisskoff argues that "material prosperity, coupled with repression and intimidation," were designed to "blunt the demand for independence."[66] Leaning on
much of the *independentista* literature, he casts a wide conspiratorial net over
Operation Bootstrap:

> Its goal was never to achieve economic improvements for all the
> Puerto Rican people, but rather through some transformation of the
> economic base together with armed repression, its goal was to under-
> mine the nationalist appeal and end the colonial status of the island.[67]

Such a conclusion ignores the fact that the Food Stamps Act of 1964 applied originally only to the fifty states and was introduced into Puerto Rico in 1973. By then the "threat" of any independence movement was long gone. Much more persuasive is another critic of the Puerto Rican model, James L. Dietz. "The island's food stamp prosperity," says Dietz, "cannot be sustained and certainly not replicated elsewhere, since nothing is being done to alter the economic base of the economy." Operation Bootstrap in his opinion is "increasingly threatened by collapse."[68] Dietz does not mince words in concluding that what Muñoz Marín and his PPD party strived for was "a relation which combines the benefits and powers that would come with being a state and an independent nation while incurring neither the costs nor the responsibilities of either status."[69]

What sustains this "structurally disarticulated" economy, says Dietz, is state welfare and ongoing outmigration.[70] Such dismal figures and such a categorical critique have to leave everyone wondering why Dietz quite evidently hopes for "a resurgence of the independent vote."[71] It is not just that the Peoples Independence Party (PIP) received a mere 3.6 percent of the popular vote in the 1984 election. It is also that Dietz (any more than Weisskoff did) makes no case for how an independent Puerto Rico might do better, nor does he point to any cases in the Caribbean which are in fact doing better than Puerto Rico.

This inclination toward independence as an option in the face of the Puerto Rican people's rejection of it is evident in much of the radical literature, whether by Puerto Ricans such as Manuel Maldonado Denis or foreigners such as Gordon K. Lewis.[72] Nowhere do they explain why the vast majority of Puerto Ricans have repeatedly rejected the independence option. As distinct from Cuba and the Philippines, where the Spanish and then American presence was deeply resented and combated, or even Panama where a century of resistance preceded the ceding of the Canal, no such movements of any significant size have existed in Puerto Rico.

Until such time as scholars can explain the Puerto Rican rejection of independence status, both the Morales and the Lewis versions of history will have to run as parallel explanations and required reading of a complex historical reality.

4

Haiti

The Origins of the Caribbean's "Terrified Consciousness" about Race

> The whole island was in a state of hidden ferment. The wealthy landowners lived in a state of constant dread, for they believed there might be a conspiracy amongst the negroes, who might be inspired to do here what they had done in San Domingo. Rumours were current about a mulatto chieftain, whose name no one knew, whom no one ever saw, but who was roaming the countryside stirring up the workmen on the sugar plantations. The literature of those "accursed Frenchmen" was hidden in too many pockets.
>
> Alejo Carpentier, *Explosion in a Cathedral*

Alejo Carpentier was talking about his native country, Cuba. In what still is arguably the greatest Pan-Caribbean historical novel, Carpentier describes similar states of dread in Guadeloupe, Jamaica, Venezuela, and French Guiana—indeed, everywhere in the Greater Caribbean. Esteban, the young Cuban protagonist who followed the French revolutionary Victor Hughes, records his final thoughts about what the revolution has wrought, concluding that "I have been living amongst barbarians." Carpentier describes the mood:

> He saw what he had left behind him in terms of darkness and tumult, drums and death agonies, shouts and executions and he associated . . . with the idea of an earthquake, a collective convulsion or a ritual fury.[1]

The Caribbean was awash with radical republican ideology invariably represented by a slave seeking not just freedom but retribution. Haiti provided the facts—or, rather, the facts as projected by a terrified white plantocracy. Everywhere in the Caribbean they reacted with a sense of terror to anything associated with Haiti. In his classic study, *The Fall of the Planter Class in the British Caribbean*, Lowell Joseph Ragatz tells the story of the cool reception given by the Jamaican population to the French planters escaping the revolutionary wars in Ste. Domingue (Haiti). The reason was that the slaves they brought with them were heard to be singing Jacobin songs which, said Ragatz, "furnished convincing argument that they should not be harbored."[2] Everything was permeated with references to the horrifying events in Haiti. When a priest based in Dominica preached two sermons in 1800 urging greater kindness toward the slaves, he was summoned before the local council and urged to leave the island. Upon his departure, the local paper described him as a "diminutive wolf in sheep's clothing" and recommended that he "exchange his gown for the party-coloured trappings of the French Republicans."[3]

By Ragatz's telling, even the debate over abolition in England began to center on events in Haiti. Those who opposed abolition cited with "lurid accounts of atrocities" what would occur in the British colonies if slavery were abolished. Abolitionists in turn predicted similar uprisings and atrocities if slavery were not promptly ended.[4] The same occurred in Spanish colonial America where racial prejudice and the brutal treatment of slaves existed. One consequence was that the Haitian Revolution created an atmosphere of terror, of collective panic everywhere, be it French, British, or Spanish *criollo* society. The instinct to hunker down, to curtail liberal thought and excessive humanitarian actions, was generalized. It was the same throughout the Hemisphere, but one place where that terror had major consequences was Venezuela. It was there that so many of the precursors and even the Liberator himself had to confront their own racial prejudices and their *criollo* caste's fear of the "contagion" of the Haitian revolt. No matter what aspect of the liberation struggle you may choose to study, the issue of race makes an appearance.

Such an example is one of the unsettled questions of the Gran Colombian War of Liberation: what were the reasons for the split between the precursor, Francisco de Miranda, and the Liberator, Simón Bolívar. Miranda, the son of a Spaniard, was not a member of *criollo* aristocracy—the *mantuano* caste—and he distrusted them. Bolívar was its representative. And yet they shared one fundamental set of values: social status and racial prejudice. Miranda always feared rule by the blacks and coloreds (*pardos*), which he equated with social anarchy. At a particular juncture of the struggle, fearing rule by the *pardos*, he surrendered to the Royalist forces. As Gerard Masur notes,

Miranda wished to avoid a civil war "in which the lower classes, the mestizo and Negros, would be the beneficiaries." Miranda associated chaos and anarchy with crime and both with race war. As Masur writes, "Miranda had a long time before he made the statement that he would prefer his country to remain another hundred years beneath Spanish oppression than be transformed into an arena for crime. He capitulated."[5]

Miranda died in a Spanish prison in Cádiz; Bolívar went into exile in Haiti and prepared to reignite the war of liberation. He realized that the racial situation in Venezuela was more roiled than ever and that if victory was to be achieved, he had to overcome his own prejudices, confront the prejudices of the *criollo* aristocracy, and so eventually secure the alliance and loyalties of the black and *pardo* masses. Without them there would not have been independence at the time. It was not an easy effort for a *criollo* of the *mantuano* caste. No one has described Bolívar's personal struggles with his own biases and the strong prejudices of his immediate family better than his aide-de-camp, the Irish general Daniel Florencio O'Leary.[6] O'Leary relates how, unlike so many others, Bolívar did liberate his many slaves, did learn to judge men in terms of their military talents, and did promulgate laws emancipating all slaves. There can be no question of Bolívar's sincerity in this personal, albeit pragmatic, wider social battle against racism and the defenders of slavery.[7]

Spanish historian Salvador de Madariaga argued that Bolívar's own mixed heritage made him at once guarded about being considered a nonwhite while also sharpening his sensibilities about the psychological impulses of the *pardos*.[8] As persuasive as this argument is, it parses a bit too finely what was essentially one social-psychological syndrome: white subordination of the nonwhites, both free and slave, and the historical fear that one day they would turn on their masters. This is what led John Lombardi, an outstanding student of slavery and emancipation in Venezuela, to argue that it is not important to know whether Bolívar wished to liberate the slaves because he needed them as troops, because he feared a *pardocrácia* if all the whites died, because he believed it absurd to fight for "freedom" while keeping major parts in slavery, or because he feared another Haiti if slavery was not abolished.[9]

Be that as it may, Bolívar was perpetually concerned about the dangers of a race war back home in Venezuela and the terrible opinions foreigners had of that situation. Spanish colonial authorities wasted no time in broadcasting the dangers of independence to the white population. During his exile in Jamaica in 1815, Bolívar tried every which way to convince the British that his revolution was nothing like that of Haiti. He explained to the editor of the *Royal Jamaican Gazette* that they should not fear the fact that Venezuelan society was divided into castes. Whites, he said, were in a minority (see table 6), but they made up for their lack of numbers by their "intellectual qualities." Indians were the majority, but they were sweet by nature and mixed easily with the whites. The problem lay with the blacks and mulattos who, encouraged by Spanish leaders to follow the example of Haiti, initially tried to eliminate white *criollo* society. Now, said Bolívar, they would join him in the War of Liberation.[10] He may have been overly optimistic.

He faced rebellion not just by Royalist *pardos* but within his own ranks. Two years later Bolívar confronted the rebellion of one of his generals, the mulatto Manuel Piar. Bolívar's analysis of Piar's "treachery" reads like a chapter from Frantz Fanon's *Black Skins, White Masks* and is worth quoting at length. Bolívar notes that Piar was born on the island of Curaçao, as was his *mulata* mother, and that his *canario* father was born in Tenerife. He was not really Venezuelan and could have no loyalty to Venezuela, said Bolívar. And then he continued with a psychological analysis of the role of race and color:

> Erguido el General Piar de pertenecer a una familia noble de Tenerife, negaba desde sus primeros años ¡¡¡qué horrible escandalo!!!, negaba conocer el infeliz seno que había llevado este aborto en sus entrañas. Tan nefando en su desnaturalizada ingratitud, ultrajaba a la misma

Table 6. Ethnic composition of the Venezuelan population at the end of the colonial period

	Number	Percentage of population
Peninsular Spaniards	1,500	0.18
Creoles of elite status	2,500	0.31
Native Canarians (immigrants)	10,000	1.25
Creole Canarians (*blancos de orilla*)	190,000	23.75
Pardos	400,000	50.00
Blacks (slaves, fugitives, and free)	70,000	8.75
Indians	120,000	15.00
Approximate total	800,000	

Sources: John V. Lombardi, *People and Places in Colonial Venezuela* (Bloomington: Indiana University Press, 1976), 132; John Lynch, *Simón Bolívar* (New Haven: Yale University Press, 2006), 10.

madre de quien había recibido la vida por solo el motivo de no ser aquella respetable mujer, del color claro que el había heredado de su padre. Quien no supo amar, respetar y servir a los autores de sus días, no podía someterse al deber de ciudadano y menos aún al más riguroso de todos: al militar.[11] ["Because General Piar proudly maintained that he belonged to a noble family from Tenerife, he denied from an early age (what a terrible scandal!!!) any knowledge of the unhappy woman that carried this human miscreant in her womb. So nefarious was his unnatural ingratitude he abused the mother from whom he received life only because that respectable woman did not share the light skin he inherited from his father. One who never knew how to love, to respect and serve the authors of his days, could not submit himself to the duties of the citizenship much less to the most rigorous of all; the military."]

Piar was hunted down, charged with "proclaiming the odious principles of race war," and executed. Whatever Bolívar's personal angst about his ethnic background and that of his white military companions, they all had a wider fear that was personal and geopolitical, as John Lynch describes it:

Race was an issue in Venezuela, usually dormant, but with potential for violence. The creoles were frightened people; they feared a caste war, inflamed by French revolutionary doctrine and the contagious violence of Saint Domingue, the future Haiti. . . . These forebodings were intensified by the horror of slave agitation and revolt.[12]

Certainly Bolívar had witnessed Haiti firsthand. He was also aware that the black and *pardo* revolt in the Venezuelan sugar-producing region of Coro demonstrated that collective fears responded to real facts and were not simple products of their prejudiced imaginations. Already the French revolutionary idea of liberty and the example of the war in Haiti had reached free blacks such as the ones who led the Coro rebellion. The theme in Carpentier's celebrated historical novel is built on that fear of the Haitian case. Even the commander of the major Spanish force that defeated the First Republic, General Murillo, believed that there was evidence that Piar had very close relations with Alexandre Pétion, "a rebel mulatto who calls himself president of Haiti." According to Murillo, Pétion and Piar "propose to create a base in Guayana from which they can dominate America."[13]

The fact that Bolívar forgave two other white officers who had disavowed his authority shed special light on the General Piar execution. Both Santiago Mariño and José Francisco Bermudez were once in open rebellion against Bolívar. Indeed, O'Leary describes a situation in Haiti where Bolívar had to draw his sword to fend off a physical assault by Bermudez.[14] Why then were there no sanctions? The case of Piar was different in the sense that, as O'Leary tells it, he was plotting Bolívar's destruction, and his actions might have caused "a slave or race war."[15] Even a cursory review of the racial divisions in Venezuela reveals just how easy, and ultimately destructive, such a war would be.

The roles that race and ethnicity played in the creation of the nation in Venezuela appear at first to be analogous to the role they played in the Haitian case. They represent, however, highly seductive analogies since, in fact, the case of Venezuela (and the Cuban case dealt with below) illustrate not the likeness but the differences with the Haitian case. Rather than serving as a positive example, the Haitian case contributed mightily to engendering and amplifying the determination of the elites of Venezuela and other countries to highlight the differences, to stop their states from becoming "another Haiti." The situation in Haiti had much to do with heightening—not creating—the fear of *pardocrácia*. The specter of a Haitian-like chaos haunted Bolívar from the time of his two stays on that island. Martha Hildebrandt, who has done the most precise content analysis of Bolívar's language, noted that he was "always concerned with the danger of a pardocrácia resulting from the growth of the *pardo* population."[16] Bolívar was concerned that *pardos* were not "paying their dues" in the war of liberation. As he wrote to Vice President Francisco de Paula Santander: "Is it fair that only free men should die for the liberation of the slaves? Is it not proper that the slaves should acquire their rights on the battlefield and that their dangerous numbers should be lessened by a process both just and effective?"[17]

The reasons for these reactions have much more to do with the perceptions of the elites in these countries than what actually was occurring in Haiti. The phenomenon is called displacement, which leads to overgeneralization on the basis of presumed similarities.[18] The following proposition on "displacement aggression" seems to fit the case of the Caribbean, indeed, the world's reaction to the Haitian Revolution: "When the actual barrier is physically, psychologically, or socially invulnerable to attack, aggression may be displaced to an innocent but more vulnerable bystander."[19]

With each victory of the Haitian rebels (especially against European armies), the more generalized the displacement aggression, the more Haiti was held up to be different from the rest of the Caribbean. Contrary to the thesis that the decolonization process in the Caribbean began in Haiti, a case can be made that the decolonization process was in fact delayed because of the way Haiti was displaced and overgeneralized in the minds of colonial and native white elites.[20] The *criollo* leaders of the liberation struggle confronted a real dilemma: they could not win without the *pardos*; they could not allow the *pardos* to be the "owners" of the victory. This explains why nowhere in the Caribbean did the Haitian War of Liberation and the eventual emancipation of the slaves fundamentally change the racial stratification system. If anything, it was reinforced by two powerful forces: the racism and economic interests of most of the *criollo* plantation owners and the scare tactics of the Spanish metropolitan ideologues, both responding to the specter of "another Haiti." Always afraid of their own slaves, metropolitan and white creoles alike feared a revolt. This was aggressive displacement writ large.

Local whites used metropolitan whites, who held ultimate power over the fates of these minute colonies, as reference groups. This is what has to be understood in Bolívar's *Letter from Jamaica* (1815) when he was seeking a European ally. Bolívar wrote, "As soon as we are strong under the patronage of a liberal nation that will lend us its protection, we will wish agreement in cultivating the virtues and talents that lead to glory." Colonial ideologues everywhere were racist and reactionary. The "white man's burden" thus combined racism with paternalism. A striking example of this was the attitude of Bolívar's very influential sister, María Antonia Bolívar, who even as her brother was leading a war of national liberation, wrote to him saying that she would have to leave Caracas because of "the insolence of the *pardos*." She could not, she said, "stomach" the idea of liberating the family slaves.[21] Bolívar's own mother continued to complain about the price of slaves.[22]

It should not be believed that fear of a *pardo* revolt was pure imagination. O'Leary describes a conspiracy spurred by the Royal authorities in Petare (close to Caracas) among "Negroes and people of mixed blood" around the time María Antonia Bolívar was writing. To the *mantuano* class, keeping the blacks enslaved and the *pardos* in their place was deemed essential to avoiding another Haiti. As Thomas Carlyle warned after observing the results of emancipation in the mid-nineteenth century, "Let him, by his ugliness, idleness, rebellion, banish all white men from the West Indies, and make it all

one Haiti . . . a tropical dog-kennel and pestiferous jungle."[23] Similar opinions came from Oxford historian James Anthony Froude.

If this was so among Europeans, is it any surprise that native *criollos*, including the great precursors Miranda and Bolívar, many of whom had found
refuge in Haiti, never understood or sympathized with the causes of the Haitian Revolution? Not at all. Despite his friendship with the Haitian leader
Alexandre Pétion, Bolívar shared the generalized dim view of the isolated
island. Haiti was Africa, the Dark Continent, the great unknown with all
the preconceptions that conjured up images of *pardocrácia*: black-led social
revolution and disorder. This is evident in his warning to Vice President
Santander on December 23, 1822, that the coasts of Colombia were threatened not only by the neighboring European colonies but also by "the Africans of Haiti, whose power is greater than the primitive fire." Haiti, he says
in the same letter, is "so complex and so horrible that no matter how you
consider it, it doesn't present other than horrors and misfortunes."[24] Soon
after his second exile in Haiti in 1817, he warned fellow Venezuelan officer
Pedro Briceño Méndez that "you are neither in Constantinople nor in Haiti.
While I can breathe and hold sword in hand, there is no tyranny or anarchy
here."[25] Again, on March 11, 1825, Bolívar wrote to Santander that the Haitian Revolution could serve as a model in certain respects, "but not in the
horrible area of destruction which they adopted." Bolívar did adopt Haiti's
strategy of total war (the war to death), but his fear was ultimately the fear
of *pardocrácia* rule or, as it was understood, anarchy, led by nonwhites. This
would appear repeatedly in Bolívar's writing, despite his efforts to overcome
his own prejudices; the roots in his social caste origins were too deep, and
his ceaseless efforts to find legitimation in European eyes were too urgent to
be easily overcome. It is crucial to understand, therefore, that Bolívar, like
Miranda, not only perceived that the Great Powers shared and understood
his social values and views on Haiti and on nonwhites generally but he also
believed that they would somehow reward him and his cause for adhering to
those commonly held racial prejudices.

It is not a trivial fact that both the writer of the memorandum citing Bolívar's rejection of inviting Haiti to the Panamá Congress, José Rafael Ravenga,
and the chief recipient and chief delegate to the Panamá Congress, Dr. Pedro Gual, had once found refuge in Haiti. Like Miranda and Bolívar, these
gentlemen held opinions that were not even faintly generous to the Haitians.
The antagonism of the Great Powers and of the United States toward Haiti

thus, while a powerful enough reason for keeping Haiti at arm's length, also provided a convenient and comfortable support for the existing anti-Haitian attitudes of the Latin American elites.[26]

While military necessity forced Bolívar to recruit nonwhites as officers, the white elite of Colombia felt no compulsion to agree with these choices. Their fear of *pardocrácia* was even more intense than Bolívar's. In fact, this was a major reason for their opposition to his rule. As an important spokesman for this group explained: "In his last years, when he became a dictator, Bolívar represented these three things: the arbitrariness of the sword, the insolence of the Venezuelans who were regarded as intruders, and the rebellion of the mixed bloods."[27] Similarly, José María Samper, an influential contemporary, in referring to the high status civilian group to which he himself belonged, revealed their value system when he noted that "it is they who guide the revolution and are the source of its philosophy. The other races or castes do nothing more than obey the impulses of those who have the prestige and intelligence, the audacity and even the superiority of the white race."[28] The fear and disdain of Haiti was part of the broader fear and disdain of nonwhites. Existing social norms had been relaxed in the military area because of the necessity and exigencies of war. Traditional conservative social norms, however, had not disappeared.

There is no evidence of a Haitian influence much less a direct revolutionary connection in Venezuela. The same cannot be said for Cuba, which, after the Dominican Republic, was arguably the territory most negatively affected by the Haitian Revolution. Foreign visitors to Cuba in the early nineteenth century were quick to notice that island's obsession with race, the mutual aversion between the *castas*, and the perceptions about the role the Haitian Revolution played in Cuban concerns. So it was with the scientist Alexander von Humboldt: "The disturbances in Santo Domingo in 1790 and those in Jamaica in 1794 had caused such great dismay among the *hacendados* of the island of Cuba that a *junta económica* passionately debated options for peacekeeping on the island."[29]

Indeed, the fear of an independent Cuba becoming another Haiti was so extensive that, in a way, it became the one issue unifying all elites in the region. A typical case was Bolívar's own prejudiced sister who had much influence over him. She opposed any attempt by Bolívar to take Cuba. She did not have a good opinion of Cuba, an opinion based on race: "They are of a treacherous spirit, and the blacks and colored men are without comparison worse than ours."[30] This prejudice and fear of blacks was true among Cuban social thinking, so much so that even those who claimed "their rightful share" of the rewards of the wars of independence—the blacks and mulattos—could not avoid the debate which was framed as "white civilization" versus "barbarian Africanization."[31] At all stages of the nineteenth-century efforts at independence from Spain, an influential segment of the *criollo* elite believed that even as they favored independence, they preferred to remain Spanish rather than open the doors to widespread African influences. While the elites wanted to enlist blacks into the wars of liberation—over 70 percent of the soldiers of the Army of Liberation (*mambises*) were black—they were determined to prevent them from dominating the island. This, in many ways, replicated the situation in Venezuela and Colombia. Hugh Thomas cites a little-known letter of Bolivar's explaining why he did not want to liberate Cuba: "I believe our league can maintain itself perfectly well without embracing the extremes of the South . . . and without creating another Republic of Haiti [in Cuba]"[32] His sister, María Antonia, was not the only one with a dim view of Haiti and blacks in general.

Charles Chapman noted that throughout the nineteenth century Cubans were obsessed with the issue of the racial balance. The whites, he said, were "in terror lest Cuba become another Haiti." According to Chapman, Cubans believed that there were too many Negroes in Cuba for the people to be willing to risk emancipation.[33] There certainly were some grounds for apprehension. In 1812, José Antonio Aponte led a black rebellion that had Haiti as a model and, according to Levi Marrero, he entertained contacts with a Haitian general.[34] Between 1841 and 1843, there were several minor slave rebellions. It was the rebellion of "La Escalera" in 1844, however, that provoked the great fright (*el gran susto*). Again, it was said that Haiti was the model for that rebellion. As Jorge and Isabel Castellanos noted, it was the fear that the Cuban blacks would make contact with blacks in Jamaica and Haiti which gave rise to a "collective hysteria." What followed were years which Cuban history knows as those of the "Gran Terror" and the "Gran Miedo." Haiti was central to these fears. Virtually every major Cuban thinker in the nineteenth century favored a reduction of the black population, citing Haiti as the reason. The Castellanos put it succinctly: "'The great preoccupation' could be summed up in one simple question: what will happen if Haiti repeats itself in Cuba? Otherwise enlightened thinkers such as José Antonio Saco looked at the Caribbean islands and said: 'Who does not tremble upon realizing that the population of African origin which surrounds Cuba amounts to more than five million?'"[35] Concerning Cuba, Saco wrote: "I passionately wish, though not by violent or revolutionary means but rather by mild and pacific ones, the reduction, the extinction if it were possible, of the negro race."[36] Whether it was Father Félix Varela, Domingo Delmonte, José de la Luz y Caballero, Francisco Arango y Parreño, or Saco, they all perceived the black slaves as irreconcilable enemies and Haiti as the place from which the leadership would come. Their abolitionist fervor was, as Leonardo Griñan Peralta put it, "hijo del temor, no del amor" [the child of fear, not of love].[37]

Evidence of the fear of any contacts with Haiti can even be seen in the attitude of Cuba's formidable independence military leader, the mulatto Antonio Maceo. Like Bolívar before him, Maceo had to find exile after initial defeat. Unlike Bolívar, however, Haiti would not be that place. Maceo's biographer, José Luciano Franco, describes how in 1891 "ofertas realmente tentadoras" were offered by the president of Haiti. Maceo rejected them "por razones obvias." Surprisingly, he appealed instead to Costa Rica where there were very strict regulations against any kind of colored immigration. Only direct appeals to the president finally allowed Maceo and some ten black families to settle there.[38]

What were these "obvious reasons" for rejecting the Haitian invitation? Franco described how Spanish authorities used the fear of Haitian racial intentions as a means of disparaging Maceo and his fellow blacks, the most effective fighters of the Cuban insurgency. The Spanish captain general of Cuba, Camilo de Polavieja, claiming that he kept several spies in Haiti, spread the "secret" information that black Cuban fighters were protected by Haitians in order to strengthen black designs to create a "Liga Antillana" that would eventually control the Caribbean.[39] Clearly Maceo would not want to contribute even the least bit to suspicions that he was part of any such scheme. Such was the fear of guilt by association that Maceo decided to go to a country that had strict legislation prohibiting immigration by blacks. Additional evidence of the efforts to avoid any contact with Haiti came in Maceo's decision to send a fund-raising delegation to various Latin American countries but not to Haiti. Several dictators were contacted, including Mexico's Porfirio Díaz and Venezuela's Joaquín Crespo. The liberal and humanist Eloy Alfaro of Ecuador was also visited. Ulises "Lilis" Heureaux of the Dominican Republic was one of those contacted. Since Heureaux was black and of Haitian descent, the choice was not racial but national.[40] Haiti had become the pariah of the Caribbean.[41] Even the great advocate of slave emancipation in France, Victor Schoelcher, had to comment on the "ruin" that had overtaken Haiti because of the mulatto hatred of the black.[42]

The fear of "Haitianization" thus hung over Caribbean and Cuban life like the sword of Damocles. It came into play again in the early twentieth century as Cuba began its independent life. At this point, U.S. racist views on eugenics and racial purity fell on receptive ears in Cuba. Racial fears even permeated the debate around the introduction of universal suffrage on the island, for, as the *New York Times* on August 7, 1899, headlined: "Cuba may be another Haiti; results of universal suffrage would be a black republic."[43] Be that as it may, Alejandro de la Fuente does record the fact that despite strong American pressure to deny black Cubans the vote, the Cuban political elite did sanction universal male suffrage in 1901. That was the law, not the practice. During the first municipal elections held under the U.S. occupation in 1900, the U.S. and Cuban authorities did everything to exclude blacks from the political process. This, it was said, would prevent "a second edition of Haiti or Santo Domingo in the future."[44] Aline Helg is masterful in explaining what she calls three "efficient icons of fear" among white Cubans: fear of the Haitian Revolution influencing black uprisings, fear of African religions and culture, and fear of Afro-Cuban sexuality, male and female.[45] These fears and the repression and discrimination they caused led to a strong reaction and subsequently to the black rebellion in 1912. Blacks protested especially the blatant discrimination in job placements and claimed, as Helg put it, "their rightful share." It brings to mind the shouts of "We put you there!" by Colonel Infante as he was led to the gallows. Predictably, the *New York Times* (May 22, 1912) headlined: "Haitian negroes aid Cuban rebels." As Rafael Fermoselle theorizes, it never occurred to these observers that the many Haitian (and Jamaican) blacks working in the Cuban sugar industry had merely gotten caught up in the middle of the Cuban warfare. The retribution meted out in 1912 to the 4,000 black rebels was ferocious. Chapman relates how President Gómez took note of the "feeling of panic" which the "ferocious savagery" of the blacks had caused among the whites in Havana and vowed to "make short work of them."[46] Over 3,000 blacks were killed.

The "terrified consciousness" of white Cubans was unintentionally heightened by novels such as Alejo Carpentier's 1949 magical realist tale of horror and superstition under King Henri Christophe, *El Reino de este Mundo*. It is the opinion of virtually all serious scholars of Cuban independence that the "race question" poisoned Cuban society and its political process. Quite contrary to the situation in Haiti, Cuban blacks were stymied at every turn from asserting any racial identity. Even José Martí, whose fervent opposition to racism is beyond reproach, once noted, "The black man who proclaims his race, even if incorrectly as a way to proclaim spiritual identity with all races, justifies and provokes white racism."[47] As Louis Pérez notes, "The image of savage spirits loomed large in the Creole imagination . . . always in the form of slave uprisings and race war."[48] Alejandro de la Fuente explains the detrimental consequences of this fear of a separate black identity very clearly: "National unity was to be achieved at the expense of racial identities. . . . Afro-Cubans would have to choose between being black . . . or being Cuban, members of an allegedly raceless nationalist force. Any possibility for blacks to voice their specific grievances and discontent was therefore explicitly rejected as un-Cuban and unpatriotic."[49]

Despite credible efforts by leaders such as José Martí to curb racism, national identity—*cubanidad*—was framed in terms of white civilization versus African barbarity, and Haiti was the living and proximate example of the latter.[50] Cubans exemplified aggressive displacement and ensured that Cuba's development was always kept different and separate from that of Haiti. This white racial identity has been so ingrained that even five decades of revolution since 1959 have not been able to eradicate completely the salience of race in Cuban life.[51] The laws, as always, are admirable, but as in colonial times, the law is "obeyed" but not carried out.

The reader will notice that this analysis does not deal with the influence of the Haitian Revolution on the American slave plantation. I accept the interpretation of Ashli White in her work *Encountering Revolution: Haiti and the Making of the Early Republic*, that there was awareness but relatively little panic about Haitian revolutionary influences in the United States. In an age of territorial expansion and with the hubris of being racially and culturally superior, which justified enslaving others, Americans were aware but not overly concerned with events in Haiti. They believed themselves to be "immune" from Haitian-influenced challenges.[52] This argument is supported by Daniel Rasmussen's detailed study of the uprising among the plantations in the Orleans Territory outside New Orleans. Rasmussen documents the American planters' insouciance: "Though terrified by Haiti, the planters refused to acknowledge or try to understand the political logic behind the slaves' actions. Their racial ideology and pride in their own accomplishments led them to miss all the warning signals of the impending revolt."[53]

Such evidence has not stopped the recent tendency of finding Haitian influences in the United States. Maurice Jackson and Jacqueline Bacon claim that the Haitian Revolution had "a profound influence on the development of African American history, culture, and political thought." They were honest enough, however, to include an essay that demolishes the myth of that interpretation by noting that African Americans "consciously avoided connecting their public demonstrations to the Haitian Revolution." Mitch Kachun asks that historians deal "with historical reality and not the historical mythology."[54]

How different the case of the Latin American and Caribbean planters and upper classes. They were as racially exclusivist as the North Americans but faced a different demographic and geopolitical environment. There the fear of Haiti's influence on "their" blacks and coloreds, slave and free, generalized a very real and present terrified consciousness. As David Brion Davis puts it, even among the most ardent British emancipationists, "the specter of Haiti haunted them and strengthened their determination to repudiate any measures that might undermine law and authority or endanger the long-term productivity of colonial labor."[55] Rather than creating "citizens," this fear of what Davis calls "a Haitian result" delayed the abolition of slavery everywhere and stymied any attempts at liberating Cuba and Puerto Rico from Spanish imperial domination for many years.

A quite different history of relations with Haiti was that of the Dominican Republic. It was the only country actually invaded by Haitians. There was a definite border between the French one-third and the Spanish two-thirds of the island of Hispaniola established by the Treaty of Rÿswerk in 1697 and confirmed by the Treaty of Aranjuez in 1777. Early Haitian leaders never respected this division of the island. Their invasions were led by Toussaint L'Ouverture in 1801, Dessalines in 1802, and Jean Pierre Boyer in 1822, an invasion and occupation that lasted until 1844. Dominicans celebrate their independence from the date of the expulsion of the Haitians. Contrary to colonial Haiti, where perhaps 500,000 slaves worked the sugar, coffee, and cacao plantations, up to 1855 the Dominican Republic's population of 230,000 consisted of 122,000 white *criollos*, 70,000 mulattos, and 38,000 blacks. Their economy was mostly raising cattle and logging on communal lands (*terrenos comuneros*).

The Dominican Republic's foremost historian, Frank Moya Pons, sets the record straight: "For about two centuries, two different societies had been evolving independently in both parts of the island under very different economic and social conditions."[56] The long overdue revisionist historiography in the Dominican Republic has been focusing attention on the fact that Dominican mulattos and slaves, especially initially, welcomed the invasion of Jean Pierre Boyer in 1822. The promise of freedom to the slaves and full citizenship rights to the mulattos had to be welcome. Not everyone, however, extended this welcome, as Moya puts it: "Because Boyer was aware that he was going to uproot a centuries-old tradition, he knew he would have to use military force against the colonial elite."[57]

During the twenty-two years of Haitian occupation, Boyer had to use force against more than just the elite. The first issue of contention was the dispute over land and how to use it. Boyer enacted the French/Haitian land tenure system, which divided the land into privately held plots and demanded that the owners cultivate sugarcane, cacao, and coffee, all for export with heavy taxes going to the state. The liberated slaves found themselves tied to a real plantation system governed by rigorous rules. The second issue of contention was language and the culture of administration generally. Boyer ordered that French be used in all official dealings, leading eventually to French being the language of the unified state. Historian Franklyn Franco, sympathetic to the Haitian presence in terms of the abolition of slavery and the legislation of the equality of all citizens, believed that this language issue joined to other radical changes created a serious cultural divide that only grew wider the longer the Haitian presence lasted.[58]

The point is that the Dominican-Haitian antagonisms are not recent productions by a small white elite. They have deep roots in the history of both countries. As a result, Haitian and Dominican intellectuals have always engaged in debates highlighting the comparative achievements of their respective societies. In 1953, Haiti's justly acclaimed ethnologist Jean Price-Mars published *La République d'Haïti et la République Dominicaine* in two volumes. It is not necessary to detail all the negative assertions Price-Mars makes about Dominican society. They were sufficiently hurtful to bring a lengthy response from Emilio Rodríguez Demorizi in a thick volume produced by the Dominican Academy of History, pointedly entitled *Invasiones haitianas de 1801, 1805 y 1822*. Whatever errors or faults Dominicans had, Haitians had them in like measure. This exchange between two highly regarded scholars only reflected an antagonism that is historical and that has to be understood to avoid arriving at simplistic conclusions regarding the Haitian/Dominican antagonism. So entrenched have the largely anti-Dominican interpretations of the issue become that it is worth dissecting a representative case of this genre. Ernesto Sagás's *Race and Politics in the Dominican Republic* is such a case: "Antihaitianismo ideology combines a legacy of racist Spanish colonial mentality, nineteenth-century racial theories, and twentieth-century cultural neo-racism into a web of anti-Haitian attitudes, racial stereotypes, and historical distortions."[59] This "hegemonic ideology" not only oppresses Haitians in the Dominican Republic but it has also traditionally been employed as an ideological weapon "to subdue the black and mulatto Dominican lower classes and maintain their political acquiescence." It is Sagás's intention to examine and "demystify" this racist ideology, perpetuated by what he terms "the light-skinned elites." Very similar light-skinned elites, he asserts, also monopolize power and exercise hegemonic control over blacks and mulattos in today's Cuba and Puerto Rico. As such, the approach of his book dovetails with the considerable literature in Haiti and the non-Hispanic Caribbean, which invariably analyzes social stratification and power relations in terms of skin color.

Given this historical interpretation, it is no surprise that Sagás repeats one of the most frequent claims made against Dominicans—their failure to recognize what he calls "their true racial identity." By not coming "to terms" with their African heritage, he claims, they exhibit a form of "false consciousness."[60] This position can be faulted on two grounds. Historically, the Dominican Republic never had a plantation system developed enough to demand large African slavery. There is, consequently, a weak African presence. Practical and ethical issues also arise: who, other than the people themselves, should decide what their "true" ethnic and national identity is? He further writes that it is the light-skinned Dominican elite who conspire to stop Dominicans and Haitians from forming "transnational alliances." Unfortunately, Sagás spends no time analyzing the nature of national identities, since in his opinion nationalism is "inevitably racist."[61] As we shall see in chapter 6, in the Caribbean, individuals, groups, indeed, whole classes move in and out of "identities" with ease. Who are we to say that they should not?

The longer-term consequences of this "terrified consciousness" about race are still evident. First among these consequences is the constant effort to be, or become, white or at least whiter. The prestige and advantages of light skin color are still the dominant feature of establishing social distance. This involves striking out at anyone attempting to upset this historical stratification, no matter how noble the efforts, whether it be in the Hispanic or the non-Hispanic cultural areas. This explains why a prominent advocate of emancipation in the French colonies, Victor Schoelcher, was generally described as "ce grand ennemi de la race blanche aux colonies" and as "le vampire de la race blanche."[62]

It is a deeply rooted set of cultural values and norms that was introduced by the Spanish with their demands for "pruebas de limpieza de sangre" and further enhanced by the tremors of panic and fear emanating from the Haitian Revolution. It is a theme that the reader will encounter in all sections of this book.

5

Haitian Realities and Scholarly Myths

A Counterintuitive Analysis

From a methodological point of view, many studies of Third World countries are challenged by the relative lack of data and previous research. No such handicap can be claimed for those working on the Caribbean generally and Haiti in particular. Garry Wills is critical of the fact that the most important historians of the Adams presidency and even of the pro-Haitian abolitionist Timothy Pickering omit any mention of the Haitian Revolution.[1] This omission has certainly been reversed by many fine studies.[2] The challenge is how to maneuver through the various theoretical schools of thought to arrive at the type of evidence necessary for short- and medium-term interpretations and for policy recommendations.

Even these new studies, however, seem to tell us, as one of the pioneers of this new interest, David P. Geggus, notes, "It is easy to list the reasons why the Haitian Revolution is important, but it is much more difficult to define how it affected the wider world."[3] True to the scholarly tradition of encouraging debate on this issue, Geggus includes in his recent anthology many essays claiming a widespread influence of the Haitian Revolution. But he also includes an essay by Seymour Drescher which argues that Haiti's significance was more symbolic than substantive: "That the Haitian Revolution remained a powerful image in the minds of most slaves is indisputable. That Haiti was itself a direct catalyst of most subsequent slave mobilizations in the Caribbean is questionable."[4]

Unfortunately, this admirable scholarly tradition has not been adopted by studies on contemporary Haiti. There have been three dominant explanations of Haiti's backwardness. First, blame the Haitian *mulâtres* (mulattos). This has been a general theme of Haitian *noir* writers. What gave it great weight was the 1928 book *Ainsi Parla L'Oncle* by Jean Price-Mars, himself a *mulâtre*. This *noirist* theme was used politically by François Duvalier and

Lorimer Denis in their 1938 bitterly anti-*mulâtre* book, *Le problème des classes à travers l'histoire d'Haïti*. The second major explanation was that the culture of the Voodoo religion encouraged fatalism of a paralyzing sort. Among Haitian scholars who emphasized this cultural factor are Remy Bastien and the founder of the Haitian Communist Party, Jacques Roumain.

Most frequently cited by far as a cause of Haiti's perennial underdevelopment has been the thesis of foreign intervention. There is no disputing the many betrayals of the early leaders of the revolution. Garry Wills describes how Toussaint, in exchange for American help, promised that Haiti would not support slave insurrections elsewhere. Since France was at the time the enemy of both Haiti and the United States, it was a simple geopolitical exchange: the enemy of my enemy is my friend. Once Toussaint was betrayed by France, the United States took a hands-off and belligerent stance vis-à-vis Haiti.[5] One also has to take into account the French demand for substantial reparations in exchange for diplomatic recognition and the nineteen years of the U.S. Marine Corps occupation. Both figure high on the guilty list. None of this, however, fully explains Haiti's historical underdevelopment. Yet the idea of foreign intervention has been part of Haitian and foreign writing on Haiti for so long that it has taken on the dimensions of a grand and largely unchallenged myth. Some recent writings demonstrate this fact.[6]

Paul Farmer's *Haiti after the Earthquake* is composed of his essay (239 out of 360 pages) and twelve contributors listed as "Other Voices," virtually all related to Farmer's Partners in Health and Zanmi Lasante medical centers.[7] These admirable centers have operated in rural Haiti and in a dozen other countries for decades. Aside from their evident dedication to caring for the poor, Farmer and his team know Haiti and are clearly eager to have their opinions heard.

The opening chapter, a two-page essay by Joia S. Mukherjee, medical director of Partners in Health, sets the book's tone. The tragedy of Haiti, she says, is that for two centuries it has been the victim of powerful foreign countries, "resulting in policies which have served to impoverish the people of Haiti."[8] From that point on, the interpretive stance of the book is essentially *frappe les étrangers* or "foreigner bashing," not least of all in the long essay by Farmer himself. Farmer had made his views evident in two previous books, *AIDS and Accusation: Haiti and the Geography of Blame* and *The Uses of Haiti*.[9] In the latter book Farmer is unabashed in his praise of Jean-Bertrand Aristide but hardly moderate in his criticism of all his opponents. One agency that was accused of "sabotage" and "covert operations to undermine Haitian democracy" was USAID.[10] He repeats his dislikes in *Haiti after the Earthquake,* except in more moderate tones. This moderation might be explained by the fact that at the time of writing he was serving as deputy special envoy for Haiti under UN special envoy Bill Clinton. His targets are many: U.S. investments (whether in tourism, assembly industries, or NGOs), the International Monetary Fund (IMF), and the neoliberal structural reforms these forces impose on weak countries. In contrast, his primary accolades are for the Cuban doctors working in Haiti, and this is in sharp contrast to his less-than-generous opinion of other foreign doctors such as those from Médecins Sans Frontières, which he characterizes as "the home base of disgruntled doctors."[11]

To Farmer, the culprit in the island's persistent poverty and underdevelopment is easily identifiable: "five centuries of transnational social and economic forces with deep roots in the colonial enterprise."[12] Even the endemic corruption of the elite is blamed on the constant "foreign intervention and meddling," especially by the NGOs that have "undermined the Republic of Haiti's capability to fulfill its government mandate."[13] In fact, says Farmer, the "free people of Haiti" have been "disrespected in their quest for democracy by an unrelenting series of dictators and coup d'états backed by Western countries."[14]

You read more than three hundred pages of Farmer's *Haiti after the Earthquake* without finding a single mention of the critical role that the U.S. Southern Command (SouthCom) played in providing aid to Haiti immediately after the 2010 earthquake. What is ignored is a fundamental geopolitical reality of the Caribbean: only the United States had and has the hospital ships, the helicopters, the heavy equipment, and the lift-and-deliver capacity essential to providing aid during the early days of catastrophes, including that of Haiti. Very rarely does one read an essay which acknowledges that fact, so thankfully this is done by another member of Farmer's team, Dr. Louise C. Ivers, chief of mission for Partners in Health in Haiti and assistant professor of medicine at Harvard Medical School. Dr. Ivers does what Farmer does not: she recognizes the important role of the American military, concluding that Haitians "are avid fans" of that assistance from the U.S. military. "Dirty Boots," the title of her chapter, comes from the many times she heard her Haitian patients say, "Look, Dr. Louise, they got their boots dirty,"[15] that is, the U.S. military was willing to do the grimy part of the work. This seems an appropriate lesson for a fact not fully developed by Farmer: both Haitians and *blancs* need to get their boots dirty to get development going.

Not everyone, however, shares the faith in the ability of foreign capital to create a labor-absorbing economy of manufactured goods for export. As noted above, Farmer disagrees with this strategy and, in a volume called *Fixing Haiti*, the widely recognized and much-quoted Haitian political scientist Robert Fatton Jr. is equally vehement in his opposition. According to Fatton, Haiti's instability and underdevelopment can be traced to two causes. The first is what he calls *la politiqué politicienne*, the unprincipled struggle for booty and public office by a "privileged or ruling minority" that "persistently manipulates the constitution to preserve its interest in the face of overwhelming popular opposition."[16] He had already developed this theme in two excellent previous books, *Haiti's Predatory Republic* and *The Roots of Haitian Despotism*. In the present volume, Fatton appears more interested in the second cause of Haiti's underdevelopment, especially its food shortages: neoliberal development programs driven by the United States and the International Monetary Fund.

Fatton's postscript, written ten months after the earthquake of 2010, presents a litany of harsh critiques of Haitian neoliberal politics and politicians and of the Interim Haiti Recovery Commission chaired by Bill Clinton. He claims that it was this model of development and these people, along with the UN peacekeeping mission MINUSTAH, which turned Haiti into a "virtual trusteeship."[17] All this leads to Fatton's central conclusion that "the neoliberal regime imposed on the country" is "the single most critical" cause of the present crisis. It is no surprise, therefore, that Fatton would recommend that Haiti abandon what he calls "neoliberal extremism."[18] Unfortunately, unless one can demonstrate how this "present" crisis differs from previous ones and unless one is ready to specify the programs that a state should abandon, blaming "neoliberalism" remains in the realm of the ideological debates that have been grist for the mill of chronic oppositionism in Haiti. This is precisely the critique of distinguished Haitian economist Ericq Pierre, who was twice nominated for prime minister but derailed for reasons he later revealed. Ironically, Fatton himself quotes Pierre's complaint: "From the very beginning of the process, I ran up against the forces of corruption. . . . I also wanted to play with my cards on the table, refusing to fall into the game of those who think they can hide indefinitely behind an anti-neoliberal mask."[19]

Another who leans heavily on the anti-foreigner hypothesis is Laurent Dubois, author of a much acclaimed book on the early years of the Haitian Independence, *Avengers of the New World*.[20] In a more recent book, *Haiti: The Aftershocks of History*, the story is updated to include the 2010 earthquake. The result is a commendable and easily accessible section on two hundred years of history that precedes his analysis of contemporary affairs. In this later part the dominant explanation for the persistent underdevelopment in Haiti returns to the role of external forces. According to Dubois, there are two main drivers in Haitian history: the steely determination of the masses to be left alone to enjoy the fruits of the postplantation system of individual subsistence plots they fought to establish, and the fact that this passionately defended peasant existence has been continually undermined by foreign interventions and interference. For Dubois, the counterpoint between these two forces explains virtually every aspect of Haitian history, from Toussaint L'Ouverture to Jean-Bertrand Aristide.

As distinct from his more refined analysis of history, this contemporary analysis is crude because it is excessively simple, devoid of the sophisticated class-based formulations of C.L.R. James in *The Black Jacobins* (to which, amazingly, Dubois never refers) or of the complex interaction of race and class by David Nicholls in *From Dessalines to Duvalier*.[21] In fact, Dubois delivers a glancing critique of Nicholls when he dismisses what he calls "the over-simplified racial explanation."[22] Yet time and again, he disregards this critique by resorting to race and color in his own analysis of the constant struggle for supremacy in Haiti. His dominant approach is to juxtapose a frankly romantic vision of peasant society to the assaults of invariably perfidious outsiders: French colonialists, American capitalists, NGOs, MINUSTAH, and even Bill Clinton. "Despite all its tragedy," he argues, "Haiti's past shows the remarkable, steadfast, and ongoing struggle of a people to craft an alternative to the existence that others wanted to impose on them."[23] The alternative that Dubois advocates and defends is subsistence agriculture. Such is Dubois's conviction that the Haitians have in fact constructed an ideal form of land tenure and agriculture that he makes the following extraordinary claim: "By combining subsistence agriculture with the production of some crops for export, they created a system that guaranteed them a better life, materially and socially, than that available to most other people of African descent in the Americas throughout the nineteenth and early twentieth centuries."[24] Dubois dismisses any analysis, no matter how well intentioned or well informed, that contends that subsistence agriculture has brought misery to Haiti's peasants. He thus rejects the shock expressed by Victor Schoelcher, who at the time (mid-nineteenth century) was fighting for emancipation in the French Caribbean, seeing "misery and sterility" and concluding that from the trees of liberty has come nothing but "bitter disappointing fruit." To Dubois, the rural culture condemned by Schoelcher "was driven by a historically constituted set of aspirations and a determined search for autonomy."[25] Going further, he says that if the peasants were so vilified, "of course, it was partly because they had been so successful." They managed to resist plantation labor "and construct something else in its place."[26] Dubois presents no evidence, eyewitness or otherwise, to support this claim of a better life. In fact, the evidence we do have tends to support Schoelcher's views.

A mission sent in 1930 by the very liberal World Peace Foundation of Boston cites study after study of the truly frightening lack of sanitation and the ubiquitous presence of contagious diseases among Haiti's peasants. "It has been estimated," said the mission, "that syphilis and yaws affected 80 percent of the population."[27] A decade later, in 1942, having recently completed his PhD at Oxford and then worked for Howard University, Trinidadian Eric Williams cautioned: "We must not be romantic about the question of peasant proprietorship . . . [which is] by itself no solution. . . . Haiti is a glaring example . . . [of the] poor, miserably poor." Citing a study of 884 rural families, 85 percent of whom ate only one meal a day and fewer than half of whom owned beds, Williams concluded that the subsistence agriculture that peasants practiced was "an impediment to progress."[28]

In 1947, an American journalist traveling under the auspices of the Inter-American Educational Foundation, much impressed with the "innate dignity," "self-respect," and "uncompromising correctness" of the Haitian peasants he met in the agricultural Artibonite region, nevertheless kept speaking of the "population problem" and described the diet of the Haitian family of this area. "The family diet," he said, "was a sweet potato for breakfast, perhaps; for lunch some mangoes or other fruit; for supper grain sorghum, called 'petit meal,' some beans, and a little rice." No wonder, he added, that he saw so many "puffy farina bellies" indicating "widespread intestinal parasites."[29]

It is telling that the great land reformer Alexandre Pétion set the ideal minimum acreage per peasant at thirty acres. Unfortunately, demography—that terrible but inescapable driver of man-land relations—has worked against

Haiti from the beginning of nationhood. The average size of peasant farms in Haiti during the past two centuries is not known, but by 1990 it was 1.3 hectare per farm and less than an acre per person. Today the topsoil on that acre is so exhausted that it provides, at best, 75 percent of the dietary needs for subsistence. The other 25 percent has to be imported or smuggled across the border from the Dominican Republic.[30] Dubois's romancing of subsistence agriculture is reminiscent of Jean-Bertrand Aristide's claim that Haitian peasants live "in a form of socialism related to their own roots." Aristide added that the people he hates most are those "liberal economists" who wish to change their lives.[31]

This brings us to the claim so often repeated by Farmer, Dubois, Fatton, and all critics of neoliberalism that, by opening Haiti's markets to imports of American rice, local production was destroyed. It is true that cheaper imports always have a chilling effect on domestic production often because of the cost differential. If Haitian rice sold at $1,200 per metric ton and imported rice at $800, there was bound to be an impact. However, this does not explain the situation in Haiti as a whole. The fact is that rice production in Haiti has been stagnant for decades, even as rice consumption has increased exponentially. For instance, between 1980 and 1987, Haitians produced on average 123,000 metric tons and consumed 60,100; by 2010, they were producing 70,000 metric tons of rice and consuming 400,000.[32] The inability of local producers to meet consumer demand is due to the disastrous erosion and loss of arable land available to farmers. In 1938, there were 540,000 hectares of arable land; in 1980, there were 225,750. As Haiti's population more than doubled, so did the consumption of wood for fuel, which went from 7 million cubic meters to 20 million.[33]

None of this is new. Haiti's most acclaimed peasant novel, Jacques Roumain's *Masters of the Dew* (1944), a work much admired by both Farmer and Dubois, paints a vivid picture of "shining gullies" where erosion had undressed long strata of rock and "bled the earth to the bone." Roumain knew where the problem lay: "They had been wrong to cut down the trees that once grew thick up there. But they had burned the woods to plant çongo beans on the plateau and corn on the hillside."[34] Deforestation results also from house construction, boat building, and most disastrous of all, the making of that fuel of the poor, charcoal. The Haitian problem is one of too many people, too few resources, starting with arable land. It is structural, a situation hardly caused by foreign intervention.

Frank Tannenbaum stressed the intractable nature of the problem. "When one looks at Haiti and northeastern Brazil, for instance, the situation seems beyond immediate remedy, no matter how heroic the effort. . . . The sum of the available natural resources and available human skills are just insufficient to deal adequately and quickly with the immediate situation."[35] Revolution in Haiti would only make matters worse.

The situation has existed for 150 years and has become progressively worse in terms of population increase and soil erosion, with more mouths to feed and heads to shelter. If one adds to this economic dimension the peasant's love of land, then the explanation of rural despair becomes clearer. Melville Herskovits noted as far back as 1937 that "there are few, among the peasants at least, who do not seek by all means to add to their heritage. . . . The drive to obtain property is an obsession with the Haitian peasants."[36] It is a sad commentary that this love of the land combined with current agricultural practices will bequeath less of it, in worse condition, to future Haitian generations. It takes nature between 250 and 1,000 years to build three centimeters of humus topsoil, which can be eroded within a few years.

George Anglade has illustrated how exhaustion and impoverishment of the rural areas over three stages has led to internal migration in Haiti.[37] One trend is the rural to urban migration, especially migration to smaller towns. It is not that the cities have that much to offer in terms of jobs, schooling, and health services, but there has been an accelerating deterioration of the rural, peasant economy. Haiti's situation is bad by any comparative standards: the annual growth of Haitian agricultural production during the early 1980s was 1.2 percent, for South America it was 3.3 percent, while the total for the Third World was 2.9 percent.

Haiti is quickly shifting from being a rural and agricultural country to a country where the rural sector cannot sustain the lives of those in the cities or, indeed, even their own. What the French call *une paysannerie parcellaire* describes a situation where 72 percent of those who own land possess less than one hectare. The traditional, and usually partly optimistic, studies of the peasantry have been replaced by a pessimistic literature that engages in debates over the residual value or lack thereof of the "atomization" of the peasantry. Atomization refers to the system of *multiculture* or mixed cultivation for family consumption, local needs, and external markets. Paul Moral, for instance, saw this as promoting disorder; he called it a system of grappling (*grapiye* in Creole), which means "grab wherever you can."[38] George

Anglade, on the other hand, sees Haitians turning necessity (that is, survival) into a virtue.[39]

Whatever the merits of this minifundia may or may not be, there is one consequence with which no one argues: given the growth of the urban population Haiti now has to import more and more of its food. Importation increased 300 percent between 1973 and 1980 and continues to grow.[40] On June 12, 2013, the World Food Programme spoke of 60 percent of Haitians struggling to meet their food needs, and in 2014 the Bill and Melinda Gates blog, "Poverty Matters," reported that instead of two meals a day as in a decade ago, "they now have one." It also reported that 1.52 million Haitians live with chronic malnutrition. The decline of the Haitian countryside goes beyond food cultivation. The pressure on the land and its timber resources continues its inexorable march to complete deforestation. The short-, medium-, and long-term assessments of rural Haiti thus are not encouraging. Haiti has only 19.4 percent of its total area suitable for rain-fed or irrigated agriculture. Table 7 tells much of the story. There is a vicious circle of poverty operating. With such man-land pressures, there can be no agricultural development, and without agricultural development, there will be no reduction in the birth rate. In sum, the candidates for migration are presently there and increasing in numbers.

Naturally, the agricultural stagnation that results extends to other food sources and explains the massive migration to urban centers, especially Port-au-Prince. That city had 152,000 inhabitants in 1950 and 720,000 in 1980, and today it has an estimated 4 million. How are these millions to be fed? By importing food. Although it is no consolation, Haiti is not alone in having to import food such as rice. Today Cuba imports 80 percent of the food consumed by its inhabitants, including 60 percent of the rice. Cuba certainly has less reason than Haiti for such a deficit in food production. According to the Cuban Oficina Nacional de Estadísticas, in 2013 Cuba had 1.05 million hectares of arable land lying fallow.[41] Obviously none of this—whether it be population growth, decline of the rural agricultural sector, or deforestation—can be blamed on foreigners. That attribution is not easily laid to rest, however, given that it has become a dominant myth. The challenge is to seek explanations derived from Haitian domestic institutions and political culture.

Two ways to test just how autonomously the Haitian political system and political culture operate is to do case studies on two presidents of radically

Table 7. The deteriorating Haitian resource base

Year	Population	Arable land (hectares)	Arable hectares (per person)	Consumption of fuel wood (1,000 cubic meters)*
1938	2,500,000	540,000	0.216	NA
1954	3,400,000	370,000	0.109	8,869
1970	4,300,000	225,750	0.052	13,125
1980	5,500,000	225,750 (Estimate)	0.041	20,000

Source: Information provided by the USAID Office, Port-au-Prince, May 26, 1987.
*Represents 75 percent of all wood consumption.

Table 8. Changes in Haitian rural and urban populations, 1950–82

	Population (000)			Annual growth rate (%)	
	1950	1971	1982	1950–71	1971–82
Total	3,097	4,330	5,053	1.6	1.4
Urban*	255	707	1,042	5.0	3.6
Port-au-Prince	152	507	720	5.9	3.2
Ten towns over 10,000 in 1982	98	180	235	2.9	2.5
Other towns over 5,000	5	26	97	8.2	12.7
Rural	2,831	3,623	4,011	1.2	0.9

Source: "Haiti: Policy Proposals for Growth," in World Bank, Haiti Agricultural Sector Study, Report No. 5375-Ha, April 26, 1985, 5.
*Towns over 5,000.

different provenance and ideology, the late Leslie Manigat and the Reverend Jean-Bertrand Aristide. They represent polar opposites in the recent political past. Manigat's rise to the presidency is a good place to begin.

The old canard that the Haitian people are not prepared to participate in electoral politics had been laid to rest in the months before Manigat's investiture. The referendum on the new constitution of March 3, 1987, had gone off without a hitch, and fully 72.55 percent of the eligible voters had enrolled to cast their ballots in the November 29 election. There were 5,721 voting stations set up for that election, as 100 photos and eyewitness accounts testify.[42] The people were out en masse as early as 6 a.m. on election day. Manigat had withdrawn from the race the previous day, claiming that the electoral process was rigged against him. Whatever the truth of that assertion might be, the fact is that on election day the Haitian military carried out a willful act of violence and bloodshed against innocent citizens standing in line to vote. This brought the democratic process to a halt when the vote was stopped and the election called off. Manigat did not condemn the cancellation of Haiti's first attempt at universal direct elections, which, from all appearances, was going to bring a coalition of left-leaning parties to power.

No such popular turnout was evident on January 17, 1988, for an election tightly controlled by the military, which had actively worked for the "right" candidate to win. Under no conditions can the regime of Leslie F. Manigat, which was selected by the military to win the January elections, be called democratic. It is an indisputable fact that Manigat was put into power in violation of the existing constitution and in defiance of the public will. Having said that, it is also an indisputable fact that Leslie Manigat and the cabinet he selected represented an outstanding team who barely had time to put the various plans and policies they announced into effect. Manigat was inaugurated on February 1, 1988, and by spring he had become engulfed in a dispute between two branches of the army. The dispute was over accusations of drug running by one of the most powerful generals in the army. Manigat had no involvement in the drug trade, but decided to support one side, which turned out to be the losing side. He was overthrown on June 19, 1988.

The Manigat case demonstrates that whether the analysis is short-term or longer, it has to deal with the inherent problems of the institutional system and the political culture. In Haiti this means understanding power, that is, the balance between opposing forces and the capacity of each contender to use raw violence. One searches in vain for the foreign hand that purposely drove such domestic events or caused these problems directly rather than unintentionally being used by competing groups.

Historically, the power of a Haitian government could be challenged only by mercenaries from the northern part of the country, called *cacos*. After the U.S. occupation and the creation of a new Garde d'Haití, the *cacos* were a defeated force. Starting with the post–World War II urbanization, official force could be met with urban violence: the *rouleau compresseur* [steamroller], roving bands of people from the slums who would force the total closing of all urban businesses and workplaces. Other than that, changes in regime have invariably required intragovernmental conspiracies, especially the subversion of the army. Manigat could use none of these methods or processes for the following reasons:

(1) The structure of the Duvalier tyranny was never fully dismantled after Jean-Claude "Baby Doc" Duvalier fled in early 1986. This left the following structures very much active and operational.

One, a national army which had been thoroughly "sanitized" by twenty-eight years of Duvalierist purges. Although it is evident that Manigat must have had some initial support in the military, it does appear that his power depended on whatever terms had been set by the existing power elite in the military, meaning the faction which won the jousting during Manigat's short tenure.

Two, a population which had been disarmed and controlled by new groups of semiprivate armies, the Ton-Ton Macoutes and the Volontaires de Sécurité Nationale (VSN). These groups, during Manigat's term, still had the arms and appeared to be coordinating their actions with elements of the military and police. An anti-Duvalierist for much of his life, Manigat was not known to have had any ties to these groups; logically, he could not count on their support.

Three, a close working relationship between some of the more politically oriented Voodoo priests and the military forces. This was especially important to the Duvaliers in those regions where there was no military presence. Manigat had previously been very critical of the use of Voodoo for political purposes; his attempt to gain the confidence of the *hougans* was short-lived and obviously ineffective.

(2) Not only were the same Duvalierist military forces in existence but there had been a compounding of their vested interests since the departure of the Duvaliers. This process resulted from the perversion and corrupt uses of those governmental economic policies advanced by multilateral lending agencies and the U.S. Agency for International Development mission. It became a case of good intentions turning sour. Those who would criticize the new policies had to state what their decisions would have been in the existing circumstances. The policy involved the dismantling of the state-run (read Duvalier) monopolies in consumer staples and utilities, as well as the opening of the market to outside goods. One result of this was heavy smuggling. Goods came across the Dominican border and through the ports and were, then as now, largely controlled by the military. Together with the control of

the illicit drug transshipments, this contraband provided individual military commanders with substantial funds. Many were reputed to supplement the salaries of their men out of their own pockets, more often than not the only guarantee of their loyalty. Manigat had no access to such funds.

These economic and marketing changes also led to two other changes, both vital to an understanding of the situation facing Manigat. First, there was a dramatic drop in the cost of staples for the masses and thus a removal of the "microeconomic" dimension of any conjectural political crisis. Second, there was a serious three-way division in the nation's economic elites between commission-agent importers, those in import-substitution manufacturing, and those in manufacturing for export. This division removed the old quid pro quo arrangement between the Duvaliers and the business elites in which the latter were left alone in return for their neutrality in politics. After 1986, the various economic elites lined up behind different contenders for power, that is, the military, thereby considerably diluting the potential effectiveness of these elites as players in the turbulent system. The consequence of this was that these economic conditions gave the military more operating space in the short term. Clearly, Manigat had no time to make any serious effort to restructure this state of affairs, even if he had intended to do so. How could he?

It was a slippery world, therefore, which Leslie Manigat entered when he agreed to have himself "elected" president on January 17, 1988. He must have believed that his exceptional talents as a political scientist would stand him in good stead as he maneuvered the treacherous waters, still infested with Duvalierist crocodiles as well as by a new breed of predator spawned by the ever-increasing drug trade. But surely Manigat knew his Hobbes, who as early as 1651 cautioned us that while military men redeem honor through war, politicians compensate for bad games by constantly reshuffling the cards. In Haiti the military were trained and disposed toward politics, not war. Honor to them was a fancy word, not an intrinsic value. They, and no one else, did the shuffling and reshuffling of the cards because they virtually owned the deck.

Manigat had lived outside of Haiti since 1963.[43] This put him at a disadvantage on two counts. First, while he had created an admirable organization in the various diasporas and with groups in Venezuela, this did not translate into organization inside Haiti. The various "problems" of the system were beyond his control, though perhaps not beyond his intellectual understanding.

In Haiti it is essential to be inside, to stay close to the *zinc* (the latest news), which the local *teleidol* (word-of-mouth communication system) keeps going. The second disadvantage was that while he had cut his political teeth in democracies such as France, the United States, Trinidad, and Venezuela, the military he would have to deal with had cut theirs in the murderous three decades of Duvalierism. It is widely accepted that Manigat had none of their killer instincts.

In 1964, Manigat tried to explain how total, and totally Haitian, the Duvalier system was: "The old, internal mechanism for overthrowing a government was no longer relevant. Traditional American steps were condemned to failure, and the elimination of Duvalier, just because Washington seemed to want it, was no longer a routine affair."[44] He also spoke of American "perplexity" about acting in Haiti.

The evidence that he was out of touch, that he had no distinct internal power base, and that once in office he was intellectually and perhaps even morally uncomfortable with his position can be gleaned from the way he argued his case. Haitians generally think metaphorically: fables of animal life, folkloric explanations of the mysteries of nature, all provide firm and clear lessons by which to act or to guard against the evil eye or other such supernatural yet very human forces. Manigat was arguing by analogy, a definite sign that he was trying to find explanations and perhaps even psychological reinforcements which transcended the Haitian experience and context. He had to. To argue in purely Haitian terms would be equivalent to placing himself in the same league with all those other politicians. No continuity in Haitian history could be tolerated. His coming to power, he told the magazine *Hemisphere* in a long interview in March 1988, was the beginning of a new era in Haitian history, the modernizing era.[45] It was, he said, a radical watershed. He had written the script for that a long time ago while in exile in Washington. His book, *Haiti of the Sixties: Object of International Concern* (1964) had always seemed a blue print for a future presidency; it certainly seemed to be in 1988.

But if the argument by analogy indicated a search for psychological and historical distance, the analogies chosen reflected heavy rationalization. He chose to find analogies with the recently occurred shifts from military to civilian rule in Argentina and Uruguay, but especially the older—but to Manigat better known—case of Venezuela where after a century and a half of military dictatorship a civilian democracy had been created. All these examples, to be sure, were worth aspiring to. They could not, however, be successfully

emulated for the simple reason that they were irrelevant to Manigat's specific historical context and reality. In those countries, democracy had been
initiated through legitimate elections. This was not Manigat's situation. He
had decided to ignore the dangers of a manipulated agenda. After his overthrow he would still claim that "what was at stake for me was the principle of
the supremacy of the civilian power over the military"—a dangerous albeit
probably sincere illusion. Specifically, how Manigat had come into office dictated what he could do once there. Much more relevant analogies, therefore,
were the history of Haitian civil-military conflicts. Manigat knew that history
better than anyone else. He appeared to be "blocking" that knowledge. This
psychological process in turn tended to give him a sense of power that was
purely illusory. The problem of oversimplification and historical generalization was in evidence. It is theoretically true that total and secure power is
best demonstrated through the occasional merciful act toward the enemy.
Such sentiments can nevertheless only follow, never precede, total power.
When Manigat dismissed and then put the head of the army and the leader
of one of the factions in conflict, General Namphy, under "house arrest," he
was showing his basic and admirable lack of bloodthirstiness—but also his
lack of power. Namphy led the assault that deposed Manigat. The reasons for
Manigat's lack of power are evident.

He had done nothing to change the basic structure of the Haitian military,
which had been in place since 1967. The cancellation of U.S. military assistance did not affect the military's power capabilities one iota. Additionally,
military political influence was enhanced by their concentration not only in
the capital but, indeed, right around the presidential palace. And then, very
fundamentally, Duvalier had cleverly divided them into three key battalions
of more or less equal size (800 men). This division was supposed to discour-
age single-minded political ideas as well as the temptation to coordinate a
"shuffle of the cards." Since each battalion had its own relative military advantage, control of only one did not guarantee control of the state. The presidential guard was located right in the presidential palace, and it controlled
the few armored vehicles on the island. Its inspector general in 1988 was Col.
Prosper Avril, the major force behind the move against Manigat.

The battalion "Caserne Dessalines" had the advantage of location, a well-
fortified garrison right behind the presidential palace, and it also had good
intelligence based on its traditional ties to the police force and to the Ton-

Ton Macoutes. Its commander up to November 1988 was Col. Jean-Claude Paul. He had become something of a household name in south Florida because of his indictment in a local court on drug smuggling charges. Paul was the closest thing to a General Noriega that Haiti had, and as such he was no pushover. It was, therefore, doubly sad for Manigat's record that he turned to this corrupt military man for critical support. He had scraped the bottom of the barrel. The third group, the "Leopards," was a battalion trained by the United States for counterinsurgency purposes. Its fighting capabilities were put in question during the invasion of the Ile de la Tortue by a ragtag band of rebels from south Florida led by Bernard Sansaricq. Its commander in 1988, Col. Abelardo Denis, was never mentioned in the local *zinc* as an important political player. The *zinc* for the months before they made their move against Manigat was all about General Namphy and his enemy, Colonel Paul. Certainly President Manigat had heard it. Namphy and members of the business community were talking openly about the need for a reshuffling.

This then was the history and the context; these were the players with which Manigat had to deal. Who initiated the fatal round of intrigues, who promised what to whom, and who betrayed whom? These are all questions for speculation and the history books. What is quite evident is that the military which overthrew Manigat had its genesis in the Duvalierist school of terror, and it gained its livelihood in the kleptocratic state augmented in the 1970s by a smuggling business that went all the way from toothpaste to Miami automobiles and guns but mainly to the drug trade.

Manigat certainly knew this: he had condemned it in his 1964 treatise. But he compromised. The military, he kept repeating, had to be negotiated with as one does with the business community or the Church. His own minister of foreign affairs and close friend, Dr. Gerard Latortue, recalls how Manigat thought of the army as "a kind of *grand électeur*." He understood that "in order to get in power in Haiti there is no way not to make a compromise with the army."[46] But negotiation implies a quid pro quo that Manigat did not have. Once his academic and international prestige failed to translate into new foreign aid and investments, Manigat was an emperor without clothes.

With so many contenders for the presidency, the "law of large numbers" guaranteed that Haitians would soon forget Manigat. Indeed, neither they nor the many foreigners who insist on the myth that the United States controls all, hardly seemed to have derived any "lessons" about Manigat's months in power before they switched their attention to the next *grand nègre* occupying the presidential palace. They would have much to capture their attention in the mystical Jean-Bertrand Aristide, another domestic *caudillo*.

Aristide never gave the appearance of being a conventional seeker of formal political office. In fact, he made a distinct point of dismissing constitutional and party politics as irrelevant. Asked as late as May 1990 whether he had political ambitions, he responded, "I do not suffer from that sickness."[47] And yet he constantly advocated and called for political change. So sudden and unexpected was Aristide's entry into the 1990 electoral campaign that he was not listed in the May 29, 1990, election handbook prepared by the National Democratic Institute for International Affairs.

Who, then, was Father Aristide? Born in 1954, Aristide was the son of an educated and devoutly Roman Catholic Haitian family. After joining the Salesian teaching order, he pursued advanced studies in the Dominican Republic, Israel, and Canada. Thoroughly influenced by the more radical wing of Latin American liberation theology, Aristide was an early member of what came to be known as the Ti L'égliz (Little Church). His antagonism to the established Church hierarchy was equaled only by his dislike of the local bourgeoisie. In sermons from St. Jean Bosco Church in the Port-au-Prince slum of la Saline, Aristide frequently used biblical passages to preach rebellion. Advocating the right of the common people to defend themselves, Aristide would quote from the Gospel of St. Luke, where Christ is cited as saying, "And he that hath no sword, I say to him sell his garment and buy one."[48] Neither Aristide nor his followers seemed to have accumulated any swords. His followers defended him by their willingness to die for him. A human shield appeared to be his only protection. No one can read Amy Wilentz's account of Aristide and not be moved by the apparently total and unconditional devotion of his supporters, even as he seemed to welcome martyrdom.[49]

In the 1988 attack during his service at St. Jean Bosco Church, Aristide had to be forcibly moved to safety by his parishioners. Whether because of raw courage or some irrational aspect of his personality, Aristide's many brushes with—and miraculous escapes from—death have become part of his charisma. "Mister Miracles" they called him. It would be a true miracle, indeed, if such constant confrontations with brutality and death did not affect his personality. They appear to have done just that. A newspaper report from the foreign journalist group that is closest to him described Aristide this way: "Nervous by disposition, Aristide suffers from periodic prostrations that leave him virtually out of touch with the world around him. He has on occasion appeared catatonic, almost haunted, as if totally overwhelmed by some frozen image of the most recent blood-letting."[50]

His was more a messianic movement than a campaign. "You see," Aristide told a veteran Haiti watcher, "I don't have to campaign. It's the people who will do the campaigning." He had, he said, "accepted this rendezvous with history." He was "one with the Haitian spirit." Certainly his status as a priest, even though expelled from the Salesian order, contributed to this nearly ethereal image. "Titide's not like the others," exclaimed a market woman. "He does not have any woman, so he wouldn't be spending the country's money on fancy cars and diamond necklaces. He's pure." Nothing here of the traditional Haitian-Caribbean macho man. The aura of purity and cleansing the Se Lavalas movement invoked was a winning combination; Aristide won nearly 70 percent of the vote in an election that attracted 85 percent of the electorate. He swept every section of the island. It was a national victory.

Midway through the Aristide administration, a source in the Presidential Palace told the press, "An adversary you can argue with is better than a blundering ally." Aristides's political problem had been evident from the start. Surrounded by ideologues and idealists, all political amateurs, Aristide never seemed able to distinguish friend from foe. Worse, he never seemed interested in the profane art of political maneuvering. In fact, he seemed to excel at turning allies into opponents. It need not have been that way. Despite social chaos and the bankruptcy of the state, Aristide had several things going for him in addition to his massive popular support. The January 7, 1991, coup attempted by former Duvalierists under Roger Lafontant was quashed by loyalist troops and massive public protests. This meant that his most dangerous known enemy was in jail, and many others were in flight. In addition, the international community responded enthusiastically to his electoral victory. French president François Mitterrand received him in Paris (the first Haitian president so invited), and the United States restored, and doubled, its direct aid to the Haitian government, which had been suspended since the aborted elections of 1987. The leading opposition figures, Marc Bazin and Louis Dejoie III, pledged to settle their policy differences in the parliament, not in the street.

But several acts of commission or omission weakened Aristide's hand early on. As Alex Dupuy noted, Aristide sent contradictory messages to his supporters and opponents alike, "and the confusion that this caused among all sectors of the population eroded confidence in him and weakened his defenders while emboldening his enemies to act."[51] He failed to speak out forcibly against mob violence by his followers. The practice of *père lebrun* (putting a burning tire around an enemy's neck) was never sufficiently condemned. More than 100 perceived Aristide enemies were executed by the burning tire method after the failed Lafontant coup. And Aristide's already strained relations with the Church hierarchy deteriorated dramatically after the Papal Nunciature and Haiti's oldest cathedral were burned to the ground and the papal nuncio and his Zairian deputy were beaten and forced to walk nearly naked down the street.

He arrested former president Pascal-Trouillot on April 4, 1991, on vague and unsubstantiated conspiracy charges, causing fear of arbitrary arrest to spread through the already wary opposition ranks. His sweeping purges of the army top command, including the retirement in July of General Heriot Abraham, who had managed the peaceful transfer of power, caused traditional Haitian military apprehensions about civilian intentions to intensify. His sudden, and some say intemperate and threatening, request in mid-April that the "moneyed classes" contribute millions of dollars to the state, giving them four days to do so, reminded some of Duvalier's notorious "voluntary contributions" campaigns.

All of this could have been managed or at least explained away if Aristide had not committed his most costly error: marginalizing, then antagonizing and even actually attacking his own political party and its followers in the legislature. This behavior best revealed not only Aristide's modus operandi but how soon and completely he had acquired the Haitian habit of emphasizing the presidency as the only significant office.

Although it held only 40 of the 110 seats in parliament, Aristides's National Front for Change and Democracy (FNDC) initially controlled the presidency and other significant posts in that legislature. Be that as it many, it was with his own party that Aristide had his major confrontations as it attempted to exercise checks and balances on the executive, the single most important feature of the 1987 constitution. Many parties had participated in drawing up that constitution, and they took their role in the new politics seriously. They were indignant about being ignored in appointments, policies, or, indeed, even informal consultations.

Not surprisingly, it was Aristide's own FNDC legislators who began to call for the resignation of Aristide's prime minister, René Préval, and it was this group that was in turn violently threatened with individual *père lebruns* if they proceeded with their plans. Under pressure from the executive, the FNDC lost control over parliament to minor opposition parties. One of these, the miniscule National Patriotic Movement—November 28, secured power in the Senate by making its leader, Dejean Belizaire, Senate president. Belizaire emerged as one of the legislative leaders opposing Aristide's return to the presidency after his ouster.

By early May the complaints voiced about Aristide's style had become a Greek chorus. The president was, they said, surrounded by incompetent "yes men"; he did not "trust people." Others spoke of a "Jekyll-and-Hyde" approach to issues. Human rights activist and Aristide supporter Jean-Claude Bajeaux summed up the situation: "Aristide has established himself as the parish priest of the National Palace."[52]

No one, however, predicted a significant political crisis. The army was thought to have been brought under civilian control. The government had secured a $422 million loan from a consortium led by the World Bank, and the United States ambassador, Alvin P. Adams Jr., commented that Aristide "has gotten off to a very credible start. The process is well begun." Even the formerly skeptical business community was cheered by what it perceived as a new realism on Aristide's part.

In September, Aristide made a triumphal trip to the UN and received keys to the cities of New York and Miami. On September 30, the day after his return to Haiti, Aristide was overthrown by what was apparently a rabble of soldiers and police. The *ti soldats* brutally suppressed public protests, and the president was courageously freed from detention and escorted to the airport by the French and U.S. ambassadors.

The charge that the Haitian elite and the army overthrew Aristide is certainly unimpeachable. But it does not tell the whole story. After all, no one, certainly not Aristide, ever entertained the illusion that the bourgeoisie were his friends. The same holds true for many of the corrupt bureaucrats and military men. Their interests were direct targets of Aristides's speeches and policies. The task is not to ask who were his class enemies but, rather, who were his steadfast friends, and did they—could they—make any difference in the boiling Haitian political cauldron?

The answer to the first part of the question can be approached from the angle of the experienced editor of Haiti's *Le Nouvelliste*, who wrote on August 30, 1991, that the "fratricidal" struggle for power between Aristide and

his Selavalassien clique and the members of the FNDC could "end in a catas-
trophe." The explanation was relatively simple: the former had the mantle of
newness, honesty, and sincerity, and the latter had the political sagacity and
contacts.

Ah, Niccolò, where were you when Aristide and his crusaders needed
you? With his constitutional-institutional space shrinking, Aristide turned
to what he did best: haranguing the masses. Day after day, from one end
of the island to the other, the president and his prime minister personally
dealt with the increasing military mutinies, strikes, food protests, and land
disputes. Aristide's efficiency plunged even as his popularity soared among
popular sectors. And this created a negative cycle: the lower the ability to
cope with "conventional" politics (in the Haitian sense), the greater the appeal to populism, which, in turn, makes the practitioners of conventional
politics more apprehensive, aroused, and dangerous. In Haiti, from time immemorial, it is the latter that have held the trump card.

Multinational military action to restore President Aristide was eventually
approved by the UN Security Council, bypassing the collective responsibility of the Organization of American States (OAS). Haiti thus exemplifies a
more generalized paradoxical situation in Latin America where a functioning regime for the promotion and protection of human rights coexists with
major and wide-ranging violations of those rights. The day after the U.S. Marines invaded and restored him to office, Aristide's op-ed piece appeared in
the *New York Times*: "I thank President Clinton for his leadership . . . and the
U.S. troops for their participation in this first critical phase of the reestablish-
ment of democracy."[53]

As uplifting and inspiring as this trend might be, the Haitian case stands
as testimony that norms and values as expressed in words are often perceived
to be of dubious sincerity unless forcefully converted into actions. Despite
the fact that, as Tom Farer writes, Haiti is arguably the most telling case of
a country which is recognized to need outside assistance, both to reinstate
a democratic mandate and then to defend it, there was no consensus on
how this should be done in the case of Aristide.[54] Inconsistency and double
talk were his modus operandi when it came to his relations with the United
States. He continually played on the myth that foreign nations disrespected
him and his country. Much of the foreign press played along with this well-
developed myth. Note how the *New York Times* correspondent Catherine
Manegold related the following scene: Aristide was addressing an adoring

crowd of thousands at a Paris gathering. The French minister of health and humanitarian assistance, sitting on the stage, was passing notes to other panelists in "a startling act of rudeness. Imperious, even insulting. But the moment tells everything—the whole story of Haiti. The small black man full of words of justice, liberty and grace. The cold-eyed white European, smelling a political death."[55]

If such acts of rudeness told "everything" about Haiti, the task of unraveling its perpetual underdevelopment and political instability could be simple. Of course, no such simplicity exists. Aristide, for one, knew this and knew how to play his only card: guilt. This got him a lengthy interview with Mitterrand (a first-ever for a Haitian president), many with Venezuelan president Carlos Andrés Pérez, and, having settled in Washington, many sessions with President Clinton. The irony (or is it strategic hypocrisy) of his move to Washington and his many appeals to Clinton reveal astonishing bravado. Just before settling in the U.S. capital, he had called Clinton "a racist," his policy toward Haiti "a cynical joke," "garbage," "a classical case of genocide," and "a holocaust."[56] The U.S. policy, he told a Dominican newspaper, "is more dangerous than the AIDS epidemic."[57] And, then, the repeated outbursts of overwrought language:

> Do they [Americans] believe the Haitian people are dumb enough to believe in this nonsense? We have our dignity and we defend out dignity. We respect ourselves. . . . We respect truth. We don't accept garbage for truth. It is a racist policy.[58]

As late as 1993, Aristide was holding on to his idea that the real enemies of Haiti were a "gang of four": the army, the oligarchy, the United States, and the Catholic hierarchy.[59] After the initial thanks to Clinton after his overthrow, not one word was uttered by Aristide about how legitimate authority was reestablished in Haiti or that the chances were slim that the democratic hopes of the Haitian people could have been restored by either internal forces or through international pressures short of the threat and use of force. Alex Dupuy has described the situation with a candor unusual among left-leaning intellectuals. "In the end," he writes, "only a power bigger than the Haitian Army could veto the army's veto of the democratic process. And that power did not reside with Aristide or his Lavalas movement but with the 'cold country of the North.'"[60]

In his superbly revealing study of Haitian politics, David Nicholls cautions that when Haitians quote the proverb *"Aprè bon dié sé léta"* [After God comes the state], "it is not the goodness or the benevolence of God that people have in mind; it is rather His remoteness, unpredictability, and power."[61] If this is true of God, how much truer it must be of the state, which is especially feared by that mass of dispossessed—and increasingly displaced—peasants. For two hundred years the meager yet amazingly munificent cow called the state has nurtured a small elite and a much larger middle sector. The Kingdom of Heaven might well belong to the 85 percent who are Aristide's beloved poor, but the key to those pearly gates is held by the 15 percent who use the state to avoid joining the great unwashed. This key eluded Aristide.

All of this to say that Farmer's celebration of Aristide, on the one hand, and Dubois's claim that the overthrow of the traditional elite by Aristide's popular forces demonstrates that Haitians were able to create "a new and better world for themselves," on the other hand, both express the triumph of hope and ideology over experience. Both Farmer, who had previously held forth on the fall of Aristide, claiming him to be a victim of U.S. and French conniving, and Dubois ignore a major part of the story of Aristides's rise and fall.[62] Farmer might consider consulting Alex Dupuy's thoroughly documented and argued *The Prophet and Power*. According to Dupuy, Aristide initially had good intentions, but all this ended when he turned to—shall we say—"chronic" authoritarianism, patronage, clientelism, and the use of terror by his gangs (*chimes*). When Aristide left Haiti in 2004, says Dupuy, he had become "a discredited, corrupted, and increasingly authoritarian president who had betrayed the trust and aspirations of the poor majority."[63] Not surprisingly, Aristide's security depended almost completely on sixty former members of the U.S. Special Forces in the employ of a private contractor, the Steele Foundation of San Francisco, California. Far from causing his overthrow, the United States and France may have saved his life by squirreling him out of the country before his multiple enemies got to him.

6

Two Popular Theories of Caribbean Ideology and Race Relations

Frantz Fanon's Theory of Liberating Violence and the Theory of Plantation Societies

> I become daily more and more convinced that all the West India islands will remain in the hands of the people of colour and a total expulsion of the whites sooner or later take place, it is high time we should foresee the bloody scenes . . . and try to avert them.
>
> Thomas Jefferson to James Monroe, Philadelphia, July 14, 1793

It is hardly surprising that given the nature of the Caribbean-wide "terrified consciousness" in race relations, certain theories of those race relations should have been widely adopted. They invariably portend restlessness in a region with if not an open propensity, then certainly an undertow of discontent. This has contributed to the enduring myth of a revolutionary Caribbean that is further enhanced by two theories in particular: the Fanonian theory of colonial terror as a "liberating" force and the theory of the nature of "plantation societies." As they are used in the literature of the postwar decolonization process, both theories speak of "terror," which in the literature of decolonization has very specific origins, meanings, and applications. These meanings can be traced to three concepts, all associated with the use of violence by the oppressed as a key weapon in the "liberation" of the oppressed.

First, George Sorel's concept of proletarian millenarian (or messianic) violence. This, according to Sorel, was "sublime work": "terrifying to the bourgeoisie but *psychologically liberating to the oppressed.*"[1] According to Sorel, to the extent that the proletariat could create a generalized myth of inevitable violence in the minds of the bourgeoisie, liberation was possible. Second, Jean-Paul Sartre's concept of the ultimate Manichaeism of the colonial situation. As Sartre saw it, if you are not a direct victim of the situation, you are irreparably an "executioner" of "race murder." Because every European is an exploiter, Sartre says, they are "bound hand and foot, humiliated and sick with fear."[2] Finally, Frantz Fanon's general sociology of colonial violence developed during his stay in revolutionary Algeria. This violence, says Fanon, is Manichaean, has millenarian dimensions, and its fundamental purpose is to have an apocalyptic outcome, that is, the "psychological cleansing" of the black man, oppressed by the fear of violence he inspires in the white oppressor.[3]

To Fanon, this race violence is different from Marxian (or even Sorelian) proletarian violence because in the latter there were still plausible, structured expectations (norms) between the adversaries. By contrast, in a colonial situation, the whole purpose of liberation is to eliminate all existing norms, all existing commonly held legitimating traditions and structures, by eliminating those who created and controlled them: the whites. Racial hatred thus does not permit proportionality of means or ends, negotiations, or other traditional methods of defining and eventually resolving conflict.

According to elite theorists such as Gaetano Mosca, since the time of the Romans the traditional way of defusing conflict and avoiding violence has been to circulate elites. White colonial racism—because it does not accept the black man or woman and their aspirations as legitimate—made such circulation and social mobility within the normative structure impossible. In response, liberation violence makes the circulation of elites equally impossible. In colonial situations, both the oppressor and the one seeking liberation engage in Manichaean strategies. Manichaean or not, to Fanon (in his Algerian phase), the intellectual task was to show why violence was the only legitimate revolutionary stance in colonial situations. It also had a deeper, more psychological function. Apocalyptic violence against the white oppressor was the only way of redirecting the violence that colonial blacks executed on themselves in the form of self-hatred, self-doubt, and psychological self-mutilation.[4] The essence of Fanon's concept of the "terrified consciousness" of the colonial white is contained in the Manichaean principle that "It is them or us." We will see later how and why this was not exactly his view before his Algerian experiences, nor was it, indeed, his view in his final years. This leads to the question: do all colonial situations and decolonization processes call for the same strategy of liberation? In his Algerian phase, Fanon was categorical:

The look that the native turns on the settler's town is a look of lust, a look of envy; it expresses his dreams of possession—all manner of possession: to sit at the settler's bed with his wife if possible. The colonized man is an envious man.[5]

The white settler, says Fanon, knows this and is terrified. It was Fanon's teacher in Martinique, the Frenchman Dominique O. Mannoni, who first called his attention to the syndrome of circumstances and relationships he called the "colonial situation." Mannoni, who had done seminal work in Madagascar, emphasized the fact that it involved economic exploitation. But he did not stop there, also noting that it embodied struggles for prestige, states of alienation, bargaining positions, debts of gratitude, and "the invention of new myths and the creation of new personality types."[6]

To both Mannoni and Fanon, the most powerful of these myths was that of racial superiority. It is race more than virtually any other factor which molds and creates the particular human dimension of the colonial situation. "When you examine at close quarters the colonial contexts," Fanon wrote, "it is evident that what parcels out the world is to begin with the fact of belonging to or not belonging to a given race, a given species."[7] This being the case, the liberation movement (which is more than a revolutionary one) cannot allow the retention of any of the old traditions, norms, and mores; it cannot admit any except those who fit the mold of the new myth and its racial embodiment. Not surprisingly, the new Algerian myth allowed only "Algerians," thus recognizing no minorities, no pluralism.[8]

If Marxian revolution involved replacing one system of production with another, the Fanonian theory of colonial liberation requires terror to replace one race with another. This explains the "terrified consciousness" of those who perceive themselves as targets for replacement. The interesting aspect of all this is that this twentieth-century advocacy of violence and the existence of a terrified consciousness is precisely what existed among whites in the Caribbean in the nineteenth century. The fact that such racial antagonisms did not contribute to black liberation in that century, and that a form of liberation came in the twentieth century without it, is an important lesson. Indeed, it was a lesson anticipated by Marx himself. Marx's position on terrorism, says Shlomo Avinieri, was that the Jacobin advocates of terror were "utterly misguided and muddle-headed" and that "their recourse to terrorism [was] immanent in their basic fallacy. Marx denounces Jacobin terror unequivocally."[9] That said, if past experience suggests that ultimately such racial Manichaeism did not prevail in the Caribbean, there is still value in asking the counterfactual question: why did it not happen the way Fanon recommended, and what lessons for race relations in the twenty-first century might this contain?

One lesson is that any theory purporting to explain complex social phenomena has to be contextualized. The Fanon who became the theorist of colonial resistance and revolution was the Fanon enmeshed and identified with the Algerian Revolution. It was that experience which led him to write his seminal book *Les damnés de la terre* (*The Wretched of the Earth*) in 1961. The work took on even more meaning when Jean-Paul Sartre wrote a preface whose message burned even hotter and was more threatening than Fanon's. "Make no mistake about it," wrote Sartre. By the colonized's "mad fury, by this bitterness and spleen, by their ever-present desire to kill us . . . they have become men; men *because* of the settler, who wants to make beasts of burden of them—because of him, and against him. Hatred, blind hatred, which is as yet an abstraction, is their only wealth."[10] This certainly was representative of Fanon's revolutionary phase. But Fanon had another intellectual phase that might better explain why the racial war was never successful in the twentieth-century French Caribbean or, indeed, in any part of the Caribbean.

In 1952, ten years before his Algerian experience, Fanon published his seminal socio-psychological work, *Peau Noire, Masques Blancs*. He introduced his text with the following words by Aimé Césaire, one of his professors at Martinique's elite school, Lycée Schoelcher, whose *Discours sur le Colonialisme* read: "I am talking of millions of men who have been skillfully infected with fear, inferiority complexes, trepidation, servility, despair, abasement." Confronted with such a dire set of psychopathological conditions, Fanon proposes "nothing short of the liberation of the man of color *from himself*." Rather than being Manichaean, he proposes to be evenhanded because to him "the man who adores the Negro is as 'sick' as the man who abominates him." Because the remedy is to be found in self-awareness and change, he rejects igniting fervor and violence. He does not trust fervor, he says: "Every time it has burst out somewhere, it has brought fire, famine, misery. . . . Fervor is the weapon of choice of the impotent."[11]

This was Fanon the psychiatrist in his Caribbean, that is, pre-Algerian, pre-Jacobean phase reflecting his environment and recommending moderation. He understood that whatever his psychological diagnosis revealed, the problem and therefore the remedy lay in broader socioeconomic structures. He made this known in an essay published three years later, "Antillais et Africains." Fanon argued that not just the individual French Antillean but indeed the whole of Martinican society had been liberated from its collective inferiority complex by three processes that changed Martinican societal values. First, the writings of Aimé Césaire, and especially his 1939 *Cahiers d'un retour au Pays Natal,* which can be said to have launched the Négritude movement and had had a profound impact on the island's intellectuals. Second, the defeat of France in World War II and the loss of credibility by its establishment of the Vichy regime, which was subject to Nazi German dictates. Third, and much closer to home, was the presence in small Fort-de-France of some 10,000 French sailors and soldiers, whose racism and cultural hubris could not hide the fact that they represented a defeated nation. All this, said Fanon, meant that black Martinicans proudly showed their blackness by taking off their white masks. "L'Antillais de 1945," he wrote, "est un nègre."[12] This explains why, during the riots in Martinique in 1959 seeking decolonization, none of the terror and murderous aspects Fanon would later witness in Algeria were exhibited.

As noted, Aimé Césaire was among the outstanding teachers at the prestigious Lycée Schoelscher. Here was another case of theorizing that has to be contextualized. Césaire, along with Leopold Senghor and León Damas, had launched the "philosophie de négritude," whose basic precept was the existence of a Negro-African civilization in Africa and everywhere the black man was colonized. Given that this was an extremely mystical and metaphysical derivation from French surrealism (as developed by surrealism's grand master, André Breton, who came to Martinique in 1941), it was hard to articulate in a post-Bandung world where "Third World" meant the search for political power among many racial groups, not just the eulogizing of black racial images and rhythms. This problem was evident when Césaire delivered an erudite speech on "Culture and Colonization" to the First International Conference of Negro Writers and Artists in Paris in 1956. His argument on the coming Negro Renaissance in a postcolonial world had not a single reference to an African thinker, but was sprinkled with references to Marx, French sociologist Maus, Hegel, Spengler, Toynbee, Goethe, Malinowski, and Nietzsche and fundamental agreement with American anthropologist Alfred Kroeber, whose analyses emphasized broad patterns of acculturation, not issues of personality. Faced with a multiracial decolonized world, Césaire had traveled an intellectual path from the racially particular to the universal. Gone from Césaire, and later from Fanon and others who had been his students, was the Fanonian thesis that in all colonial situations "violent forces ... blaze up" because the violence which the colonizer used to colonize "will be claimed and taken over by the native at the moment when, deciding to embody history in his own person, he surges into the forbidden quarters."[13]

Clearly, neither Fanonian colonial violence and terror nor Césaire's Négritude could explain the nature of Caribbean race relations. Nothing exemplifies more clearly the polymorphic nature of those relations than the different way Breton and surrealism were received and adopted or not adopted in the region. In her encyclopedic *Historia de la literatura hispanoamericana*, Jean Franco mentions only one author influenced by Breton, the Mexican Octavio Paz, and even he "adopted surrealism in a very personal way" and only in one phase of his career.[14] Kenneth Ramchand apparently found no surrealist influences in the rich English-speaking literature, since there is no mention of it in his *West Indian Novel and Its Background*.[15] Even Gabriel R. Coulthard, very much in touch with the literature of the whole area, said:

> Some critics were deceived into thinking that the products of *négritude* were Surrealist, and, indeed, it was André Breton ... who took up Césaire and to some extent launched him. However, in spite of superficial resemblances, on closer inspection it is quite clear that *négritude* is different from Surrealism.[16]

Coulthard argues that surrealism is found almost exclusively in Césaire.[17] The point is, first, that each linguistic area of the Caribbean sought its literary influences from the main literary thrusts of the particular metropolis with which it was associated. There are, of course, exceptions such as that of Gabriel García Márquez, who admits to the influence of the American writer William Faulkner. Second, in none of the literature contextualized in a Caribbean setting does the theme of "cleansing violence" in its socio-psychological sense dominate or even appear. Social protests occur, even violent ones, yes, but these are social movements seeking collective redress for injustice, not the Fanonian violence as the mechanism of personal redemption.

The quest to explain Caribbean race relations with one comprehensive theory was also evident when students began to hypothesize that Caribbean societies were "plantation societies." The paradigm was expanded into a "race-colonialism-plantation-capitalism" framework that predicted a high probability of racial violence. This was not the original formulation of the pioneers of plantation economic theory, Lloyd Best, George Beckford, and Kari Polanyi Levitt. Theirs was a sophisticated economic analysis. The problem was their level of generalization. The central thesis of Lloyd Best and Kari Levitt in their very popular *Essays on the Theory of Plantation Economy* is that the Caribbean economy as a whole has undergone little modernization, little structural change since the establishment of the slave plantation over three hundred years ago. Further amplifying the concept, Lloyd Best theorized that "the Caribbean islands" fell into a class of economy and society called "plantation economy and society":

> Politically the system lacks community support. Economically it is an appendage of a metropolitan economy and therefore has no internal dynamic for accumulation, technological change, and taste formation. Socially, it is stratified by reference to metropolitan criteria . . . and to the extent that people are imported willy-nilly from different spheres and at different times, segments of race, religion, and culture emerge side by side.[18]

At this level, it is no wonder that the "plantation society" thesis would lend itself not just to sophisticated economic analysis that challenged the dominant models at the time but to anyone concerned with the ongoing nature of race relations everywhere in the Caribbean.[19] Even though debates over the role of race in the Caribbean were common in the nineteenth century, the issue took on special relevance in the late 1930s because both in the United States and the Caribbean, black citizens were stirring politically and economically. It is true that in the Caribbean, rioting spread from island to island and from plantation to plantation, but "plantation society" theorists have not been able to answer convincingly these persistent questions: Why did each island show idiosyncratic termination modes? If the Caribbean as a whole was shaped by ideas and practices characteristic of a generic sugar plantation society, how do we explain the wide variety of "styles" and expressions persevering in Caribbean race relations? Was there more than one type of "plantation society"? Did other forces, such as those argued by Tannenbaum and Williams, transcend the plantation's institutional and material conditions? If the answer to this last question is yes, what were these forces?

Whether it was Fanonian colonial violence or the plantation society thesis, the debate's vivacity and scholarly level indicate that the Caribbean, with its rich variety of colonial legacies and wide array of responses to colonial systems, is an extraordinary laboratory for the study of continuities and changes in race relations. This is best illustrated by describing the continuities and transformations that are evident in the race, color, and class relations of six Caribbean societies of different sizes, colonial histories, and contemporary political situations. The comparisons are matched: Cuba, the Dominican Republic, and its contiguous neighbor, Haiti; the much smaller Trinidad, an ex-British colony; Martinique, a present-day French Department d'Outre-Mer; and Curaçao, an autonomous part of the Kingdom of the Netherlands. We start with Spanish colonialism, the first to settle and exploit the New World.

Since much was said about race relations in Cuba in chapter 2 and chapter 5, here we pick up the story but repeat only the most salient features of those relationships in order to introduce two Cuban novels about the slave plantation.

Rather than being engendered by the New World plantation, race relations patterns were brought to the New World and governed all aspects of life in Cuba. Among the many ideas and practices the conquering Spaniards transferred to the New World, the idea of racial differences was crucial. The belief in or concept of racial purity—*limpieza de sangre*—had been an integral part of the *Reconquista*, the eight-century struggle to regain Spain for the Catholic kings. The definition of "limpio" was the old Christian without traces of Moorish or Jewish blood ("el cristiano viejo sin raza de moro ni judío"). The opposite of limpio was to be "de mala raza."[20] Similarly, the corollary of natural aristocracy was natural servitude, "since the more perfect should hold sway over the less." This emphasis on racial purity and its association with a "natural" leadership class was not invented in the New World; it had deep roots in medieval Spain, indeed, in medieval Europe. To be a *caballero*, a *hidalgo* (*hijo de algo*, literally), you had to have a singular or particular demeanor, a lifestyle that became known as *decoro*. Because it was a form of ceremonial behavior intended to reflect on both the individual and the group to which he belonged, *decoro* was surrounded by both positive and negative rules of deference. The positive rules were meant to show explicit appreciation, the negative proscribed and set taboos on relationships with others. This corporativist association of the individual with the social order was the essence of medieval stratification—rooted in Thomistic doctrine—and it was passed intact into the New World.[21]

It would be a mistake to assume that the age of discovery and reconnaissance was a liberating age. Even among humanists, it was a conservative and extremely respectful form of authority. Besides, to the extent that the conquest of the New World was an extension of the Spanish Reconquista, and especially the vanquishing of the Moors at Granada, it perpetuated the racial and religious prejudices of the Spanish crusade.[22] The unprecedented harshness with which the Queen dealt with the Moors of Granada, says J. H. Parry, "represented a deliberate rejection on the Queen's part of the African element in Spanish culture."[23]

Naturally, in a colonization experience composed mostly of males, race mixing could hardly be inhibited by laws. Demographics and human nature ensured considerable race mixing. Gilberto Freyre once suggested that the Portuguese colonized in bed. Other Europeans may not have been so sensuously prone, but they were hardly abstemious. This one-sided sexual and biological democracy, however, did relatively little to minimize the emphasis on social status and the critical role that race and color played in the assignment of status. As Jean Descola put it, perhaps overstating the case, "The Colour of [an individual's] existence depended on the colour of his parents' skin."[24] The important point is that there tended to be a close relationship between race and socioeconomic status. The dominant ideology secured the maintenance and exclusivity of that status. The mechanism was invariably endogamy and generally loyalty toward family and groups. As François Chevalier notes, in societies where written contracts are not customary, traditions based on blood ties and personal bonds are the only contracts with real importance.[25] In these situations race and ethnicity were synonymous and influenced all aspects of social stratification. Verena Martínez-Alier's study of marriage, class, and color in nineteenth-century Cuba demonstrates that the metaphysical notion of blood as the vehicle of lineage equalities was very much part of the white Cuban's attitude, "a legacy of the much older Spanish concern over purity of blood reinforced by the special socio-economic conditions obtaining in the colonies. Interracial marriages were rare; race mixing resulted only from consensual unions."[26]

It was in Cuba that the first novels dealing with life on the slave plantation, race mixing, and discrimination generally appeared. They were all written by Cuban whites. The first to be published was Anselmo Suárez Romero's *Francisco*, an explicitly antislavery novel. Probably written in 1839, it was first published in 1880 in New York. The plot is standard theme: black slave (Francisco) seduces young household slave and is brutally punished by the son of the plantation owner, who had his own designs on the mulatto girl. The punishments meted out to Francisco are described in realistic detail. These passages were surely intended to portray slavery for what it was: a system which degraded the slave but degraded the master even more. Predictably, in the nature of classical Spanish tragedy, Francisco hangs himself upon hearing that his love has given herself to the young master as a means of minimizing the punishments meted out to Francisco. Of course, this novel was not known in Cuba in the nineteenth century.

By far the most celebrated novel of nineteenth-century Cuban race relations is Cirilio Villaverde's *Cecilia Valdés*, published in Havana in 1839 and later in New York by the exiled Villaverde. It describes the terrible situation on the plantations, but its central thematic thrust was the race-conscious life of free mulattos in Cuba. It is a narrative that explores the complex question of the status-seeking by the light-skinned Cecilia through her relationship with a white man, Leonardo, which makes the novel worthy of the early Fanonian psychological analysis. Pimenta, the black man whose advances Cecilia has rejected, laments, "They take away attractive colored girls from us and we dare not even look at white women." Once again, the ending is typical of Spanish tragedy: Pimenta stabs Leonardo to death and suffers the terrible consequences.

The theme of the Cuban mulatto (in this case far removed from the plantation) is developed in works on the mulatto by Gabriel de la Concepción Valdés, known as Plácido, who A. M. Elegio de la Puente calls the most popular poet in Cuban history.[27] Plácido's mother was a traveling Spanish actress, and his father was the mulatto barber attending theater people. Born in Havana in 1809, the record of his baptism certificate specifies a boy who appears to be white ("un niño al parecer blanco").[28] Plácido grew up to become a well-known poet in the town of Santa Clara. It cannot be said that Plácido wrote black poetry, as Juan José Arrom notes, "He had little of the Negro in his blood and less so in his poetry" (De negro tenía muy poco en la sangre y aún menos en sus versos).[29] And yet, because he was a mulatto, he associated and lived with fellow people of color.

In 1843, Cirilo Villaverde, author of *Cecilia Valdéz*, made Plácido the protagonist in his novel *La peineta calada*.[30] Not only was Plácido a great poet but his tragic death in 1844 made him a martyr of the early Cuban black efforts at rebellion. It has never been established whether Plácido was involved in what is known as the conspiracy of La Escalera, but he was executed, along with all those who lived in the house where the mulatto intellectuals met. The court verdict revealed the terrified consciousness of the whites:

> The negroes and mulattos used to meet periodically in this House under the Presidency of the conspiratorial negro Plácido, conspiring against the government and the white race.

> [Que en esta case se reunían periódicamente los mulatos y los negros, bajo la Presidencia del sedicioso negro Plácido para conspirar contra el Gobierno y la raza blanca].[31]

Such was the infusion of fear, suspicion, and open hatred between the races in Cuba that José Martí himself had to intervene to defuse conflicts between his white and black soldiers (*mambises*), all fighting to liberate Cuba. Continually pleading that "debiera bastar ... Debiera cesar esa alusión al color de los hombres," Marti rejected the idea that any race has special rights; neither the black man nor the white can speak of their race as being superior. Anything else, he said, is "a sin against humanity."[32]

Even as many Cuban planters sought independence from Spain, their attitudes tended to be more anti-black than anti-Spanish. The white *criollo* resented the Spaniard for his unwillingness to show deference and the accompanying demeanor, precisely the deference he demanded—without expectations of reciprocity, of course—from his nonwhite fellow citizens. As Simón Bolívar complained to an English friend in his famous 1815 Jamaica Letter, "We should also have enjoyed a personal consideration [from Spain], thereby commanding a certain automatic respect from the people."[33]

Being a Spanish colony, the same attitudes toward race and social status existed in Spanish Hispaniola, later called the Dominican Republic. This, of course, did not stop race mixing. As far as attitudes toward race are concerned, there was little difference between those in Cuba and those in Spanish Hispaniola. The proportions, however, were radically different. Also very different were the situations between the Spanish and the French parts. On the eve of Haiti's first military invasion of its neighbor in 1801, the respective population compositions were as shown in table 9.

Quite evidently, any society as conscious of race and color as Spanish His-

Table 9. Race in the Dominican Republic and Haiti in the late eighteenth century

	Dominican Republic (1794)	Haiti (1789)
Whites	35,000	40,000
Slaves	15,000 to 30,000	450,000
Freed/mixed	38,000	30,000

Sources: Pedro Andrés Pérez Cabral, La comunidad mulata (Caracas: Gráfica Americana, 1967), 106–7; David Nicholls, From Dessalines to Duvalier: Race, Colour, and National Independence in Haiti (Cambridge: Cambridge University Press, 1979), 19.

paniola would look with alarm on a neighbor such as Haiti. As it turns out, Dominicans, as they began to call themselves, had other reasons as well to be in a veritable panic about their recently liberated neighbors. As already described, several invasions and an occupation from 1822 to 1844 established that fear of Haiti as a permanent trait in Dominican culture.

In his social history of the Dominican Republic, Harry Hoetink traces variations in race and color emphases over the half century following the Haitian occupation.[34] He found that the essentially aristocratic-patriarchal Dominican society, with clearly established criteria of stratification and social distance, demonstrated a remarkable adaptability. While the Haitian occupation increased the black and mulatto populations (by Haitian settlements and white flight) and reinforced the African dimensions of Dominican culture, it also "softened" race relations among Dominicans themselves. Given their reduced numbers (on the eve of the Haitian occupation, only 63,000 inhabitants resided on 18,712 square miles), the elite attempted to unite all Dominicans in a national liberation struggle against the Haitians. This effort to create a strong, independent national identity was not totally successful—in 1860 important sectors of the white elite invited the Spaniards to reoccupy the island. Fear of the Haitians overwhelmed any sense of national sovereignty.

By 1865, however, independence-minded Dominicans again called on Dominicans of all colors, in the name of nationality, to defeat the Spaniards. The Spaniards' defeat, and the flight of many whites who had supported them, further democratized the Dominican stratification system. This explains how a black of Haitian descent, Ulises Heureaux, could govern for the last twenty years of the nineteenth century. As soon as the fear of foreign occupation by Haitians or any others abated, however, Dominicans returned to divisions of race and color. Heureaux was persistently hounded with racial epithets and accused of favoring Haitian settlement. When he showed an inclination to concede to a U.S. naval base, his enemies warned that North American racism would oppress Dominican blacks and mulattos. The political use of racial fears could go in all directions. Even during the U.S. occupation from 1916 to 1924, the Dominican white elite refused to cooperate in certain reforms or to join the new constabulary, opening the doors to members of the colored middle class. This mobility was especially true in the military, where Rafael Leonidas Trujillo—considered nonwhite by the elite—used U.S. sponsorship to catapult himself, and his many relatives and friends, into a twenty-nine-year dictatorship.

Again, the Dominican capacity to use race and color identifications when convenient was evident in the Trujillo years. The dictator simultaneously became the most ferocious enemy of the traditional white aristocracy (which on more than one occasion snubbed him in his requests for membership in their clubs) and yet, paradoxically, the greatest promoter of Hispanic white identification. The combination of democratization on social mobility, through state sponsorship, and a conscious effort to identify with Spain and its heritage affected all parts of Dominican life. At the height of the Trujillato, color considerations were so pronounced that even a pro-regime sociologist could lament that "since Dominicans are not predominantly of pure race, we have a complex about ethnicity, we are constantly noticing the different skin colors, hair textures and degree of white blood. Three dominant drivers are noticeable: those who do not have white blood want to acquire it; those who have some, improve it; those who are white want to preserve this gift (*don*)."[35]

There exists no better account of the behavioral results of a regime that tried to at once open up opportunities for social mobility while not disrupting a stratification system emphasizing color than the 1977 memoirs of Joaquín Balaguer, which carry the extraordinarily submissive title *Memorias de un cortesano de la "era de Trujillo."* Balaguer served Trujillo throughout his stay in power, and later—whether as president for seven terms or out of office—dominated Dominican politics for decades. He died in 2002 at age ninety-five. To Balaguer, one of Trujillo's greatest accomplishments was to have "swept away everywhere the claims to aristocracy (*los pergaminos sociales*)." Yet Balaguer relates how the color-conscious dictator would pass his hands over a child's hair and say, "But how surprising, he's got good hair." The element of surprise indicates the dictator's concern was not over biological race (genotype) but over racial appearance (phenotype), and the latter had to do with perceptions of acceptable demeanor. According to Balaguer, it was concern over demeanor, and the impact it might have on the deference paid by outsiders, that led Trujillo to dismiss his most effective collaborator because his "rough" Negroid features were an embarrassment during a sojourn among Spain's aristocracy. The much less competent Roberto Depradel, on the other hand, was always retained; he was white, with blue eyes and easy speech. "Men of good looks and good appearance," writes Balaguer, "were always especially pleasing to the Dominican dictator."[36]

Dominicans' capacity to adjust to difficult circumstances—to be accommodating even with their most intrinsic racial identities—is evident in Balaguer himself. From his explicitly racist book *La Realidad Dominicana* (1947), in which he argued Haitians' racial inferiority, to his later *La Isla al revés: Haití y el destino Dominicano* (1990), in which he merely argued Haiti's cultural inferiority, Balaguer made anti-Haitianism the linchpin of his concept of Dominican nationality. In 1937, he defended the right of Dominicans to eliminate—to massacre—those Haitians who had crossed the border into Dominican territory. Had he been there, he told the U.S. chargé d'affaires, he would have probably participated in the killings.[37] And yet in 1990 he ends with a plea for a confederation between his country and Haiti: "By forgetting the past we can have a rebirth, two countries forcibly joined as neighbors by geography and history can create a new union, a more honorable and lasting indivisibility: that of the awareness which men on both sides have of their economic and cultural links as well as common destiny."[38]

It would be illusory to believe that this political veteran ever gave up his basic identity—his private prejudices—as a Hispanic Dominican. But the politician who in 1937 could hardly conceal his approval of the slaughter of 10,000 to 15,000 Haitian squatters faced in 1991 quite a different demographic and economic reality. In 1937 Dominicans estimated that some 52,000 Haitians were living in the Dominican Republic; in 1991 they calculated the number to be 1 million. By that time Dominican agriculture depended on Haitian labor, as did much of the private construction industry and significant sections of the ever expanding economy. At the dawn of the twenty-first century, as in the past, arguments against the Haitian presence is made on ethnic and national grounds: the distinctiveness of the Spanish language and history, especially the links with Spain and the struggle to retain their identity against all invaders, Haitian and North American. The inclusive power of culture and history is not to be minimized, which explains the grossly irregular decision to change the traditional granting of citizenship to anyone born in the Dominican Republic (*jus soli*) with the right to citizenship by blood descent (*jus sanguinis*) and then—in defiance of any principle of universal jurisprudence—making it retroactive to 1926. All of this, however, occurred without any massive deportations of the vital Haitian workforce. It was to the credit of the CARICOM nations that the law was modified. In May 2014, all three branches of government lay out new procedures for the eventual naturalization of Haitians born in the Dominican Republic of parents who were there illegally; only time will tell whether they carry out the legal provisions.

Continuity in using nationality in the Dominican Republic reveals the strategic subordination of race and color distinctions, which are otherwise evident in private. The fact is that black politicians' rise to political prominence reflects a relaxation of public attitudes toward racial and color attributes in their leaders. The distinction between color and nationality, however, is still important in the island's politics, as the case of José Francisco Peña Gómez illustrated. The accusation that he was of Haitian origin played an important part in some of the electorate's perceptions of his not being "presidential" (*presidenciable*). It was not a generalized response but enough to cost him the 1996 election. On the other hand, the equally black musician Johnny Ventura, a political protégé of Peña Gómez, suffered no such handicap. Significantly, Johnny Ventura is the leading proponent of the island's music, the *merengue*, generally regarded as a major unifier of Dominicans' sense of nationality.[39] The fear of the Haitian in Peña Gómez was clearly accentuated by opposing elites who no longer seemed to find the racial or color issue strategically advantageous. As already described in chapter 1, such was the hatred of the Haitian element that Balaguer joined with his historic enemy, Juan Bosch, to stop the election of Peña Gómez in 1996. Bosch, in turn, had no evident objections to Balaguer's anti-Haitian sentiments, since it ensured his party's (PLD) victory. Race was pliable; being "Haitian" was not.

All this is to say that under no circumstances can the Dominican Republic be described as a "plantation society" in the classical definition of that term as set out by Lloyd Best and Kari Levitt. Nor do we find evidence of a Fanonian propensity to antiwhite violence. To cite another case where the two theories did not apply was the Netherlands Antilles. Among the region's earliest non-Hispanic settlers were the Dutch in Curaçao. Here the Protestant white elite and the Sephardic Jews trace their roots back to the mid-seventeenth century.[40] The amount of change in the stratification system over the years has been minimal, even as the political and economic situation changed. It was never, however, a plantation society. There was a simple reason: neither the land nor the inclinations of the original settlers lent themselves to establishing plantations. They put all their efforts into establishing Curaçao as a trade entrepôt and were very successful.

In Martinique, on the other hand, you certainly had and have an economically dominant white group (*bekés pays*) whose power was originally the plantation and, once that waned, landownership. On that island a researcher found a white creole elite composed of 150 patronymic *beké* names whose roots could be traced as follows: 28 families (39 percent) arrived before 1713; 37 families (22 percent) arrived between 1713 and 1784; another 35 percent arrived in the nineteenth century; while only 4 percent of the whites were first or second generation Martinicans.[41]

To the *bekés,* race, class, family, and an ideology shaped by a sense of their historical role on the island formed the pillars of their identity and ethnocentrism. Each *beké* child was first socialized into "the cult of the family name" and then into the "sacred duty" of maintaining the *beké* group's social characteristics. The mechanism of this group's hierarchical stability has always been endogamy; any marriage outside the group's strict norms was regarded as a "stain." This explains not just their survival as a group over the ages. It is evident that their continued social and economic status cannot be explained exclusively through the theory of the plantation society, since Martinique stopped being a plantation-based economy a long time ago. And, certainly, Fanon's fiery theories do not apply either. The "departmentalization" carried out in 1946, according to Fred Constant, meant the equivalent of decolonization with the emergence of new black and mulatto elites to political and administrative power.[42] According to Constant the *bekés* survive by strategically accommodating themselves to changes on the island and in France. Accommodation, that is, in everything except its continued endogamy. Of course, the other side of the coin of this is that growing black and mulatto prosperity and political recognition in France allows the new black elites to tolerate the racial exceptionality of the *bekés*—as long as they are seen as entrepreneurs who add to the economy and not as political competitors.

Despite this permanence of a white elite, intellectuals on both Martinique and Guadeloupe (starting with Aimé Césaire described above) have developed sociological explanations far removed from both Fanonian and plantation society theories. Not that they were not concerned with racism and class exploitation; they certainly were, and are. But their central concerns have been the complexities of culture, language, and political autonomy as it affected the individual and the society as a whole. The intellectual depth and general sophistication of French West Indian theorizing can be seen in the discussion of the concept of *creolité* pioneered by Patrick Chamoiseau and Raphael Confiant. One hardly does the theory justice by reducing it to a theory of cultural and racial homogenization. *Metissage* involves linguistic, biological, and cultural dimensions, all major characteristics of *creolité*. The emphasis is on the fact that everyone (even the *beké pays*) speaks *Créole* and all share in its wider cultural expressions. Following the highly intellectualized discussion of *creolité* came a debate over the broader meaning of Antillanité, equally removed from any theorizing about violence. In this latter debate, the role of Édouard Glissant (1928–2011) was fundamental.

It was arguably Glissant who transformed the Martinican discourse over race and class into a discussion of Caribbean-wide relevance. Glissant argued that there was something which could be termed "Antillanité" which all Caribbean people, regardless of race, shared. Antillanité describes a consciousness of place, of the Antilles, which is the glue that binds cultures across any barriers posed by different languages. His fundamental work, *Le Discours Antillaise,* was first published in 1997.[43] It is composed of fifty short essays on a variety of topics, from analyses of the Creole language and its role in shaping an Antillean identity to essays on Chile and Jamaica. Regarding the latter, Glissant published the speech he delivered at CARIFESTA in Kingston, Jamaica, in 1976. Confronting the critique that Martinicans have no great populist leader à la Toussaint L'Ouverture, José Martí, Simón Bolívar, or Benito Juárez, Glissant argued that the absence of such heroes reflected "the particularities of a people secure in their identity."[44] Nowhere in Glissant can one find the concepts of self-hatred and self-doubt. Indeed it could be, said Glissant, that in addition to Victor Schoelscher, the white Frenchman who pushed for abolition in 1848, they also have Aimé Césaire. Neither were "men on horseback," but they certainly were the molders of the national identity. Neither Fanonian colonial violence nor plantation society postulates apply to their actual comportment.

Besides being a poet, a novelist, and a philosopher, Glissant excelled as a sociolinguist. One of his deep dislikes was the intellectual "paralysis" caused by "monolingual prejudice," which maintains that "my language is my root."[45] Glissant wished to do more than just celebrate the richness that Creole added to the French Caribbean. He wished to know its origins, as he explains in his 1990 book, *Poétique de la relation,* translated as *Poetics of Relation*:

> An idiom like *Créole,* one so rapidly constituted in so fluid afield of relations, cannot be analyzed the way, for example, it was done for Indo-European languages that aggregated slowly around their roots. We need to know why this *Créole* language was the only one to appear, why it took the same forms in both the Caribbean basin and the Indian Ocean, and why solely in countries colonized by the French; whereas the other languages of this colonization process, English and Spanish, remained inflexible as far as the colonized populations were concerned, their only concessions being pidgins or other dialects that were derived.[46]

Whatever historical and sociolinguistic truth there is in Glissant's analysis, it was incomplete. It was the translator of Glissant's book who corrected Glissant on this score:

> Another language of the region that would be an exception to this statistical rule is Papiamento, which has a Spanish lexical basis in countries (Curaçao) that are no longer Spanish, it seems that, in this same region of the Americas, more and more linguistic microzones are being discovered in which Creoles, pidgins, and patois become undifferentiated.[47]

Indeed, one could add Surinamese Sarang Narong and Jamaican patois to the list. Glissant is under no illusion that his concept of Antillanité described a united Caribbean. There is, in fact, no harmony in the region. Caribbean intellectuals might all resort to the metaphor of Próspero and Caliban, but whether used by the Martinicans Fanon and Césaire, the Barbadian George Laming, or the Cuban Fernando Retamar, the metaphor tends to describe specific national, linguistic, and cultural realities; in other words, expressions of the polymorphic nature of the region. This appeal of the local scene, complex enough everywhere in the region, influences all writings about their

island's realities no matter what ritualistic verbal allusions they make to regional communalities. This is what explains the existence of what Ivar Oxaal
called "plural disassociation" and in Martinique is referred to as *chacun dans
sa chacunière*, that is, a live-and-let-live collective attitude.

None of this is to be explained by any grand theory but rather by understanding paradox. As Richard Burton explains, "Perhaps the Martinican
intellectual is never more 'French,' never more assimilated than when precisely, he opposes assimilation."[48] There is also the epistemological dimension as Gabriel Coulthard theorized. The ideology of Négritude, he says,
seeks redemption in attacking Western reason and eulogizing primitivism
("the cult of the drum") rather than from secular social revolution. It invariably ends up being a quest for personal identity reparation rather than broad
social change.

These "French" Antilleans would eventually succumb to the pressures of
their more conservative environment. As George Padmore had done before
him, Césaire resigned from the French Communist Party in 1956. As he wrote
to the French Communist Party's secretary-general, Maurice Thorez, an
alternative path existed to the "fleshless universalism" of European communism: "Black Africa, the dam of our civilization and source of our culture." Only through race, culture, and the richness of ethnic particulars, he
continued, could Caribbean people avoid alienation. "What I wish is that
Marxism and Communism be utilized to benefit the man of color, not the
man of color to benefit Marxism and Communism."[49] Césaire founded the
Martinique Progressive Party. In the final analysis, the tension between a
Communist secular ideology and a black Caribbean experience resulted in
the pursuit of an identity—a black identity.[50]

This consequence of the individualism of Négritude was later critiqued by
others. In his later years Césaire and Négritude came in for heavy criticism
for continuing to write in French and supporting French "colonialism." At
the Pan-African Cultural Festival in Algiers in 1969, Négritude was openly
rejected as outmoded and even colonialist by the Marxists who attended.
"*Négritude*," said the head of the Guinean delegation, "is really a good mys-
tifying anesthetic . . . [not] an arm of economic and social liberation."[51] This
brings us to Haiti where, one would suppose, both Césaire's concept of
Négritude and the concept of plantation societies were theoretically most
applicable, since it is generally agreed that plantation economy reached its
apogee in Haiti. As it turns out, it also met its crisis and dénouement there.

Because of the heroic nature of its revolution (at once a war of liberation and an independence movement) and the heroism of its leaders, it is indeed an exceptional case. This, however, has not stopped generations of Caribbean intellectuals from turning it into a morality play.[52] One who resisted such a stance was David Nicholls. Nicholls began his seminal study of race and color in Haiti by asking what appears to be a paradoxical question to anyone accustomed to a bifurcated "black-white" system: "How is it that racial pride should have been among the principal causes of Haitian independence, while colour prejudice should have been one of the chief factors undermining this independence?"[53] It was a question Victor Schoelcher had also asked.

The response is that each emphasis—on race and color—served a different strategic purpose. In the confrontation with white colonial domination, for instance, the emphasis was race. This made sense not only in terms of alliances, which all nonwhites found necessary to combat the external enemy, but also in terms of the way the white enemy classified all nonwhites. Whites certainly recognized shades of difference, but in the final analysis black and colored alike were "soiled" by Africa. This explains why the first Haitian constitution defined the nation as *noir* and all its citizens as black. It also explains why, during the U.S. military occupation of 1915–34, the nationalist reaction among otherwise divided black and mulatto elites was couched in terms of a rediscovering of their collective African past. In the Haitian resistance to North American racism, ethnography became the central organizing discipline: nationalists of all shades of color drank at its font. Perhaps the most impressive of these nationalists was someone we have already met, Jean Price-Mars. Price-Mars's *Ainsi parla l'oncle* was a call to his countrymen especially *gens de couleur, mulatos*, to come to grips with the African past and context.[54] The racial principle—as biology, but also as cultural protest—made sense in the face of evident North American racism, which was both biological and cultural. However, once the racial protest was made and the North Americans withdrew, color differences took hold just as they had after the independence struggles of the early nineteenth century.

The material and political context, however, had changed. While the U.S. occupation forces showed a distinct bias toward the educated mulatto elite—even creating a new army (*gendarmerie*) staffed with their sons—they had also helped create a new black middle class. Through various technical schools and other practical social and public programs, a generation of black lawyers, doctors, teachers, and agricultural extension technicians soon rose to challenge the power of the mulattos. Not surprisingly, differences in color and culture (in which language differences were critical) reappeared as the operative aspect of social, economic, and political competition.[55] Micheline Labelle discovered a precise and nuanced color classification scheme, not unlike Moreau de Saint Méry's, which survived from colonial days. But a "color ideology"—always present—really came into full operation around economic, and especially political, competition. Labelle maintains that it has been the Haitian variant of class conflict.[56]

Nicholls's question is answered, therefore, by noting that in Haiti one has to differentiate between intrinsic ethnic identities of color and strategically varying identifications, which can be of class, race, and/or color.

The 1991 election of Haitian president Jean-Bertrand Aristide is generally recognized as the first truly democratic poll in the island's history. It was also the first major political campaign in which race and color played no major part, at least not explicitly. Aristide's cabinet also reflected an indifference to color distinctions. Aristide's populism was quite different, therefore, from that of the Duvalier regime, a dynasty that made color distinction a central piece of its existence for twenty-six years. With Duvalier followers attempting to revive the black versus mulatto strife during the 1990 campaign, it became strategically important that the opponents of Duvalier not make color an issue, as indeed they did not, with enormous electoral success.[57] Whatever other weaknesses and failures were evident in the Aristide government, that interlude indicated that color strife did not have to be the basis of a national mobilization in Haiti.[58]

There is no need to repeat the description of the fall of Aristide, as it was done in chapter 5. The interest here lies rather in demonstrating the little analytical utility such monolithic, generalizing formulations such as Négritude, decolonization through Fanonian terror, or the plantation society model have. Duvalier ran on a race theme, Aristide—initially—on a Theology of Liberation one. In the midst of the always present race, class, and color antagonisms, Haitian elites have options: they can be creative and flexible. This is further illustrated by the fact that it was in Haiti that some of the foremost intellectuals rejected the concept of Négritude as formulated by Aimé Césaire. The writings of René Dépèstre, J. Stephen Alexis, and especially Jacques Roumain rejected the concept as ignoring the hard objective realities of their island or indeed any Caribbean island. Their critiques of Négritude are analyzed by J. Michael Dash in a highly persuasive critique of all generalizing theories which deny an individual island's original creativity. In an interpretation that brings to mind that of Rebecca Scott discussed in chapter 2, Dash argues that such myths negate the individual's autonomy to confront (not negate) the past through "a complex process of adaptation and survival." He calls this a "counter-culture of the imagination," which he sees exemplified in "marvelous realism" of the Carpentier type.[59] Similarly, what Dash discovers in the "Marvelous Realism" of Alejo Carpentier is how awareness of "the creative continuum of history" contributes to the emergence of "a literature of renaissance which concerns itself with survival rather than conquest." Even the past of dominant alien culture contributes to "the vitality and hardiness" of the Third World personality. No need to turn to Fanonian "liberating violence," Césaire's Négritude or to assume that every society exhibits the persistent traits of the "plantation." Caribbean man and woman have been modernizing, laying their own paths to a better future. If, at certain stages of their history, whites were "terrorized," it was a creation of their own projections. It is all the more reason to understand—and celebrate—the fact that the new, decolonized black elites never behaved as those projections predicted they would.

Figure 1. Eric Williams. Courtesy of Eric Williams.

Figure 2. President John F. Kennedy meets with president-elect of the Dominican Republic, Dr. Juan E. Bosch. Photograph by Abbie Rowe. White House Photographs. John F. Kennedy Presidential Library and Museum, Boston, image AR7655-A.

Figure 3. Arturo Morales Carrión and Luís Muñoz Marín, 1958. Courtesy of University Interamericana, San Juan.

Figure 4. Gordon K. Lewis.
Courtesy of David Lewis.

Figure 5. *Left to right*: Cheddi Jagan of Guyana, Alexander Bustamante of Jamaica, Errol Barrow of Barbados, and Eric Williams of Trinidad and Tobago. Jamaican Information Services.

Figure 6. C.L.R. James (*center*) on his return to Trinidad in 1958 after a long absence. Shown with him are Eric James (*left*) and Carlton Comma (*right*), Port of Spain chief librarian. By permission of the *Trinidad Guardian*.

Figure 7. *Left to right*: Michael Manley, prime minister of Jamaica; Maurice Bishop, prime minister of Grenada; Kurt Waldheim, secretary-general of the United Nations; Fidel Castro, president of Cuba. Photographed September 2, 1979, at Havana airport during the arrival ceremony for the Non-Aligned Countries Summit beginning September 3. Rod MacIvor, copyright Bettmann/ Corbis/ AP Images. By permission of AP Images.

Figure 8. Forbes Burnham with President Lyndon Johnson, 1966. Photograph by Yoichi Oka-
moto. Courtesy of the Lyndon B. Johnson Library and Museum.

Figure 9. Aimé Césaire (1913–2008) of Martinique. Courtesy of the Martinique Tourism Authority.

Figure 10. A pencil-drawn portrait of Captain Andrew (Tattoo) Cipriani, a white French Creole who founded the first socialist movement in the English-speaking Caribbean. From the author's collection.

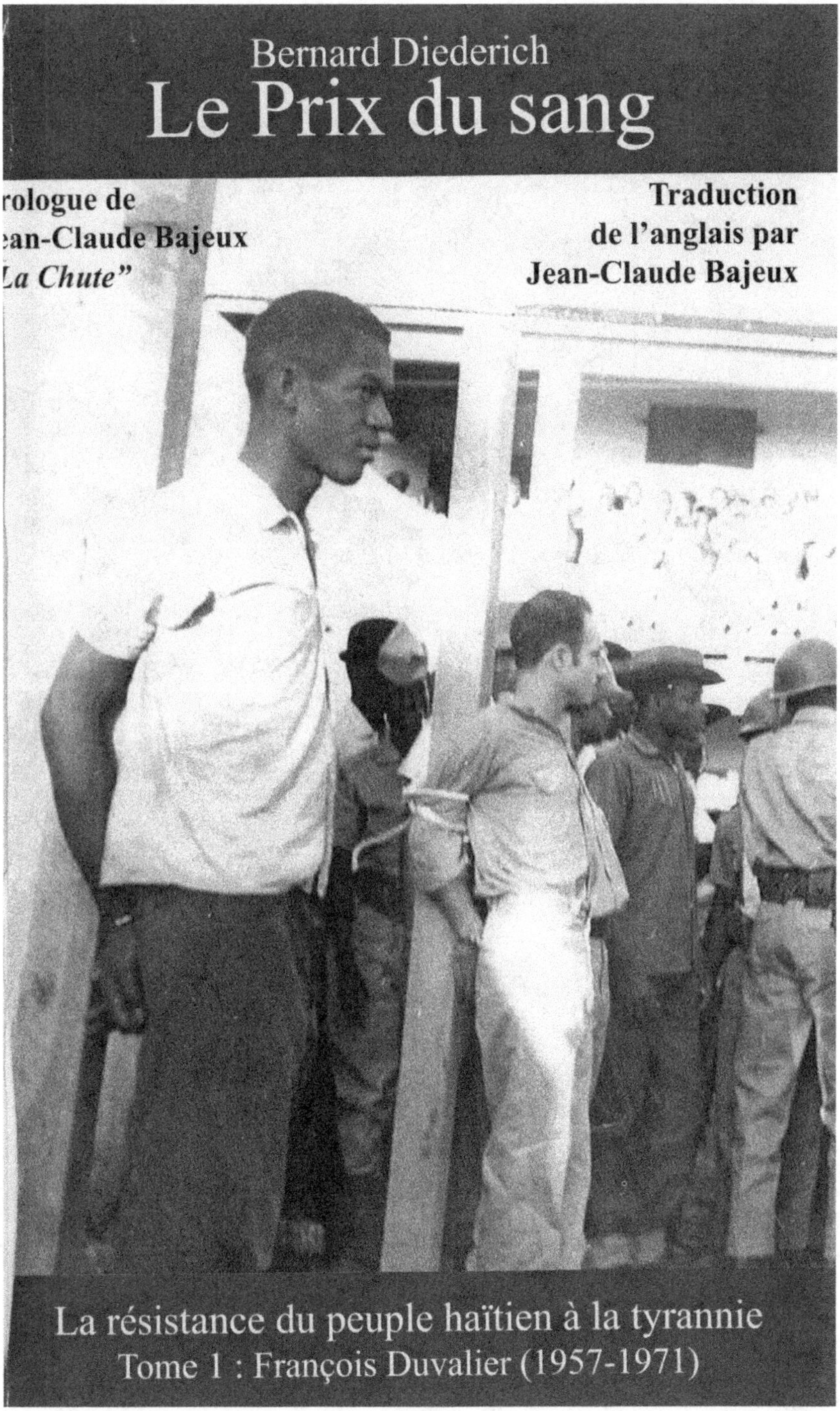

Figure 11. Marcel Numa and Louis Drouin facing execution, June 8, 1967. Cover of Bernard Diederich, *Le Prix du Sang* (Port-au-Prince: Editions Antila, Centre Oecumenique des Droits Humains, 2005).

Figure 12. Dame Eugenia Charles, "Iron Lady" of the Caribbean. Permission of Special Collections of the Sidney Martin Library, Cave Hill, Barbados, University of the West Indies.

Figure 13. Grenada Revolutionary Army on parade. Photograph by Tony Buxo, Grenada, 1982.

Figure 14. Revolutionary graffiti in Grenada, 1982. Photograph by the author.

Figure 15. Heavy equipment used by Cubans working on the Grenada airport, 1982. From People's Revolutionary Government (PRG), *To Construct from Morning* (St. George's, Grenada: Fedon, 1982).

IN EVERLASTING MEMORY OF
PRIME MINISTER MAURICE BISHOP

FITZROY BAIN
NORRIS BAIN
EVELYN BULLEN
JACQUELINE CREFT
KEITH HAYLING
EVELYN MAITLAND
UNISON WHITEMAN

ANDY SEBASTIAN ALEXANDER
SIMON ALEXANDER
GEMMA BELMAR
ERIC DUMONT
AVIS FERGUSON
VINCE NOEL
ALLEYNE ROMAIN
NELSON STEELE

KILLED AT THIS FORT, OCT. 19, 1983
THEY HAVE GONE TO JOIN THE STARS
AND WILL FOREVER SHINE IN GLORY

ERECTED 19TH OCTOBER, 1993
WITH THE CO-OPERATION OF THE GOVERNMENT OF GRENADA
BY THE MAURICE BISHOP AND MARTYRS FOUNDATION

Figure 16. Plaque honoring Maurice Bishop and colleagues executed at Fort George. Photograph by the author.

Figure 17. Joaquín Balaguer. From Joaquin Balaguer, *Memorias de un cortesano de la "Era de Trujillo"* (Santo Domingo: Editora Corripio, 1989).

Figure 18. In a rare case of a multiracial alliance in Trinidad and Tobago, the leaders of the National Alliance for Reconstruction ("One Love") team, who were victorious in the 1986 elections. *Right to left*: John D. Humphrey (Minister of Works and Infastructure), Basdeo Panday (Deputy Leader and Minister of External Affairs), Arthur N. R. Robinson (Prime Minister and Minister of Finance), Trevor Sudama (Junior Minister of Finance), Anthony P. Maingot (Visitor conducting interviews in December, 1987). All three ministers were soon thereafter dismissed from the cabinet, and politics returned to the usual racial polarization. Author's photograph.

Figure 19. The surrender of self-appointed iman Yasin Abu Bakr of the Jamaat-al-Muslameen, July 1990. Photograph from "The Year in Pictures, 1990," *Daily Express*.

7

C.L.R. James, George Padmore, and the Myth
of the Revolutionary Caribbean

Small islands are certainly capable of producing big thinkers. St. Lucia has produced two Nobel Prize winners, Sir W. Arthur Lewis in economics and Derek Walcott in literature. Trinidad and Tobago, aside from a Nobel Prize winner in literature, V. S. Naipaul, and an outstanding historian-politician, Eric Williams, produced two of the most recognizable Marxists of the Third World, Cyril Lionel Robert James and George Padmore, born Malcolm Nurse.

C.L.R. James is indisputably the best known theoretical Marxist of the English-speaking Caribbean and perhaps the whole Caribbean. That said, a critical handicap to anyone wishing to write a full analysis of James is the fact that he never wrote a full autobiography. The closest he came to leaving an autobiographical record is on pages 30–46 of his celebrated book on cricket, *Beyond a Boundary*, and in a few of the two hundred letters he wrote to his love, and later wife, the American actress Constance Webb. According to Anna Grimshaw, the editor of these letters, it is in these letters, full of intimate sentiments, that "James found a way to articulate much that gave meaning to his own life and work."[1] James, born in Tunapuna, Trinidad, in 1901, was known affectionately to his family and friends as "Nello." Both his parents were educated. His father was a rural schoolteacher, and James would later describe his mother in a way that probably explains his own eclectic reading habits. "She was a reader. She read everything that came her way. . . . As she read and put it down I picked it up."[2]

In 1910 James won a scholarship to attend the prestigious Queen's Royal College (QRC). Following graduation he took up teaching at QRC. One of the pupils he tutored was the future political leader Eric Williams, with whom he would share a lifetime of scholarly interests and, later, political involvements. During his postsecondary school years, James began participating in the avant-garde literary and nationalist group gathered around *Beacon* magazine. That group represented the first awakening of national identity and literary talent on the island. Besides literature, James's other interest was cricket, studying and playing the sport. Politics, literature, and cricket would become his lifelong passions. During this early period on the island, James published two important short stories, "La Divina Pastora" and "Triumph," both realistic descriptions of the island's urban working-class culture. In December 1929, James joined a Portuguese-Creole, Alfred H. Mendes, in establishing another magazine, *Trinidad*, and James became a most polemical contributor to the only two issues ever published. Undeterred by the closing of the magazine, James continued to write and in 1936, four years after his arrival in England, he managed to finish the manuscript of a novel, *Minty Alley*. His evolving radicalization was evident in the central theme of the novel: the rise of the black bourgeoisie and its alienation from the masses. James never abandoned this interpretation of the racial and class distortions wrought by colonial and capitalist society to the colonial political aspirant. He never published another book of fiction. As he noted in *Beyond a Boundary*, "Fiction-writing drained out of me and was replaced by politics. I became a Marxist, a Trotskyite."[3] Marxist politics became what he always called his "beacon." It is only in 1963 in that same quasi-autobiographical *Beyond a Boundary* that he describes something of the colonial atmosphere of his early schooling. It took him many years, he says, to understand "the limitation on spirit, vision, and self-respect" that was imposed on the local students. Everything, curriculum, code of morals, "began from the basis that Britain was the source of all light." Sadly, according to James, both masters and boys accepted it as in the nature of things.[4] That described the solid foundations of the island's conservative colonial society.

James's early host in Lancashire, England, was the Trinidad cricketer Learie Constantine, who in 1933 published a much acclaimed book, *Cricket and I*. Constantine was later knighted and became the first black member of Great Britain's House of Lords. James notes that he assisted Constantine in writing that book, but he also acknowledges how the older and "more political" Constantine influenced him. "Within five weeks we had unearthed the politician in each other. Within five months we were supplementing each other in a working partnership which had West Indian self-government as its goal."[5] In addition to playing and writing about cricket, Constantine was also deeply interested in issues of socialism, race, class, and social change, all later recorded in a 1954 book, *The Colour Bar*. Soon after his arrival in Lancashire in 1932, James published *The Life of Captain Cipriani: An Account of British Government in the West Indies*.[6] Demonstrating that socialism, not merely race, was his central concern, James's study of Capt. Arthur Andrew Cipriani, a white French Creole, described Cipriani's early battles for trade unionism and fair play for the black working masses. Sadly, it remains the only study done of this socialist pioneer—a reflection of the race-consciousness of later radical generations. Constantine funded the private publishing of the early version of this monograph, but in 1933 the Hogarth Press republished it as *The Case for West Indian Self-Government*. In England in the mid-1930s, James wrote for the *New Leader*, the newspaper of the Independent Labour Party, and also worked as a cricket correspondent for two newspapers, the *Manchester Guardian* and the *Glasgow Herald*. This was invaluable experience preparing him for work on his popular 1963 book on cricket.

James's life changed when world events drew his attention to Africa. Mussolini's invasion of Ethiopia (Abyssinia) in 1935 agitated blacks everywhere but arguably most intensely in Britain. James joined a fellow Trinidadian, Malcolm Nurse, by then known as George Padmore, in organizing the African Service Bureau, a news and information service agitating world opinion on the Ethiopian case. Despite this heavy organizational involvement, James managed to publish two books, *Abyssinia and the Imperialists* in 1936 and *World Revolution* in 1937. The latter was a Trotskyite history critical of the Stalin-dominated Communist International movement (Comintern) to which Padmore had once been an important official. But James was determined not to be either a member or, even less, a simple party pamphleteer for any political party. He was already pursuing his interest in the history of black revolutionary movements and doing archival research on the topic. His considerable efforts bore fruit in 1938 when his history of the Haitian independence revolution, *The Black Jacobins: Toussaint L'Ouverture and the San Domingo Revolution*, appeared. This became the seminal study of the Haitian Revolution, always sticking to the facts that were revealed by his research in French and British archives, never overwhelmed by his own Trotskyite proclivities. That same year, he published *A History of Negro Revolt* (republished in 1985 with the title *A History of Pan-African Revolts*), which argued with more passion than fact that black people were "inherently revolutionary" and ready at any time to smash bourgeois society.

With his reputation growing as an articulate Trotskyite intellectual, he accepted an invitation from the United States Socialist Workers Party to visit the States in 1938. James (using the pseudonym "Johnson") joined Trotsky's former secretary, Raya Dunayevskaya (who used the pseudonym "Forest"), in organizing the "Johnson-Forest Tendency" of the Trotskyite Socialist Workers Party. With Dunayevskaya as co-author he published two long essays, in 1947 *Dialectical Materialism and the Fate of Humanity*, and in 1950 *The Class Struggle*, both highly theoretical works that had limited circulation. Also in 1950 with the collaboration again of Dunayevskaya and Grace Lee, James published a full-length book, *State Capitalism and World Revolution*. It is in this book in particular that James's independent, even contrarian nature and ideological positions are revealed. The book is a robust but always thoughtfully articulated argument against "Stalinism, fellow travelers, and Trotskyism." The critique of Trotskyism is explained by the fact that he and the small Johnson-Forest Tendency group had broken with the Socialist Workers Party, and James was presenting his own theory of revolutionary change. James is categorical in his rejection of two of the cornerstones of Trotskyist theory and policy that he unabashedly calls "fetishisms": the idea of immediate and total nationalization of the economy and the Leninist theory of the Vanguard Party. To James, both policies were necessary to Lenin's circumstances in 1917–23, but were no longer suitable after World War II. Although his advocacy of socialism would never abate, *State Capitalism* was the last major work James would write with a Marxist methodology and theoretical thrust.

By 1950 he had been in the United States for twelve years and was already a popular lecturer identified as a Trotskyite, but he could never be pigeonholed ideologically. Paul Buhle notes that James "struck many of his political associates not only as a brilliant and encyclopedic Marxist thinker but also as an extreme eccentric. Others disagreed regarding him variously as a mystic, crypto-anarchist, or Black Nationalist."[7] Buhle was on target when he wrote, "Probably only a small circle *could* accept perspectives so radically out of kilter with existing doctrines."[8] Indeed, it was thought that at most the Johnson-Forest Tendency had seventy followers, although James admitted that they "never exceeded 35 people."[9] Membership size did not seem to matter to James and his colleagues, since they declared that their fundamental role was explaining Marxism and socialism to groups of intellectuals and workers.

Little is known about the activities of the Johnson-Forest Tendency group after 1950. Indeed, little could have been achieved because James was arrested in 1952 and deported from the United States in 1953. The charge was that he had overstayed his visa, but surely it was also a case of Cold War anti-communist hysteria. Be that as it may, James had not wasted his years in the United States. He researched the American working class, its popular culture, and especially film and developed an interest, even affection, for the United States. This sentiment is quite plainly evident in the book he wrote in 1953 while incarcerated on Ellis Island, *Mariners, Renegades, and Castaways: The Story of Herman Melville and the World We Live In.* Here James, already fifty-one, avoids polemics. He appears much more interested in Melville's use of metaphors to describe a complex world and the psychological nature of man's search for answers to problems of an existential nature. In the final chapter of this book, James explains the reasons why he became an anticommunist and describes his health problems (a duodenal ulcer and the beginnings of Parkinson's disease). Also for the first time he relates briefly his life as "essentially a writer" and with obvious pride reprints several significant reviews of the various works produced.[10] In the final analysis, however, he admits that the book was written as a plea to the American people to grant him U.S. citizenship.[11] The plea did not help him avoid deportation.

With his deportation to England, the phase of James's writing under the pseudonym "Johnson" and his work with the Johnson-Forest Tendency ended. James did not spend much time in England before he was invited by the nationalist leader of Trinidad and Tobago, Eric Williams, to return and help organize the movement toward independence. He returned in 1958, the first time since having left his native island twenty-eight years earlier, and was made editor of the *Nation,* the People's National Movement's newspaper. It was not long before the two erstwhile friends had a falling-out and James resigned as editor. The causes of the Williams-James split have been speculated on by many, including the protagonists themselves. Arguably the two most authoritative sources, however, are Ivar Oxaal and Selwyn Ryan. Oxaal notes that to radical interpreters, Williams's agreement to negotiate with the Americans over the return of the World War II base Chaguaramas, rather than seizing it outright, was a betrayal of the nationalist movement and the cause of the split with James. Oxaal disagrees with this interpretation, basing his analysis on James's own history of the split in *Party Politics in the West Indies* (1984). Oxaal notes that "Eric Williams was no revolutionary;

and James, although he had curbed his radical instincts, was no bourgeois reformer."[12] But there was more. It was the resentment that the more conservative original core of PNM stalwarts felt of the radical James's sudden claim to
leadership which eroded the Williams-James partnership. In one of the three
private meetings I had with Prime Minister Williams, Williams claimed that
James's editorship of the *Nation* was a disaster and that James's multiple columns did little more than promote his ideas and political prospects.[13] Ryan,
author of the fundamental biography of Williams, traces the break to the
"ideological disconnect" between the Marxist James and the strictly pragmatic Williams.[14] It is evident that James's propensity to proselytize was not
well received in the nationalist movement, much less the wider conservative
society.

After leaving the *Nation* and simultaneously the PNM, James gave a series
of five lectures for the public library's adult education program. He advised
his audience from the very beginning that he was a Marxist, but not of the
Communist China or Communist Russia kind. Despite promising not to
"propagandize," James finished with this: "If this course of lectures has stim-
ulated you to pursue the further study of Marxism we will have struck a blow
for the emergence of mankind from the darkness into which capitalism has
plunged the world."[15] Evidently James had not abandoned the emergence of
a socialist world nor his desire to proselytize.

James left Trinidad and Tobago for England just before Independence in
1962. A year later, he published his remarkable analysis of cricket and politics
in a colonial context, *Beyond a Boundary*. This was further evidence of his
boundless intellectual energy; he was already involved with events in West
Africa, specifically in Ghana. Many of his friends from the International
African Service Bureau were there assisting Ghana's Kwame Nkrumah's nationalist independence push. Once again, however, James found it difficult
to remain engaged. In his 1962 book *Nkrumah and the Ghana Revolution*, he
only half praises Nkrumah. "Like Cromwell and Lenin, he initiated the destruction of a regime in decay, a tremendous achievement; but like them, he
failed to create the new society."[16] In 1966 he wrote an even stronger critique
of the Ghanaian case, *The Rise and Fall of Nkrumah*.[17] By that time, a call
from his trade union friends in Trinidad led him to return to help organize a
left opposition to the PNM. Despite gathering a bevy of leftist intellectuals
and trade unionists, his Workers and Farmers Party was soundly defeated
in the 1966 elections. Once again he left Trinidad, this time to return to the

United States. Between 1968 and 1981 he was a professor at the University of the District of Columbia and lectured widely in U.S. academic circles. In 1981 he returned to England where he supported the Black Power Movement. He died in Brixton in 1989.

Beyond the standard sociology of knowledge explanations regarding social and economic context, how does one explain the varying interpretations of this celebrated Trinidadian's life and work spanning more than five decades and covering four continents? Is it Wilson Harris's explanation that James had a distinct ability "to appear very different in contrasting lights"?[18] Were James's bold political maneuverings and capacity to adjust and prosper intellectually due to what Anthony Bogues in a brilliant biography of James calls his "Caribbean audacity"?[19] Might it have been James's Caribbean "plasticity," that is, one steady in identity but constantly shifting identifications strategically?[20] Or might it be that James wrote on so many topics, was involved in so many political groupings without ever being personally, ideologically, or dogmatically subservient to any, that his appeal has remained broadly humanistic in a universal sense? Might it be all of these in combination? Arguably, the clearest assessment of James was that of Anna Grimshaw, his secretary in England during his final years, who wrote that although James was claimed by different constituencies, he was never an intellectual who could be confined, because his vision "was truly universal." The result has been, as one of James's closest followers says, that "everyone has his own C.L.R."[21] Whatever the interpretation, it is a fact that there has been no other West Indian personality who has served as model and exemplar for so many different movements or causes.

In a trenchant analysis of James's enduring appeal, Humberto García Muñiz describes the wide range of Jamesian American, Canadian, and West Indian followers in academia, trade unionism, and cultural studies.[22] They represent a veritable constellation of outstanding performers. Evidence of all this is the enormous body of work on him. In the years since his death in 1989, there have been at least three dozen scholarly books written on James, including five biographies and the appearance of a "C.L.R. James Journal." There is now a C.L.R. James Institute, but there have long been C.L.R. Centers. Ralph Gonsalves, prime minister of St. Vincent, relates how as a student at Manchester University he deepened his knowledge of Marx by paying regular visits to the C.L.R. James Center of that city.[23] Significant evidence of James's stature is that even V. S. Naipaul has gotten into the act, and as we have come to expect, he is hardly flattering. In his 1994 book, *A Way in the World*, Naipaul returns to his oft-repeated theme of the unrealistic ambitions of black radicals resulting from personal humiliations. The character of Lebrun, according to literary critic Bruce King, is C.L.R. James, a man misled by the hardly compatible combination of Marxist dreams and Black Nationalist urges.[24] It is no surprise, therefore, that in 2001 the director of the American studies program at New York University argued that C.L.R. James had attained a stature "now matched only by Du Bois."[25]

Predictably, as each person pursues the James of his or her choice, there have been occasional manipulations. In 1978, in a new edition of James's 1953 *Mariners, Renegades, and Castaways*, the editors left out the final chapter of the original.[26] One can readily understand that when James states in that final chapter that the book "is also a claim before the American people, the best claim I can put forward, that my desire to be a citizen is not selfish nor a frivolous one,"[27] it would grate on the sensibilities of the partisans, and they would decline to print that admission. Similarly, officials of James's estate refused to allow publication of one of his essays, "My Life with Women."[28] It was hardly a guarded secret that James liked women, and as Caryl Phillips of the *Guardian* wrote, he "freely indulged" in many affairs.[29] How sad that we cannot have James's own version of this crucial aspect of his life.

In 2010 two new volumes appeared on James reflecting his universal appeal and also reflecting the fact that each author conveys the James that suits either their intellectual or their political agendas. Andrew Smith, a Scottish sociologist, reproduces his own articles in several scholarly journals dealing with the sociology of sport, theory, and culture. This explains the particular focus of the book. He is explicit as to "his" James: "in what follows, I have acted as proponent for James."[30] It is the James of eclectic and independent intellectual disposition, of a peripatetic life, of a "supple, creative and humanist Marxism," the man with a "glint of utopianism" in much of what he wrote. But fundamentally, "'my' James is particularly the cricket-loving James."[31] Of course, Smith shares James's love of the game. Thus it is not surprising that absolutely the best parts of the book deal with both the macro-sociological and individual fine points of James's approach to the "style" of the game. James, says Smith, places a much more concerted emphasis on understanding the "specific intrinsic qualities of cultural practice than have most writers in the sociology of culture." For those not acquainted with the arcane ways of cricket, some of Smith's elaborate details will be hard to follow. On the other hand, true aficionados will relish Smith's forays into the rituals and forms of both cricket players and cricket audiences across continents. Those same aficionados, however, will be confused by the following assertion by Smith: while James does go beyond what most Marxists do, "James perhaps owes more of a debt here to Trotsky than he sometimes admitted: compare Trotsky 1991 [1925]."[32] For one not versed in Trotsky's approach to the sociology of culture, this is, to say the least, the kind of assertion which puts James in an enigmatic light and as such deserved more elaboration from Smith. There are other assertions in Smith's book that cannot go unchallenged. It is outrageous, for instance, for Smith to claim that James broke with Ghana's Kwame Nkrumah because Nkrumah "followed" Eric Williams's "path into autocracy and reaction."[33] This is taking the advocacy of James beyond the pale, distorting both Ghanaian and Trinidadian history.

Equally questionable is Smith's assertion of the oft-repeated story that James had the decisive part in the origination and virtual writing of Williams's doctoral thesis and later book, *Capitalism and Slavery*.[34] This claim cannot be substantiated. It was given some authority by Ken Boodhoo, who quotes a letter from James saying that he not only suggested the thesis but actually sat down and wrote what the dissertation should be.[35] There can be no denying that the James-Williams relationship was a mentor-student one going back to their days at Queen's Royal College in Trinidad. One has to exercise certain caution, however, in such claims made by James. He was positively, paternalistically possessive about his influence on those he considered his "pupils." In a long letter to Constance Webb (whom he calls "my most precious pupil" from whom he "expects even more than from Bill [Williams]"), he says the following about Williams (PhD Oxford) and also about Grace Lee (PhD Columbia) and Raya Dunayevskaya (economist): "Now I am as confident about you as I am about them and when I began with them, with every one, *they had no real idea of their own talents*."[36] Are we to believe that Dumayerskava, who was for years Leon Trotsky's secretary and translator, learned nothing from Trotsky?

It is, of course, true that Williams acknowledges on page 268 of *Capitalism and Slavery* that "the thesis advanced in this book is stated clearly and concisely and, as far as I know, for the first time in English on pages 38–41 of James's *Black Jacobins*." It is good that he specified "in English," since anyone who wishes to revisit those celebrated pages will notice that James introduces his theoretical framework with the words "This section is based on the work of Jaurès' *Histoire Socialiste de la Révolution Française.*"[37] Indeed, French socialist Jean Jaurès establishes the role of the capitalist *negrières* slavers in Nantes, Bordeaux, and Marseille and their self-serving advocacy of abolition in the British colonies. According to Jaurès, financial gain, not religion or humanitarian impulses, dictated their stance. Williams had made French history one of his fields of concentration, and he was fluent in French. It is no surprise, therefore, that he read and cited many of the French historians who followed Jaurès's historical materialist interpretations of the relationship between slavery and capitalism. Williams's conclusion that "what was characteristic of British capitalism was typical also of capitalism in France" follows logically from his readings.[38] Selwyn Ryan is only partly correct when he notes that despite the originality of Williams's contribution to this issue, "his book appeared at a time when the thesis was dominant, and he must have been influenced by the prevailing neo-Marxist discourse."[39] The thesis was dominant in France but hardly in England. Williams explains why this was so in several pointed and bitter passages in his autobiography, *Inward Hunger.* He recalls how even the Fabian Harold Laski was not well thought of at Oxford and how the most left-wing publisher in London would not consider his manuscript on *Capitalism and Slavery* because the materialist thesis was "contrary to the British tradition."[40]

These facts are crucial beyond the historiographical issue at hand. In England, or in the United States for that matter, history students would have had difficulty finding a Marxist tutor, much less a politically active one. In France, the Marxist and Socialist activists dominated the highest echelons of higher education, and Jaurès was their leader, their "tribune," according to H. Stuart Hughes.[41] Jaurès shaped a whole generation of socialist intellectuals who went on to dominate political life in France in the 1890s. He had attracted the best young scholars, including no less a figure than Émile Durkheim, to the "moral passion" of Marxism. This difference in educational structure and milieu explains in part why no Marxist socialist (as distinct from Fabian socialist) ever came to power in the English-speaking Caribbean. In the French Caribbean they not only held the highest departmental posts but they held them for very long periods. Aimé Césaire, as we shall see, is only the best known of these.

The second book on James published in 2010, the David Austin reader, is another which illustrates the search for a particular James. Austin's James is the James of what is generally called the "Walter Rodney" period, the period of Black Power–cum–Marxist Mobilization in Canada and the West Indies in the late 1960s. The "Rodney affair," that is, the banning by the Jamaican government of Walter Rodney, a professor of politics at the University of the West Indies (UWI), is judged by many to be a watershed event. He calls it "the key event stimulating the postwar renascence of Anglo-Caribbean radicalism." "Over the next few years," says Charles W. Mills, "black nationalist and, later, Marxist-Leninist groups would spring up in Jamaica and across the anglophone Caribbean, as people challenged the racial and class structures inherited from hundreds of years of colonialism."[42] Rodney's impact on the Caribbean radical Black Power movement is beyond dispute. What can be disputed is any claim that this was Marxist in ideology. In fact, Rodney exemplified the confusing counterpoint between race and the radical ideological currents at the time. A reading of Rodney's own account of the 1968 events and beyond reveals a crude racial perspective. He wrote, "If you are not white, then you are black." Notice how he defined the goals of the Black Power movement:

(1) the break with imperialism, which is historically white racist;

(2) the assumption of power by the black masses; and

(3) the cultural reconstruction of society in the image of the blacks.[43]

It is not clear what influence C.L.R. James—who was with Rodney in Montreal—had on his thinking. There is some evidence that James did not have much influence because he was a Marxist not at all given to what Marxists call "particularisms."

It is interesting that the David Austin reader of James's speeches in Canada during this critical period should be published by AK Press, self-admitted "anarchists," since neither James nor most of his many followers were any such thing. The volume's real value for Jamesian scholars is not just the up-to-now not available speeches and interviews James delivered in Canada in 1966, but the inclusion of an interesting exchange of letters between James, his ideological adherents, and the latter with each other. Together they provide an exceptional insight into the vivacity and excitement surrounding James that sustains the impulse and attraction his words had decades later. Again, there are gaps which future research will have to fill. One such is the possible role of James in the various radical movements that agitated the region in the 1970s, including the attempted coup d'état in Trinidad in 1970.[44]

Be that as it may, what one finds in the documents is the consistently radical but also consistently ideologically independent James. Perhaps the most revealing interview in terms of the thesis of modern-conservative societies is a 1962 interview in the *McGill Daily*, October 11–12, 1968, entitled "You Don't Play with Revolution." He was asked about the search for African roots:

> *James*: I don't know that people should go into African culture with the idea of bringing elements of the African culture to the West Indies and America. First of all, the West Indies and America are two very different places. America has a culture of its own. It has an attitude to the world—social, political, and otherwise. To bring African culture to that is quite a problem. I don't see it as something realistic. But what I think one can learn is a sense of nationalist politics. The West Indian is very backward in regard to that, and the African has no trouble in being an African nationalist. That, I believe, he can learn. But I don't know that that is a part of culture in the sense in which we are using the term.
>
> *Reporter* (asking about revolution): I would like to quote once more from your book *Party Politics in the West Indies*. You say here that "Political power, a dynamic population which knows its political power, a backward economy. That is a potentially explosive situation." And you have a footnote here which says, "Marxism equals 'communist' equals r-r-revolution. That is the fashionable logic. I am a Marxist, I have studied revolution for many years, and among other things you learn not to play with it." Could you elaborate on this?
>
> *James*: By the way, let me say that *I do not believe it will be easy for any autocratic regime to impose autocracy on the Caribbean population* (emphasis added). I say there are the two alternatives [a left-wing or a right-wing coup] and I would like to say the domination, the forced domination and submission of West Indians by an autocratic government would be very difficult. It would be wrong for me to go further, speculating as to what will happen . . . but I pose the two alternatives.[45]

Here is the peripatetic James, ranging brilliantly across a variety of topics but unwilling to be pulled along mindlessly by any of the ideological currents of the moment. To be sure, scholars and politicians will keep searching for "their" particular James, but as with Marx, beyond the opportunistic reading, there has to be ultimately the honest assessment: he was an intellectual who marched to his own drummer. That drummer beat two fundamental notes—tenets which no amount of historical rewriting, intellectual juggling, and vulgar hagiography can erase: James was categorically opposed to any form of state capitalism and opposed also to the idea that the revolutionary masses had necessarily to be led by a Stalinist "vanguard" party. James, in short, was a Marxist for the ages, not just the one we opportunistically find convenient for our present agenda.

Given that James was always an anti-Stalinist and never a member of any organization controlled from Moscow, it might be surprising to some that he sustained a close personal relationship with George Padmore, who was affiliated with Moscow most of his adult life. To those who knew both, there was nothing surprising about their friendship: the bond was their common birth in Trinidad, but they also supported the cause of the decolonization of Africa and the advancement of its multiple diasporas.

Born Malcolm Nurse in Tacarigua, Tunapuna, Trinidad, in 1908, Padmore attended secondary school on the island and migrated to the United States in 1922 to enroll at Fisk University, a traditionally black university in Tennessee. By then he probably was already imbued with radical ideological and racial inclinations—ideological because of his friendship with James, one of the island's earliest socialists, and racial because of his admiration for another Trinidadian, Henry Sylvester Williams, who had founded the African Association in London in 1897 and organized the First Pan-African Conference in 1900. Padmore always claimed that he was a nephew of Sylvester Williams.

At Fisk, he stood out for his articulate and well-versed knowledge of the main issues of race and colonialism. In 1926 he transferred to New York University and then to Howard University. The first of three active phases of his life began in 1927 when he joined the U.S. Communist Party (USCP). The United States had not yet recognized the Bolshevik government of the Soviet Union, and its activities in the United States were under constant surveillance. Especially spied on were the activities of the Communist International (Comintern), established in 1919. A study prepared by the U.S. War Department General Staff in 1919 stated that American "revolutionaries" were directed and controlled by the Communist Party of Russia through the Comintern. By 1920 the United States was in the grip of a Red Scare, "a state of collective hysteria."[46] It was no surprise, therefore, that Malcolm Nurse would adopt a nom de guerre, George Padmore.

He rose rapidly in the Party's ranks, and his articles in the USCP's *Daily Worker* brought him much visibility. In 1928 he was chosen to attend the Second Congress of the League Against Imperialism in Frankfurt, Germany. By that time he had been appointed head of the Negro Bureau of the Communist Trade Union International, the Profintern. This put him in close contact with the Comintern. As we already noted, James never had anything to do with this "church." Padmore, on the other hand, became its first black member. This fact is usually mentioned in the literature of the West Indies as just another stage in Padmore's political life. It was, but not "just another" stage. He was put to work on race issues in two societies where the Comintern had hit a stone wall, the United States and Great Britain.

Just as the Comintern made few advances in the United States, the British Communist Party never amounted to much electorally. However, the UK did have a non-Communist alternative promoting anti-imperialism and decolonization, Fabianism. The Fabian society, through its Colonial and International Bureau, did reach every corner of the Commonwealth. And its colonial policy, to which a young St. Lucian, W. Arthur Lewis, contributed greatly, appeared sufficiently radical for the times and for those conservative societies. This is how the official record of the society put the case: "It was the right of all peoples to benefit from the natural resources of their own territories, that colonial economies should not be geared to the profit of the white settlers and that . . . advance to self-government was only achieved by forcing the British Government's hand."[47] Among the politicians who read and "trusted" the Bureau's literature, of which Professor Harold Laski was one its leading lights, were Hastings Banda, Jomo Kenyatta, Norman Manley, and Nnamdi Azikiwi. Padmore would later describe Laski and American professor Ralph Bunche of Howard University as having the greatest influence on colonial students.[48] Certainly Michael Manley was influenced by Laski and Eric Williams by Bunche, who was his departmental chair at Howard.

Individuals in the Hispanic Caribbean, on the other hand, did come into closer, and often oppressive, contact with the Comintern. While the Monroe Doctrine did not apply to the English, French, and Dutch territories in the region, its application in the rest of the region more often than not meant landing the U.S. Marines. Consequently, it is not surprising that Comintern operators (usually coming from Mexico) operated with César Augusto Sandino in Nicaragua and with the Farabundo Martí peasant fighters in El Salvador and in Costa Rica where the Communist Party was legal.[49] In Venezuela, the oil industry had given rise to an industrial proletariat which the Comintern struggled mightily, but unsuccessfully, to control.[50]

This is the world George Padmore became part of when he was appointed Moscow's American and colonial specialist in the League Against Imperialism and for National Independence (LAI). As such, he did Moscow's bidding, for as James Hooker points out, Padmore was at all times "under party discipline." In one of his pamphlets written for the Comintern, *Negro Workers and the Imperialist War—Intervention in the Soviet Union,* Padmore ridiculed Marcus Garvey as "a decayed bombast," called Dr. W.E.B. Du Bois a "petty bourgeois Negro intellectual," and in general denigrated other "reformists" frowned upon by the Comintern. In 1931 he published his first book, *Life and Struggles of Negro Toilers.* It was a standard Marxist-Leninist approach to the black proletariat generally, but not yet to what he would later call "my people" in a strict racial sense.

To understand the dramatic nature of George Padmore's life as a member of the Communist International, you must understand something about Communist Party doctrine before Gorbachov: it was homogeneous, exclusive, and sacrosanct. "Marxism," says French political scientist Maurice Duverger, writing in the early 1960s, "is not only a political doctrine but a complete philosophy, a way of thinking, a spiritual cosmogony." It represented up to the mid-1980s a veritable "catechism" which, like a true religion, excludes all other systematic explanations of history. To cite Raymond Aron, a thinker Duverger calls "an intelligent conservative," "Iranian Shiites and Marxist-Leninists belong to the same family, since the Shiite clergy wants to rule over civil society as the Soviet Communist Party does."[51] After the October Revolution of 1917, it was the Bolshevik Party which enforced doctrinal obedience while Lenin created the Communist International (Comintern) to spread and defend the faith worldwide.

Additionally, some understanding of what the Comintern was and was supposed to do will go a long way in explaining why Padmore eventually broke with it. One who understood the operation of the Comintern was American diplomat George F. Kennan. He had accompanied the first U.S. ambassador to Moscow in 1933, served there as second secretary until 1937 (critical years in Stalin's operation of the Comintern), as minister counselor from 1944 to 1946, and finally as ambassador from 1952 to 1953. "The Comintern," he wrote, "was a highly disciplined and extremely serious organization, partly political, partly military, the purpose of which was revolution abroad."[52] Jane Degras, who edited the papers of the Third Comintern Congress (1921), quotes a Comintern directive in order to convey her opinion that it was a ruthless organization: The members were ordered "to keep alive in the minds of the proletariat the idea that at the time of insurrection it must not let itself be deluded by the enemy's appeals to its clemency. It will set up people's courts, and with proletarian justice settle accounts with the torturers of the proletariat. . . . We are the deadly enemies of bourgeois society. . . . It is the historical mission of the Communist International to be the gravedigger of bourgeois society." She notes the frequent use of terms like "iron discipline" and "uncontested authority" of the Soviet Communist Party and the advice that "Communist parties must proceed with periodic purges of their organizations to eliminate all members who are petit-bourgeois or have ulterior motives."[53]

Given the totalizing Marxist ontology of world history, both James and Padmore had to accept that eventually even the Caribbean would go Communist. To both it was an article of faith that it was only a matter of time before Communism would reign everywhere. The difference was that while James's Trotskyite adherence merely represented a loose alliance of similar believers in world revolution, Padmore had the Soviet State and Communist Party and the Comintern behind (and over) him. James was part of a loosely operating sect, whereas Padmore was a disciple and official of a vertically organized party with global ramifications. Neither approach appealed, however, to the small islands of the colonial Caribbean.

After the failure in the United States, the larger countries of the Greater Caribbean were being directed from Comintern headquarters in Mexico and financed by the Communist Party of the United States. Padmore operated out of London, where the task was to gain adherents in organized trade unions and among intellectuals, as a way of penetrating the British Labour Party and by extension the colonies.

Because Stalinism deliberately subordinated the interests of the Comintern to those of the USSR—making the USSR their spiritual fatherland—there were many rebellions among Third World followers. Anthony Cave Brown and Charles B. MacDonald quote American Whittaker Chambers as saying upon his own defection from Communism, "Nearly every Communist that breaks with the party, breaks over the question of Russia."[54] Padmore's break with Moscow came after the Comintern, following Stalin's Popular Front accommodation with the West, disbanded the anti-imperialist ITUG-NW in June 1934. Padmore's explanation of this action was published later in the journal *New Leader*. His words are worth citing at length because they explain the end of his first phase as a loyal party man and the beginning of the next and critical phase, the Pan-Africanist. Race trumped ideology in this phase. The Soviet government, he said, decided to "put a brake upon the anti-imperialist work of its affiliate sections and thereby sacrifice the young national liberation movement in Asia and Africa. This I considered to be *a betrayal of the fundamental interests of my people,* with which I could not identify myself. I therefore had no choice but to sever my connection with the Communist International" (emphasis added).[55]

Padmore appears to have taken his expulsion with extraordinary sangfroid. Normally an expulsion would be accompanied by accusations that the individual was a "Trotskyite," a "left-wing deviationist," and other vilifications. He got away lightly, "as my sin was merely petty bourgeois nationalist deviationist." With that, Padmore threw himself body and soul into the anticolonial movement, combining Black Nationalism, socialism, and Pan-Africanism and, as James Hooker notes, never joined another non-Negro organization. By 1935, back in London, he joined his old friend, James, who was directing the International Friends of Ethiopia, and together they launched the International African Service Bureau. Despite the heavy organizational burdens, Padmore began writing. In 1936, his second book, *How Britain Rules Africa,* was published in Switzerland in English and German. His third book, *Africa and World Peace,* was published in 1937 with a foreword by Sir Stafford Cripps, a Fabian. Clearly Padmore was relinquishing his old dogmatism and seeking allies for the anticolonial campaign, whatever their race or affiliations. His sights shifted to the West Indies and, together with W. Arthur Lewis he published *The West Indies Today.* He never returned to the islands; as far as we know, he was never invited.

His organizational efforts did not stop, however, and in 1945, together with F. Kwame Nkrumah and W.E.B. Du Bois, he organized the widely influential Fifth Pan-African Congress in Manchester, England. This was followed by his attendance at the World Trade Union Conference. Padmore edited the papers presented at what he called the first time in the history of international labor that colored colonial workers—"the most oppressed and exploited section of the world proletariat"—were given "the opportunity of voicing their grievances and of expressing their hopes." He repeated the principle that "Labour in the white skin cannot emancipate itself while Labour in the black skin is enslaved." These were not exactly Fanonian, Manichaean sentiments. Padmore's foreword to the collection of presentations indicated that his thinking had evolved from a narrow form of racial nationalism to one of international class solidarity and commitment to socialist development.

Padmore's interest in the process of decolonization led him to study experiences other than that of Britain. This explains his book *How Russia Transformed Her Colonial Empire*.[56] The book confirms Rupert Lewis's conclusion that Padmore—even after he broke with Moscow—was more than a Marxist interested in theory; he was a Leninist interested in what he believed Lenin had achieved and what decolonization was. The latter, he argued, was one of Lenin's great achievements. It also revealed that as involved as he was in a major decolonization battle, he could not allow himself to publicly criticize Soviet foreign policy. He never gave up his belief in the historical correctness of Marxism-Leninism. This was based on his lifelong belief that national and cultural independence among multiracial societies was possible only if a centralized, planned economy was put in place. On the other hand, since he was, according to Hooker, under no illusion about Stalin's imperialist actions in the Baltic states, Finland, and Poland, this indicated that he never seemed to come to grips with the essential contradiction in his defense of the Soviet Union and his absolute opposition to Stalinism. Where there was total consistency was in his determination to be an independent Marxist. His identity as a black man demanded this. Padmore's greatest objection was to being subordinate to any international movements not led by revolutionary blacks. His 1935 "Open Letter to Earl Browder," secretary general of the USCP, stands as testimony to this and predates Aimé Césaire's 1954 *Lettre à Maurice Thorez*. They both made the same point: black socialists would no longer be subordinate to Moscow. Césaire wrote to Thorez, secretary general of the French Communist Party, who, like Browder, was totally subject to the dictates of Moscow.

Unfettered by Comintern restrictions, Padmore's intellectual growth was revealed in a solid text of colonial analysis, *Africa: Britain's Third Empire*. The book covers an enormous swath of West African colonial history but reserves its most devastating and condemnatory words for the situation in South Africa. The analysis confirmed Padmore's admonition that "as a life-long Anti-Imperialist, I make no pretense (as is the fashion among imperialists writers on Colonies) to impartiality."[57] Despite these fighting words, and never abandoning his proselytizing for decolonization and socialist development, Padmore now sounded a more moderate note by calling for a more nuanced understanding of the complexities of decolonization. "Both Britons and

Africans," he wrote, "have much to share to their mutual advantage." After listing a series of British institutions worthy of emulation, he concluded by saying that the sterling qualities found among the British "are found among no other imperial race" and that once colonialism was dismantled, "nothing will stand in the way of genuine friendship and solidarity between Africa and Britain."[58] With such a moderate discourse he could have been confused for one of the anticolonial Fabians so demonized by the Marxist-Leninists.

Further evidence of his ideological evolution was his next and arguably most influential book, *Pan-Africanism or Communism?* which he finished in London in 1955 and which carried an important foreword by black American writer Richard Wright. It was an apt accompaniment, since Wright had left the U.S. Communist Party, disgusted by their attempts to use him and his angry black novels to advance the policies of the USSR. Later, Richard Crossman would include Wright's account of his disillusionment with Communism in an edited book, *The God That Failed*, containing similar accounts by luminaries such as André Gide, Ignacio Silone, Stephen Spender, Arthur Koestler, and Louis Fischer. Wright explained why true intellectuals could not abide by the authoritarian rules of the Soviet-dominated party, but in his case, as in the cases of Padmore and Aimé Césaire, it was even more difficult for a black intellectual to give up his freedom of thought. As if leaving a church, Wright vowed to "never again express such passionate hope . . . never again make so total a commitment of faith."[59] Padmore, however, still could not resolve his ever more acute ideological dilemma: he continued to believe that Marxist theory and especially Lenin's approach to colonial peoples was ontologically, theoretically, and practically on target. Later Marxists would not unravel his dilemma. In another case of literary ideological sleight of hand, Padmore's widely read *Pan-Africanism or Communism?* was republished after his passing in 1959, when it appeared as simply *Pan-Africanism* and included an introduction by Harvard professor Azinna Nwafor that did not seem to have much of a relationship with Padmore's last will that the decolonization process be democratic. Nwafor's words seemed rather to reflect the radical turn of the American Black Power movement in warning that the issue was not political independence but whether Africa will continue to exist in a "state of refurbished servitude" or whether it will definitively rise to break its chains of subjugation. This alone, Nwafor writes, "constitutes the real revolutionary alternative for the liberation of Africa. Measured in these terms, Pan-Africanism did not offer a revolutionary choice." Professor

Nwafor then ends dramatically—and, let it be said, in a non-Marxian fashion—by quoting Goethe: "He only earns his freedom and his life who takes them every day by storm."[60]

Padmore, who by the 1950s had taken a more conciliatory, even conservative, stance, was describing himself as "a socialist and democrat," and he had abandoned any revolutionary aspirations and goals. As the original title suggests, Padmore believed that aggressive black nationalism such as Pan-Africanism was the only antidote to Moscow-dominated Communism's spread in Africa. Communism and Pan-Africanism had similar developmental goals; they both advocated rapid industrialization and rural development. That said, the ultimate overall results would be different, since Pan-Africanism could "fulfill the socio-economic mission of Communism under a libertarian political system."[61] At a theoretical level, Padmore believed that at the national liberation stage, Africans might seek both their independence and the assertion of their national identity as Africans and blacks but also look "above the confines of class, race, tribe, and religion."[62] At the more practical level, however, he understood that tribalism "is a present menace," easily exploited by opportunistic politicians, and that there were cleavages which had "assumed a form of class conflict." The hope lay in the newly emancipated younger generation "with a detribalized outlook," and the ultimate goal had to be a federation of self-governing countries, a United States of Africa.[63]

Contrary to the attempts by those seeking to use Padmore to bolster the myth of a revolutionary-prone Caribbean, Padmore's final thoughts were about Africa, the fate of the black man, and the preference for a democratic anticolonial movement. Aside from his passionate promotion of black assertiveness everywhere, his final political thoughts were not dissimilar to those of the radical wing of the Fabian decolonization group. In fact, Fitzroy Baptiste believes that one of the reasons why the British political directorate was not alarmed by the Pan-Africanists' claims that they were implementing socialism was because it was not unlike the Fabian socialism in postwar Britain, that is, some state intervention in the public sectors in the domestic economy.[64] Because he was writing for intellectuals and about Africa, Padmore never received much attention in the Caribbean. Indeed, as distinct from James, Padmore never returned to the Caribbean. Nonetheless, his influence among decolonizing elites in Africa and the Caribbean cannot be doubted. His was, however, an antidote to Communism. As Rupert Lewis quite rightly said, because of Padmore's independent political stance and final ideas, there was hardly a Communist in Africa or the West Indies.[65]

Like James, Padmore would end his long crusade against colonialism and imperialism facing real disappointments. Just as James was received with distrust in Trinidad, so Padmore received the cold shoulder from the Ghanaian nationalists. Hooker says that there was "substantial Ghanaian opposition to his presence. He was West Indian and there were too many of them prominent in Accra."[66] Similarly, journalist Colin Legum reported that "there was never a time when there was no pressure on George Padmore to leave."[67] The Party, the civil service, the cabinet—they were all against him. He survived because of his steely determination to fulfill his and Nkrumah's Pan-African dream and Nkrumah's equally steadfast loyalty to his friend and mentor. Eventually, it was sickness and death in London in 1959 that tore him from his grand enterprise. On October 6, 1959, Nkrumah announced that "freedom fighters all over the continent of Africa are mourning the loss of Comrade George Padmore."[68]

By erasing—or rather purging—the final ideas of Padmore and much of James's opposition to racial revolution, Caribbean Marxist-Leninists contributed to the myth of a revolutionary Caribbean. The victory of the Castro forces in Cuba in 1959 nearly coincided with the rise of Black Power and radical student activism in the United States. As Black Power and revolutionary talk spread throughout the Caribbean, the international press began to describe the region in a sort of prerevolutionary ferment. Typical was the reporting of veteran UPS foreign correspondent Georgie Anne Geyer, repeatedly citing the secretary general of the Jamaican Communist Party, Trevor Munroe. She warned that if "in the next five years" the governments of the region do not improve the economic life of the masses, "Black Power may really become the 'revolution.'" Geyer noted that some of its "overzealous adherents" contend that it is already revolutionary.[69] Other stories expressing similar beliefs that the region was in a prerevolutionary phase appeared in the *New York Times* (November 9, 1969), the *Economist* (May 2, 1970), *Time* magazine (May 4, 1970), and the *Wall Street Journal* (December 22, 1970). Even local journalists, writing in hindsight, argued that "the period of 1970 and thereafter in Trinidad and Tobago and elsewhere was a revolutionary and historical one."[70]

It is true that the Black Power movement in 1970 in Trinidad can be considered revolutionary in the sense that the mass black social movement came close to overthrowing the government of Eric Williams.[71] Had the mutiny by part of the Defence Force succeeded, there would have been a military revolutionary regime of some sort in power. This probably would have been for a brief time. Without any known leadership, the multiple groups participating in the Black Power movement would most surely have disintegrated through in-fighting, and the Williams regime restored, probably with American, British, and Venezuelan intervention. The reasons why the mutiny failed were that the police and the coast guard, commanded by a retired British merchant marine captain, defeated the mutinied troops, and second, the Indo-Trinidadians and black and colored middle classes refused to join the movement. To these essentially conservative groups, the revolutionary movement was a university-led youth movement influenced by North American events and in no way representative of the broader society, not even the highly organized trade unions.

One of the tragic aftershocks of the Black Power movement was the rise of the National Union of Freedom Fighters (NUFF), which began an urban (*foco*) guerrilla movement. The leaders were all black middle-class university students, thought to total three hundred youths, only two dozen of whom were believed to be armed. Guy Harewood, son of the head of the Department of Statistics and the University of the West Indies (UWI), was their leader. His younger brother and a cousin joined him. From their proclamations and from their tactics, it seemed they were following the Brazilian Communist Carlos Marighella's *Minimanual of the Urban Guerrilla* as much as Ché Guevara's idea of the foco. The robbing of banks, the killing of policemen (for their guns), and the execution of suspected "spies and informants" within the group all followed Marighella's *Minimanual* dictates. Every one of these tactics caused repulsion in the society, resulting in the NUFF remaining in isolation and widely labeled as "bandits" for three years. It was soon evident that the many well written revolutionary proclamations were the work of a small group of professors at the University of the West Indies, St. Augustine.[72] One was Bernard Coard, whom we will encounter again in Grenada; another was the leader of a small Marxist party who eventually migrated to the United States to teach at an exclusive liberal arts college.

On October 8 and 9, 1973, I published two lengthy columns in the *Trinidad Guardian* arguing that the conditions which Ché Guevara and Fidel Castro confronted in Cuba and Marighella confronted in Brazil, that is, brutal military dictatorships, did not exist in Trinidad. Nor was there colonialism such as the atrocious French colonialism that Frantz Fanon confronted in Algeria. In sum, there was much to argue in favor of the existing system and much to argue against any type of "subjective" foco theory of revolution. Knowing through contacts that the remaining NUFF fighters in the hills were sick with dysentery and surrounded by a combined police-army commando force, I secured a promise of amnesty from the very popular Roman Catholic archbishop, Anthony Pantin, and the commander of the army, Joffre Serrette.[73] The police (who had lost three officers) refused to join in guaranteeing an amnesty.

Given the myth of revolutionary "preconditions" in the society, it was not surprising that a number of university faculty attacked my columns. It became the most extensive set of responses to a column in the *Trinidad Guardian* up to that time. Marxist-Leninist Michael Als (later to play a role in the Grenada debacle) wrote, "Dr. Maingot, like all bourgeois intellectuals, trembles before the might of the workers" (October 12). Lecturer Marcus Balintulo—in a response of considerable length peppered with references to Lenin, Che, and Marighella—concluded that "the Guerrillas are the spark that lights the fuse" and that Dr. Maingot's opinions carried no more weight than those of "any taxi-driver who cherishes the status quo" (October 18). Several others joined the fray, all justifying revolutionary action. On October 21, the other daily newspaper, *Trinidad Express*, published an editorial by Jeff Hackett, calling for an amnesty. It was too late. Ten days after the publication of my columns, on October 18, 1973, Guy Harewood and several others were killed. The "revolution" was dead. The toll was fourteen NUFF fighters killed, twelve wounded, and four executed as "informants" by their own comrades.

The myth of a revolutionary society was laid to rest in Trinidad, but six years later many of the comfortable Marxist-Leninists' proclamation writers would carry their attempt at a Marxist revolution to Grenada. Additionally, since rebellious instincts still lingered in the hearts of others, some of the participants in the 1970 Black Power movement later abandoned their Marxism and reappeared as Black Muslims in an attempted coup d'état in 1990. By a selective reading of Marxists such as C.L.R. James and George Padmore, they distorted their final positions and also distorted the nature of their society. It is sad that so many promising students had fallen for the siren's call of revolution.

8

What Type of Socialism?

Marxists and Social Democrats Vie for Leadership

In what is arguably the first major multi-island study of the new elites that took the British West Indies to independence, Wendell Bell and his team studied the critical decisions they made regarding nationhood.[1] Their conclusion was unequivocal.

> In fact, the new and near nations of the British West Indies may be particularly instructive in this regard, since they have managed so far to establish and maintain political democracies based on universal adult suffrage and public liberties while at the same time . . . succeeding in their attempts to grow economically at relatively rapid rates.[2]

Twenty years later, a Canadian political scientist whose proclivities toward socialism were hardly hidden was complimentary of the Jamaican social and political system. Noting that the island serves as a test case for the viability of a left-of-center social democratic program in a Third Word context, Michael Kaufman assessed the story of Jamaica as "a rich and exciting one." Jamaica, he said, is one of the comparatively few Third World countries that had a number of the preconditions often associated with a reform-oriented social democratic approach. Kaufman pointed to a functioning parliamentary system, a strong trade union movement, a history of state economic intervention, and a high degree of literacy by Third World standards.[3]

Why then did Jamaica of all the countries in the region have the most intense and often violent competition between a Marxist socialist and a democratic or Fabian socialist approach to governance? Three reasons can be adduced. First, in Michael Manley Jamaica had the most charismatic leader the region had ever seen. He had inherited the prestige of his less charismatic but intellectually accomplished father, Norman. Second, Manley's decision to shift to the left energized socialists in Jamaica and elsewhere in the Caribbean. Third, Jamaica had a small but sophisticated and engaged Marxist-Leninist movement with a long history of involvement in Jamaican, University of the West Indies (UWI), and trade union politics. Finally, both the charismatic leader and the Marxist-Leninist members of the movement believed that the "correlation" of forces in the Caribbean had tilted sharply left. The secretary general of the Workers Party of Jamaica (WPJ), Trevor Munroe, described the situation in 1977:

> In Cuba, a communist party holds state power; in Guyana, the ruling party declares its adherence to socialism and its openness to Marxism-Leninism; the opposition party is recognized by the world communist movement as a fraternal party; in Jamaica, for the first time in twenty-five years, ideological debate on "socialism," "capitalism," and "imperialism" is an important factor in national politics. General elections in the current period in a number of territories, for example in Trinidad and Grenada, bring to the fore questions of Socialism and Communism in political propaganda and agitation. Marxist-Leninist ideology is gaining influence among sections of the intelligentsia and communist political groups, and trends are taking shape in Jamaica, Barbados, St. Vincent, Grenada, and Trinidad.[4]

Despite his admirable academic credentials, including a Rhodes scholarship, Munroe's many monographs read more like political manuals than scholarly pieces. There are ample references to what Marx, Lenin, and especially Stalin recommended regarding the "National and Colonial Question." Especially relevant, said Munroe, citing Frank Hill, the historic mentor of Jamaican Marxist-Leninists, is Stalin's 1925 manual, *The Political Tasks of the University of the Peoples of the East.* Munroe was a lecturer at the UWI and when given the opportunity to revise the most used reader in politics, *Readings in Government and Politics in the West Indies,* in 1971, he made sure to include several readings on "the radical and revolutionary traditions." Very prominent was a reading by British Marxist Ralph Miliband, a severe critic of political pluralism who taught occasionally at UWI. Not surprisingly, several of the other essays by UWI staff also criticized the parliamentary system and rejected the idea that Jamaica had achieved true independence because it had not had a revolution. As an outspoken faculty member put it, the absence of a direct struggle against imperialist control and colonial rule meant that Jamaican independence was little more than the "symbolic manipulation and the myth of democracy." Real independence, he asserted, was to be found in Cuba and Tanzania.[5] A perusal of the literature produced by this theoretically and ideologically committed group at UWI reveals the formidable thrust of Marxist theory at the time. Nowhere is there evidence of a revisiting of the final phase of George Padmore's anticolonialism or other black intellectual breaks with Moscow, such as that of Aimé Césaire.

That said, the Left did not have it all their way. Traditional anticommunist *caudillismo* was already present and active. The closest any West Indian politician came to being the equivalent of a Latin American *caudillo* was the Jamaican Alexander Bustamante, known as Busta. Born Aleck Clarke, the tall, light-skinned young man grew up riding horses and having what his biographer George E. Eaton calls the "physical prowess and sporting skills" likely to endear him to his rural audiences. If any Jamaican politician could reap the fruits of Marcus Garvey's early political (and anticommunist) mobilization of the island's black populace, it was Busta. Even Munroe had to admit Busta's success when he noted that the anticommunist Bustamante with his Bustamante Industrial Trade Union (BITU) "was the genuine leader of the workers, [and] embodied their highest level of development at the time.[6] Similarly, Gordon K. Lewis, who considered Busta's anticommunism "sterile" and "a raucous and bogus radicalism" demonstrating "a colonial mentality," had to conclude that, up to independence and even beyond, "'Busta' seemed much more than his archrival [Norman Manley] to embody the self-image of the Jamaican populace."[7] Despite this assessment, Lewis, writing in the late 1960s, was neither the first nor the last to assume that regardless of Busta's popularity, working-class unity and a socialist ideology "were natural even logical and necessary conditions of the Jamaican and West Indian masses." That was the theory; the political reality was different. A two-party system was in its incipient stages, and Busta dominated one of the parties.

Is one to believe that Busta was a Jamaican re-creation of the Latin *caudillos*? No, he was a man who played by the rules of Jamaican colonial parliamentary politics. The incipient institutions of those rules were elections and political parties anchored in trade unions. In other words, they were colonial replicas of the British political system. By 1938, Busta was a fundamental part of the generation that engendered the nationalist spirit and class consciousness of the equally deeply religious Jamaican people.

The upshot of all this was that the history of Jamaican politics from that time up to the early 1970s was the history of the counterpoint between Bustamante's anticommunist populism and Norman Manley's intellectual socialism. "The Bustamante-Manley polarization," notes Rex Nettleford, "is seductive. The rival cousins, each with undoubtedly major talents, have provided an excellent scenario for the nation's political drama."[8] That scenario incorporated a solid two-party system that was based on a spoils and patronage network but that also harbored a propensity to violence.

In 1940, the People's National Party (PNP) proclaimed itself a socialist party. To Norman Manley at that time, socialism meant "a fundamental change . . . a demand for the complete change of the basic organization of the social and economic conditions under which we live."[9] Manley included in his definition the notion that "all means of production should in one form or the other come to be publicly owned and publicly controlled." Lest he be misunderstood by the largely socially conservative Jamaicans, Manley did add that "you are not being committed to revolution or to godlessness." Not surprisingly, a fundamental characteristic of Norman Manley's socialism was its foreign intellectual origins, which Nettleford tells us included the "exposure of a few bright self-made intellectuals to Fabian socialist thought then current in Britain. Sir Stafford Cripps of the British Labour Party's left and Golancz's Left Book Club publications were important intellectual and inspirational sources in the Jamaican genesis and adoption of the creed."[10]

Under attack from members of the colonial government, Norman Manley noted as early as 1940 that it was the socialisms of Norway, Sweden, Ireland, Denmark, New Zealand, Australia, and the British Labour Party that were the PNP's ideal. In the mid-1950s Manley wrote that he was a democratic socialist, which was "the essence of British socialism . . . and that is the socialism to which I subscribe."[11] This approach held a wide appeal for the educated middle class. They joined the PNP, as Wilmot Perkins notes, because it "appropriated not only the country's leading intellectuals and artists . . . but the very idea of intellectualism in politics."[12]

Norman Manley demonstrated his adherence to democratic parliamentary principles and his aversion to "alien" (that is, nondemocratic) ideologies in 1952, when he expelled some of his most important Left allies from the PNP on the grounds that they had formed a Marxist caucus within the party. Expelled from the executive committee of the PNP were Ken and Frank Hill, Richard Hart, and Arthur Henry—known as the "4 H's." Norman Manley's son, Michael, returned from England to head up a new union to counter these Marxist trade unionists. He became the head of the National Workers Union (NWU), the main labor base of the PNP up to today.

Yet Manley and the PNP were always vulnerable to opposition attacks on two grounds: race and the "foreign" origins of the party's philosophy. To the opposition the PNP was a party of socialist, middle-class "brown men." As George Eaton has noted: "Bustamante . . . elected to fight the PNP on the issue on which they were most vulnerable and one which they themselves had interjected, namely, ideology. . . . Socialism was equated with Communism and Communism meant tyranny and slavery. Besides, as the PNP was also the party of the urban middle classes . . . a PNP victory would mean tyranny and slavery."[13]

Bustamante's Jamaican Labour Party (JLP), founded in 1943, could never rival the PNP among the middle class in terms of the glamour of its following. The JLP, Wilmot Perkins maintained, was "repellent to the status-conscious "brown skinned intelligentsia."[14] With Bustamante's JLP successfully pushing an anticommunist populist line and the radicals within the PNP at bay, the latter party's commitment to socialism weakened over the years. Nonetheless, its ideological dependency did not. Only its economic program shifted: to the Puerto Rican model of development through "industrialization by invitation." Socialism would not be brought to the forefront again until the electoral victories of Norman's son, Michael Manley, in 1972 and 1976. The point is that even as Norman Manley moderated his socialist inclinations, Michael (whose early actions appeared quite conservative) was undergoing a very gradual ideological transformation.

In 1952 Michael Manley wrote that his own analysis of society had been "inhibited by the socialist doctrine which I had unquestioningly accepted," but that his trade union experiences added "a humanist and individualist focus concerned with the human equation within society as distinct from a more general and structural focus to be found in socialist doctrine." These words were penned after he had been exposed to socialist Harold Laski, his "most influential professor" at the London School of Economics. As late as 1972, after a massive electoral victory, Manley told an interviewer, "I totally distrust these cliché words like socialism, capitalism . . . methodologically I am a pragmatist."[15] This was very much the line of the whole generation which took the West Indies into independence. With the exception of Cuba and Guyana, there was little occurring in the Caribbean before 1970 to justify talk of a massive move to the left.

Despite the efforts of Marxist intellectuals to paint the entire West Indies as responding to similar pressures from a radicalized labor sector, the fact is that each island showed real idiosyncrasies in the relationships between labor, unionism, and political party formations. The Jamaican link between trade unionism and political party organization, for instance, was not replicated in Trinidad. There, the first significant socialist political organizer, Captain Andrew Cipriani, did not come onto the scene until after the First World War. Cipriani, a member of a white French Creole family, became president in 1919 of the moribund Trinidad Workingmen's Association, which within a decade under his leadership became the largest and best-organized labor-oriented political movement in the British West Indies. He affiliated the Association with the British Labour Party and the Labour and Socialist International, and made it a point to always be present at the Biennial Empire Conferences of the British Labour Party, "looking for your help and support."[16] Cipriani was a strong defender of parliamentary politics. He opposed violence as a strategy and was a devoted adherent of Roman Catholic strictures.

The next stage in the development of Trinidad's more activist labor movement came in the 1930s when a considerable rise in labor consciousness led to active trade union organization, trade unions having been legalized in 1932. But the 1932 ordinance made no provision for the right of peaceful picketing and gave unions no immunity against action in tort—both part of Great Britain's union legislation since 1906. The deep-rooted dependency of the Trinidad Left was again evidenced when Cipriani's Association, in protest, refused to register as a union, a decision taken on the advice of the International Department of the British Trade Union Congress.[17]

It is interesting to speculate on the consequences of Cipriani's decision not to register his party as a trade union. The 1930s were the period when the two most significant groups of workers in Trinidad—blacks in oil and Indians in sugar—were joining two newly registered unions, the Oilfield Workers' Trade Union (OWTU) and the All-Trinidad Sugar Estates and Factory Workers' Trade Union. When labor unrest escalated in 1937 and Cipriani opposed this escalation, power seemed to pass from his hands, and others grabbed the leadership of labor. One of these was Uriah Butler. Given the colonial structure of the government, Cipriani found that by entering the political arena he had cut off his room to maneuver. Part of Cipriani's problem, aside from his white, upper-middle-class background, was his dependency on British legalistic approaches to labor and his Roman Catholic–based opposition to the divorce bill, which was very popular among non-Catholics at the time. Butler had no such restrictions and could fit his methods to local needs, which involved mostly bread-and-butter issues but also racial ones—for instance, protesting the employment of white South Africans on the oil companies' staff.[18] Butler did energize politics, but totally lacking in any organizational talents or political ideology himself, he was unable to grasp the political opportunity the times presented, and leadership shifted to others less activist but more politically savvy.

The fall of Cipriani had major consequences for the future of political parties on the island. His attempt to emulate the British Labour Party's structure did not conform to the island's fast-changing economic scene driven by the modernization of the oil industry. By not converting the multiracial Trinidad Workingmen's Association into a legal union and making it a branch of his Labour Party, Cipriani paved the way for the effective separation of trade unionism from parliamentary politics and consolidated a conservative bent among the members which then divided on racial grounds. Labor in both oil and sugar expected its leaders to deal with bread-and-butter issues, no matter what the ideology of the union leadership. By 1956 this had permitted a totally pragmatic, nonideological politician named Eric Williams to organize and launch a racially based political party, the People's National Movement (PNM), with a link to the small Teachers Union, but without association with any other major union structure and leadership. This in turn permitted Williams to exclude from party membership any radicals whose outright loyalty he doubted. Given the Indian-black division in the society that had already crystallized, and given the relatively unorganized state of Indian political thought,[19] the black unions had no alternative but to support the predominantly black PNM, as did some Marxists (whose grounding in Marxist doctrine was not always a sure thing).[20]

The dramatic consequences of this separation of radical trade union leadership from the masses and from parliamentary politics can be seen in election results. In the 1956 general elections for the legislative council, the Marxist West Indian Independence Party (WIIP) contested only one of a possible twenty-four seats. Its candidate received 3.8 percent of the vote in that district. In 1961 the WIIP ran no candidates. In the 1966 parliamentary elections, the radical groups ran under the banner of the Workers and Farmers Party (WFP) and competed in thirty-five of the thirty-six constituencies. This radical Left alliance did not elect a single member; in fact, its total vote was 3.46 percent. Table 10 indicates how the most prominent Marxists in the WFP fared against the black PNM and the Indian Democratic Labour Party (DLP) in that 1966 election.

All these WFP candidates had long histories of direct or indirect ties with the labor movement and were a mix of black, Indian, colored, and white Trinidadians. They had strong personal ties with different parts of the island. George Weekes was an executive with the largely black Oil Field Workers Trade Union. Basdeo Panday was a leader and lawyer with the totally Indian sugar workers, and the others, especially C.L.R. James, were well-known and respected intellectuals. Jack Kelshall was a white Trinidad Marxist who had helped Cheddi Jagan in Guyana and his People's Progressive Party (PPP) adopt a Marxist philosophy. The Marxist message of this prominent radical group could not compete with the racial appeal of the PNM and the DLP. Their defeat in 1966, four years after independence and two decades after universal suffrage, was very clear proof of the fundamental societal conservativism and, consequently, weakness of the radical Left movement in Trinidad. Politics had already become a racial matter in which ideology played a minimal part. After two successive PNM governments, the number of declared Marxist-Leninists on the island had been reduced to insignificance.[21] Understanding the racial basis of politics and in keeping with a "critical support" program followed by other movements in the Caribbean at the time, a "popular front" of labor union–based radicals called the United Labour Force (ULF) competed in the 1975 elections. Led by the charismatic Basdeo Panday, the ULF won ten of the thirty-six

Table 10. Parliamentary elections in Trinidad, 1966

WFP candidate	Percentage of vote	PNM candidate (%)	DLP candidate (%)
Lennox Pierre	0.355	54.6	40.9
Eugene Joseph	0.891	88.9	4.5
C.L.R. James	2.8	53.8	40.8
George Weekes	4.9	28.06	51.2
Basdeo Panday	3.5	15.0	65.8
Stephen Maharaj	5.5	39.2	53.9
John Kelshall	1.2	49.9	46.2

Source: Report of the Parliamentary General Elections, 1966 (Trinidad, 1967).

seats—all in the predominantly Indian areas formerly controlled by the Indian-based DLP.

In early 1977 a group of Marxist-Leninists united in a semi-secret organization called the National Movement for the True Independence of Trinago (NAMOTI) attempted to carry out an anti-Panday coup within the ULF, thereby hoping to carry the membership of the major trade unions with them.[22] It soon became evident that this radical Left group had no mass support and even less unity. Soon a Maoist versus pro-Soviet split rendered them even less effective. Panday, who in early 1978 recaptured command of the party and who was himself an old ally of the Left, had occasion to reassess the political-ideological terrain and his own political chances: "These armchair ideologists," he told the press, "have no conception of how our people feel and think. They mislead themselves into believing that the working class cares what is happening in China, Cuba, and the Soviet Union, or that our people are ready to accept, lock stock and barrel these foreign systems."[23]

The significance of race and the ideological dependency of socialist organization, central to the political evolution of Trinidad, can also be seen in the case of Guyana (the former British Guiana). For example, the Marxist-Leninist leader Cheddi Jagan, who was educated in the United States, notes in his autobiography that the first thing he became very conscious of in the United States was the question of color, for him an entirely new experience. "I, too, had imbibed the psychology of fear which had gripped the U.S. Negro."[24] In the United States he married a young socialist, Janet Rosenberg, and adopted her more educated approach to Marxism-Leninism. Jagan's ideological maturing was completed through his travels to Trinidad in the 1950s to meet radical labor union and political leaders, of whom he writes, "These were some of the 'gods' I then worshipped." Indeed, one of his main advisors was Kelshall.

It was not until July 1969, however, that Jagan announced that his People's Progressive Party (PPP) was being reorganized along the lines of Communist parties of the Soviet bloc. (In June Jagan had attended the Moscow Conference of World Communist Parties and had formally enrolled the PPP in the Communist movement.) A purge of the internal opponents of that open identification with Moscow immediately began to take place—not the first such purge in the PPP's history. The split with Jagan's original political ally, Forbes Burnham, was an opportunistic move on Burnham's part. To hear Burnham tell it, it was Jagan's open affiliation with Moscow which led to the break: "We will not and cannot permit persons who consider an international reputation for being communists more important than the success of our struggle."[25]

Much more accurate a description of the ideological split is the analysis of Percy Hintzen, who found that Burnham understood the society better than Jagan. Despite all the talk of socialism, only ten Guyanese leaders (32 percent) were socialists; the rest were pro-capitalists. "In other words," says Hintzen, "they [socialists] were in ideological disagreement with all the major political parties in the country."[26] Almost all the powerful leaders were capitalists. Burnham knew he had to depend on the latter, at least during the early stages of his regime. Later, his continued stay in power was guaranteed by "absolute control of the electoral machinery and a resort to electoral fraud."[27] Burnham died in 1985. The PNC governed under Desmond Hoyt until Jagan returned to power in 1992 and governed without much Communist talk until his death in 1997. The radical phase in Guyanese history, like that of much of the Caribbean, had passed with the deaths of these leaders.

Surely this history of crude racially based political discourse and organization in Trinidad and Guyana and the failure of Marxists to transcend that political level was known in Jamaica where the intellectual level of party leaders was considerably more sophisticated. Contributing greatly to this was the presence of the UWI in Mona and the contributions of Michael Manley. Knowing of the failure of radical political mobilization in the rest of the Caribbean, why did Manley move so sharply to the left in the mid-1970s? Contemporary students of Jamaican politics are fortunate to have a record of this evolution through the many books authored by Manley or his speeches compiled by others. Other West Indian leaders left autobiographies (some prematurely penned), but there is no Caribbean, indeed even Latin American, equivalent of Michael Manley's written legacy. That legacy provides an excellent opportunity to trace the evolving political tussle between Communists and social democrats in Jamaica.

Manley's first full-length book was *The Politics of Change: A Jamaican Testament* (1974). By then he was prime minister, had had a successful career as the leader of the National Workers Union, had won a seat in the PNP "safe seat" constituency of Central Kingston, and upon his father's retirement in 1969 had been elected political leader of the PNP. He led the party to victory in the general elections of 1972. He wrote, he said, to clarify his own "ideals and principles" as well as to explore a new "philosophical road" for Jamaica.

He quickly dismissed several existing prescriptions for that road: "The anarchists, the racialists and the extremists of the radical left and intransigent
right have offered labels interspersed with fragments of advice. These prescriptions, however, have added up to something rather less than a viable
strategy."[28]

What followed was a thoughtful discussion of the options open to the
small, underdeveloped island. Unrestrained capitalism was discussed early
because, Manley noted, it involved so much exploitation. No further discussion of that option seemed necessary. On the other hand, Marxism came in
for a serious review and was found lacking. Marxist laws of the immutability
of capitalist development and eventual dénouement was wrong, said Manley,
because Marx had failed to see the "historical resilience" that characterized
capitalism and that lent itself to social and political reforms.[29] Manley then
confronted the advocates of the one-party state, arguing that they did not
understand Jamaican society and its "natural tendency" to be individualistic,
disputatious, and suspicious of any authority that cannot be changed. The
preference for settling disputes through a vote—the principle that "majority
must carry"—comes naturally to the Jamaican. A clearer description of the
conservative middle-class society could not be made. Manley then explained
the role of tradition and the paradox that democratic inclinations gestated
in an authoritarian colonial context. Democracy, he argued, resulted from a
long tradition of respecting traditions, even colonial ones:

> [It] is partly a consequence of all that we have learned during the colo-
> nial experience, partly a product of building society meetings stretch-
> ing back for over a hundred years in which men learned to set down
> and debate and argue and take a vote to decide; partly the influence
> of the Church, and partly the interaction of all these things upon each
> other.[30]

The parallel with British attitudes toward authority was clear. Even under
colonialism, said Manley, Jamaican attitudes "were designed in the shadow
of the Westminster model of democracy."[31] All this brings one to the conclusion, he said, that the one-party state was "unthinkable to the Jamaican."[32]

During these years Manley's speeches paralleled his writing.[33] To the
House of Representatives (November 20, 1974) he explained at length the
difference between Democratic Socialism and Communism. He would repeat the analysis on several other occasions, testament to the fact that from

its very inception the PNP had two ideologically opposed factions. Manley did not wait long before publishing another full-length book, *A Voice at the Workplace: Reflections on Colonialism and the Jamaican Worker*. Published in 1975 as a personal account, it carries an introduction by Carlyle Dunkley, a fellow officer of the PNP associated with the National Workers Union. It is an account of Manley's twenty years in the trade union movement, and its central focus is the interaction between class attitudes and the workers' movement. Manley began by admitting his intellectual debt to his father, Norman, and his professor at the London School of Economics, Harold Laski.

Manley wrote about the investigation into activities of the Marxist wing, already "simmering" by the time he returned to Jamaica. In 1951 the Marxists were expelled, and they left with their Trade Union Congress and formed a separate party, the National Labour Party (NLP). In response, the PNP launched the National Workers Union (NWU). Manley was now displaying a sharper criticism of capitalism, but still maintained a clear social democratic philosophy: it is not who owns the factors of production but how the worker is treated: "egalitarianism" was the ultimate goal, a "humanist and individualistic focus."[34] Again he confirmed his democratic credentials:

> I have been confirmed in the belief that the true objectives of socialism can only be achieved in terms of the most careful development of democratic processes for the management of both the political and the economic system.[35]

The most daring and controversial measures being taken at this time were the worker participation in ownership and decision making and some nationalizations. Fifty-one percent of Kaiser Bauxite Co. and Reynolds Mines and major public utility companies were nationalized. Manley was still speaking—and campaigning—on the moderate social democratic platform, which had been that of his famous father and the party.

All this changed as Manley swung sharply left in the mid-1970s. The question is why? Was it an aberration, or did those intense and dramatic years reflect a natural intellectual and political evolution and fruition of the "real" Michael Manley? How predictable was it that a politician steeped in pluralist parliamentary politics would suddenly take on dictators (Brezhnev, Castro, Bishop, and Burnham) as his closest—and most admired—international allies? How to explain that the politician who in 1954 had done battle with and then swept some of the most popular Marxist-Leninists out of his father's party, would in the 1970s allow the miniscule and unrepresentative Workers Party of Jamaica (WPJ) and its secretary general, Trevor Munroe, such influence in his own party and government? At a much more personal level, how does one explain that the man who was known to be a stern husband with his first three wives suddenly appears to be meekly supporting the extreme left-wing radicalism of wife number four, Beverley Manley?

It was during the elections of 1976 that Manley brought a radical ideology center stage. Part of that was accepting the offer of the WPJ and Trevor Munroe to campaign jointly. The membership of this party was calculated at one hundred but, as already noted, they did represent many faculty and university workers through their University and Allied Workers Union (UAWU). It could hardly be claimed that they contributed much to Manley's great electoral victory in the 1976 elections. Political mobilization momentum was building, and the voter turnout in 1976 was higher than in 1972. The decisive vote was taken as evidence that there has been "a fundamental realignment" in Jamaican politics. This, however, was a misreading of the nature of the island's electorate. Proof that there was nothing permanent and structural about this came in 1980 when the electorate turned out in even larger numbers and gave the JLP and its conservative leader, Edward Seaga, an even larger "mandate." Neither ideology nor race could explain such tectonic shifts. A plausible explanation for these swings points to the interaction between the Jamaican electorate and the intractable economy. Jamaican politics are about bread-and-butter issues, but since the economy had proven to be so consistently resistant to significant improvements in the general standard of living, votes tended to be used more as punishment of incumbents than support for particular ideologies.

There is a danger in assuming that all social conflict takes place along clear class lines and that these divisions are accurately reflected in the election results. In fact, as table 11 illustrates, in Jamaica both parties show a relative polyclass composition.

"Mandates" and "fundamental realignments" tend to be short term, certainly not more than four years, the span between islandwide elections. Manley seemed to have lost sight of this. The clearest path to an understanding of the divisions and constant civil strife during the 1976–89 period is contained in his book *Jamaica: Struggle in the Periphery*, written after his defeat in the 1980 elections. The very cover design foretells that this is an angry

Table 11. Cross-tabulation of social class and partisan preference, 1973

Social class	PNP (%)	Independent (%)	JLP (%)	Anti-Party (%)
Business	19	10	71	0
Professional	40	20	37	3
Small business	47	0	43	10
White collar	60	16	16	8
Self-employed artisan	59	13	14	14
Working/blue collar	48	12	29	11
Lower class	28	10	41	31

Source: Carl Stone, *Class, Race, and Political Behavior in Urban Jamaica* (Mona, Jamaica: University of the West Indies, 1973), 43.

Note: Figures for lower class total 110 percent in the original.

book: the presumably American eagle flies ferociously over the Caribbean. The factor on the dustjacket, half visible, half unseen, is U.S. power. Manley was unbowed, saying, "I write from the position of electoral defeat but not from the perspective of failure."[36]

In his book Manley analyses every major East-West geopolitical contest—Cuba, Nicaragua, Angola, Chile, Grenada—from what can only be called an anti-U.S. perspective. One has to wonder why little Jamaica, already engaged in confrontations with the U.S. bauxite companies, the IMF, political and gang-related violence, and myriad other domestic issues, should take on other fights. Did Manley truly believe that he could defy the United States and its long-standing and aggressively enforced spheres of influence in the Caribbean? Defying this geopolitical reality was only one of the three rationalizations described in the book about decisions which turned out to be politically costly. How does one explain the categorical posture: "As far as I am concerned, Cuba represents a non-negotiable point of principle about the kind of world in which we live."[37] After all, the U.S.-Cuba enmity dated to 1959, four years before Jamaica became independent, and independent Jamaica had lived with intractable geopolitical problems for thirteen years after independence. In addition, both parties in Jamaica had agreed to maintain cordial relations with socialist Cuba; the presence of thousands of Jamaicans, many of whom had been in Cuba for decades, made diplomatic ties a necessity. Then there was the question of feeble support for radical economics. The empirical evidence that the initial enthusiasm for a radical politics, especially widespread nationalizations, was waning had been presented by the island's foremost pollster, Carl Stone. Unlike some other Third World countries where the indigenous capitalist class was the target of popular hostility, this was not the case in Jamaica. "Policies of greater economic nationalism," said Stone, "can only be introduced by overriding the tremendous influence this sector exercises on both public opinion and middle stratum political leaders who head the multiple class coalition parties."[38]

The central issues in the heated 1980 campaign were not about either race or Caribbean geopolitics but about economics. And yet two other issues stood out because they figured prominently in the PNP's rhetoric even though they seemed to contribute so little to Manley's electoral strength: Manley's decision to accept the close collaboration with Jamaica's miniscule Communist Party, and his argument that adopting the "noncapitalist" path to development was an original Jamaican idea rather than the idea the USSR was recommending to Third World parties.[39] Additionally, the question was often raised as to what benefit was derived from such close relations with Cuba given the very deteriorated state of the Cuban economy? Seaga—who had none of the soaring speaking style of Manley—asked that question and described Jamaica's own economic problems with the clinical precision of a domestic accountant. Fundamental was Seaga's point that between 1972 and 1976, revenue increased only slightly from 19.4 percent of GDP to 21 percent due mainly to the new revenues from the bauxite levy (from U.S. $19.2 million in 1973 to U.S. $180 million in 1974). On the other hand, expenditures doubled from 21.4 percent to 41.2 percent of GDP. Economic growth plunged from positive 7.8 percent of GDP to negative 6.3 percent; in Seaga's words, it was "an unbelievable precipitous fall of 14.1 percent." These realities seemed to bolster the opposition's argument that Manley was more interested in distribution than production and growth.[40] There were no disclaimers or corrections of the data Seaga presented. There was only a claim that the economic downturn responded to a destabilization strategy by the United States.

There can be no doubt that the radical rhetoric and the new initiatives of the charismatic Manley gave radicalism a great boost in the region. Was that radicalism essential or even mildly beneficial to Jamaica's interests? And did it represent the will and wishes of the Jamaican people? In both cases, the answer is no. As Evelyn Huber Stephens and John D. Stephens, two American scholars very well disposed to Manley's search for a socialist path, noted: "The policies, the rhetoric, the Cuba relation and the deteriorating economy were tied together in the minds of many of the business people to whom we talked." Of these, it was the close relation with Cuba which was "the single most important factor in causing the rift with the U.S." The most damaging effect of Manley's rhetoric and especially his anti-Americanism was to alienate the local technical and moneyed bourgeoisie without winning votes from the masses: "More distance from Cuba and less rhetorical anti-Americanism would have had further favourable effects on the government's relationship to these classes, besides sparing Jamaica some of the effects of U.S. suspicion and hostility."[41]

If his government could not mobilize any particular resources in Jamaica, if, as Manley himself admitted, U.S. investments were not an obstacle to expansion of state initiatives (to which the U.S. government did not object), and if there was no real evidence that the United States was attempting to "destabilize" the Manley program, why pick a fight? Since the radical rhetoric seemed to have outpaced the radical practice, its results were especially counterproductive. Note the language of Manley's interview with Soviet journalist V. Veraikov republished in the *Daily Gleaner* (February 3, 1977): Manley vowed to "take Jamaica out of the British sphere of influence" and "hoped to be able to put to use the rich experiences of the USSR of building a new society." Cuba, he added, had given the whole Hemisphere "a marvelous example of how social and economic problems must be solved." The reaction was immediate and not at all timid. The *Daily Gleaner* (March 28, 1977) warned in a front page editorial that Manley "appears to be in the act of mortgaging us to the Soviet-Cuba communist expansion." This was exaggerated and alarmist but hardly surprising, given the overwrought radical rhetoric of the campaign.

The charge that was repeated by many during these years, that the United States had "destabilized" the regime in the same way it had done in Allende's Chile, was received with wide skepticism. Manley himself listed a series of events and concluded, "The events appear to be more consistent with an orchestrated plan to bring a society to the very verge of chaos and paralysis." He then defined the process as "destabilization."[42]

Because the newspaper most frequently targeted as a destabilizing agent was Jamaica's *Daily Gleaner*, it is all the more ironic that that newspaper was the most widely quoted source for both parties. Something must be said in commendation of a newspaper that was consistently labeled "reactionary" and "neocolonial right," but which still managed to provide factual stories to scholars of all ideological stripes. This was partly what led British scholar Anthony Payne, arguably one of the most perceptive students of Jamaican politics at the time, to recommend that Jamaicans ask the question, "What does destabilization mean?" Payne suggested distinguishing between a "broad" and a "narrower" definition. The broad definition involved awareness of the opposition of sectors who perceived their interests to be threatened. That opposition, says Payne, "should not be considered surprising or beyond the capacity of radical leader to anticipate." The narrower type, such as direct actions by the CIA in league with local interests, did seem, in Payne's opinion, to be involved. Given the margin of Manley's electoral victory, however, Payne concluded that it did not seem to have had much effect. What did take a toll on Manley's popularity ("beyond repair," according to Payne) was the decline of the Jamaican economy after 1976. "For this phenomenon," Payne concluded, "explanations have to be sought beyond destabilization."[43]

Even as they lambasted the *Daily Gleaner,* there were two journalists they could not, and did not, accuse of being CIA agents: John Hearne and Carl Stone. Hearne had been one of Manley's closest advisers and speechwriters, but he turned against him and the PNP on grounds that they had betrayed the ideals of democratic socialism. Stone, as already noted, was Jamaica's and the West Indies' most accurate pollster. His polls before the 1980 elections should have been the handwriting on the wall.

Other views in 1978 ran toward the moderate end of the scale. Even among the urban working class, the most radical in the sample, attitudes had moderated: only 19 percent favored government expropriation of land, and

Table 12. Social class and ideological position in Jamaica, 1978

Social class	Support for ideological principles, February 6, 1978 (%)			Views on increasing government ownership, January 30, 1978 (%)	
	Capitalism	Democratic socialism	Communism	Support	Oppose
Kingston middle class	45	25	3	27	73
Kingston working class	20	38	14	48	52
Small farmers	4	33	2	21	79

Sources: Dr. Carl Stone Poll, *Weekly Gleaner*, February 6, 1978, 1; Dr. Carl Stone Poll, *Weekly Gleaner*, January 30, 1978, 1.

Note: Percentages are of those with views on these ideologies.

only 12 percent saw the private sector as "exploiters" (though 48 percent saw it as "selfish").[44] Even more surprising was Carl Stone's finding that fully 63 percent of the urban working class disliked Trevor Munroe and 65 percent disliked D. K. Duncan, the two most visible radicals on the Jamaican political scene. Fully 42 percent of the small farmers could not even identify them.

And then came Stone's devastating analysis explaining Manley's evident political decline:

> Michael Manley's overwhelming popularity among the electorate in 1976 has dramatically declined while [the JLP] Hugh Shearer has emerged as the most popular leader in the country and Eddie Seaga as the man seen by the voters as most equipped to manage the affairs of the country in its present state of economic crisis. In 1976 the JLP was tarnished with an image of being a party provoking violence while the PNP had a very clean image in the minds of most voters. In 1980 both parties are seen as being involved in political violence, although voters had more fear of the PNP guns. In effect, the 1980 campaign is virtually a replay of the 1976 campaign. The real difference lies in the fact that the mood of most of the country has swung against the PNP primarily because of the deteriorating economic situation.[45]

PNP's attacks on Seaga, wrote Stone, were not hurting the JLP. Those voters who had shifted from the PNP were not voting for the JLP out of any love or fondness for Seaga but out of a sense of frustration. Their belief and hope was that Seaga could create a climate in which foreign and local business activity would recover and thereby create some jobs. Indeed, paradoxically, the PNP was aiding Seaga's credibility by labeling him as the man with powerful friends and connections in the United States and among overseas investors.

In a 1974 poll, Stone discovered that only 9 percent of a representative class and community sample admitted hostility or anger toward whites, and in an April 1978 poll of those Jamaicans who perceived conditions to be "getting worse" (84 percent in urban Kingston felt that way), 70 percent blamed "the government" first, whereas only 17 percent put the blame on "capitalists and political enemies of the government."[46] In January 1978, "governmental mismanagement" and "radical talk" consistently outpolled the "private sector" as the main culprits in the opinion of those who saw the situation as deteriorating.[47] Michael Manley's crowd appeal was no longer the force it had been in 1976. The rural people sensed that his confidence had been shattered and that the impact of the PNP's media arm, the Jamaican Broadcasting Corporation (JBC), was not very strong outside of the urban areas where it played an important role redefining the issues and discrediting the JLP.

To many sympathetic left-leaning foreign observers, the litmus test of Manley's socialist credentials was the divisive issue of whether Jamaica should accept the economic reform strictures of the International Monetary Fund (IMF) or not. After a description of the alignment of forces with the PNP, for instance, Darrell Levi explained Manley's final and agonized decision to go with the IMF by saying: "The goal of economic sovereignty and self-reliance was sacrificed on the IMF altar."[48]

Levi's explanations for many of the critical events during those years are essentially those given by the Jamaican and foreign Left, many of which have yet to be factually established. Such, for instance, was the case with the shift in President Jimmy Carter's attitude toward the Manley regime in mid-1980 from strong support to suspicion. Carter's change, said Levi, responded to "right-wing pressures," and it was these pressures which led Carter to use covert CIA activities to "destabilize" Manley, just as had occurred under President Richard Nixon in Allende's Chile.[49] However, Levi provided no examples of such destabilization actions.

By 1974 Carl Stone had already concluded that "in Jamaica there is neither a will to achieve the socialist alternative nor the necessary political supports to sustain it even if such a will existed."[50] By 1978 Jamaican elites had not defined the nature of the "socialist" system they were striving for. What was clear by 1978, however, was that the majority of people were in no mood for radical Left experiments in "scientific socialism," as the data in table 12 indicate. Surely such findings were not lost on the Jamaicans who, unlike the Guyanese and Trinidadians, did not vote race and consequently were capable of switching votes in subsequent elections. Again in contrast to Guyana, where both parties claimed to be socialist vanguard parties, Jamaicans had a choice between "democratic socialism" and the "nationalistic laissez-faire" of the JLP. That Jamaican parliamentary democracy survived the hectic 1976–80 period is in itself an accomplishment not to be minimized. Predictably, they would soon become restless with the meagre benefits derived from the JLP victory in 1980. Seaga's friendship with incoming president Ronald Reagan was not producing the expected rewards.

By Seaga's midterm, Jamaica's historically independent and disputative electorate was showing its discontent. With the 1989 elections looming, Manley launched a campaign characterized by modest language and moderate promises. Compared with the recent past, his platform contained little if any ideology and certainly not one word about "democratic socialism." It was as if 1973–80 had been an interlude in the life of a basically moderate and pragmatic politician. How his thinking had evolved is very evident in his last book, *Up the Down Escalator: Development and the International Economy.* Manley explains that the book was completed in 1980. However, there are citations well beyond that date. Manley now presented a sober and detailed analysis of the world's production and trading system in which Jamaica had to function. There was still fire in his pen regarding imperialism being the "root" of all the world's problems, but not necessarily of Jamaica's problems directly.[51] It was a quite different Manley who was now writing with the benefit of hindsight and having regained the friendship of many of his former American allies.

The story of the epic battle between social democracy and Marxism-Leninism in Jamaica would not be complete without relating what transpired after Manley dropped the left wing of his party and discontinued any ties with Trevor Munroe's Marxist-Leninist Workers Party of Jamaica. First, and predictably, came the fissures so frequent in Marxist-Leninist parties. On August 29, 1989, the *Weekly Gleaner* published the letter of resignation from the WPJ of a prominent member, Professor Don Robotham. Robotham claimed that the WPJ's Marxism-Leninism "is narrow and dictatorial and its organization forms require that individual members are subordinated, manipulated, and stifled." Padmore and Césaire, even C.L.R. James, would have concurred.

This break came two months after Munroe had led a party delegation to the USSR to observe the "restructuring" taking place there in the Communist Party. With Robotham and other dissidents out, Munroe was reelected unopposed as the WPJ's secretary general at the party's Fourth Party Congress, held September 11–13, 1989.[52] It was not all defeat. The WPJ-affiliated UAWU won the right to represent a sector of the sugar industry. The irony of this, however, was that it was upon appeal to that British Imperial Court, the Privy Council, that it got the green light to contest that leadership. Clearly, the usually disparaged but impartial "imperial" institutions still had a role to play in guaranteeing fairness.

Despite the secrecy surrounding internal party affairs, it is known that the dismal electoral performance of its first try as an independent political force (0.2 percent of the vote in the 1986 municipal elections) left the party membership further dispirited. Things had not been going well since the debacle in Grenada in October 1983 revealed that Munroe and other WPJ members were key advisors to the hardline Bernard Coard faction that destroyed the Maurice Bishop regime. That said, the most important reason for the almost complete invisibility of Munroe and the WPJ in the 1980s had to be the ideological metamorphosis of Michael Manley. Explaining his distancing from the Communists and the hard left wing of the PNP, Manley argued, "I think we have all grown a little older, a little wiser, a little more mellow with years."[53] He then added that he would not "rock the boat" or create any sudden ideological "lurches." Before a Miami audience of bankers and businesspeople, and later in an interview with this author, he was adamant: "We do not ever intend again to allow the relationship with Cuba to become internally divisive or a source of trouble with Washington."[54]

The propitious circumstances of the 1970s that gave Munroe and the WPJ much greater prominence than the party's size seemed to warrant had vanished. Jamaican Communists had to make do on their own merits. This explains why Munroe later explained that the party was now engaged in a "process of fairly 'profound rethinking'" of tactics and concepts. This was necessary, he admitted, "because there is no popular upsurge on the agenda."[55] He called for a new "humanism" in the party's agenda. Since it was not defined, it is unclear what that meant. What was clear was that his traditional attempt to combine appeals to both race and ideology had not changed. Munroe concluded that the interests of the Caribbean people and the interest—in fact, the "core"—of Marxism-Leninism as a revolutionary doctrine require that "we Caribbeanise, indeed, we 'blacken,' Marxism-Leninism to link with our people and for our people." As much as Munroe attempted to take the well-traveled path of a George Padmore and an Aimé Césaire, quite evidently he could not sustain that ideological posture in Jamaica. Neither his theory nor his understanding of the nature of Jamaican race relations received a positive response. Within a few years, Munroe had undergone another one of those Caribbean ideological transformations: he accepted appointment as an independent senator presenting himself with a most moderate discourse to that traditionally conservative body.

Even as the Jamaican electorate has moved beyond the turbulent 1970s, foreign Marxists have never reconciled themselves to the defeat of Manley's socialist project. As an author in the Marxist *Monthly Review* put it:

> Because he was socialist he instituted universal free education, but because he was democratic he did not prevent Jamaican college graduates and professionals from leaving the country.... Why did he not take the unemployed Kingston throngs, put machetes in their hands, and send them to the cane fields? Because he could not. He lacked the power.[56]

It might well be true that he "could" not. But there were two reasons other than that open-ended "could." First, Jamaica was not Cuba, nor was Manley Fidel Castro. As he told the *New York Times* (February 29, 1976), "[I am,] to my backbone, a democrat!" Second, he had to know his Jamaican and West Indian history, about which C.L.R. James, who did know about revolutions, warned:

> You may have a military dictatorship, you may have an autocratic regime, but a totalitarian, communistic kind of dictatorship or fascist dictatorship, that is most unlikely.... The domination, the forced domination and submission of West Indians by an autocratic government would be very difficult.[57]

Typically, the Marxist-Leninist clique in Grenada was not listening.

9

The Failure of Socialism and "Militarism" in Grenada, 1979–83

The idea that any state or city-state should be small in size and population dominated western philosophies of democracy for centuries. Aristotle went so far as to set the optimal size for a state as a place where the whole population could assemble to listen to a speaker. As Robert Dahl and Edward Tufte note, both Rousseau and Montesquieu argued that opportunities for citizen participation always vary inversely with size. "Equality, participation, effective control over government, political rationality, friendliness, and civic consensus all must decline as the population and the territory of the state increase."[1]

But there was a built-in dilemma in the preference for smallness: a state too small would always be in danger of subjugation by a larger state, and one too large tended to be destroyed by internal forces. Montesquieu resolved this by advocating the federation of small states. Later philosophers argued that the dilemma could be solved by instituting representative democracy. The founding and evolution of the American state was the first to prove that by federating, a representative republic could be established in a large country.[2]

Given that many outstanding studies have been done on the small islands of the Eastern Caribbean, it is good to understand that size in itself has neither ensured nor deprived them of democracy.[3] Be this as it may, small size is what persuaded political scientist Archie W. Singham to choose Grenada, the smallest of the islands in the Eastern Caribbean, as the site of a major study. Barely 120 square miles in area, the island had a population of less than 100,000.[4] Singham saw clear advantages in the study of such a small polity. First of all, the question of size or "scale," as he called it, is an important variable in political analysis, and in his opinion his study clearly demonstrates just where that importance lay. Second, Grenada, at least during the period under analysis (basically the decade 1951–62), embodied many of the problems found in the process of decolonization, which usually brings intense mobilization of native political forces and personages. Third, the reduced size of the polity enable these processes to be observed in their "functional whole"—in the relationship to the rest of the institutional and dynamic forces in the society.

Singham analyzed the context of the "total" system in terms of what he called the "colonial condition," essentially a state of social, economic, and psychological dependency, "a deep-rooted state of mind."[5] Having set the stage in time and space, Singham discussed the constitutional development of Grenada, leading up to a critical political and constitutional crisis in 1962 that forms the bulk of the book. Singham maintains that in Grenada political interests are aggregated and articulated not through a western-type political party structure but rather through the nearly symbiotic relationship between a "hero" and the "crowd." Total legitimacy is centered on one individual (the "hero"), making politics personalistic and thus dangerously prone to conflict—a danger from which, he makes clear, Grenada did not escape. In fact, an uneven conflict ensued when the flamboyant native politician—Eric Gairy, the "hero"—confronted the "rational" civil servant in Her Majesty's service, bound by tradition and duty. One consequence of this struggle between charisma and rational authority, according to Singham, was that by 1962 Grenada had lost many of its constitutional gains and, in terms of democratic governance, was behind other colonies of the Windward chain.

Gairy certainly was a hero to his largely rural followers, but to those he called "the upper brackets" he was a demagogue who terrorized his enemies. As Grenadian historian George Brizan explained, for twenty-eight years Gairy had used harsh tactics to become the arbiter of the political fortunes of Grenada. "The mere mention of his name conjured up for most people scenes of violence, arson, intimidation, and death."[6] Singham was fully aware of this dark dimension of Gairy's rule, so it is altogether puzzling why he argues that Gairy had only one path to power open to him. It is open to question, he says, whether Gairy could have developed a different political style, since both the social structure and the political system "encouraged demagoguery rather than genuine charismatic leadership." Singham's empirical findings do not support his theory of a hero ("genuine" or not) and a crowd. A crowd appears only occasionally on the scene, the predominant leader-follower relationship being described as one of "very weak links between the leaders and the masses."[7] What worked was terror for the enemies and patronage for the followers. Gairy succeeded easily enough in scaring off a few remaining resident plantation owners and then dividing the land among the so-called black planters. The traditional omnipotence of the employers of agricultural labor, says Brizan "was not only effectively challenged but broken."[8] As Patrick Emmanuel noted, Gairy's mobilization of the black workers also brought about the political displacement of the traditional political elite. By destroying the plantation system, Gairy had carried out a social and economic revolution, and these peasant landowners became strong financiers of his regime.[9] They were not his preferred social milieu, however, since he constantly strived to get admission to the social clubs of the remaining "upper bracket." Their rejection, says Singham, "rankled" him, but he pursued social mobility by learning to play tennis and speak with a "cultivated English accent."[10]

This point had already been made by Simon Rottenberg, who found that Gairy did achieve much for his black followers but that he also sought money and enhanced social status.[11] Rather than pursuing Frantz Fanon's *Peau Noir, Masques Blanc* line of analysis, however, Singham erroneously leans on Fanon's concept of the "colonial situation" in his *Wretched of the Earth* to explain Gairy's hatred of the urban brown skin class. This is a perplexing choice, since nowhere in Singham's description of Grenada's reality is there anything akin to the Algerian situation Fanon analyzed. It is evident that the myth of a colonial revolutionary situation in the Caribbean was very much alive at this time. Just as questionable is Singham's equating what he calls "the basic pathological nature" of West Indian society with George Balandier's Africa-based explanation of "personality types" characterized by "anomie, rage, compulsion and withdrawal" in a society where "hostility is always latent." The middle class, says Singham, are "anxiety-ridden" because they suffer from a "crisis of identity."[12]

Because Singham seems not to be able to find any redeeming qualities in any of Grenada's politicians (they are all, he says, engaged in superficial "pantomime" and "entertainment"), it is not surprising that he argues that it is all caused by a combination of the island's small size, the "colonial heritage," and the inherent inadequacy of the parliamentary, Westminster system.[13] In other words, Singham had dragged to Grenada the radical theoretical baggage already widespread in West Indian political and university circles. What system then did Singham believe adequate to a society of such a "pathological" nature? None is suggested by Singham. Writing in the mid-1960s, he did argue that the urban sector, perhaps more than the rural folk, also needed a hero, because their anxiety is more acute and this "makes them prone to identify with a hero-type leader who also emphasizes personal leadership, despite the lip service they pay to institutional or party leadership." In other words, Grenada needed a *caudillo* but of a different stripe (that is, class and ideology) than Gairy. Singham was prescient in anticipating the arrival of just such an educated *caudillo* just a few years later:

> In response to their peculiar needs, the middle-class hero stresses somewhat different qualities and goals than the mass hero. The former is apt to stress his education as qualifying him for leadership, and he often adopts the posture of the savior who has sacrificed his career and opportunities for this task. His ideology is usually populist; for him the rhetoric if not the content of Marxism or radical socialism fulfills a very useful role by enabling him to sustain the vicissitudes of politics in the lights of the sacrifices he has had to make.[14]

Singham could find no middle-class hero of this type "during the period with which we were concerned." Of course he had no way of knowing that one precisely of that type would emerge a decade later. His name was Maurice Bishop.

On March 13, 1979, Maurice Bishop went to the radio to announce that the New Jewel Movement (NJM) was now in complete control of the island. Not a single member of the NJM had been killed in the coup d'état, but four of Gairy's ninety troops had died, one accidentally. Bishop promised that "all democratic freedoms, including freedom of elections, religious and political opinion, will be fully restored to the people." How sincere was he? Not very if we are to believe the plans he had outlined two years earlier. The few in the English-speaking Caribbean who read Spanish would have read how Bishop had already explained to the Cuba weekly *Bohemia* that "our party began to develop along Marxist lines in 1974, when we began to study the theory of scientific socialism."[15] Given the attachment that Grenadians, like all West Indians, had to the parliamentary system and especially elections, Bishop was clearly holding his ideology and political designs close to his vest. In fact, it was not at all easy to discern exactly what the ideological underpinnings and political goals of the leaders of the Grenada Revolution were prior to 1979.

Maurice Bishop and his closest ally in the Eastern Caribbean, George

Odlum of St. Lucia, had initiated in 1978 a series of forums to discuss the changes they believed were necessary in the islands. It was later revealed that they had met secretly on Rat Island off St. Lucia to discuss their plans.[16] Odlum understood that "there is a certain Romance in the Cuban Revolution which appeals to the youth of the Caribbean" but that such sentiments needed proper leadership.[17] In other words, they spoke about freedom, civil rights, and honest elections, but did they ever intend to govern that way? Two books published before 1979 by key leaders of the revolution provide a window into their ideological proclivities that had little if anything to do with Westminster-style constitutionalism.

In the proceedings of a conference organized at the University of the West Indies (UWI) in 1974, two of the key ideologues of the 1979 coup and subsequent regime revealed some vital political thoughts. Political scientist Richard Jacobs was explicit in his concern that one of the things holding the revolutionaries within the NJM back from openly declaring for a Marxist regime was "the impact that a public commitment to socialism would have on the Grenada masses." Secrecy was of the essence because they needed to form coalitions with more conservative forces, that is, those seeking power through "traditional constitutionalist goals." Such a subterfuge, if held long, involved a risk to their ultimate goals, said Jacobs, because "in any event, such a coalition would encourage a movement towards pragmatism, and the socialist proposals of the NJM would be among the first causalities."[18] Jacob's paper was followed by a rambling presentation by Bernard Coard, who would play a key (and ultimately nefarious) role in the PRG and its denouement. According to Coard, "All of these Caribbean developments are basically reformist and survival oriented that is, 'neocolonialist. . . . ' Unless a radical restructuring of the internal economic and political structures is undertaken, linked with Third World–wide action to do the same . . . political independence will remain a dream yet to be realized."[19]

It took the independent pen of another UWI lecturer, Carl Parris, to point out that Coard, in his long reiteration and criticism of Caribbean "constitutionalism," never broached the issue of actually bringing socialism to power. Parris argued that given the nature of the society they described themselves, Coard had "begged the question." Under what conditions can such a socialist regime be installed, and more important, how can it be maintained?[20] No answer was forthcoming, of course, since the true agenda of the Grenada revolutionaries was not yet to be revealed. As one of the commentators on the conference, I reminded the various authors that "a moral state can never be built on immoral acts." My commentary addressed the presentation by Archie Singham, who recommended the study of the Chinese, Russian, and Vietnamese use of class-based analysis "and then in turn to see to what extent that analysis can be applied to the Caribbean."[21]

Two years later, Richard Jacobs edited the transcripts of the trial for sedition of Trinidad labor leader Uriah Butler. The book was not so much a biography of the perplexingly complex Butler but a trashing of the reputation of Fabian socialist Capt. Arthur "Tattoo" Cipriani, calling him insidiously and erroneously "a cocoa planter and a race horse owner" and a servant of the upper classes. There was the usual blending of race and class analyses, so that Cipriani is described as "a Caucasian (white) liberally infused with humanitarian ideas" that only served to "confuse the mind of the colonized." He was a "reformer," not a "revolutionary." Beyond that, Jacobs shows his hand when he concludes that the politics of constitutionalists such as Cipriani, Albert Gomes, and Eric Williams demonstrates "that in colonial and neo-colonial situations, the cards are so heavily stacked against the proletariat that only efficient organization backed by a revolutionary ideology could usher in the final victory." This, of course, is what occurred in 1979, after which their full agenda became clear, including the plans to build a major airport.[22]

In the *Bohemia* interview mentioned above—again, fully two years before the coup—Bishop repeated the NJM's opposition to a supposed U.S. and World Bank offer to build a new airport, arguing counterintuitively that it could be used militarily by Cuba's enemies because "its importance for the military circles in the Pentagon is also obvious given Grenada's strategic position in the Caribbean and on the routes to Africa and Europe."[23] He also repeated his opposition to tourism as a corrupting force that made such an airport a luxury. Both the conservative Grenada National Party (GNP) and Gairy's Grenada United Labour Party (GULP) had advocated building the airport, but the Bishop-Coard NJM's Manifesto was categorical in its opposition. Because the NJM emphasized agriculture, they opposed the typical Third World emphasis on what they called "prestige dream" projects and declared, "We are not in favour of building an international airport at this time. The present airport is more than adequate for our needs." Besides, such an airport would encourage tourism, "always a corrupting" force. This was in keeping with the 1978 report of the World Bank that warned against overly ambitious airport construction projects in the smaller islands.[24] Evidently, Bishop and his NJM colleagues had not been fully candid.

After taking power in 1979, Bishop revealed that he had had a conversation with Fidel Castro about the airport at the Nonaligned Conference in August 1979 and again at the UN meeting in October 1979. Bishop argued on March 29, 1981, that a new airport was needed and that it had long been "a dream" of Grenadian governments and people. He explained that they had raised the issue with just about every country and donor organization, including the U.S. government itself, "but met with little prospective feedback." The airport, he said, was needed to bring "all this tourism development," even though the hotels had not yet been built. Only Castro had offered to build it, but even with that, Bishop explained that it was "clear from the outset that our fraternal friends in Cuba could help only in certain fields within their possibilities." He then added that when the promised aid started arriving in November 1979, all Grenadians were sure that "our ancient dream of our own international airport was at long last on its way to reality."[25]

Cuban heavy equipment arrived, and some five hundred Cuban workers began building that airport. Two questions immediately come to mind. First, Maurice Bishop maintained:

> Our hospitals are without medicines, sheets, pillowcases, and proper equipment. Our schools are falling down. Most of our rural villages are in urgent need of water, electricity, health clinics, and decent housing. Half of the people in our country who are able to and would like to work are unable to find jobs. Four out of every five women are forced to stay at home or scrunt for a meagre existence.[26]

So why go ahead and undertake the largest project in the nation's history as well as think of establishing your own airline? There were no hotels, roads, or other infrastructure in place, and as far as the argument that an airport would help with the island's exports, Grenada's exports of spices, cacao, and mainly bananas amounted to $13 million, but Grenada imported over $32 million worth of food and goods. Second, it defies any geopolitical logic that in the context of the Cold War, the U.S.-Cuba antagonisms, and the history of U.S. imperialistic actions in the Caribbean, you could continually voice anti-American rhetoric asserting which side you were on in that Cold War and not expect retaliation of some sort. It is an ideological stretch to argue that by not acceding to requests for funds to finish the airport, the United States was retaliating, much less that it was engaged in a "destabilization" campaign in the sense that the U.S. embargo on Cuba truly was. Having chosen sides in a Cold War context, it was illusory to expect U.S. assistance. As British political scientist Tony Thorndike noted, "The acceptance of Cuban arms and military advisers—which by mid-1979 the People's Revolutionary Government (PRG) did not conceal—placed Grenada fairly and squarely into the developing post-détente new Cold War between the Superpowers."[27]

How the existence of such a large and expensive airport would integrate into and stimulate the economy was never specifically spelled out. There were, however, many grand promises made, such as the statement by Deputy Prime Minister and Minister of Finance Bernard Coard during the presentation of the 1982 Budget and National Plan:

> Let us think about our own International Airport . . . with it will come a massive growth in the riches of our country, . . . more schools, more hospital beds, more and better roads, more chances to export . . . more tourists, more direct communication outside our island to plant us even more firmly in the mainstream of world events.[28]

Given the economic realities on the island, these were idle promises camouflaging the cost of the airport. A look at the allocation of the budget for capital expenditure of $67.83 million is illustrative: airport—$38.7 million; agriculture—$8.749 million; communications—$11.293 million; industrial development—$0.5 million; and health—$0.4 million.[29] Even with the most generous help from Cuba, it was soon evident that this grand airport project was absorbing the greatest share of Grenada's budget.

It was not necessary to be an antisocialist to realize that the official renderings of their economic plans were unrealistic. Note the critiques of Marxist economist Jay R. Mandle. First, the NJM elite had to know that the airport was a project whose feasibility was entirely dependent on foreign assistance. Second, there was "a profound paradox for a leftist government like the PRG to be promoting tourism." Finally, Mandle raises the ideological-cum-geopolitical point that since it would be American tourists that they hoped to attract, which would require a U.S.-Grenada air treaty, the airport-tourism strategy "would have strengthened the American bargaining position."[30] Since the airport would be economically viable over the medium to longer term only if the North American market was secured, there had to be a slow realization by the Central Committee "that anti-American sloganizing was counterproductive."[31]

The airport project also took up much of Bishop's time, and there were costs to this. He spent an enormous amount of time traveling, seeking funds for the building of the airport. There can be little doubt that one of the greatest costs to the revolution was Bishop's absence not just from party/government work but from his contacts with the masses. He was the only one with something of the aura of the "hero" Singham wrote about. What was occurring, in fact, was that the overwhelming costs in budget and time of building this monumental project were causing some real strain. Not even much island labor was hired, since the Cubans brought their own workers. Given how the new NJM leadership described their society, it is evident that the monies for such a project, as Mandle says, had to come from abroad, and it is clear that at least Bishop knew ahead of time that more than Cuban workers and machinery would be needed. Bishop explained:

> It was certain from the beginning that we would still need assistance to complete: (1) the runway—a section needing much oil and asphalt; (2) the terminal and tower complexes; (3) the communications and navigational equipment; (4) the additional infrastructure in terms of roads, electricity, pipe-borne water, etc.; and (5) of course, the new hotels that we would need to get built rapidly to ensure that we had a sufficiently large capacity to accommodate the greater number of tourists. . . . In addition, it was clear that considerable sums of money would be needed to complete the project. This year alone, for example, we will need U.S. $32 million to keep the project going forward on schedule.[32]

Meanwhile Bishop and his colleagues had to consolidate the power they had gained, not through an election, which could have given them a measure of popular support, but through a coup d'état. None of this was lost on the Reagan administration's over-the-top "national security" strategy and Cold War rhetoric. Highly respected Caribbean scholars wrote and lectured on the influence of such rhetoric on a supposed militarization of the Caribbean.[33] Adding to this was the position of Gordon K. Lewis, who argued that once history showed that the imperial dogs of war had been unleashed in the Caribbean, they were there to stay.

It is an interesting fact that in none of the literature alleging the "militarization" of the Caribbean are either Cuba or the PRG of Grenada cited as "militaristic." Also absent is any attempt at defining "militarism." Drawing on the classical literature on militarism,[34] one can accept Alfred Vagts's distinction between a military project and militarism proper.[35] As such, one must conclude that of all the islands Cuba was by 1970 the most militarized and, in the Eastern Caribbean, Grenada was the one where the tendency of the PRG government was toward increasing militarism. Indeed, the militarization in Grenada began from the regime's very inception. Bishop himself began using military garb, complete with a pistol strapped to his waist. Within one month of his coming to power and without any internal opposition of significance, Cuba had supplied the PRG with 1,000 infantry weapons and 36 artillery pieces and the necessary advisors. As the captured documents revealed, Grenada received 2,000 military uniforms from Nicaragua, and a "top secret" document revealed that in 1980 the USSR was to deliver, free-of-charge, the following: 12 mortars, 24 antitank grenade launchers, 54 machine guns, 1,000 submachine guns, and 18 antiaircraft guns. Another top secret agreement was signed in Havana on February 9, 1981, calling for shipments between 1981 and 1983 of 8 armored personnel carriers, 2 armored reconnaissance vehicles, 1,000 submachine guns, and 12,600 complete sets of uniforms for an army of 6,300 men.[36] A third top secret agreement was concluded in Moscow on July 27, 1982, which promised that between 1982 and 1985, the USSR would deliver, shipped through Cuba, 50 armored personnel carriers, 60 mortars, 30 antitank guns, 50 portable rocket launchers, and 2,000 submachine guns, plus a long list of equipment for intelligence operations for the Ministry of the Interior. Grenadians were being trained in the USSR and Cuba, and Soviet trainers were to be housed in Grenada. There was also technical assistance from East Germany, Bulgaria, North Korea, Czechoslovakia, and Vietnam. Although the U.S. invasion in October 1983 interrupted the delivery of many of these weapons, U.S. forces nevertheless recovered enough weapons to equip an army of 10,000 men. The army under the Gairy regime had been 100-man strong, similar in fact to all the other islands in the Eastern Caribbean.

The PRG leadership's description of the society contained in the "Line of March" memorandum is the most revealing of all the secret documents captured by the invading U.S. Marines.[37] Because of the repeated use of the first person singular *I*, it appeared written by one person and, given the straight-forward Marxist language about "historical stages" and the assertions such as "only the working class can build socialism," it was probably written by Maurice Bishop. Bishop argued consistently for putting the party on, as three sympathetic English scholars put it, "a firm Leninist footing . . . adapted to that of the Soviet Communist Party."[38] Given Bishop's description of Grenada's basically conservative society, one has to wonder how, other than through militarizing it, this could be achieved. As Bishop explained:

> What we have in Grenada primarily, of course, is a very large petit bourgeoisie, particularly a large peasantry—the rural petit bourgeoisie—small farmers who own small means of production and who must therefore work as they cannot live off their own plot of land alone. Some of them employ labour; some do not. . . . Then there is the urban petit bourgeoisie in terms of shopkeepers, garage owners, craftsmen, small restaurant owners, and such like.

Bishop noted that such a petit bourgeoisie, because fooled and deluded by bourgeois ideology and propaganda, "have bourgeois aspirations." Therefore, the struggle to win this petit bourgeoisie involves "a very serious intense struggle." And, then, the vital question:

> The question we must now pose, comrades, is whether a society such as ours with their primitiveness, with so little infrastructure, with so little development of productive forces, with such a small working class can really build socialism.[39]

No evident answer was given in the "Line of March" document. It does tell us, however, that the claim by the Jacob brothers, two key NJM ideologues, that the revolution had overthrown a "capitalist economy" was nothing short of ludicrous.[40] Even the so-called land reform the PRG was promising had little to do with the existing peasantry. In fact, the peasants were not even allowed membership in the party. The reasons were three. First, the majority of the peasants had received their land from the Gairy regime's campaign against the larger landowners and were therefore owners and independent farmers, not a "working class." Second, Bernard Coard believed that 2,500 unemployed youth ("the reserve army of labour," he called them) should be placed on large-scale cooperatives and state farms.[41] Finally, when you consider that at its highest, the Party had only three hundred full members, you realize that they were applying Lenin's dictum: "better fewer, but better." This led to widespread dissatisfaction. Jamaican scholar Charles W. Mills interviewed a number of former NJM members who were disaffected and essentially in exile in Toronto. They described Bernard Coard and the leadership as intellectually arrogant and elitist, ignoring popular sentiments and opinions. Even people who had long fought Eric Gairy's regime were ignored in favor of those coming from abroad speaking the language of Marxism-Leninism. All decisions were made without any public consultation.[42]

The clearest evidence that the beautiful egalitarian vision of those who took over Grenada on March 13, 1979, was set aside and had become militarized came in June 1981. A group of twenty-six Grenadians, including Alistair Hughes, who had bitterly attacked the previous Gairy regime without retribution, put out a mimeographed newspaper called the *Grenadian Voice*. In the absence of any opposition parties, they editorialized, it was important to have an independent source that would praise or criticize the revolutionary regime as need be. This was the last issue of the *Voice*. People's Law No. 18 of June 19, 1980, made sure of that.

This is not the place for a full history of the evolution and then disintegration of the revolutionary leadership. That story is told competently elsewhere.[43] Here we describe the fall of the PRG. The first real sign that a succession battle typical of Marxist-Leninist parties was unfolding was when Deputy Prime Minister Bernard Coard resigned from the Central Committee (CC) in June 1983 and went to live on one of the Grenada Grenadine islands. Coard was known to control a somewhat secret "cell" within the New Jewel Movement, the military-civilian Marxist discussion group called the Organization for Educational Advancement and Research. His military man in that group was Grenada's ambassador to Cuba, Major Leon Cornwall, who returned to Grenada just in time to play a key role in the events that ended in the execution on October 19, 1983, of Prime Minister Bishop and four of his closest NJM associates. It was Cornwall who had emerged on October 15 to announce that while "the party" recognized Bishop's contributions during the past ten years, "our process as it develops is becoming more complex," making changes necessary so as to fundamentally "strengthen the work of the Party and the Revolution." The honeymoon period, he intoned, was over because the masses were "deeply frustrated."[44] Commander Edward Layne, another military man, was even more alarmist:

The situation is that the revolution now faces the greatest danger since 1979. There is great dispiritedness and dissatisfaction among the people. . . . The state of the party at present is the lowest it has ever been. The international prestige of the party and revolution is compromised, e.g., the CC delegation visit to the S.U. . . . The party is crumbling, all mass organizations are to the ground. . . . The CC is on a path to right opportunism.[45]

Finally on the third day of such deliberations, Coard appeared at the meeting, but Bishop was absent. Arguing that there were two trends in the CC—petit bourgeois Revolutionary Democratic and Marxist-Leninist—he warned that "within six months the party will disintegrate totally unless a fundamental package of measures are done." The die was cast. Bishop, Coard's allies demanded, had to submit to the leadership of "true" Marxist-Leninist revolutionaries or resign from the CC. Events led to a dramatic sequence: Bishop was arrested, the "crowd" gathered to liberate their "hero," but Bishop and his closest allies (and his pregnant girlfriend) were taken up to Fort Rupert and executed. U.S. president Ronald Reagan ordered the military to undertake Operation Urgent Fury on the pretext that American students at the St. Georges Medical School were in danger of being taken hostage.[46]

The militarists came out in full force after Bishop's murder. The Revolutionary Military Council that took power was composed totally of army officers loyal to Coard. They immediately announced a "shoot-to-kill" curfew. How that clique would have governed Grenada will never be known because the United States intervened four days later. What is evident is that armed to the teeth and with no organized opposition, they would have governed the way Phyllis Coard is said to have constantly recommended, with "manners," a Jamaican word for strict and uncompromising rule. Some inkling of what was in store for Grenadians could be gleaned from the very first laws the regime began to implement. George Brizan, an original member of the NJM, who left after studying the trend toward dictatorship, describes People's Laws No. 17 and 21:

People's Laws No. 17 and 21 provided for the establishment of Preventive Detention. Under this law the Minister of National Security could order the detention of anyone whom he had reason to believe and was satisfied may act in a manner prejudicial to public safety or public order or defence of Grenada or with a view to subverting or otherwise sabotaging the PRG. Persons detained under this law would be allowed no bail; the writ of habeas corpus would not lie in the case of any person denied bail by or under this law, and the Supreme Court under any rule of law or other authority had no jurisdiction to grant such bail. No such detention could be called into question in any court.[47]

The tragedy of the Grenadian Utopian dreams and the fate of the airport has led to several puzzles. There is no mystery or surprise in the actions of the Reagan administration which, as Fidel Castro said, Coard and his small group "served the United States, on a silver platter, ideal conditions for the invasion of Grenada." Without this, said Castro, there would have been no invasion. In an interview with Castro, former U.S. congressman (born in Trinidad) Mervyn Dymally asked one of the key questions about the Cuban response to the whole affair: "Given your close relationship with Maurice Bishop . . . why did you not know about the intrigue that went on while Bishop was out of the country? Where did Cuban intelligence break down?"[48]

Castro responded by making several points. First, Cubans do not spy on a country with which they have a relation of friendship. But was "spying" necessary? Strange, indeed, that many in the small island, and in fact in much of the region, knew what was going on, but not the Cubans? With Cuban "internationalists" working in agriculture, education, the army, "and even in the Ministry of the Interior," it defies credibility that Cuba was in the dark. In fact, at the CC meeting of September 15, Grenada's ambassador to Cuba, Commander Cornwall, asked the CC to "address the Cuban Ambassador's problems . . . because of the problems we face . . . because they already know the problems . . . if not they will see us as jokers." Castro admitted to Elliot and Dymally that after his last visit to Cuba, "Bishop went to our embassy in Grenada and explained that there were problems. . . . He said he feared . . . that they might even attempt to assassinate him."[49]

On October 15, 1983, Castro sent a letter to the Central Committee of the NJM. He referred to "certain references" from members of the PRG to the Cuban ambassador that there was the "supposed notion" that Bishop in his recent visit to Cuba had informed him of the problems inside the Party. "This," wrote Castro, "is a miserable piece of slander. We are indignant at the very thought that some of you would have considered us capable of meddling in any way in the internal questions of your Party. We are people of principle, not vulgar schemers or adventurers." Castro did try to prevent the assassination of Bishop through a phone call to General Austin, the military leader, just prior to the execution. On October 19, he lamented Bishop's death and then sent 150 to 200 army troops under the command of Col. Pedro Tortoló Comas to reinforce the Cuban construction contingent. Their orders were to take no offensive action, only to defend themselves if attacked. Because Cubans were all barracked at the airport, and that is where the first U.S. paratroopers landed, combat was highly likely.

Was the airport at Point Salinas primarily for Soviet-Cuban use, as the Reagan administration claimed? Mark Falcoff records that the notebook of a Central Committee member explicitly notes the "airport to be used by Cuban and Soviet military" and that the British Special Branch reported that the workers in Point Salinas regarded "the Cubans as building a military base."[50] That it could have a military function—of course; that it was built specifically for that purpose—not yet proven.

What caused Bishop to make such a major change of plans, calling the airport "an ancient dream" of his and of his comrades? Given his stout programmatic (and ideological) opposition to the airport and tourism, is it not more probable that it was Fidel Castro, not Bishop, who raised the issue of the airport? It was already revealed that Cuban planes were using first Barbados and then Guyana as refueling stations on the way to supplying Cuban troops in Angola. An airport in the Eastern Caribbean beyond U.S. interference was certainly a welcome option. The enormity of the Cuban expenditure in capital and labor weigh against the widely accepted interpretation that this was done as an act of "fraternal" solidarity. Cuba moved nearly 400,000 troops in and out of Angola between 1975 and 1991, keeping some 50,000 men, 150 planes and helicopters, and 1,200 tanks there at any given time. Just the logistics of this 10,000 kilometers supply line was a monumental, even heroic— and successful—military operation. Cubans were also fighting in the other Portuguese colonies of Mozambique, Ginea-Bissau, and the Cape Verde Islands and had a substantial mission in Nicaragua. As Cuban general Gustavo Chui, in charge of logistics, explained, the old turbo-prop Britannias used in the airlift flew in three legs: Cuba, Guyana, and Sal Island off the coast of West Africa before reaching Luanda, Angola. "We put the entire country behind the effort," recalls Chui.[51] Further information on the logistical problem was provided by General de Brigada Juan Escalona Reguera answering a journalist's questions. When asked why they flew to Guyana, the general replied, "When they stopped us from using the airport in Barbados, Fidel sent us to ask the president of Guyana, Forbes Burnham, for authorization to land our planes there—with the wounded and without arms." Burnham said, "Tell Fidel that I will provide the airport. Everything else is his problem."[52] It would appear that the Cubans needed an airport they could control and the Grenadians provided it. That said, did the Grenadians generally approve of the Cubans building their airport? The polls are clear. Fully 93.9 percent believed that by building the airport, Cuba had helped Grenada. In 2009 the airport was renamed the "Maurice Bishop International Airport," and relations with Cuba were again on a normal course. So were relations with the United States, whose military intervention had been supported by large numbers.

Was the military intervention legal under international law? Probably not. It was, however, supported by the majority of the American people. Similarly, the request by the Organization of Eastern Caribbean States (OECS) for a military intervention was of doubtful legality in terms of the OECS, UN, or OAS charters. And yet, in these deeply law-abiding states, which for nearly five years respected Grenada's right to shape its own destiny, the intervention enjoyed wide support.[53] When polled, 89 percent reported that they wanted the United States "to save them from Coard." The people's reasons are a complex blend of revulsion at the brutal murders and a sense of communal solidarity with those believed to be oppressed. There are an estimated 120,000 Grenadians living in Trinidad; is it any surprise that their concerns were also the concerns of the rest of the Grenadian population? Finally, University of the West Indies pollsters found that the biggest objection their respondents had to the PRG regime was "not holding elections" (70.1 percent felt that way). Contrary to Singham's dismissal of pluralist elections and the NJM's claim that parliamentary elections represented "5-minute democ-

Table 13. Feelings about the landing of American troops

Response	Number	Percentage
Favorable	340	88.1
Unfavorable	42	10.9
Mixed	4	1.0
Total	386	100.0

Source: Patrick Emmanuel, Farley Brathwaite, and Endine Barriteau, *Political Change and Public Opinion in Grenada, 1979–1984*, Occasional Paper no. 19 (Cave Hill, Barbados: Institute of Social and Economic Research, 1986), 44.

racy," Grenadians, like all West Indians, want and respect the vote. There had been eight general elections in Grenada between 1951 and 1971 with turnouts as high as 82.6 percent in 1972 and as low as 53.0 percent in 1961, for an average voter turnout of 70.1 percent. Such enthusiasm for the right to vote was and is evident in the rest of the Eastern Caribbean.

What then, is to be made of the claim by so many academics that the United States had "militarized" the place? Was there, post-1983, an atmosphere of militarism and, as Gordon K. Lewis maintained, a continued "imperial" presence? Because bare statistics seldom probe the nature of modern-conservative societies, I decided to do basic field research on the first post-invasion election in 1984.[54]

St. David's was the parish to study for that election. A traditional stronghold for the party of former prime minister Eric Gairy (GULP), the constituency seat was held by his wife, Cynthia. The area was also the birthplace of the Joint Effort for Welfare, Education, and Liberation (JEWEL), later to join Maurice Bishop's Movement for the Assemblies of the People—to become the New Jewel Movement (NJM) and later the People's Revolutionary Government (PRG). It is a most beautiful and agriculturally productive part of Grenada, a series of valleys rich in cultivations of cocoa, coffee, bananas, and spice trees, the mainstays of the island's important small peasant farmers. With 5,341 registered voters, it was the largest constituency. Tony Buxo, the island's only optometrist as well as its only graduate from Britain's Sandhurst Military Academy, was legitimately worried about how his party, the New National Party (NNP), would do there.[55]

A coalition of one old and two recently formed parties, the NNP was hammered together on Union Island under pressure from the prime ministers of Barbados, Tom Adams, Dominica's Eugenia Charles, and St. Vincent's "Son" Mitchell. The United States was delighted with the outcome, having invested money and prestige in a bring-out-the-vote campaign and in making sure the NNP's Herbert Blaize was adequately funded. But the United States was not the only outside influence. Eric Gairy, returned from exile, was also receiving strong support from Grenadians based in Trinidad. In addition, the Maurice Bishop Patriotic Movement was also competing and receiving assistance from friends in the United States, England, and allegedly Libya. Grenada, it appeared, had not stopped being an object of international concern. And yet, after the Eric Gairy revolution of the 1950s and 1960s which politicized the peasantry, and the New Jewel Movement's four and a half years of revolution which politicized the urban youth and the middle classes, no one in the know would predict that outside forces would determine the outcome of this first election since 1976.

Buxo—who himself had helped organize a telephone campaign to force the NNP merger—was not sitting still; on the eve of voting day he wished to test the mood of St. David's parish for the NNP and its candidate, Dan Williams. In one of those strokes of theatrical genius that makes West Indian elections such spectacular affairs, Buxo appropriated his daughter's doll-house and strapped it to the roof of his car. The house became the new symbol of the NNP. Gairy's GULP star was quite well known, and the Maurice Bishop Patriotic Movement's airplane was an obvious allusion to the airport, which the Cubans had built for the murdered ex-prime minister. These then were the competing symbols of this new effort to get pluralist politics back on track after a decade of Gairy misrule and nearly half a decade of Bishop's "socialist" and militaristic monologue. After some hours of meandering through the villages of St. David, Buxo decided that the majority of reactions had been decidedly in favor of "de house." While Buxo was tallying reactions, I was attempting to gauge the mood. What was the atmosphere like? Was it militarized? Not in any way.

Maybe the real challenge would not be either Gairy's GULP or the MBPM, but rather disinterest reflected in a high voter absentee rate. After all, every report since the October 1983 invasion had highlighted the fact that Grenadians wanted as little to do with politics as possible. Our tour through St. David's, however, showed that the mood had changed dramatically. The enthusiasm for the star, for the plane, but especially for the house was conveyed with such energy that it soon became enveloping and contagious. At least the people of St. David were showing as spontaneous a collective joy as I had witnessed anywhere in the Caribbean. Buxo's unique polling had been a smashing success; it gave him something quantifiable about the general mood and presented me with the first lesson I would bring away from Grenada: the people's political instincts and interests in free elections had survived the multiple tragedies of their young history. It confirmed what Grenadian social scientist Beverly Steele wrote before the PRG regime held on to power: "The Grenadian is obsessed with politics; he lives for political discussion, excludes most other topics from conversation, and politics is one of the only things he can get excited about."[56] Previous elections in Dominica, St. Kitts, St. Lucia, and Tobago and the subsequent election in Belize showed that Caribbean Man and Woman love politics and the opportunity to vote periodically for the party of their choice. It is their basic conception of what political rights—their citizenship—are all about. In the more or less contemporaneous elections in St. Vincent, 89 percent of the electorate turned out despite torrential rains and tropical squalls. That Grenada gave every evidence of coming close to that performance was made evident with force that same evening.

Expecting a motorcade of perhaps a dozen or so vehicles, we had discussed whether the two of us, both light-skinned West Indians, should join in; would this contribute to the accusation of both the GULP and the MBPM that the NNP was a "bourgeois" party? Was the Gairy and the Bishop-Coard inspiration in the Black Power Movement still alive? We decided that the morning's experience with the dollhouse made our presence not only possible but, indeed, desirable. And so I learned Lesson No. 2: except in Guyana and Trinidad with their Afro-Indo divide, West Indian racial (or better, color) tension, always latent, tends to recede dramatically during periods that require collective, democratic participation. Elections, like carnivals, sporting events, or religious processions, seem to bring out that intrinsic sense of humanity and fellowship which makes West Indian social relations so unique. But this lesson contains its antipodes: that same fellowship can turn into raw hatred and anger in the face of the people's collective sense of moral outrage or indignation. It had built up against Eric Gairy and against Bernard Coard.

Happily, this was not the mood in St. David, so we drove toward the caravan, and it was a sight. Snaking its way through St. David's magnificent valleys was a line of vehicles of every conceivable type, jammed with Grenadians of every conceivable color singing to the beat of their especially composed calypso, "Dan Is the Man in the Van," for the NNP candidate, Dan Williams. Beating on bottles, pans, and car doors, the caravan wound its way like a giant "jump up" (the West Indian version of the Cuban conga line) to the screams of delight from clusters of humanity in every village they passed. By the time it reached the meeting place—a typical crossroads where traditionally Caribbean peasant meets urban man—a large assembled crowd of all ages was already "jamming" (a mutual erotic rotation of the hips) to the tune of a popular Trinidad Indian-imitating calypso, "Kuchibadbach," which the earthy Grenadians had translated in sexual terms. And then, as if by well-practiced synchronization, a voice called them to open the meeting with the

Lord's Prayer, the calypso went off the air, and the crowds settled down to pray in unison. That religious note set the tone for the rest of the meeting: no more hatred and violence, no more jails, no more killings; Grenadians were to behave as the big Christian family they had been before, with not a trace of militarized police in evidence.

Lesson No. 3 stared me starkly in the face: Caribbean politics can be described as a counterpoint between conservatism and the rebellion against virtually all constraints: the interplay between deep-rooted respect for religion and its corresponding themes of family, the Christian rearing of children and respect for one's elders, and an explosive—even nihilistic—"do-as-you-damn-well-please" syndrome of attitudes. After all, weren't most of these young people only yesterday raising clenched fists and shouting, "Power to the People!" Who, one might ask, are the "real" Grenadians? No answer is possible because the question is not quite relevant. Once you take into account differences in style, expression, and presentation of self, all people have the capacity and the tendency to shift moods and loyalties. The difference is that democracy, by defending the right to be different, invariably seems more unruly or chaotic than the disciplined order of institutionalized "revolution."

It is precisely this flexibility which disproves absolutely the Marxist theory of social change. Societies, that is, social classes, do not move inexorably forward through an increasing social conflict, nor is it a question of Lenin's "Two steps forward, one step back." It can be forward or backwards, sideways—all movements quite unpredictable—unless, of course, there is a straitjacket of the militarized police state. That fortunately was not Grenada and St. David's in 1984. There was no censuring of films, limiting freedom of movement, or recruiting "armies of production" for regular militia. Those had been the facts which contributed as much as the deteriorating economic situation to the division and then self-destruction of the PRG. In St. David's Dan Williams received 60.5 percent of the 87.7 percent who turned out to vote; Gairy's GULP candidate received 37 percent, and the late Bishop's MBPM candidate, 2.3 percent. And the story was repeated in all but one of the fifteen constituencies.

It is a fascinating comment on the irony of politics in general that it is precisely the four and a half years of New Jewel Movement rule which generated this political awakening. Virtually all the leaders on the present political scene had been victimized by the "revolution": Gairy and Winston Whyte on the right, Blaize, Alexis, and Brizan in the center, and even those stout Bishop loyalists, Radix and George Louison on the left. Grenada's apparent commitment to parliamentary pluralism, to freedom, is probably more authentic than most, based as it is on bitter experience with militarism and an authoritarian Marxist-Leninist theory. Thanks to the Cubans and some American money, Grenadians had their airport, and also had, thanks to the U.S. Marines, the removal of the militarists, which allowed free elections. The Marines did not have to teach Grenadians about electoral politics, since Grenadians already had this ingrained in their political culture; they merely made it possible for an unarmed people to exercise this cherished tradition.

Because every Caribbean island has dreamed of having an international airport, the paths to achieving that dream have been many and often involved much political sagacity. We have seen how Cold War geopolitics and Cuban logistical needs resulted in Grenada having an international airport. But prior to this, François Duvalier of Haiti voted for the expulsion of Cuba at the Organization of American States (OAS) meeting in Punta del Este in exchange for an American-built airport in his country,[57] and Dominica's prime minister (1985), Patrick John, made the building of an airport a major condition in his negotiations with a U.S.-based cartel interested in creating an island-within-an-island of casinos and other illicit offshore activities. In order to achieve their goals, they had to overthrow the elected government of Eugenia Charles. In a courageous act of civilian rule, Charles had disbanded the Defence Force and relied on the Dominican Police and the U.S. Federal Bureau of Investigation (FBI) to uncover and arrest the band of mercenaries John and his cartel friends had contracted before they left from Louisiana. Contrary to stories of Charles's militarization because of a potential threat from revolutionary Grenada, Charles had rejected an American offer to participate in a very much larger security force based in Barbados and the other islands. "If they have a new army [in Dominica]," she told the press, "it will not be in my time."[58]

Demilitarized, and having rejected the Mafia option, Dominica still does not have an international airport.

10

Transcending Race

Self-Interest and Self-Determination in the Non-Independent Territories

Two of the persistent myths in the Caribbean are that the region contains many colonies and, following from that, that many of the racially based social and economic conflicts in the region have had as goals not just decolonization but movements toward independence and socialism.

It is not difficult to understand where the idea that independence is the necessary prerequisite to development came from. Waves of decolonization in the post–World War II period made this virtually axiomatic. "Seek ye first the political Kingdom," intoned Ghana's Kwame Nkrumah, "and all things else shall be added unto you."[1] Such was the urgency of self-rule that little thought was given to latent and unforeseen consequences. Again, Nkrumah describes his choice: "We prefer self-government with danger than servitude with tranquility." This was the typical stance of those nationalists who sought posthaste sovereignty for their states. By sovereignty they meant the quality of having supreme (or ultimate) independent authority in their territory. They rejected outright the colonialism that enforced the hegemonic principle that "the strong do what they want and can, and the weak put up with what they must."

This decolonization movement also reached the Caribbean, where up to 1961 there were (with the exception of the briefly independent Federation of the West Indies) only three sovereign countries: Cuba, Haiti, and the Dominican Republic. Even after the movements toward independence in the British West Indies, several territories remained—with a variety of constitutional arrangements—not independent. This has led to the belief that the Caribbean is a region of colonies, governed by conservative elites subordinate and subservient to Metropolitan dictates. This is an enormously mistaken view. What exists in the twenty-first-century Caribbean are territories that have democratically decided not to break the Metropolitan tie, elites who understand that in a globalized world, their small territories have little to gain from political independence. Indeed, they perceive many a vulnerability in outright independence. If Nkrumah chose risking "self-government with danger" over a condition of tranquility, many Caribbean elites have freely chosen tranquility. As Luís Muñoz Marín put it:

> I learned among the simple people the nationalist concept does not exist, because in its place there is a deep understanding of freedom. I learned that in their wisdom they prefer *if they have to choose* one who governs respectfully from a distance to one who governs despotically from nearby.[2]

Muñoz was not deciding this in an authoritarian fashion; he had submitted the idea of a Free Associated State with the United States to a referendum. It carried with 373,554 votes in favor, 82,777 against. Political scientist Rupert Emerson believed in 1960 that Puerto Rico was the only case in the Third World where rational planning for the future overcame hasty moves toward independence.[3] Events in the Caribbean have shown that there were many other such cases. In fact, in much of the Caribbean, decolonization has been interpreted as being the freedom to decide independently what political-constitutional status is desirable. In both the British and Dutch cases particularly, say two Dutch scholars, "Caribbean obstruction successfully blocked the effort to accomplish a full retreat [from colonialism]."[4] "Victory" was defined not by the successful storming of the colonial barricades but by the successful stymieing of European desires and efforts to sever the colonial bonds that were regarded as expensive and psychologically unrewarding. Of the four major colonial powers in the region, only the French were ever consistently determined to hold on to their former colonies regardless of cost. The French islands became, and still are, transfer economies, that is, costly parts of the French nation. After the failure of their scheme of a West Indian Federation, the British managed to push the major islands overboard, while keeping a few "British Overseas Territories," two of which, Bermuda and the Caymans, were already self-supporting, just as the British Virgin Islands and Turks and Caicos soon would be. The Americans, who would probably prefer to avoid the heavy cost of statehood or, indeed, of the present Commonwealth status for Puerto Rico, have no recourse but to wait for the Puerto

Ricans to make up their minds. Such local decision-making autonomy did not always exist in what has historically been a colonized region.

Since the Spanish-American War and the opening of the Panama Canal in 1914, the dominance of the United States in the Caribbean has been such that one sophisticated historian can continue to argue that "the United States practices almost total control in the Caribbean."[5] This was certainly the case not so long ago, when strategic considerations led to the militarization of the area through a ring of military bases and one island in particular, Puerto Rico, served as a veritable regional fortress for the United States.[6] So persistent and so total was U.S. hegemony that terms such as "the Marines," "Banana Republics," "Dollar Diplomacy," and "American Lake" all originated with U.S. action in the Caribbean. By the end of the twentieth century, however, virtually all U.S. bases had been closed and U.S. defense is now controlled from the U.S. Southern Command (SouthCom) based in Miami. The U.S. presence is reduced to a limited number of "forward operating bases," that is, planes based in civilian airports (viz. in Aruba and Curaçao, Netherlands Antilles), serving mostly counter-drug-trade functions. With the exception of relations with Cuba, the post–Cold War era witnessed the beginning of what can accurately be called a period of interdependence between the United States and the Caribbean. It is true that the more recent activities of Venezuela as an important actor on the Caribbean's geopolitical scene have added complexity to the policy environment of these small states (as I explain in the conclusion), but this hardly changes the post-hegemonic reality in any fundamental way.

This complex interdependence goes well beyond purely economic and military relations to include both bilateral and multilateral relations on a continuum from cooperation to competition to open discord. In such a complex environment, both hegemonic inclinations and strident nationalist claims of sovereignty have been modified, and what exists should properly be called a "post-hegemonic" environment.[7] If this is so, how does one explain the persistence of the myth of Caribbean colonialism? One possible explanation is the intellectual inertia—driven by the clear ideological preferences of a few—in the United Nations agency tasked with dealing with this issue. As of 2014, there were seventeen non-self-governing territories (NSGs) listed by the UN Special Committee on Decolonization. This committee operates under General Assembly Resolution 1514 (XV) of December 14,

1960, and it decides which are the candidates for decolonization. That said, it is not at all clear how given territories are included in the list targeted for decolonization. For example, the British list as self-governing territories the Falklands-Malvinas islands and Gibraltar, but the UN lists them as NSGs. On the other hand, Spain's enclaves in Morocco, Ceuta, and Melilla are not listed as NSGs. French Polynesia, a territoire d'outre-mer (TOM), is included, but St. Pierre et Miquelon, a French overseas community (CTOM) in Canada, is not. Nor is it evident that the principle of self-determination, that is, the will of the resident people, is the determining factor. In the cases of the Falklands-Malvinas and Gibraltar, recent referendums show support of well over 99 percent in favor of keeping the present relationship with the United Kingdom. The case of Puerto Rico is illustrative of the problem.

The people of Puerto Rico have voted repeatedly in referendums and island elections with parties representing all three possible status options competing. Since at least 1948, the independence option has never received more than 5 percent of the vote. Yet every year the UN Special Rapporteur on Puerto Rican decolonization "Reaffirms the inalienable right of the people of Puerto Rico to self-determination and independence." This is usually followed by a statement with which few if any Puerto Ricans will disagree; it reiterates that "the Puerto Rican people constitute a Latin American and Caribbean nation that has its own unequivocal national identity."[8] At a minimum, the repetition of this last point demonstrates how great the distance is between the insistence on what is called decolonization and the issues of self-determination and national identities in the Caribbean. As is the case in the French West Indies, so in Puerto Rico the arguments over "identity" have a complex history, replete with sophisticated debates which, however, have none of the bitter undercurrents of the debates in, for example, Catalonia and the Basque country in Spain, or the Flemish-Walloon antagonism in Belgium, or Scotland in the UK. Puerto Ricans are adamant that Spanish is their national language and the foundation of their national culture, and they see no contradictions in having a political association with an English-speaking Metropolis. Making the situation even more complex is the fact that the use of the word colony is not exclusive to Left independentistas, since those favoring entry into the U.S. union as a state also use it to describe the present status. To the estadistas, U.S. statehood would represent true decolonization. They have yet to convince a clear majority of Puerto Ricans that this is so.

The French West Indies and Puerto Rican cases illustrate another myth:

that true national identity requires full political sovereignty, that is, independence. This belief is nurtured by the various conflicts that involve issues of race or at least tensions between "metropolitans" versus natives. However, this involves a complete misunderstanding of the capacity of Caribbean people to use race and color strategically and situationally for political and economic gains. This use of "strategic ethnicity" described in chapter 6 is evident in the various serious conflicts that have shaken Caribbean societies in the past three decades, especially those where there has been a mix of Black Power and some variant of Marxism.[9]

However, if that was true in the 1970s and 1980s, it is questionable whether the assertion of Ivar Oxaal still holds—that in the West Indies, "Black Power demands are, in the nature of the case, socialist demands."[10] Certainly it was the case three decades ago. Note how Tim Hector, Antigua's leading Marxist, reminisces about his relationships with then Grenadian leader Maurice Bishop and Enzi Kawayna, co-leader of Guyana's Marxist Workers and Peoples Alliance. There was, he said, "a unique and unbreakable bond" between them that was "forged in the Black Power movement; socialism was nothing more than a logical extension of that." The question is, of course, what was the nature of that "logical extension," and how many in the region understood it? It is a fact that nowhere in the Caribbean was a Black Power movement followed by the establishment of socialism. Grenada might be the only case, and even there it is debatable that the people, as distinct from the elite, saw the revolution as representing Black Power and socialism. The cases of Curaçao and Trinidad will illustrate different instincts and needs and how in democratic societies, the pursuit of both race and Marxism has tended to have mutually neutralizing effects.

To observe pictures of the leadership of Curaçao's Frente Obrero i Liberashion in their Castro-style fatigues and caps (similar to those of Bishop and Odlum) during the May 1969 movement and to read their rhetoric, which combined Black Power, Curaçao linguistic and cultural nationalism, and Marxism, is to realize the powerful mix of ideas behind race and ideology in the region and Curaçao at the time. It is no wonder that the movement's ideological leader, a white Curaçaoleño named Stanley Brown, felt it necessary to mix his anticapitalist rhetoric with repeated reminders that his grandmother was black.[11]

To be sure, despite the existence of major differences between Curaçao and the rest of the Caribbean, especially the British West Indies, there were some commonalities. What all the islands that had experienced racial unrest had in common was a powerful influence from students abroad. In the case of Curaçao, it was students in the Netherlands, and in some other islands they used the U.S. Black Power movement as their guide. The movement had begun in Jamaica in 1968 when students rioted to protest the ban on the reentry into Jamaica of their indisputable leader, the Guyanese Dr. Walter Rodney. Other than this, race and ideology evolved idiosyncratically. Curaçao's Official Commission of Inquiry, which looked into the May 30, 1969, troubles, noted that Curaçao and Aruba were exceptions to the rule prevailing in the rest of the Caribbean where black elites governed. Curaçao in 1969 was governed by a party led by the long established white Protestant elite. The Dutch Commission noted that despite Hemisphere-wide influences of Marxism, the Curaçao movement was quite specific in its targets: it did not follow a Marxist pattern, nor did it attack *all* white groups.[12] In fact, the true economic elite, the Sephardic Jewish banking and commercial sector, was not a direct target. The Curaçao Movement's singling out of the island's Protestant white elite as also being the "economic establishment" (always used in English in the radical journal *Vito*) was sociologically and factually incorrect but politically useful. From a strict Marxist perspective, therefore, the movement was hardly revolutionary. Anger was aimed at the *political* elites, composed of native Protestant whites, a traditional group that, as Curaçaoan sociologist René Romer pointed out, had lost its economic position over the years and now ranked well below the Sephardic Jews and expatriate whites on the economic and even the social scale.[13] All this led the Dutch Commission of Inquiry to note (with no small amount of irony) the historical paradox that it had been the white Protestant group that was the originator of a nationalist, anti-Dutch stance which brought about the rapidity of social and political change in the movement toward autonomy in the early 1950s. Paradoxically, they were now accused of being "foreign exploiters."[14] Yesterday's reformers were today's "oppressors."

What was involved was less class conflict than a classic case of rebellion against blocked political mobility and the process of ethnic group succession. With the top economic slots taken by the long-established Sephardim but also more recently arrived immigrant groups such as Indians and Lebanese, the only areas open to both local established Protestant whites and newly emerging and highly educated black and colored elites were government jobs. Decolonization and democratization had unleased a competition between these two groups, and the whites won politically in the early 1950s by advancing a more progressive and nationalist modernization program. By the late 1960s, however, they were overtaken by the very political evolution they had engineered and became the targets of what was essentially a competition for power. This was not to be confused—as it indeed was in much of the literature at the time—with total social revolution; it was conflictive social change, legitimate protests against dominant ethnic groups blocking the political rise of newly educated and propertied classes. As in the rest of the Caribbean, people freely articulate and mobilize for their demands for change, and where the avenues for legitimate social mobility are blocked, they tend to react aggressively and occasionally violently. It is an ongoing process of domestic self-assertion, not total social upheaval, at least, in the non-independent Caribbean.

These social movements were seldom calls for political independence. The dominant focus on revolutionary decolonization often obfuscated this fact. In a rare retraction of a position taken in 1987 by one of the best informed Caribbeanists in Britain, Paul Sutton pulled back on his statement that by the end of the twentieth century "colonization in the form known in the previous century will have all but gone. Only the rocks will remain."[15] In fact, there have been no newly independent countries in the region since the late 1960s. What could conceivably still occur, said a more accurate Sutton in 2009, might be at least various degrees of internal decolonization and fragmentation, best termed "constitutional devolution." But Sutton was still not rid of the idea of independence; he concluded that despite his opening remarks retracting his 1987 prediction, "it is perhaps still too early to finally call it a day on the exercise of the independence option."[16] He leaned again on race, citing Bermuda where 60 percent of the population is black and might opt for independence. It is unclear what the evidence for such a conclusion could be, since the independence option was soundly defeated in a 1995 referendum, even as the heavily black electorate was voting for new black political elites. In other words, one has to be careful not to confuse oppositional identity politics—especially those ethnically based—with a logical or "natural" choice for independence. The cases of the French DOMs and the Dutch territories demonstrate that reality quite clearly. To follow the continual reorganizing and realigning of the various French territories, usually after being approved by a vote, is to understand that democratic self-determination is alive and well in those areas. The fact that a given population does not opt for independence does not in any way mean that it has opted out of its struggle for autonomy and its national—and especially ethno-national—identity and pride. Most recently, in the Caribbean, the islands of Saint Martin and St. Barthélemy voted to secede from the DOM of Guadeloupe and become overseas collectivities of France (COM). In 2005, the Martinicans and Guadeloupians, few of whom have argued for independence, reacted vehemently to the suggestion by France's then-minister of the interior, Nicolas Sarkozy, that their schools should begin teaching about the "positive" features and roles of original French colonization. What? Glorify French colonialism? Even Aimé Césaire was said to be "scandalized." Fearing massive protests, Minister Sarkozy not only withdrew the suggestion but also canceled his planned trip.[17]

Clearly, there is nothing simple when racial and ethnic sentiments provide the context for international and constitutional issues involving self-determination. That said, it is not an issue that can be avoided; it has to be dealt with. This is where the terms *colony* and *decolonization* have to be revisited, at least in the Caribbean. One might start by deciphering the following story appearing in Dutch Sint Maarten's *Daily Herald* on December 21, 2011, reprinted in the *Overseas Territories Review* in November 2013. The report dealt with the joy expressed by many members of the Dutch Second Chamber of Parliament at the rumor that Curaçao would seek independence. They were reported as saying, "They [the Dutch] want to make it as quick as possible." Part of the Dutch irritation was with the Curaçao government's cancellation of the Kingdom Consensus Law of Financial Supervision as well as Curaçaoan resistance to presenting a balanced budget. One parliamentarian appeared to see through the bluff, however. They will not, he said, leave the Kingdom of the Netherlands. "They only want less supervision by the Netherlands after the money has already been wired."

This Dutch attitude is precisely what two Dutch scholars explain with admirable frankness and thorough scholarly reasoning in an exemplary, unvarnished geopolitical analysis. Gert Oostindie and Inge Klinkers deal head-on—but counterintuitively—with what *colonialism* and *decolonization* mean in the contemporary Caribbean. Based partly on an extensive analysis of Dutch Foreign Office documentation and on interviews on both sides of the Atlantic, their study reads like one of those colonial commissions of inquiry which, let it be said, has left in many a metropolitan country such an extraordinary historical record. One can thus excuse the stiff, even plodding, narrative style—surely made all the worse by being translated from the Dutch original—none of which detracts from the enduring importance of the book as a contribution to the study of post–World War II decolonization in the Caribbean. It makes refreshing reading also because it avoids making any concessions to political correctness and ideological certainties. True, the title *Decolonizing the Caribbean* is somewhat misleading, given the central thesis of the book. It is not about decolonization à la Haiti, Algeria, Indonesia, or Angola, which involved heroic but bloody movements, or even the peaceful ones, à la Jamaica or Trinidad and Tobago. It is rather about a twentieth-century Caribbean willfully and consciously resisting any of those routes. By the authors' own telling, twentieth-century Caribbean people have prolonged and delayed decolonization by playing some astute and quintessentially polite and peaceful political games. It brings to mind the analysis of Arturo Morales Carrión regarding Puerto Rico's adept game-playing with the Americans, a combination of the islanders' keen political negotiating skills and their acute sense of the individual and collective psychological vulnerabilities of American politicians. Similarly, the leaders of the Netherlands Antilles finessed the Dutch, thereby bringing about what they call the "final denouement" of the decolonization process.[18]

Oostindie and Klinkers do not mince words in asserting that for the past fifty years, in economic terms and in spite of idle hopes of "reciprocity" described in the original Dutch Kingdom Charter of 1954, assistance has remained a one-way affair. "The Caribbean," they generalize, "has never been the window of opportunity sought by the Dutch—neither in the time of slavery and their aftermath nor in the twentieth century. And this is not likely to change."[19] Their arguments are pursued through a detailed and well-documented review of Metropolis-colony relations in four spheres: (1) constitutional goals and actual outcomes, (2) migration, legal intentions, and real results, (3) economic policies and their consequences, and (4) cultural policies, fundamentally teaching familiarity with Dutch culture and language skills. They see the outcomes as paradoxical in all four areas. In the face of Caribbean "passion," a Dutch colonial "guilt complex" over their truly brutal actions in Indonesia and a concern with not being seen as "imperialists" led to constant "overcompensation" as they confronted Dutch-Caribbean demands. This response, they argue, increases Caribbean social and psychological satisfaction but deepens the economic dependence of the "colonies." The authors call this syndrome "decolonization upside-down."

That said, the plausibility of the authors' "decolonization upside-down" thesis weakens when they analyze the case of Suriname. Again, there was no mass anticolonial movement in that colony, since in many ways Surinamese were the ones who, of all the Caribbean "colonials," best assimilated Dutch language and culture.[20] Dutch political scientist Albert L. Gastmann argued in 1968 that "the greater part" of Surinamese did not favor independence. Those agitating for it were the Suriname students in Dutch universities.[21] Be that as it may, the Dutch were absolutely determined to truly decolonize, that is, to cut and run, because stopping the flow of Surinamese into the Netherlands (60 percent of the population migrating before independence closed the door) was worth a "Golden Handshake." This is what the Surinamese got: 3.5 billion Guilders, representing at the time more or less 10,000 Euros for each Surinamese. Rather than holding a plebiscite on independence (which the authors claim would have failed), the Dutch went along with the sitting government's designs. "The whole procedure," they tell us, "which was far too short, between February 1974 and November 1975, had an exceptionally feverish character."[22] The consequences of full independence were not long in coming: ethnic violence, a coup d'état followed by political assassinations, and the entrenchment of a veritable drug mafia.

The results of this Surinamese decolonization were hardly recommendations to the few in the Antilles who wished to move toward independence. Already frightened by the 1969 riots and violence in Curaçao, the Surinamese case truly stiffened the resolve of those who would not be pushed into total independence, which is what the Dutch desired. If the events in Suriname were among the disincentives, important incentives for not decolonizing were freedom of migration and the retention of Dutch citizenship in the context of an open-borders European Union (EU), as well as opportunities to establish profitable financial centers at home. Fortunately for the Dutch, with Suriname cut loose, the relations with the Antilles were manageable. "In the end," say the authors in their forceful and candid way, "the burden of postcolonial relations has never weighed heavily enough to make The Hague opt for really radical—and possibly judicially contestable—policies. This dossier has never caused much commotion or difficulty within Dutch politics."[23] In other words, the Empire could absorb and live with the decisions of the "colonials."

Even inter-island conflicts such as the historical antagonism between Aruba and Curaçao could be—and have been—finessed by a neat new Dutch constitutional arrangement called Status Aparte. The fact that Sint Maarten later acquired a similar status hardly seems to rattle anyone in The Hague. This process of decentralization was in some ways similar to what occurred in the other metropolitan areas. The colonial Metropolis settled down to managing what can only be called a situation of "complex interdependence" within the Kingdom of the Netherlands. All this represents a big change from a decolonization usually defined in terms of blood, sweat, and tears. Perhaps this peaceful Caribbean process should be described by a word other than *decolonization*. A process of widening and deepening of local autonomy seems more apropos. The mix of gains and losses for the islands in this complex and ongoing bargaining process can be summed up as favoring the islands.

First and foremost, there would be the benefits of better management of the migration flows despite the new demand that there be linguistic and cultural preparation of Antilleans for life in the Netherlands. In an age when the politics of identity reign supreme, this last goal might prove to be the most intractable. The Leeward Islands of Aruba, Curaçao, and Bonaire (ABC) appear no more eager than before to give up their beloved Papiamento, and the Windward Islands cling perhaps tighter than ever to their English. As of 2013 Papiamento is an official language in the ABC islands, along with Dutch, and every effort was being made to introduce it into the school curricula and exams. This explains why Aruba's Culture Department declared 2013 the "Year of Papiamento." In addition, in the face of such cultural-linguistic resistance, the Dutch appear little enthused about engaging in a *mission civilisatrice* regarding language. Just "muddling through" has worked before, and chances are it will work again for these pragmatic people. Neither the English nor the French Caribbean citizens confronted any such linguistic—or indeed, cultural—difficulty.

However, the linguistic strain for the ABC islanders is more than compensated for by their access to the European Union with all the advantages that brings. Another benefit would be assistance in promoting good governance, especially in combatting administrative corruption and waste. This has certainly included some controversial involvements in what the islanders consider their autonomous sphere of operations, especially in the area of international finance. Finally, and very controversial, there is the understanding that the islands would seek assistance from the Netherlands and its allies in the European Union and the United States in combatting the drug trade and any illicit operations in the offshore world. Even here, however, the

Dutch appear unwilling to come down too decisively on the various smuggling schemes operating out of Aruba.[24]

It is more than evident that a true understanding of internal self-determination and the formation of a national identity is not to be had from listening to the often over-the-top speeches on colonialism by self-appointed representatives abroad or politicians and ideologues with minimal following back home. These processes are best understood by analyzing decisions in areas where the locals mostly cooperate and occasionally confront powerful Metropolitan and international forces. Such an area is the growth of the financial offshore industry in much of the region, defended with equal fervor by independent and non-independent territories alike. Political status makes little difference in how each state or territory pursues its national interests. The freedom with which a territory such as the Cayman Islands manages its financial sector differs little from how an independent Switzerland manages its own. As a major French study of *fiscal paradises* notes, "Dans tous ces paradis fiscaux, les banquiers privés font la même chose qu'à Genève." The difference lies in the relative importance of the offshore sector in each economy. In Switzerland it represents 3 percent of GDP whereas in the Bahamas and Caymans it is 40 percent.[25]

At a meeting of Florida International University's Journalists and Editors Workshop, May 6, 2011, Professor Wenran Jiang of the University of Alberta, Canada, presented a paper on "China's Energy Policy toward Latin America." Part of the presentation dealt with China's use of Caribbean offshore banks to finance the operations in China, the United States, and Latin America. The sums he spoke of in these offshore centers seemed extraordinarily large, certainly larger than warranted by the nature of the transactions. The issue was soon closed as other speakers took up the issue of the panel's theme, "Geopolitics and Conflict," dealing mostly with Cuba and Venezuela. This was closed but not ignored, since those Chinese holdings offshore came back into the headlines with a bang three years later.

The first to break the story was the *New York Times* in 2012 when it revealed that ex-prime minister Wen Jiabao's family had a fortune of U.S. $2.7 billion. Then on January 21, 2014, *El País* of Spain, the *Guardian* and the BBC of the UK, *Le Monde* of France, and *Asahi Shimbun* of Japan simultaneously published the findings of what became known as "Chinaleaks," first revealed by the International Consortium of Investigative Journalists of Washington, D.C.[26] "Chinaleaks" involved over 2 million files from the major Chinese offshore bank, Portcullis Trust Net, and Commonwealth Trust of the British Virgin Islands (BVI). The documents cover the period up to 2010. With a population of only 27,000, this British territory was reported as having over 1 million "societies" registered, 40 percent of which are from mainland China and Hong Kong. The BVI was the second largest investor in China after Hong Kong.[27] It was calculated that in 2011 some U.S. $150 billion left China. "Chinaleaks" revelations can be summarized as follows: some 22,000 Chinese hold accounts in the BVI including 1,000 members of the National Popular Assembly and 13,000 who belong to what is known as the "Red Aristocracy." Among the political elite, one member's family had U.S. $2.7 billion, and one businessman from the private sector had U.S. $10 billion. It was not revealed how much the state petroleum triumvirate—Petrochina, Sinopec, and China Offshore Oil Corporation—had in their accounts. Acting as middlemen in the establishment of the offshore holdings were firms such as Price Waterhouse, Coopers, Credit Suisse, Citigroup, UBS Bank, JP Morgan, and Deutsche Bank. Meanwhile, a Chinese lawyer who had protested against the corruption in the Chinese Communist Party leadership was being tried for "disturbing the public order."[28] The *New York Times* described the complexity, the "gray world" of offshore business. "Offshore bank accounts, trusts, and shell companies are not in-and-of themselves illegal," reported the *Times*. But offshore companies can also be used to launder money, avoid taxes, and hide an individual's stake in a company.[29]

What is called "offshore" describes a whole range of businesses, including banks, insurance companies, ship registers, and international business corporations (IBC). These are not, by definition, illegal, but the main dimension of the offshore is that it operates outside the control of a central bank or of the state control under which national banks operate. It is not my intention to argue that Caribbean territories are the major actors in this gray world, only that, given their size and regardless of whether they are independent or not, Caribbean elites have battled for their rights and interests—variously defined—to engage in this global enterprise.

It is not difficult to choose a tax paradise. The requisites for the creation of an international company are few, and in the majority of cases the business is created electronically and, if not immediately, at least within the next twenty-four hours. These institutions attract not only criminals who seek a way to launder their money but also those who are not legally "criminals" but who seek places where they will be exempted from taxes and will enjoy absolute confidentiality and secrecy. This confidentiality is what legal and illegal businesses seek. For the licit client, it is crucial that tax evasion in the original country is not considered a crime in any of the offshore centers. The latest trend in corporate tax avoidance is called "inversion." Under U.S. law, companies owe taxes on their worldwide income. But they pay these only if they bring those profits home to the United States. This explains why by 2009 some 7,827 businesses had located their earnings in offshore tax havens.[30] Three of these havens in the Caribbean—Bermuda, Cayman Islands, and the British Virgin Islands—"earned U.S. $129 billion in 2010." This amounted to U.S. $873,611 for every person living in those islands. Just to cite one case, in 2013 General Electric had U.S. $110 billion in foreign earnings on which they paid no taxes in the United States.[31] Gabriel Zucman calculates that 8 percent or U.S. $7.6 trillion of the world's financial wealth is hidden in fiscal paradises. This includes the 20 percent of U.S. corporate profits that are shifted offshore.[32] Clearly you do not have to be independent to offer such a service. What does require status as an independent country, that is, sovereignty, is the increasingly popular "sale" or granting of "economic citizenship." New passports with new names are available. Other than that, sovereignty is not necessary to operate "offshore." These centers offer to launder the money but also to clean the identities of the people and institutions involved. According to Ronen Palan, the following assets are managed there:

- 80 percent of all global transactions;
- almost all of the U.S. $2 trillion in exchange transactions;
- 20 percent of the global private wealth; and
- 22 percent of the external assets of the banking world.[33]

The very volume of studies dealing with the problems of the links between traditional capital flight, international organized crime, and the world of offshore banking is in itself evidence of the dimensions of the problem. These studies include early works by Moisés Naim, Misha Glenny, and R. Thomas Naylor.[34] In 2013, the Brookings Institution published *Dangerous Liaisons*, an edited book by experts on the growing corruption by international organized crime of democratic institutions and political parties. Arguably the most interesting and informative for the purpose of this chapter, however, is the 2004 Alan Block and Constance Weaver book, *All Is Clouded by Desire*.[35] Drawing on British and U.S. intelligence sources, the authors unravel the world of "hot money" in international banking and the role of organized criminal gangs in money laundering and the financing of terrorist groups.

What concerns us here is the role of certain Caribbean-based banks, especially those in non-independent European territories. As argued, these territories have such a sharply defined sense of their autonomy and are so tenacious and aggressive in promoting their national interests that they can hardly be called colonies anymore. To repeat, there is no difference between the offshore banking in the non-independent and independent states.

It is good to keep in mind that there was often a history of Metropolitan colonial action at the origins of many an offshore center when colonial geopolitical interests demanded them. A case in point is Panama, one of the oldest offshore banking and service sectors in the Caribbean. From 1855, when a railroad first connected both oceans, Panama's destiny as a mercantile, transit economy was established. Its destiny as such a center was arguably institutionalized in 1904 when the new republic, hardly a self-determining sovereign state, signed a monetary agreement with the United States.[36] The U.S. dollar was adopted as local currency, and Panama agreed not to establish any currency exchange restrictions of any sort. In 1927 Panama took a page from the Delaware and New Jersey corporation laws and passed its first General Corporation Law in order to attract offshore financial business. Aside from providing favorable tax treatment for any capital invested, it also guaranteed confidentiality, and it established that any two people of legal age—whether Panamanian or not, whether resident in Panama or abroad—could establish a corporation. The basic elements of the Panamanian offshore center had come into being. Later, under fuller sovereign decision making, Panamanian elites expanded the operation of the offshore industry.[37] Panamanian Law 18 of 1959 added coded (secret) bank accounts. Both the 1927 and the 1959 legislation were consolidated and amplified by the Banking Law of 1970. Not only did the 1970 law further lower taxes and make the movement of funds free. It also provided complementary legislation in the Criminal Commercial and Labor codes to enforce bank secrecy obligations and guarantees. Panama remains an important offshore center, protective of its role in international finance.

One should note immediately that the French DOMs have not been included in the various official inquiries into what is legal and what is illegal in the offshore world. It is the Dutch and the British islands (including many of the newly independent ones) which repeatedly come up for scrutiny for illegal offshore activities. In 2000, the International Monetary Fund (IMF) listed the following non-independent territories as "Offshore Financial Centers": among the British territories—Anguilla, Bermuda, British Virgin Islands, Cayman Islands, Montserrat, and Turks and Caicos; and among the Dutch territories—Curaçao, Aruba, Bonaire, Sint Maarten, and Sint Eustatius.[38] The boom of the offshore business in the Caribbean reached such heights that a small island like Anguilla, with only 7,000 inhabitants, had 45 banks with 3,500 registered companies. Montserrat, with 15,000 inhabitants, had 350 banks, only one of which even had a vault.[39] There was such a scandal that the British government had to intervene and close the majority of the banks and companies in Montserrat. The Cayman Islands is one of the most important tax paradises in the Caribbean, and it was the second offshore center in the world after Switzerland until overtaken by the British Virgin Islands (BVI). Full of Chinese money, according to the BBC of London, the BVI, as of 2014, holds 45 percent of all the offshore companies of the world. It has become the preferred offshore site for 65 percent of all the companies and personal fortunes offshore.[40] If history contains any lessons, it is that to close down or even roll back these centers is futile. A few cases will illustrate.

The British action to intervene in Montserrat was followed in 2000 by the Organization of Economic and Community Development (OECD) and its Financial Action Task Force's action threatening to sanction centers that appeared in a list of countries and territories characterized by their bank looseness or laxity. The Caribbean was more than present in that list: Bahamas, Cayman Islands, Dominica, Panama, St. Kitts and Nevis, and St. Vincent and the Grenadines. The OECD continued publication of a "black list" until 2004 when the IMF complained that it was difficult for that institution to carry out cooperation for development in these small territories. With or without being on the list, the Caribbean continued to be popular mainly for geographic reasons: its offshore centers are in the same region that serves as a bridge for 50 percent of the drugs that flow from the biggest producer, Colombia, to the biggest consumer, the United States. But there is also a human dimension that explains the concentration of these offshore banks in the Caribbean. The main goal of any criminal is to enjoy his profits in some tropical paradise, especially if it is located in the zone where he operates his criminal activities.

Prior to their role in "Chinaleaks" in 2013, the single largest investigation into the offshore world was done over fifteen months by the Center for Public Integrity, parent of the International Center for Investigatory Journalists

(ICIJ), a consortium led by British, French, German, and American newspapers in 2013.[41] It involved eighty-six journalists from forty-six countries. Here in summary is what they uncovered:

- They accepted the verdict of Jack Blum, former U.S. Senate investigator, that the offshore world remains a "zone of impunity. . . . There's been some progress, but there's a bloody long way to go."
- They cite the fundamental study by James S. Henry, former chief economist at McKinsey and Company, who estimated that there was between $21 and $32 trillion hidden in offshore havens. This was roughly equivalent to the size of the U.S. and Japanese economies combined.
- Of the 177,020 British companies with directors in offshore jurisdictions, 17,959 are located in the British Virgin Islands, with one director for every 1.3 residents of the islands.
- When investigators focused on the tiny Channel island of Sark, a pair of British expats relocated their empire of 2,250 company directorships to the Caribbean island of Nevis.
- The French might not have any official offshore centers, but as the ICIJ study revealed, many French use Monaco, Andorra, Liechtenstein, and Luxembourg to hide their money.

There can be little doubt that the British government has made real efforts to gain control over the use of their overseas territories for illegal offshore activities. Aside from several multilateral efforts to combat illegal offshore activities such as those of the Basel Committee and the OECD's Forum on Harmful Tax Havens, the following standards were set as a result of two specifically British initiatives, emphasizing the still-dependent status for the Overseas Territories:

Minimum Standards for the Supervision of International Banking Groups and Their Cross-Border Establishments

- All international banks should be supervised by a home country authority that capably performs consolidated supervision.
- The creation of cross-border banking establishments should receive the prior consent of both the host country and home country authority.
- Home country authorities should possess the right to gather information from their cross-border banking establishments.

- If the host country determines that any of these three standards is not being met, it could impose restrictive measures or prohibit the establishment of banking offices.[42]

Just how effectively these standards are enforced is debatable. So the attorney general of the Cayman Islands demonstrated real independence when he informed his island's legislature on the MLAT negotiations:

> We, the Government of the Cayman Islands, have a specific, categorical undertaking from our Sovereign Mother, the United Kingdom, that there will be no further offence added to this list, even though the United Kingdom and the United States both agree, without specific consent, Sir, of the Government of the Cayman Islands. *We have say so. They cannot do it without us.*[43]

Similarly, Premier Walter Brown of Bermuda, after being summoned to London by Prime Minister David Cameron to a meeting of the UK Overseas Territories and Crown Dependencies, said emphatically that Cameron's efforts "came across as petulant political posturing" and had extended the reach of the UK "beyond its constitutional powers with regard to Bermuda." This was hardly the language of a "colonial" in its proud assertion of independence. As Brown continued:

> If Britain continues down the path of meddling in the economic affairs of overseas territories and seeming to dictate a course of action, particularly while the territories are already working to meet international obligations, there will be a battle akin to that of David and Goliath. But for the David that is Bermuda the recourse may simply be the path to autonomy.[44]

And there was more: there was the threat of future independence led, said Brown, "by an unlikely group—business leaders." It is interesting that in Martinique, the traditional white elite, the so-called *bekés pays*, had become so resentful of "foreign" French Metropolitan rules and regulations that a possible move toward independence led by them was perceived as possible by a leading scholar.[45] This scholar should have known that elites, be they in British non-independent territories, French DOMs, or Dutch islands, are all skillful at bluffing.

Despite the tough talk, the Cayman authorities have always understood that they benefited from the stability provided by their non-independent status. As their financial secretary once put it, "As you see, the economic stability of our region [the Caribbean] is questionable. Yet, in Cayman, in the midst of it [economic turmoil], we enjoy a very stable economy and marginal inflation."[46] On their frequent advertisements regarding their sterling banking tradition, they are always ready to make pointed reference to their good educational level (in English, of course), their superior infrastructure, and communication network. Given that, at least before the Chinese began arriving in the 1990s, 90 percent of its clients were Americans; it is a classic case of British protection for American—and now Chinese—money. They also make a credible case that they have cooperated with U.S. authorities since the 1980s. And yet despite decades of efforts to control the offshore world, as late as November 2012 the United States was still engaged with over 50 countries attempting to "improve internal tax compliance" and reporting requirements of the Foreign Account Tax Compliance Act (FATCA). The U.S. Department of the Treasury announced that it was "working to explore options for intergovernmental engagement" with Bermuda, the Cayman Islands, the British Virgin Islands, and Saint Martin.[47]

The fact is that Caribbean secrecy havens have benefited from the persuasiveness of free enterprise arguments. They have taken these arguments as their own raison d'être. They invariably highlight the words *financial independence, personal freedom,* and *avoiding state oppression.* Note the statement of philosophy of the Omnicorp Financial Group in St. Vincent: "We believe that authorities and governments have made basic rights difficult [through] oppressive taxation, over-regulation, invasion of privacy." In the United States particularly there have been efforts to rein in the autonomy of these offshore jurisdictions. What the terrorist act of September 11, 2001, did was to strengthen the state's argument that while the practice of tax avoidance might have its "rational" side, it cannot be justified in an "age of terrorism" for two reasons: it deprives that state of the additional resources needed to combat terrorism, and it serves the terrorist networks. The enactment of the Patriot Act of 2001 and the new money laundering legislation passed by a 412–1 vote in the House reflects the public's mood. That act enhances the government's ability to carry out the three F's—find, freeze, and forfeit—by mandating the following:

(1) facilitating and sharing of financial information through "a highly secure communications network";

(2) keeping a central register of all banks in the United States and abroad;

(3) banning all correspondent accounts with "shell" banks (banks that have no physical offices anywhere); and

(4) extending the definition of money laundering to legally acquired funds which end up in terrorist organizations (so-called reverse money laundering schemes).

The U.S. action was nearly immediately emulated by the thirty-one-member Paris-based Financial Action Task Force on Money Laundering (FATF). In late 2001, for the first time, the FATF focused on the role of money laundering in supporting terrorism fund-raising generally.

It should come as no surprise that one of the first types of transactions the Paris-based FATF looked at was credit card fraud. For years the U.S. Internal Revenue Service has known that perhaps 2 million U.S. citizens hold credit cards issued by offshore banks. Lack of funds and authority prevented much investigation. Of the 1,500 cases in just the Cayman Islands that the IRS felt needed investigating, only 10 were eventually looked at. With the Patriot Act's far-reaching authority, Master Card alone handed over the records of 230,000 credit card accounts issued by offshore banks.

This being the case, one can argue that one subject which could use some creative hypothesizing is the issue of corruption when there is little or no government intervention and regulation. Without denying that there might be other benefits to be derived from deregulation, "downsizing," and liberalization, several Caribbean cases demonstrate that it has yet to be proved that reducing corruption is invariably one of them. In fact, the opposite appears to be the case in areas such as the one researched here: offshore banking centers. Not called "secrecy havens" for nothing, these rapidly multiplying businesses are thriving with the new globalization of capital flows and emphasis on "deregulated" environments, which boast a minimum of transparency and a maximum of autonomy of private action. The function of the state, independent or not, is to ensure that very privacy and secrecy by keeping encumbering regulations to a minimum.

Professional help and growing complexity in money laundering schemes are only two of the reasons why this process will not be easily defeated. Another is that, as James Morgan of the *Financial Times* noted, in this issue of offshore banking, "everyone finds someone else to blame for crime." All this should caution us against the contemporary doxa that eliminating many rules, regulations, and supervision is a prerequisite for the reduction of corrupt behavior. The situation with the offshore secrecy havens would tend to indicate the exact opposite. As noted, there has been a broad, even worldwide, awareness of the role which these offshore centers play in enabling organized crime to sustain and fund its activities. What there have not been are mechanisms by which this awareness can be translated into disincentives to deviant behavior.

The United States has multiplied the number of its foreign policy instruments designed to force the compliance of foreign states: from "certification for good behavior" to economic incentives and disincentives, to authorizing the Federal Bureau of Investigation to operate overseas. In 2010 the United States passed the Foreign Account Tax Compliance Act. It was another attempt to force banks to disclose accounts held abroad by U.S. residents. Severe sanctions have already been carried out. But as Zucman argues throughout his well-researched book, the very wealthy always have teams of lawyers and accountants ready to come up with even more elaborate tax evasion techniques. Whether this will work completely has yet to be seen, but it does serve to reflect the frustration with the problem and the futility of leaving a solution to the marketplace.

Transparency International is not engaging in idle chatter when it asserts, "The whole world is demonstrating outrage at the scale of bribery and kickbacks involving leaders of business and politics." That outrage can be converted into action only by a worldwide, coordinated set of rules and the mechanisms for enforcing them. That might eventually even influence China to rein in its corrupt elite. This means—as far as the offshore phenomenon is concerned—more government involvement, not less. There might be real material reasons for choosing rectitude. Given the globalization of economic enterprises and their reputation or goodwill, the fear of being sanctioned or tainted by a powerful U.S. or international agency—and thus the fear of losing status and/or reputation—has both national and international dimensions. Small conservative societies would be expected to recoil from such a prospect.

The question remains: What would lead a non-independent territory, enjoying an enormous advantage in income over an independent territory (as indicated in table 1) and sitting on mountains of capital earned and "parked" by legitimate U.S. corporations, to want to change that situation? There are powerful mutual financial interests at work that can only gain strength as new players such as China enter the search for safe havens. What all this means in the final analysis is that given the contemporary trends of "upside-down decolonization," the world will have to learn how to live with these very independent-minded non-independent territories. This in turn will require new theories of governance and development. The racially based theories of violence as having a "restorative" function or of plantation societies that call for being rid of white elites have exhausted their explanatory capabilities.

11

Barbados

Tradition and Modernity in a Model Small State

In June 2014 Barbadians (known as Bajans) were dismayed by the news that the credit rating agency Moody's had again downgraded the island's creditworthiness. There had been a previous reduction in 2013 from Ba1 to Ba3 and a year later from Ba3 to B3. Standard and Poor's had already reduced it from BB-plus to BB-minus. Additionally, the International Monetary Fund (IMF) had set off alarms noting that Barbados's debt burden had risen from 60 percent of GDP to 70 percent in the course of one year. This, to be sure, was lower than the norm for Caribbean states, which in 2013 stood at 143 percent of GDP. No consolation was to be had from this, as the government's opposition was quick to remind the people. Calling on the minister of finance to resign, Leader of the Opposition Mia Mottley addressed the issue of Barbados's international reputation: "Bloomberg last weekend and now *Forbes Magazine* . . . are now referring to Barbados as . . . 'Cyprus West'!"[1] Shock and disbelief followed dismay when former prime minister Owen Arthur warned that the never-devalued Barbadian dollar—third strongest after those of Cayman and the Bahamas—might have to be devalued.[2] But the bad news did not end there. Insult was added to injury when the chief economist at the Caribbean Development Bank (CDB) recommended that Barbados and other Eastern Caribbean states take a page out of Jamaica's fiscal reform.[3] What? Bajans learning from Jamaicans?

In spite of the fact that the spokesman on finance for the opposition denied that there was any danger of devaluation and that the Central Bank had "adequate" foreign reserves,[4] Bajans were still skittish about the situation—and with good reason. With an open economy that depends on the earnings from tourism, the licensing of small offshore companies, and a small manufacturing export sector for its foreign currency, it was not doing well between 2007 and 2014, the years of the global recession. And the fact that it made no difference that Bajans kept reminding everyone that they were not an offshore haven but a low-taxation country run with admirable transparency injured their well-developed national pride.

The question is why, given that the island had had negative growth in the past five years, were Bajans so shocked now? One plausible explanation is that the Bajans' historical conservatism and tendency to abide by semi-sacred traditions (viz. never devalue)—part of their strengths and weaknesses—engenders a strong propensity to block anything that disrupts their search for harmony and balance in their lives. Even if this were true, however, it cannot explain the whole Barbadian narrative. As such, the counterintuitive question has to be asked: if such a cultural propensity is capable of producing negative results in the short term (viz. a five-year period), might the same cultural propensities have produced positive results over the long term, that is, over four centuries, and therefore be an intrinsic strength rather than a structural cultural weakness? My answer is yes, and this in turn leads to the prediction that based on what the historical record shows, Barbados will probably return to economic growth in a few years, overcoming this blip in its history.

In the face of IMF encouragement, the Barbados government decided to undertake some drastic belt-tightening. Central government employment was targeted to be reduced by over 3,000 jobs, and the salaries of ministers, government legislators, and all other "political appointees" was to be reduced by 10 percent. What was striking about these measures was the way the society responded, starting with the ones taking the deepest cuts, the trade unions. The National Union of Public Workers (NUPW) decided to delay any pronouncements until they had had discussions with the administration and leaders of the private sector. Sir Roy Trotman, general secretary to the Barbados Workers Union (BWU), called for "hope and the usual Barbadian resilience." He was being Barbados-proud, but also accurate, when he stated that recuperation would occur because the island's people were "perhaps the best educated body of persons in the region and in many other parts of the world."[5] In January 2014, the foremost economic publication specializing in the Caribbean, *Market Dynamic Caribbean*, echoed Trotman's steely optimism. It noted that the Bajan Public/Private Partnership was upbeat and that the improving world economy and the tough measures taken would return the island to health.[6] This assessment was also that of the governor of the Central Bank of Barbados.[7] Such optimism or positive thinking may or may not lift the island's fortunes in the short term, but it is in keeping with the general political culture of the island and the strategic culture of its elites. Even one as critical of the conservative policies of the Barbadian Central Bank as Terrence Farrell, former deputy governor of the Trinidad and Tobago Central Bank, had to acknowledge that Barbados "is easily the most disciplined of Caribbean territories" and that this will allow them to "swallow the bitter" IMF medicine. He was optimistic about the island's future.[8] There are strong historical reasons for taking these opinions seriously.

Of all the countries of the Greater Caribbean, Barbados has most successfully combined a deep respect for tradition with a constant attempt to modernize. Evidence of this is found in Richard Ligon's *True and Exact History of the Island of Barbados* (1657). An educated man of the minor English aristocracy, Ligon had very clear ideas about the administration of a plantation colony. First, prosperity was to be ensured by a respect for order and social harmony. Adherence to the laws of England was essential to keeping order. Not that those laws were invariably equitable and just or "Christian," as Ligon saw it, since both the European indentured servant and the African slave were treated with equal brutality. "Truly," he lamented, "I have seen such cruelty there . . . as I did not think one Christian could have done to another." Such cruelty explained why first Irish indentured servants and then African slaves attempted to overthrow their masters. But Ligon was prescient when he described three traits which characterized Barbadian political culture then as they do now: a strong and loyal identification with the island (call it a protean national identity); keeping order and harmony among the elite by encouraging fair play; and a general disposition to work hard. Ligon was adamant on this: "[Neither] the voluptuous or lazy persons . . . are fit to inhabit on this land. . . . So much is a sluggard detested in a County, where Industry and Activity is to be exercised."[9]

Despite such early evidence of what Max Weber would certainly have called the Protestant ethic, which is conducive to a spirit of capitalism, few scholars paid much attention to Barbados. A rare case is that of Columbia University economist Otis P. Starkey, who traveled to the West Indies in 1938, when the whole region was very much in the grip of labor unrest. He was struck by how Barbados differed from the other islands and decided to probe how these differences arose.[10] Starkey did a longitudinal study of three hundred years of Barbadian history (1647–1931), looking at the impacts of overpopulation, hurricanes, droughts, pests, and "accidents of history." He concluded, "Nature has not spared the rod and spoiled the child in Barbados." Perhaps because of this, Starkey argued that there were "hidden advantages to environmental handicaps." One of the advantages was that, as distinct from what he witnessed on other islands, Barbadians appeared to draw on a "collective will" to confront these adversities. He was particularly struck by the fact that on Barbados, "planter and laborers alike have built permanent homes and developed a loyalty to the island."[11]

Unfortunately, Starkey's idea of Barbados exceptionalism never caught on in the literature on the region. In fact, that literature seldom took the island into account. Even Sidney Mintz's admirable attempt at providing a more operational framework for the study of the Caribbean reflects the absence of significant studies on Barbados. This explains why at least three of his nine major features of Caribbean regional commonality do not apply to Barbados. First, in Barbados, as distinct from the rest of the Caribbean, there was no interplay between the plantations and an existing small-scale yeoman agriculture. Land was simply too expensive. Second, Barbados—as distinct from Trinidad and Guyana, for instance—never experienced the introduction of "foreign" (e.g., Asian) populations into the lower sectors of island social structures. Finally, and crucially for the argument presented in this essay, Barbados was not characterized by what Mintz called the "absence of any ideology of national identity that could serve as a goal for mass acculturation."[12] The fundamental reason for this lack of national identity in the Caribbean, according to Mintz, was that the planter groups were less likely to come to settle; they were, rather, "temporary exiles." Whatever the case was in the other islands, in Barbados as Ligon discovered in the 1650s and Starkey in the 1930s, large numbers of those who came voluntarily stayed, as did those who were "transported" against their will (black and white). Planter absenteeism was not a significant part of the Barbadian historical background. Barbados was and is different. The question is, can we learn something of universal, or at least Caribbean-wide, applicability from these differences?

Any social scientist who knows the island and is willing to "see" and not just "look" will wonder why its successful development has been ignored by the substantial theorizing that has been done on the region. Its standard of living and quality of life are by any sociological measure visibly better than that of the other islands of the Caribbean and not just the English-speaking ones. These observations are supported by the hard data supplied by both domestic and international banking and/or development agencies. Observe that the United Nations Development Program (UNDP) ranks Barbados the number one developing country in the world, 31st out of 177 countries. Consider the rankings in the 2007–2008 Human Development Index —Barbados: 31; Bahamas: 49; St. Kitts/Nevis: 54; Antigua/Barbuda: 57; Trinidad/Tobago: 59; Dominica: 71; St. Lucia: 72; Belize: 80; Grenada: 82; Guyana: 97; and Jamaica: 101. In the Heritage Foundation/Wall Street Journal Index of Economic Freedom, Barbados ranks 28th in the world. And, fundamentally, while there are two other islands which have achieved relatively good standards of development, that is, the Bahamas and Antigua/Barbuda, these have been characterized by high levels of corruption and openness to the flow of suspicious monies that helped build their tourism infrastructures.[13] Not so in Barbados. The most complete study of corruption in the Caribbean gives Barbados the highest marks. Barbados, says Michael Collier, avoids corruption "through a strong sense of consensus and public participation in politics—conditions lacking in many of the other former British colonies."[14]

Indeed, beyond the hard measure of successful modernization, the sociologist takes note of the very civic demeanor of public interaction, the courtesy of Barbadians' public address with that distinct cadence and syntax of their English, their penchant for making points with metaphors, and the uniqueness of their vernacular architecture. Critically, in a Caribbean wracked by crime, Barbados is relatively crime-free. Hard data and long-term observations all point to the culture of this 430-square-kilometer island of 270,000 people as indeed being "different."[15]

Of course, to assert a difference is not the same as demonstrating its origins and causes. The student can begin to unravel those origins through the comparative analysis of three areas: first, the distinct Barbadian pattern of complex interdependence between its plantation system and its civil society; second, its unabashed adherence to "tradition" and the idiosyncratic consequences of that for its society and culture—consequences which helped transcend somewhat the very deep division of race and class; and third, the rational choices of its political elite, which has invariably favored moderation over radical populism, be it of ideology or race. The engaged student will discover that the presence of these three secular processes over a very long period helps explain why Barbados is not just different but indeed more developed than the rest of the islands.

From the time Lowell Joseph Ragatz published his monumental 1928 study of the decline of the planter class in the British Caribbean,[16] the study of the sugar plantation has been in vogue. It was St. Lucian economist W. Arthur Lewis, however, who laid the fundamental intellectual foundations of what would become known as the "theory of plantation societies." Lewis asserted that all Caribbean societies were "plantation" societies, characterized by a "traditional" plantocracy which had shown "no dynamic initiative over a hundred years," and land which had reached its maximum carrying capacity. He noted that the British islands in the 1950s had 294 persons per square mile when it could accommodate at most 60.[17] Given these features, Lewis argued that the only way out of underdevelopment was to abandon the plantation system in favor of an urban-centered industrialization somewhat along the lines of the Puerto Rican model of "industrialization by invitation."[18]

As we saw in chapter 6, this idea of doing away with not just the plantation but all the "traditions" that it had generated was adopted by a group of West Indian intellectuals whose ideas on the plantation system evolved into one of the two dominant paradigms of Caribbean political economy. This New World Group argued that "politically, the plantation system lacks community support; economically it is an appendage of a metropolitan economy and therefore has no internal dynamic for accumulation, technological change, and taste formation." Even more serious was the fact that socially, it is stratified by reference to metropolitan criteria, that is, race.[19] To these intellectuals, the "old" and the "traditional" were stumbling blocks on the road to change and progress. They argued that "from time to time there had to be a revolution." Strangely enough, they did not necessarily mean a Cuban-style revolution but rather "as with Adam Smith, Marx or Keynes."[20] This strange mix of ideologists responds to the fact that to plantation society theorists, ideology did not matter that much as long as all the plantation societies of the Caribbean were "shaken" once in a while. The point was that if you did away with these, you did away with the white plantocratic elite as well as its economic base, the sugar plantation.

Largely on W. Arthur Lewis's authority, but also on the political impulse of the New World intellectuals, eventually all the islands with the exception of Barbados did accomplish this in one form or the other. In Cuba, Antigua, St. Kitts, and Grenada, the planter classes were essentially pushed out of the economy. In Guyana and Jamaica, the state took over the failing plantations. In Trinidad, Dr. Eric Williams, who often ridiculed what he called the "brown sugar mentality" of the planter class, kept the plantations going under state ownership, fearing that a sudden closing would put some 20,000 Indo-Trinidadians out of work. Barbados's experience with plantation society differed from all of these other cases.

By the early eighteenth century, Barbados had a population of 65,000, and contemporary maps show the entire surface of the island covered by 976 plantations. Perhaps 5,000 of the 65,000 inhabitants were English, Scottish, and Welsh planters and merchants. These were the "gentlemen." The rest were 30,000 African slaves, 20,000 Irish indentured servants, and some 1,200 Scots who had been "transported" in 1745. Many of the white population were unable to find land and so emigrated, making the plantation more and more dependent on African slaves. By 1671, immigrants from Barbados composed half the population of South Carolina and were already identified as arriving with a "Barbados attitude." In his political history of South Carolina covering the period 1663–1763, M. Eugene Sirmans tells of the impact these men had on early Carolina:

> The Barbadians . . . were ambitious, experienced, and occasionally unscrupulous men who had little interest in Lord Ashley's dream of erecting a perfect society in Carolina. Trained in the island colony to be enterprising and self-reliant, they were primarily concerned with making their own fortunes.[21]

This is the attitude George Washington and his half-brother Lawrence remarked on after a three-month stay in Barbados in 1751. Lawrence, sick with tuberculosis, was seeking the reputed healing qualities of the island's climate. It was, he said, "the finest island in the Caribbean," while George wrote in his diary of the "hospitality and genteel behavior of the gentleman inhabitants."[22]

Of all the plantation societies in the region, Barbados, after emancipation in 1838, was unique in two fundamental respects. First, it was a "closed" economy in the sense that there was no land or employment outside the plantation, and the cost of land outside the plantation was completely out of reach for newcomers (see table 14). Therefore, neither a small yeoman sector nor maroon enclaves developed as they did elsewhere in the region. Second, the island was so geographically isolated and so difficult to navigate to and from that former slaves had no opportunity for escape to the mainland or to other islands. The post-emancipation scene in Barbados was one of de jure liberty but a de facto accommodation through a "law of necessity" to the existing plantation. Hilary McD. Beckles, Barbados's most severe and consistent critic of the white plantocracy, notes that "all signs along the road to emancipation . . . led to the Great House as the centre of power in the new dispensation . . . [S]cattered as they were along the landscape, they formed a network of monuments to terror and military might."[23] They also became a formidable domestic reference group, since their rule and the constraints of their environment led to two paradoxical processes which advanced the foundations of any development process: a hunger for education at all levels, and out-migration with its flows of remittances and attitudinal changes.

Education, on the island as elsewhere, is acknowledged as a major element in modernization, contributing directly as a factor of production or indirectly as a complement to other factors of production. On an island with few natural resources, this is the place to begin. The Barbados National Commission of Sustainable Development stated: "Education is the major vehicle to bring about positive, relevant changes within our society."[24]

When a scholar like Beckles observes, virtually in passing and without a tinge of irony, that emancipation "nonetheless" opened up possibilities for blacks to pursue education, he is describing one of the few avenues to which they could displace their anger and frustration and aspire to a better future. "There developed," he says, "a 'cult' of education among the older generation who insisted upon their children's acquisition of formal schooling."[25] Indeed, despite constant opposition from the planter elite, this cult slowly

Table 14. Land values in the West Indies in the late 1840s

Colony	Average price range per acre (£)
Dominica	1–3
Trinidad	1–13
Guyana	1–30
Jamaica	4–20
Antigua	40–80
Barbados	60–200

Source: Hilary McD. Beckles, *Great House Rules* (Kingston: Ian Randle, 2004), 80.

but surely broke through the barriers and prepared the island's black middle and working classes for some of their greatest future challenges. One cannot understand Barbadian society's great strides, whether it is the success of its many out-migrations or the relatively smooth transition of its economy as it confronted external challenges, without understanding its emphasis on education. In addition, the fact that schooling was in Standard English and carried out in each parish by the established Anglican Church created a uniformity of language, religion, and loyalty to the British traditions of the parish very often lacking in the other more culturally plural islands. Contributing to the historical cultural cohesiveness of the island is the notable absence of pidgin dialects, any significant nonwestern religions, or syncretic cults such as exist in virtually all the other islands. All theory informs us that cultures are strongest when the various component parts have relevant linkages and are in relative harmony.

The emphasis on education did not come easily or cheaply. The data show that the island has been willing to pay for this critical aspect of development. The English-speaking Caribbean's expenditure on education is higher than that of Latin America, and Barbados's expenditures are the highest in the region, as both a percentage of gross domestic product (GDP) and expenditure per capita. In 2003, and including expenditures for health, Barbados's spending was 13.2 percent of GDP, compared with 7.54 percent for oil/gas-rich Trinidad/Tobago and 3.42 percent for resource-rich Jamaica.[26] The results in the critical area of secondary education are evident: Barbados's enrollments in 2004 were higher than the Caribbean average as well as those of Korea, Hong King, and even the United States.

The fact that historically there was little land outside the plantation and that what was available was beyond the means of the working-class whites, let alone the emancipated blacks, means that migration has always been a fact of life on the island. There developed a true culture of migration. The movement to the American mainland has already been noted, but it is worth repeating that in the seventeenth century, some 30,000 of the Irish and Scottish who had been transported to the island migrated, mostly to the Eastern Seaboard and especially South Carolina. In the eighteenth century, another 20,000 migrated.[27] Originally migration of blacks was discouraged in order to keep an ample supply of low paid labor on the plantations. Only during periods of crisis in the market for sugar and thus on the plantation were blacks encouraged to migrate as a matter of national security. This explains the mass movement to Panama at the beginning of the twentieth century. Between 1904 and 1912, 44.1 percent of the laborers in the Panama Canal were from Barbados, where they were generally referred to as "West Indians." This represented 10 percent of the island's total population and 40 percent of the adult male population at the time. The character of the Barbadian working class became a matter of admiration, as David McCullough wrote:

> Generally speaking, the West Indian worker on the Panama Canal was soft-spoken, courteous, sober, very religious, as nearly everyone associated with the work came to appreciate. John Stevens once remarked that he never knew such law-abiding people and the records show the crime rate, as well as the incidence of alcoholism and venereal disease, among the black employees to have been abnormally low throughout the construction years.[28]

Again, a peculiar Barbados attitude was evident in Panama and among those who returned to the island. "The returned Panama Canal labourer," commented one observer "is an uncommonly vain fellow." This same commentator presciently observed that "returnees to Barbados brought with them a less subservient attitude and a new cosmopolitanism. They would be at the forefront of the social upheavals of the 1920s and 1930s that eventually led to political decolonization."[29] Be that as it may, what this migration really created were the first accumulations of capital that allowed the island's working class not so much to buy as to rent in leasehold land and start businesses. And, let it be said, as Starkey observed, none of this disrupted the culture of deference which had already crystallized. Traditions were upheld from the first settlement in 1625, including the recognition of the British colonial past and its institutions as an integral part of their history. Niall Ferguson's assertion that "the difficulty with the achievements of empire is that they are much more likely to be taken for granted than the sins of empire"[30] might be a truism, but it does not apply to Barbados. This island refuses to turn its back on its colonial past, traditions, and legacies. Predictably, this attitude explains much of the derision of outsiders bent on "decolonization." As Courtney Blackman, a former governor of the Barbados Central Bank, once said, outsiders have found Barbados "guilty of the crime of crimes, to have been English from 1625."[31] The criticisms did not stop.

In his justly praised 1968 treatise on the growth of the modern West Indies, Gordon K. Lewis opens his discussion of the Barbadian case by stating that "it is difficult to speak of Barbados except in mockingly derisory terms." Lewis is correct in saying that Barbados has always borne the brunt, if not of outright ridicule, at least of biting banter by fellow West Indians. "Little England," the "Tropical Isle of Wight," and "black Englishmen" are but some of the derisory names used. This carries over into popular imagery and comparisons not always meant to ridicule. When Trinidadians, upset with local umpiring in cricket, say "they do not do such things in England or in Barbados," only the tendency to ridicule the island would lead anyone to consider this unflattering to the Barbadians. But so it is, and Lewis himself contributes to that derision. "If Trinidad is West Indian Byzantine," Lewis argues, "Barbados is an English market town." Things are even worse than that, according to Lewis, because Barbados continues to hold on to what was essentially a stereotype of a kind of English town that passed away after 1914. Barbadians, he concludes, are a people stuck in time, living with a kind of "antiquarian nostalgia for the old folkways and pastimes . . . under the omnipresent shadow of a romanticized past." None of this is encouraging for development, says Lewis, because "it is doubtful that one could ever modernize a society so deeply traditionalist."[32] Thus Gordon Lewis agrees with W. Arthur Lewis and the New World Group thesis that pure plantation systems are incapable of innovation.

Gordon Lewis is not the first British observer to treat Barbadian adherence to tradition with irony and even ridicule. It is this Barbadian attachment to tradition which led the English scholar Anthony Trollope in 1859 to describe Barbadians as "a little self-glorious. . . . No people ever praised themselves so constantly; no set of men were ever so assured that they and their occupations are the main pegs on which the world hangs."[33] Arriving three decades after Trollope, the English scholar James Anthony Froude noted that 250 years of British occupation had imprinted strongly "an English character" on the island's inhabitants and that they "cling to their home with innocent vanity as though it was the finest country in the world."[34] This, of course, contradicts Mintz's assertions that plantation societies do not engender a sense of national identity.

These oft-repeated observations and admixture of admiration and scoffing were not limited to scholars and the Victorian travelers of the nineteenth century.[35] The Englishman P. L. Fermor visited after World War II and could not hide his disdain for what was already an identifiable Barbadian character:

Barbados reflects most faithfully the social and intellectual values and
prejudices of a Golf Club in outer London ... or of the married quarters of a barracks in Basutoland, which are not England's most interesting or precious contributions to world civilization.[36]

The juxtaposing of the golf club and the barracks refers to the class/race
divide on the island. That divide was the closest thing to what would later
be called "apartheid" in South Africa. Indeed, the South African comparison
was often made, and censured, by other West Indians.

Few cases illustrate the region's dislike and distrust of Barbados social
structural (i.e., racial) realities better than the search for a capital city for the
newly formed state of the West Indies Federation in 1948.[37] The choices were
three: Jamaica, Trinidad, or Barbados. Unable to agree among themselves,
West Indians accepted the Colonial Office's appointment of a three-man
commission. Barbados, in order to enhance its claim, quickly passed its first
law outlawing racial discrimination in public places. This belated recognition
of its terrible record of race relations did not change the region's attitude
toward the island, a fact duly noted by the commission of three Englishmen.
They made a specific reference to the pervasive criticism of all the other islands, "that Barbados had a prejudice against colour not found elsewhere."
The commissioners admitted that this was so but recommended the island
as the site anyway. The grounds they cited were worthy of a Burkean dictate:
stability, they said, was of the essence for a federal capital city and that history has shown that "changes occur more slowly in a stable society."[38] This
did not persuade the other islands. They rejected the choice of Barbados
and eventually selected Trinidad as the site of the capital of the short-lived
experiment in West Indies federalism.

The striking aspect of Barbadian history is that even the most severe—and
persistent—critics of the long history of white rule in Barbados eventually
turn to the great paradox that, whatever injuries racism caused individuals, it
did not have longer-term negative results for the collectivity. The understand-
able difficulty of dealing with this contradiction and paradox objectively,
more often than not, results in an obvious non sequitur. In the most widely
used text on the island's history, Hilary Beckles consistently lambastes the
injustices of a society in which the white "manipulation planter-merchant
oligarchy" perpetually kept a "stranglehold" on all aspects of society only to
conclude, "The country has certainly lived up to the challenges of nation-

hood, and citizens pride themselves for being among those American nations with the highest material living standards and democratic freedoms."[39]
Similarly, Linden Lewis, in a lengthy essay that calls for a structural change
in the nature of the Barbadian economy, begins his analysis with two quota-
tions: the first from George Lamming and the second from "Mighty Gabby,"
a calypsonian:

> Barbados has always been ruled by fear. There was no black man of my
> generation, irrespective of class or occupation, who was not afraid of
> white people. There was no black boss who did not see it as his role
> to intimidate his black subordinates: and to do so on behalf of white
> power. This legacy of fear, created and nourished by an ideology of rac-
> ism, has never been overcome to this day.

> Barbados is a little South Africa of the past. But certainly, racism is a
> highly denied realism in Barbados.

Lewis follows their observations with his own analysis:

> Barbados has an exceptionally high rate of literacy—believed to be
> somewhere around 98 percent. Its infrastructural development is ex-
> cellent, and it finds itself in a position to boast of its accomplishments
> in housing, health, education, and public utilities and in the areas of
> tourism development, sugar production, and the export of quality
> rum. Barbadians pride themselves on being a model of stability and
> prudent management, perhaps even to the point of arrogance.[40]

Contrasting statements such as those of Beckles and Lewis need explaining,
but this is never done. Similarly, Michael Howard outlines in detail the "deleterious impact" of centuries of colonization by the "planter-merchant alliance" and what he calls the "functional dependence" of the society intended
to continue elite economic power. He then concludes that the island has had
a very successful development due to three things: high levels of political
stability guaranteeing "smooth transition" from colonial to modern times, a
reasonably disciplined workforce with high levels of literacy, and sound governmental economic policy and management.[41] Nowhere is there an attempt
to explain how a society dominated by such selfish elite power manages to
have such a democratic development history. Are the Beckles and Howard
versions "Tales of Two Cities" or simply illogical and fallacious because they

do not account for the paradoxical in the evolution of their island? At a more theoretical level, one has to ask whether holding on to traditions, including the objectionable ones, is an insurmountable obstacle to development as argued by W. Arthur Lewis, the New World Group, and Gordon K. Lewis. As already noted in the prologue, Edward Shils rejects the widely held thesis, and modern sociological theory understands what Edmund Burke understood, that even objectionable values can have very positive functions over the long run. Because of this key interpretation, Shils's arguments are worth repeating in the Barbados case.

At least since the French Revolution, says Shils, western intellectuals have made anti-institutionalism and anti-traditionalism central to their theoretical formulations. They had to combat "the inequity of tradition." Unfortunately, tradition "has become a term of polemic and not an object of analysis.[42] Traditional beliefs, Shils argues, are beliefs that contain an attachment to the past, to some particular time in the past, or to a whole social system or particular institutions which (allegedly) existed in the past. Beliefs that are considered traditional are those which assert the moral rightness or superiority of institutions or a society of the past and which assert that what is done now or in the future should be modeled on the past patterns of belief or conduct. Far from being a barrier to change, Shils argues, the survival of traditional beliefs, even in latent form, contributes to the continuity of personality systems and certain institutions, like the family and religious communities, which manage to withstand, at least partially, the rapid and far-reaching changes in other spheres. Traditions provide the personality systems with a measure of toughness and continuity. Even after periods of severe deprivation and disorganization, says Shils, they tend to reassert themselves with most of the same properties they possessed before disruption. Many traditional beliefs that become assimilated into the personality system by virtue of the implicit or explicit dispositions toward authority become main supports of what Shils calls "the need-system."[43] On this, Shils is very much in the sociological tradition of thinkers such as Burke and Tocqueville.[44]

Contrary to the assumption that respect for the traditions and institutions of their colonial past created what Trinidad writer V. S. Naipaul calls, with his usual acidity, "Mimic Men,"[45] men who, lacking order and discipline, mistake words for power, in Barbados it created some tough, independent-minded leaders, first white and now black. From the very inception of colonization, the settlers demanded equal rights. Notice the tone of a memo to the king in 1684:

> After a King has given unto any People, being under his Obedience and Subjection, the Laws of *England* for the Government of the Country, no succeeding King can alter the same without Parliament. And therefore as the Inhabitants were by the first Grant invested with all the Rights, Privileges, and Franchises of *English* subjects, ... it has been adjudged, 'That tho' this Island is Parcel, of the Possession of *England*, yet 'tis not govern'd by the Laws made in *England*, but by its own particular Laws and Customs.[46]

The critical aspect of Barbadian political culture has always been its capacity to combine deference to the symbols of the British monarchy without ever losing its functional and psychological independence from that monarchy; deference, yes, submissiveness, never. Because it was never a Crown colony ruled directly from London, as were so many of the islands, including Trinidad and Jamaica, Barbados governed itself little differently from the way the British governed themselves.

It is in this vein that the first prime minister of independent Barbados, Errol Barrow, upset by some slight, wrote the *New York Times* in September 20, 1966, that since George Washington had witnessed his first truly independent assembly in Barbados, it is there that Americans learned their first lesson in self-government. This letter was no mere fluke on the prime minister's part. During the confrontational conference in London on Barbados's independence, Barrow lectured the British secretary of state for the colonies and his staff in what is now known in the same Barbadian treasury of historical myths as the "No Loitering on the Premises" speech:

> When in 1639 your own country had been governed without a Parliament for 11 years, the English inhabitants of Barbados settled a Parliament for themselves and thereby created the Legislative institutions which we have since, without any disturbance, enjoyed. In this respect, Barbados shared only with Virginia, Massachusetts, and Bermuda the solid comforts of representative government.

Again, without showing the least concern for the British secretary's discomfort, Barrow continued:

In 1651 when Englishmen were cowering in their homes under the whip of Cromwell's major-generals, and when they who had lopped off the head of a king sought to enmesh the people of Barbados in their saintly tyranny, Barbadians stubbornly defended their respective institutions from Cromwell and in the famous Charter of Barbados which they signed, they have managed to preserve for three centuries the supremacy of parliaments and the liberty of the subject.[47]

Finally, none of this development could have been sustained through the Caribbean's "lost decade" of the 1970s without Barbados's judicious handling of its race relations, moderate ideology in domestic and foreign policies, and level-headed understanding of the geopolitical limits, regional and international, of being a small state.

As already noted, Barbados's success could not have been predicted by the writings of West Indian intellectuals who were convinced that holding on to tradition was the formula for developmental failure. Writing at the end of the 1950s, a distinguished economist at the University of the West Indies joined the chorus of those who believed that the development prospects for Jamaica, British Guyana, and Trinidad were solid. "By contrast," he continued, "a survey of the history of the Barbadian economy since 1938 leaves one with the impression of stability and even rigidity."[48] Even a Jamaican anthropologist who theorized that the islands were all "plural" societies could not help striking at the elite of the plantation society. "The overriding concern of this elite," wrote M. G. Smith, "is to maintain its links with the metropolitan power and the imperial government." What they fear most, he said disapprovingly, is "instability."[49]

There is no better example of the antiestablishmentarianism of West Indian intellectuals than the extensive and well-funded study of populist politics in the region in the 1960s, Archie Singham's *The Hero and the Crowd*, discussed in chapter 9. Not once making reference to the stability next door in Barbados, Singham spoke of "the inevitable crisis in colonial societies" due to the "indiscriminate imposition" of the British Westminster system. Personal rule, he concluded, was "an almost inevitable concomitant of colonial politics." Native middle classes all suffer from "anomie and rage" because they are all "anxiety ridden" about their identity, a failure of plantation societies that were fundamentally "dependent" societies.[50]

All this is to say that while there is abundant interest in studying "revolution," there is lamentably little interest in studying either the consequences or the benefits of postrevolutionary stability.[51] Indeed, there are no studies of just how much the "antiestablishment" movement of the 1970s set the region back. It is a fact that these racial and ideological upheavals reached every corner of the Caribbean with one exception: Barbados. There, domestic policy extended to foreign affairs showing moderation and caution in ideological and geopolitical terms. Not a single major politician in Barbados followed Jamaica's Michael Manley's sharp ideological turn to the left during his second term in office (1976–80). No major politician in Barbados believed that the People's Revolutionary Government in Grenada (1979–83) was anything more than a revolt against a despised government, opportunistically turned into a "revolution" with Cuban support. To the extent that it was articulated, Black Power in Barbados—on the rise in politics and the economy—took on a much more intellectual tone and set of goals. This did not involve censorship evident by the fact that one of the books most widely assigned at the Barbados campus of the University of the West Indies was a text by the Jamaican George Beckford articulating a thesis that the only path to economic, social, political, and even "psychological advancement" in the Caribbean was the complete destruction of the plantation system.[52] In Barbados, the governor of the Central Bank answered such theses with the pragmatism that was already part of the political culture. Noting that it was still popular to project the image of an all-white power structure such as existed in Barbados prior to 1937, Blackman warned: "If we continue to base our conduct on the 1937 image, we will certainly succeed in impoverishing a few hundred whites; in the process we shall also destroy our major agricultural industry and reduce the standard of living of the remaining 240,000 or so non-white Barbadians."[53]

Just as Jamaica and Guyana (and to a lesser extent Trinidad) witnessed the drying up of direct foreign investments and a massive flight of human talent and capital in the 1970s, Barbados was experiencing its first significant infusions of international and domestic capital. While the others were rejecting the Puerto Rican and W. Arthur Lewis model of "industrialization by invitation" they had all adopted earlier, Barbados was implementing it to build the industrial and tourist infrastructures it now enjoys. Even that radical (in Barbadian terms) Errol Barrow, lambasted and excoriated by Caribbean radicals in the 1970s for his moderation, did not hesitate to admit that he and his new nation would march to their own drummer. "I have certain principles," he said. "They may be Victorian and you may consider them ingenuous."[54] But, he said, there was nothing ingenuous about his understanding of two fundamental features of Caribbean geopolitics: because of the deep roots of the diasporas in the United States and the historical importance of the remittances sent to people on the island, it was virtually impossible to turn these people into ideological anti-Americans, and because the leadership in the islands had been historically Fabian socialist and tightly aligned with democratic trade unions, they were intrinsically adverse to Communism.[55]

But moderation in the midst of regional instability was also evident in the area of economics. In the most authoritative study of comparative economic performances in the region in the 1970s, Barbadian economist DeLisle Worrell notes that since external prospects were the same for all the islands, the different political and economic outcomes have been due to the policies chosen. Fiscal and monetary conservatism won out. "Orderliness," he writes, "must be the watchword of policymakers in small economies."[56] Barbadian moderation also characterizes the society's attitude toward the private sector, one of the most contentious areas of Caribbean society. The reasons are evident: there has been historically a high correlation between race and class and between race and the private sector. "White oligarchy" is the most benign of those terms used throughout the region, even in staid Barbados. The debate over race and control of the private sector has never been purely academic. It has been fuel for West Indian social-political movements from the days of constitutional reform at the end of the nineteenth century to the Black Power movements of the mid-twentieth century. Whether it is the "High Street Boys" of the Bahamas, the "Parasitic French Creole Oligarchy" of Trinidad, the "Exploitative Portuguese" of Guyana, or the "ethnic minorities" (Jews, Chinese, and Lebanese) of Jamaica, the question is invariably this: Is it the purposeful opposition of these ethnic minorities that has kept the black majority out of the private sector? The answers usually show that where you stand depends on where you sit. In Barbados in 1992, only 10 percent of whites believed that color was an important factor in business advancement, while 44 percent of blacks believed that it was.[57] Researchers Errol Barrow and J. E. Greene present data showing the overwhelming white dominance of the private sector yet speak of a black "perception . . . whether real or imagined" of this dominance and consider it an important psychological factor in holding back black entrepreneurship. Nothing imagined about it, the historical dominance of whites has created a self-fulfilling prophesy. But need it, and can it, continue, given the new realities of the islands' economies?

There is evidence that Barbadian attitudes are changing, but not without strife. A case in point was the so-called Mutual affair, the battle to integrate the all-white board of directors of the Barbados Mutual Life Insurance Company. Given that the vast majority of policyholders were black, the resistance of the all-white board to do what appeared to be perfectly just, that is, including blacks on its board, was obdurate and irrational. It logically and justly generated widespread racial resentment. When the board finally integrated, it did not do so voluntarily but even in its grudging way avoided affecting the viability of the company. Again, it is worth turning to the trained eye of an outsider to put the Mutual affair battle in its proper Barbados context. Given the tensions involved in the Mutual affair, wrote the *Economist* on July 8, 1989, "perhaps the surprise is how little racial tension there is in Barbados today. . . . There has been a lot of social change with remarkably little sound and fury. After all the fuss at the Barbados Mutual, board and objectors look as if they are following the island's *much maligned* tradition of consensus and compromise."[58]

The fact is that when the issue is studied systematically, the common folk tend to have a more nuanced view of race and economic power. In Trinidad, Selwyn Ryan sought responses to the assertion: "Panday (leader of the majority Indian party) has characterized the 'French Creoles' as a 'Parasitic Oligarchy' which controls the country behind the scenes. Do you think there is any truth to his assertion?"[59] Here are the answers: True 0 percent; Partially True 28 percent; Not True at All 50 percent; Don't Know 22 percent.

It is paradoxical, given its long history of white domination, that it should be in Barbados where black attitudes toward starting businesses are changing most rapidly. The opening of business schools at the Cave Hill campus of the University of the West Indies, the establishment of the Barbados Development Bank, and the opening of the Barbados Institute of Management and Productivity are all geared toward helping small businesses. Important also is the publishing of serious inquiries into the history of business on the island. One such contribution is that of Henderson Carter, who studied several black businesses that went from great success to bankruptcy. He concludes that despite the acknowledged obstacles of race prejudice, "no single causal factor explains the failure of some of the black businesses in

Barbados."[60] He does conclude that things are changing. Of the sixteen pictures of "Outstanding Business Leaders of the Modern Period" Carter includes in his book, eight are black. He attributes the increasing success of blacks and whites in business to two fundamental processes. First is the role government has taken in development, through legislative enactment, tax concessions, infrastructure support, and by giving certain government agencies such as the Fair Trading Commission some teeth to enforce a word that commission often uses: *equity*.[61] None of this is exclusively Barbadian; all Caribbean states have enacted sustainable development plans in an attempt to involve all sectors of the society in the process. What does have a distinctly Barbadian bent, however, is the second reason Carter gives for the island's success: the social partnership among the government, the private sector, and the unions, "which have shown responsibility and restraint" and been "a critical agent of social stability." Carter is referring to the social compact first formalized in 1993–95 and renewed every two years through a "protocol" among government, employers' representatives, and workers' representatives called "social partners." Although not created by an act of Parliament, the group's final meeting is always chaired by the prime minister, and its report is submitted to Parliament. The fundamental goal is industrial harmony through tripartite consultation. Emphasizing the fact that Barbados is a small open economy in a world of globalization and trade liberalization, the 2008 protocol spells out the new attitude toward the private sector. After admitting the obvious—that not all sectors of the society have "been afforded their full opportunity"—the representatives pledged to eliminate all forms of discrimination even as they acknowledged that "the Social Partners realize that the private sector provides the vital engine of growth in the economy. . . . The Partners recognize that while fair and balanced regulations are necessary, every effort should be made to ensure that these regulations support a culture of entrepreneurship."[62]

No precise comparative data on industrial relations among the islands are available to this author. From a purely anecdotal perspective, however, Barbados would appear to have relatively fewer disruptive industrial disputes than its counterparts. But, according to my informants, the number of wildcat strikes had been increasing. Indeed, Labour Department data show that although the number of work stoppages decreased from forty in 2005 to thirty-one in 2006, the total number of man-days lost increased from 2,606 in 2005 to 4,228 in 2006, and the number of workers involved in work stoppages was 55 percent higher in 2006 than in 2005.[63] None of this involved any violence, road blockages, or illegal occupations of premises, however. Barbadian civility seems to reign even in the midst of serious grievances. This does not mean that the Barbadian worker is not capable and prone to forcefully asserting his or her rights. What they also appear to be capable of doing is keeping legitimate labor disputes as just that, disputes over fairness. Seldom are these carried over into areas best called "unrealistic," that is, class or racial conflict that cannot be settled in labor-management negotiations. Those disputes are best left for the political arena where they are "settled" by free elections. It is this system of contested but ultimately peaceful class and economic sector relations that helped Barbadians overcome a similar financial crisis in 1991, and odds are that it will help the island emerge from the crisis it faces today.

As we study how Barbados maneuvers to extricate itself from the very severe fiscal crisis it faces, we would do well to pause and reflect on the admirable historical transition this small, densely populated island has made from a total sugar economy dominated by an all-white plantocracy to an economically and racially diversified society governed by a freely elected black elite today. That history demonstrates that even a total plantation society can evolve and progress when there is, as in Barbados, the political will to do so and the educated populace who know how to elect leaders with just such a will.

12

Cuba, the Last Holdout

"Organic" Intellectuals Defend the Revolution
by Abandoning Marxist-Leninism

> The learning process of revolutionaries in the field of economic con-
> struction is more difficult than we had imagined. . . . We have cost the
> people too much in our process of learning.
>
> Fidel Castro, speech, Year of the 10-Million-Ton Zafra, July 26, 1970

During the 2009 Summit of the Americas in Port-of-Spain, Trinidad, Venezuelan president Hugo Chávez pressed forward to give U.S. president Barack
Obama a copy of Eduardo Galeano's 1971 book, *Las venas abiertas de América
Latina*. The book was the iconic statement on American imperialism and
hegemonic exploitation of the Western Hemisphere. It sold in the millions.
Chávez called it "a monument to our Latin American history," but his gesture, while theatrical, was utterly futile. Not only did Obama show little if
any interest in meeting Chávez but he also showed little interest in hemispheric affairs as a whole. As it turned out, Galeano himself later admitted
that he believed the theme of his book to be passé. He would not, he said,
read, much less write, such a book again.[1] The ideological and geopolitical
confrontations that were legendary in this hemisphere, said Galeano, from
the multiple military interventions (à la Haiti and the Dominican Republic)
to the efforts at destabilization (à la Chile of Allende or the Contras in Nicaragua) were things of the past. Whatever validity his treatise might have had
in the past, by his own admission, today it has none. Reality today, Galeano
noted, is much more complex. That said, there is one arena of confrontation
which has shown little change: U.S.-Cuban relations. Cuba's style of governance has not changed that much, and U.S. policy toward the last Marxian

holdout in the hemisphere has done little to engender the change that the United States sought.

No need to argue with the fact that for the past five decades U.S. policy toward Communist Cuba has been dominated by a policy that can be characterized by what in game theory is called "endgame strategizing." The main characteristic of that strategy is called "the gambler's fallacy": the blind faith that eventually the dice will roll in one's favor. The end was initially perceived as "neutralizing" Fidel Castro, either by assassination[2] or by contriving to have his beard fall out or causing some other form of physical deformation that would cost him his charismatic appeal. The argument was that, absent the charismatic leader plus the pressures from a stifling embargo, Cuban politics would take a different course. Even one as knowledgeable as Frank Tannenbaum predicted as early as 1961 that Castro would be overthrown by the Cuban people. "The people," he said, "will throw themselves into the streets by the thousands, perhaps even by the millions."[3] This became what Don Bohning rightfully calls a strategic "obsession."[4] Rare indeed have been the contrary opinions such as those of Senator J. William Fulbright, who as early as 1964 called on U.S. policy makers to abandon "the myth that Cuban communism . . . is going to collapse or disappear in the immediate future." We have to accept, he advised, that it will long survive "as a disagreeable reality."[5] As chairman of the Senate's Foreign Relations Committee from 1959 to 1974, Fulbright had a holistic understanding of how superpower status could blind a nation's elite's comprehension of complexity in international relations. Call it hubris. "Power," he wrote, "confuses itself with virtue. . . . Once imbued with the idea of a mission, a great nation easily assumes that it has the means as well as the duty to do God's work."[6] Fulbright, of course, was right then, and his opinions are still right today, since there is no evidence that despite the known generalized popular discontent, Cubans are ready to storm the ramparts of the state. Be that as it may, both the international and the domestic situations of the revolutions have been changing. As Galeano explained, it is a more complex world, both inside and outside Cuba.

That is the kind of complexity Mikhail Gorbachev must have had in mind when he announced in 1987 that the USSR was now going to start charity at home, that they were "pragmatists, not adventurers," and, as such, were not going to exploit anti-U.S. attitudes, "let alone fuel them," nor were they going to "erode the traditional links between Latin America and the United States."

Consequently, he said, there were going to be changes in Soviet strategies in the Third World starting with a reconsideration of relations and economic assistance to Marxist-Leninist vanguard parties. It was premature to conclude, however, that the handwriting for Cuban Marxism was on the wall.[7] That was twenty-seven years ago, which only goes to prove that the past cannot be erased with a book of opinions or even the collapse of an economic system—certainly not a revolutionary past such as that of Cuba. There were profound historical reasons for the three major revolutions that occurred in this hemisphere: the Haitian, the Mexican, and the Cuban. Each had its "moment" on the world scene, but each was different. In the case of Haiti, as we noted in chapters 4 and 6, everything conspired to contain that revolution to that one country. Similarly, the Mexican Revolution, despite some symbolic transnational influences, was also a one-country phenomenon. The Cuban Revolution has had a global impact in terms of ideological trends and direct intervention.[8] As English Marxist Eric Hobsbawn noted, "In the third quarter of the century all eyes were on the guerrillas." And it was Cuba ("oddly," says Hobsbawn) which "put the guerrilla strategy on the world's front pages." No revolution, says Hobsbawn, could have been better designed to appeal to the Left of the western hemisphere and the developed countries or to give the guerrilla strategy better publicity: "The Cuban revolution had everything: romance, heroism . . . ex-student leaders with the selfless generosity of their youth—a jubilant people, in a tropical tourist paradise pulsing with rumba rhythms. . . . Fidel's example inspired the militant intellectuals everywhere."[9]

This highlights a fundamental characteristic of the Cuban Revolution: it was, as Senator Fulbright warned, not imposed by an outside power but was an authentically Cuban grassroots affair that was initially wildly popular. Even the Castro-Guevara theory of the revolutionary *foco* was original. And yet, Hobsbawn concludes, five decades after thousands of true-believing intellectuals had died (including many on the island of Trinidad), the whole foco or guerrilla thing was "a spectacularly misconceived strategy."[10] Indeed, since the collapse of the Soviet Union in 1990, Cuba has been struggling to save its own revolution. As far as revolutionary international involvements are concerned, Cuba has gone from activism to what Michael Oakeshott called "quietism," an essential feature of a conservative political culture. Its international involvements are largely in services: medical personnel, teachers, and sports coaches. All, to be sure, are handsomely paid for by the many host countries. Additionally, Cuba now acts as good faith intermediary trying to bring groups such as the FARC of Colombia into electoral politics. In other words, Cuba is contributing to the dismantling of guerrilla movements it once encouraged and assisted.

That there have been changes in the U.S. public's attitude toward Cuba has been in evidence for some years, but especially in 2013 and 2014. Small but not insignificant movements were evident in policy on both sides of the Florida Straits. From the U.S. side, President Obama—perhaps encouraged by the fact that he carried Florida in the 2012 presidential elections and that 35 percent of Cuban Americans voted for him—began to relax the laws on travel and remittances. The results have been dramatic: 600,000 Cuban Americans and Americans traveled to the island in 2013, and 173,550 Cuban Americans traveled during the first three months of 2014. Approximately 63 percent of Cuban Americans remit money to Cuba, and in 2013 that amounted to $2.7 million, 90 percent of which came from the United States. Opinion polls supported these changes. The best longitudinal polling has been done by the Cuban Research Institute at Florida International University, and it reconfirms the steady downward trend in the support by Miami Cuban Americans for the embargo: in 1991, 87 percent supported it; in 1997, 78 percent; in 2004, 66 percent; in 2011, 56 percent; and in 2014, only 48 percent of Cuban Americans supported the embargo.[11] Similarly, the Atlantic Council revealed on February 11, 2014, that its national poll on U.S.-Cuba relations indicated that 56 percent of Americans—63 percent among Florida adults and 62 percent among Latinos—favored a change in U.S. policy toward Cuba.

This popular change of public opinion has been accompanied by important lobbying efforts in favor of opening and even lifting the embargo. The *New York Times* editorialized on October 12, 2014, that "The Moment to Restore Ties to Cuba" had arrived. Most surprising was a letter to the president signed by forty-four former high-ranking civilian and military figures and some key Cuban American businessmen. They included John Negroponte (former director of national intelligence), Admiral James Stavridis (former commander of U.S. Southern Command, Miami), Andrés Fanjul (Florida sugar magnate), Gustavo A. Cisneros (Venezuelan media mogul), and Jorge Pérez (The Related Group).[12] Reflecting the changed mood, in May 2014 the president of the U.S. Chamber of Commerce led a large delegation of businesspeople to Cuba. Joining the push for changes, the Peterson Institute for International Economics published a policy-oriented book suggesting

that both the United States and Cuba stand to gain a lot from greater economic integration.[13] This was also the opinion of Eric Schmidt, president
of Google, who visited Cuba in June 2014.[14] In May 2014, Charlie Crist,
Democratic candidate for governor of Florida, declared that he intended
to travel to Cuba. Although he later canceled, it is significant that in a poll
published by the *Miami Herald* (June 8, 2014), 67 percent of the Miami-
Dade registered voters declared that his proposed trip would have no influence on their vote. It seemed in 2014 that, except for certain sectors of the
Cuban American community and the *Miami Herald*,[15] Americans, including
Floridians, were open to a more flexible and liberal policy toward Cuba.

Before dismissing movements on the Cuban side as insignificant, one
has to take note of the difficulty of any Cuban attempts at restructuring, not
just the institutions of the island but indeed its entire political culture. Five
decades of revolution are not easily reversed. As early as the 1960s, Richard
Fagen had recorded the dramatic revolutionary efforts to erase the past and
to create what Che Guevara called a "New Man."[16] Despite major changes,
however, it cannot be said that even fifty-five years of such efforts managed
to do in its entirety what Che Guevara and Fidel Castro intended. Nevertheless, it is evident that Cuba is not what it was in pre-Castro days. Breaking out
of the all-inclusive grasp of the state, political and economic, is not going to
be smooth sailing. All the signs, however, point to a slow but unmistakable
move toward decentralization as the command economy is being chipped
away and charismatic authority is replaced by greater pragmatism. No one
has analyzed this excruciating process more acutely than Carmelo Mesa-
Lago, here speaking of Fidel Castro's ideological cast of mind:

> He reluctantly grants piecemeal concessions (his brain responding to
> the reformers, whose arguments are bolstered by Cuba's economic de-
> bacle) but regulates them to death (his heart supporting the orthodox,
> who still believe that both the revolution and socialism can be saved).
> Yet the Cuban crisis is of such enormous magnitude that it demands an
> ideologically integrated team capable of designing and implementing
> a comprehensive and coherent economic reform. Meanwhile, Castro
> is gradually losing power to market forces, and the reform process ap-
> pears irreversible.[17]

At the level of the erstwhile diminutive private sector, a poll done by the
Havana Consulting Group in Miami concluded with some hyperbole that

the actions of the diaspora were "without a doubt . . . transforming the style of life of the Cubans on the island."[18] Many of the changes, such as reducing state employment by 500,000 workers, made encouragement of private enterprise an inexorable necessity. Other reforms followed, such as the right to buy and sell houses and cars and to travel abroad. Most dramatic, given the closed, centralized nature of the system, was the new law regulating foreign investments, including those by Cuban Americans. The new investment law sounds (at least on paper) vaguely similar to the original Puerto Rican model: tax holidays, exemption from payroll taxes, special arbitration procedures, and a clause ensuring no nationalization in the future. In preparation for what Cuba hopes will be many investments in import, export, and manufacturing, Cuba (with Brazilian money) expanded its port of Mariel and built an adjacent Free Trade Zone. Beyond what these ongoing changes demonstrate, there are other reasons for believing that the reform process is irreversible.

Historically, one has to understand three critical things. First, despite the authentically domestic nature of the revolution, Cuban Communism or Marxism-Leninism as an ideology is, and has always been, skin deep among the people. Second, important sectors of what Antonio Gramsci called "organic intellectuals" have been agitating for a major shift in economic policies (not "regime change") for a long time. And, third, far from being a weak, transitory leader, Raúl Castro has proven to be a strong leader, motivated to change, with whom negotiations are possible. In order to understand these three points, it is necessary to do a review of the roots of communism in Cuba.

The birth and development of Cuban communism starts with the Spanish immigrant laborers who first brought radical ideas to Cuba. These syndico-anarchists continued to have close ties with their Spanish homeland and the movements there and in other parts of Europe. Not surprisingly, the first socialist party would be organized by a Cuban, Diego Vicente Tejera, whose residence in Spain and Paris exposed him to both the misery of the working classes of those countries and the socialist intellectuals who addressed themselves to possible solutions.[19] Tejera's major works were written in Paris (in French), and even after his return to Cuba, his closest intellectual associates were to be found not in Cuba but in radical circles in the Florida cities of Key West and Tampa, both settled by Cuban tobacco workers. Neither Tejera's Partido Socialista Cubano (est. 1899) nor the one that followed its demise in

1900, the equally short-lived Partido Popular, had any impact on the Cuban laboring classes. For one, these classes were too deeply divided on ethnic grounds, with native Cubans (*criollos*) resenting the Spanish workers.[20] In fact, Cuban intellectuals did not find relative ideological cohesiveness until Lenin and then Stalin organized the Third International and its organizing arm, the Comintern.

The origins of the Cuban Communist Party in 1925 showed just how persistent conservative Cuban society was, making the protean and small Cuban radical groups highly dependent on foreign Marxists. Although the guiding spirits of local Communists were undoubtedly the young Cuban university students Julio Antonio Mella and Carlos Baliño, foreigners played critical roles in the organizing stages: Mexicans, Yiddish-speaking Poles, and Catalan-speaking Spaniards, so much so that a translator was needed for these early meetings.[21] Crucial financial aid came from the American Communist Party (USCP), which meant the Cuban Communist Party readily accepted the leadership of the USCP, which was, in turn, subject to commands from Moscow's Comintern. Mella himself had a deep mistrust of any and all national bourgeoisies, especially the reformist ones, and he looked upon the Third International and Moscow as the "pivot" of all Latin American socialist movements. He continually sought "inspiration" from that source.[22] According to Robert Alexander, the lines of communication ran Moscow/Paris/New York/Havana.[23] Crucial decisions made during the early phases of the Cuban Communist Party indicate its close dependence on external factors. This included the initial working alliance between two new labor unions (the Confederación Nacional Obrera and the Federación Obrera de la Habana), allied in 1925 to the new Communist Party, which eventually split after the Stalin-Trotsky rift. Cuban Trotskyites (who controlled the Federación Obrera de la Habana) left or were expelled from the Cuban Communist Party and formed the Partido Bolchevique Leninista. The leaders of both wings of the movement were under no illusions as to their condition of dependence on events in the United States. Victor Alba notes how even the Trotskyites believed that "there could be no revolution in Cuba so long as socialism remained a minor force in the United States, because of the island's economic dependence on the United States."[24]

If splits within the Cuban movements reflected the situation in the Soviet Union, so did the Cuban Communist Party posture regarding vital Cuban national problems. Such a problem was the "Negro question." There can be no argument that the Cuban Communists were the first to really deal with race relations—historically a burning issue in Cuba—and that they were the first to make a truly concerted effort to change what was a shameful state of affairs. But their efforts did show a high degree of dependence on the Soviet Comintern's posture in both the United States and Cuba: the Negro question according to the Comintern was to be dealt with as a "national" rather than a "racial" question. In Cuba that meant that black "self-determination" was to be built in the "Black Belt" of Oriente Province. The Cuban approach was identical in goals and even wording to the posture adopted by the USCP on the Negro question in the United States.[25]

Throughout the 1930s, leaders of the USCP, such as Earl Browder, Robert Minor, James W. Ford, and William Z. Foster, were frequent guests and speakers at various activities of the Cuban Communist Party. Similarly, Cuban Communists were frequently in the United States, especially after the Comintern ordered, in 1934, a shift from the anticapitalist "Third Period" to a collaborationist "Popular Front" stance. In 1936, Blas Roca, secretary general of the Party, went so far as to tell the *New York Times* that he was in the United States in order to ensure "continued financial aid" from the U.S. Communists.[26] The behavior of the Cuban Communist Party, including its "critical support" of the Batista regime (1940–44), was quite in keeping with the "Browderite" program of national unity mandated by the Comintern for the USPC and its hemispheric peers, which led to the break of key black members with Moscow.

Thus the first decade and a half in the life of the Cuban Communist Party showed a high degree of programmatic and financial dependence not only on the Comintern but also directly on the USCP, part of the broader dependence of Cuban society on the United States. One fundamental aspect of this U.S.-Cuban relationship was the fact that the absence of a significant American socialist party left the Cuban Left with no major representation beyond the Communists. In this they differed from the European colonials in the Caribbean who could, and did, turn to Fabian and Social Democratic parties in the Metropolis.

After the defeat of the broadly left-wing "revolutionary" movement of 1934 against dictator Gerardo Machado, the Cuban Left was absorbed by the Communists, especially as the latter became more respectable in Cuban and U.S. eyes. Compared with the ideologically centered Communists, it is hard, in hindsight, to regard the Auténtico party of Grau San Martín and

Prío Socarrás as ideologically centered parties. They were little more than patronage-distributing electoral machines. Even Eduardo Chibas's Ortodoxo Party was more populist than socialist. On the other hand, the Communists attracted many intellectuals and came to represent an educated and disciplined force. They had no particular following in the working class, urban or rural, however, which meant that they were not a significant electoral force but were always opportunistic in their alliances.

Because the Cuban Communist Party—like the French and Italian—attracted so many intellectuals, call them Cuban Organic Intellectuals, it is useful, and at the same time paradoxical, that one of the better ways of looking at Cuba today is through the theories of a Marxist theoretician-practitioner. Antonio Gramsci (1891–1937) was, in the words of two prominent Gramsci scholars, "the greatest Marxist writer on culture."[27] He certainly was one of the first Marxists to use a sociology of knowledge conceptual framework, which is why he was known as "the theoretician of the superstructure." Contrary to other Marxists who followed a dogmatic interpretation of the primacy of the "base" over the "superstructure," Gramsci believed that ideas, language, and intellectual production (especially the written word) were not merely ancillary consequences of the factors of production but also had significant causal effects of their own. He was particularly interested in the role of intellectuals. All men, he argued, are, in a way, intellectuals, but every society assigned, explicitly or implicitly, specific statuses and roles to those who either defend the ideational status quo or those who challenge it. He called those who occupy those roles "organic intellectuals," individuals who battle over the conception of the world.[28] He viewed this as a process of "elective affinity" that characterizes the world of modern communications where many intellectuals share common ideas and knowledge in specific fields. These are said to belong to "epistemic communities."[29]

Karl Marx certainly understood the vital role of globalization and of epistemic communities of intellectuals. To quote from the Manifesto of the Communist Party (1848):

> The bourgeoisie has through its exploitation of the world market given a cosmopolitan character to production and consumption in every country. . . . In place of the old local and national seclusion and self-sufficiency, we have intercourse in every direction, universal inter-dependence of nations. And as in material so in intellectual production.

The intellectual creations of individual nations become common property. National one-sidedness and narrow-mindedness become more and more impossible, and from the numerous national and local literatures there arises a world literature. (Emphasis added)

This is Marx the historian and economist, not the Marx driven by ideological and ontological schemes. He fully understood how globalization exposed intellectuals to the wider world, creating epistemic communities.

The emergence of epistemic organic intellectuals in Cuba helps in the formulation of the following hypothesis, pregnant in irony: Cuba today represents the reverse of the process of social change that preoccupied Gramsci. Being a Marxist, he was particularly interested in the role of organic intellectuals in the challenge to the bourgeois political, cultural, and ideological "hegemony." How, Gramsci asked, could revolutionaries defeat the intellectual hegemony of the conservative status quo, including the Vatican and the Roman Catholic Church? How to bring about what he termed the necessary ideological "crisis"? This, he said, tended to occur during periods he called "transformism," which consisted "precisely in the fact that the old is dying and the new cannot be born." Of course, according to the Marxist ontology, the one straining to be born was the next stage, socialism. Today, it is decidedly just the reverse in Cuba, where what is striving to be born is capitalism. Because Gramsci was both theoretically and politically interested in the role of language, he would have been interested in the implications of the evident abandonment of radical dependency/world system language and paradigms and the rise of common technical languages among skill-based or epistemic communities in Cuba and in the global economy. Economists and political scientists, no less than petroleum engineers, "know" and communicate this knowledge in fairly similar ways and more and more in English, directly or in translation. This is a global phenomenon of which Cuban intellectuals, particularly social scientists, are part.

This brings us to the evidence that the language of social scientists in Cuba is changing. To those who would argue that the content analysis presented in table 15 and other analyses of ideas are mere impressionistic approaches that tell us nothing "objective," one should keep in mind just how closely Gramsci's ideas fit into well-established modern theories of sociolinguistics, which argue that transition in language necessarily means a transition in ideas. "Necessarily" because two principles in the widely accepted Sapir-Whorf hypothesis in linguistics tell us that new words and language are invented to reflect new realities and that language is not merely a reproducing instrument for voicing ideas but is itself a shaper of ideas.[30] It is, in the language of Edward Sapir, "the programme and guide for the individual's meaningful activity." In other words, language shapes or "frames" our perception of reality.[31]

Gramsci was ahead of his time not only in sociolinguistics but also in his understanding of the role of language (national and foreign) in creating epistemic communities. As he put it, the capacity of intellectuals to be in touch with "the great currents of thought which dominate world history cannot be long blocked." He was one with Marx, the social scientist. While no major groups in Cuba (as of 2014) are calling for a full switch to political pluralism or to a complete market (capitalist) economy, the new language they are using makes it evident that a new, open debate is taking place over the nature of Cuba's national economy and the desirability and requirements (even inevitability) of its insertion into the competitive global market. All state attempts to block the diffusion of ideas by independent bloggers and others have failed. Evidently, as reforms allowing freer travel by the United States and Cuba expand, the less control the state will have.

Intellectuals have long asked whether the highly centralized—even totalizing—socialist model so dear to Fidel Castro and other top leaders can be retained, or should it move toward some form of market socialism or quasi-capitalism? In January 1989, faced with Mikhail Gorbachev's dismantling of the socialist system, Castro was adamant that he would reject any reforms that "reek of capitalism," vowing "socialism or death."[32] "I despise capitalism," he said to the National Assembly in 1993. "It is excrement!" But in a clear admission that there were challenges to the existing monolithic official ideology and party, he then lamented, "It seems that we are afraid to shout: long live socialism, long live communism, long live Marxism-Leninism!"[33] He called for a "Battle of Ideas." He was neither having the final word nor assuring all others that in Cuba it is the organic intellectuals, in touch with epistemic communities internationally, who continued to challenge the official views and often suffered the consequences. This is exactly what occurred in 1996 when the most outstanding group of economists and social scientists working in the Centro de Estudios de America (CEA) were purged for opinions not in line with those of the regime.[34] Cases such as this certainly had a chilling effect on intellectual debate, but this did not stop the organic intellectuals from conceptualizing what changes were needed.

That said, it is still unclear whether what has been transcending in the orthodox discourse in Cuba since the end of the twentieth century is a productive intellectual debate or an intellectual protest going nowhere.[35] In either case there is ample evidence that many Cuban intellectuals involved in the "Battle of Ideas" hew closer to economic and developmental pragmatism than to any Marxist "laws of development." Also rejected is the purely voluntaristic idea of Che Guevara that the revolution had created a "New Man" who could develop the society on "moral" rather than material incentives.[36] This is not to say that it is evident that the organic intellectuals had won the "Battle of Ideas," but there was evidence that at least they were holding their own in that battle. Even some of those purged in 1996 continue to debate from exile. As in any intellectual battle, there is first a need for space, for the opportunity to expound. They have partly achieved this under Raúl Castro. For anyone accustomed to the monolithic discourse for the past fifty-five years, it is surprising to read the following words from two professors at the University of Havana's Center for the Study of the Cuban Economy, who seem to represent widely held views.[37] They recommended a shift in the teaching of economics and of what exists in other countries:

> One of the problems in moving toward policies which emphasize economic growth is of a technical nature. For one, it is not at all evident that Cuban decision makers have the skills and knowledge to achieve a change. This is due to the fact that for fifty years they have been trained in a context with mechanisms with origins in the present problems.... Even when they do not use the language, it is evident that Cuba is moving toward a market economy . . . more akin to what exists in other countries.

The search for epistemic communities in countries that have had greater economic development is clear. While all this reveals the beginning of generalized transformation, it is arguable that, at least in Cuba, it is the economists who have been the most important organic intellectuals of this search for reform. In their comprehensive and very revealing 2005 book, *Cuba's Aborted Reform*, Carmelo Mesa-Lago and Jorge Pérez-López review the work of those they identify as some of Cuba's most recognized economists. They chose Julio Carranza, Alfredo González Gutiérrez, Hiram Marguetti, Pedro Monreal, Juan Triana, Anicia García Alvarez, Omar Everleny Pérez Villanueva, and Viviana Togores García. Mesa-Lago and Pérez-López note that these scholars were loyal adherents of the revolutionary regime, evident by their rejection of neoliberalism and explicitly stated support of the socialist system. However, while there were differences among them in interpretation and emphasis, "their identification of current problems is markedly similar."[38] Mesa-Lago and Pérez-López analyze seventeen areas of substantial agreement. I will highlight six of the problems the Cuban economists cite to explain why Cuba still confronts a "failed" or stalled recovery:

(1) Cuba has been unable to generate sufficient internal resources to invest for a sustained recovery.

(2) Cuba's international creditworthiness is poor; there is limited access to external credits and loans.

(3) It is "impossible" to restrict consumption further in order to divert resources to investment, since consumption is already depressed.

(4) There is a need to increase domestic efficiency and a spirit of enterprise competitiveness.

(5) The enterprise management reform process (*perfeccionamiento empresarial*) is new and being implemented very slowly; "verticalism" and enterprise centralization and concentration continue to have deleterious effects.

(6) Finally, and critically, there were the political, social structural impacts, including a decline in real wages, an increase in disguised unemployment, steeper income stratification, and concentration of bank deposits by, and prebends for, the elite.

Not surprisingly, all the Cuban economists recommend changing property relations, decentralizing economic decision making, and promoting domestic competition.[39] As is well known, few, if any, of these recommendations have been fully implemented. The reason, according to Mesa-Lago and Pérez-López, is defensive: the fear that economic decentralization will cause a political weakening of the regime.

Prominent Cuban social scientist and historian Rafael Hernández, known for his firm defense of the regime in domestic and international forums, was nevertheless brutally candid in admitting that "the hothouse in which the system and the culture of socialism could flourish, was shattered more than ten years ago."[40] The negative impact of the growth of tourism, the growing gap in social equality, the presence of fashion, and behavior foreign to socialism in everyday life is already sufficient, he says, to consider that challenges associated with a reencounter with capitalism do not belong to a faraway and improbable future; they are already present. Even so, Hernández believes the "new" Cuba will retain the major gains of the revolution but not without serious challenges. Hernández argues that the fundamental question is "what a system (or the project of a system) is worth that cannot endure the merciless blast from the [capitalist] elements outside of its hothouse and flourish on its own." The system, the culture, and the values of a possible socialism, he argues, cannot be protected by "an ideological condom," but only through acquired immunities that permit it to survive even in the face of the virus coming from contact with the outside. "This vaccination, this acquired immunity," he concludes, "has been taking place for 12 years now, not without cost, but still without showing signs of fatal illness."

Not nearly as optimistic is Haroldo Dilla, one of the victims of the 1996 purge of the most internationally recognized think tank on the island, the Centro de Estudio Sobre América (CEA). In exile in the Dominican Republic and then Chile since the late 1990s, Dilla argues that the idea that Cuba can open up to global capitalism without internal changes is an illusion.[41] He maintains that there will have to be three major structural changes. First, the state will need to modify the strident nationalist discourse, basic component of its legitimacy; second, a reinsertion into the global market will intensify the cultural/ideological links between domestic and exiled communities; and third, it can be assumed that a distention will erode the standing of the "hardliners" (*sectores duros*) and open spaces for more moderate figures on both sides of the Florida Straits. One institution that will not disappear in Cuba, says Dilla, is the military, "the most coherent and efficient of the Cuban system." It will continue to operate in the world of business and "in any transition toward a liberal regime, [it] will aspire to play a leadership role."[42] The historical record since the beginning of the reforms in the 1990s tends to support the Dilla thesis. There is considerable evidence that even the modest openings of the early 1990s had a significant impact on Cuban social mobility and stratification. Recording these impacts has become a task for Cuban social scientists. Their studies are now part of the established literature.

Further empirical evidence of the evolving intellectual milieu in Cuba is found in table 15, which lists eighteen of the most internationally recognized contemporary Cuban economists. There is ample evidence that, to use Gramsci's term, the "hegemony" of the orthodox Marxist ideology of the Cuban revolution regarding the economy is being challenged by organic intellectuals gathered in a number of think tanks and at the University of Havana. They are presenting their ideas in a much more eclectic and flexible fashion, utilizing frames of reference widely accepted in the international epistemic community of scholars. The emphasis on economists is in keeping with Gramsci's ideas on their role. He was of the opinion that while all social tasks require a degree of skills, economists require more. "In the first instance," he noted, "these occupations are associated with the particular technical requirements of the economic system."[43] We note the sources and references used by these economists to illustrate why we call them part of the epistemic community of scholars studying the global economy. Their language and principal economic arguments are strikingly similar to those found in any report from, for instance, the Economic Commission for Latin America and the Caribbean (ECLAC), while their criticisms of "neoliberalism" do not sound much different from those of liberal U.S. economist Joseph E. Stieglitz in his 2002 book, *Globalization and Its Discontents*.

The data in table 15 bolster the central argument that Cuba is experiencing an *apertura* which, at least on its surface, would indicate a much greater tolerance for dissent on the part of the authorities. Given that the new discourse

Table 15. Scholarly references cited by a select group of reformist economists

Scholar, publication year	No. of references	Marxist references*	World systems/ dependency theory	Global development theory	No. of references in English**
Omar E. Pérez Villanueva					
2003	31	0	0	31	1
2004	38	0	0	38	10
2005	11	0	0	11	3
Pedro Monreal					
2004	21	0	0	19	9

Scholar, publication year	No. of references	Marxist references*	World systems/ dependency theory	Global development theory	No. of references in English**
José M. Sánchez Egozcue					
2004	63	0	0	63	61
Mayra Espina Prieto					
2004	39	3	0	36	2
Viviana Togores González, Anicia García Alvarez					
2004	52	1	0	51	1
Juan Triana Cordoví					
2005	27	1	0	26	16
Mariana Martín Fernández					
2005	5	0	0	5	2
Anicia García Alvarez, Hiram Marquetti Nodarse					
2005	32	0	0	32	13
Anicia García Alvarez, Eislen Guerra Boza					
2005	27	0	0	27	5
Gabriela Dutrenit, Alexandre O. Vera-Cruz, Argenis Arias Navarro					
2005	53	1	0	52	38
Humberto Blanco Rosales					
2005	22	0	0	22	7
Jorge Ricardo Ramírez, Silvia García García					
2005	21	0	0	21	2
Dayma Echeverría León					
2005	14	0	0	14	2

Sources: Jorge I. Domínguez, Omar Everleny Pérez Villanueva, and Lorena Barberia, eds., *The Cuban Economy at the Start of the Twenty-First Century* (Cambridge: Harvard University Press, 2004); Juan Triana, *Cuba: Crecer desde el conocimiento* (Havana: Editorial de Ciencias Sociales, 2005). Most of the authors in this volume are members of El Centro de Estudios de la Economía Cubana.

*Includes reference to Fidel Castro's speeches.

**Includes translations.

of the organic intellectuals precedes Raúl Castro's call for new measures to "modernize" Cuban socialism, might they have had a role in encouraging such a call? There has been candid discussion of the hardships of the Special Period and very detailed analyses of what it will take for the island to reverse the deterioration and reinsert itself into the global economy. Marxist or other radical paradigms appear to have little space in these efforts.

It is true that at this point the organic intellectuals are only challenging ideas about economic arrangements in a reformist or gradual way rather than in a "total opposition" way. Note, for instance, the sophisticated analysis by two Cuban scholars of the confusing dual monetary system where there is a "national" peso (the CUP) and a convertible peso (the CUC, equivalent to the U.S. dollar) which is worth twenty-five times as much. Monetary reform is widely believed to be unavoidable if any modernizing measures are to succeed.[44] According to these scholars, the dual system, the *peso duro* (the so-called CUC) and the common peso, equal to 4 cents of the U.S. dollar, cannot be sustained, though the change should be gradual rather than all at once.[45] These scholars call for caution because they understand what the sociology of knowledge informs us: beyond the manifest functions of any action there are the latent, unintended consequences. One would have to conclude that it will probably be the unintended consequences which will be the most serious challenges to the hegemony of the Marxist state. They will define the outcome of the real "Battle of Ideas" in Cuba's transformation.

Finally, all the evidence, as of 2014, is that this battle will unfold in Cuba among Cubans and within the transition that they themselves are constructing. And, to be sure, not everyone inside Cuba believes that the changes are significant. The veteran Cuban economist resident in Cuba, Oscar Espinoza Chepe, argues that Raúl Castro is making just enough reforms "so that, in the final analysis, everything stays the same."[46] He does agree that there is evidence that a new debate is unfolding, more of a protest, regarding economic policies, which falls short of what the literature on revolution has called "the abandonment of the intellectuals."[47] The consensus is that Marxist frameworks and language are being abandoned. Our hypothesis is that these changes should not be minimized and that changed language foretells changes in policy. Indeed, events in 2014 are clear indications that this is occurring. The logical corollary of this is that *hostile* attempts from outside Cuba to determine the course of the Cuban transition will fail just as they have failed for the past five decades. It is illusory to believe that now that

Cuba has produced its own homegrown organic intellectuals, it will be ready to cede to outsiders the directions it should take. Cuba will certainly seek out congenial epistemic communities. But nationalism and the desire for self-determination will continue to be the operational impulses in this long-lasting drama. In addition, even the most enthusiastic intellectual will have to recognize that what anchors the present political system is a modernizing military institution, very much a creation of Raúl Castro. It is crucial that policy makers try to understand what drives this leader.

Two French authors dedicate 650 pages to analyzing the long delayed (but, in their minds, inevitable) fall of Fidel Castro. They pause long enough to ask, "What is a Raúlista?" They answer with a refrain which has been around since the beginning of the revolution: "Raúl's men may slip, but they do not fall."

> The concept of a *raúlista* is useful, not because it is opposed to that of a *fidelista* but rather to indicate a fact: throughout his career Raúl Castro has recruited, protected, and occasionally shaped leaders who remain in their positions, are loyal to him, and have ended up forming the essence of the high political command.[48]

Lacking his brother's charisma but fully understanding the need for a disciplined and technically trained institution at a time when virtually all other mediating groups were being dismantled or exiled, Raúl Castro took the path so many others have taken in the Third World: building a modernizing military elite or oligarchy.[49] The French authors repeat Raúl Castro's assertion that the Cuban army is a "political" army from which four things are expected but only one of which is a strictly military attribute. First, they are required to act as political cadres with "high political, ideological and moral qualities." Second, they must be highly skilled military professionals. Third, they must all have "the basic skills of food production and agriculture." And finally, and critically, they must have "a rudimentary knowledge of economic affairs."[50]

This approach to an understanding of Raúl Castro is supported by Hal Klepak's *Cuba's Military, 1990–2005*, which carries the enigmatic but highly suggestive subtitle *Revolutionary Soldiers during Counter-Revolutionary Times*. The exceptional access this Canadian military scholar had to so many military individuals and institutions could only have come from higher authority. That said, this access does not detract from the objectivity of the book; in fact, it adds to its utility. It is, up to now, the best insider's view of the Cuban Armed Forces (FAC). The FAC, says Klepak, will be "the key player in any transition." He develops this argument systematically and documents each of the following key points:

(1) While Raúl Castro has none of the charisma of his brother, the importance of this should not be exaggerated. "Those closest to him . . . are usually quite impressed by him."

(2) Raúl Castro established his credentials as a military commander and regional administrator as commander of the Eastern Front.

(3) He has been instrumental in forging the institutional links with the other key pillars of the society.

(4) He has been the one most keenly interested in raising living standards by improving economic performance.

(5) While open to discussions with the United States on a range of issues, this will have to be done on as level a field of sovereign states as the enormous and historical asymmetry allows.[51]

It is widely accepted, then, that the Cuban military has the professional and institutional resources and nationalist motivations to play a modernizing role. Clearly, one of the fundamental characteristics which put it in such a position is organization, that is, bureaucracy with "discipline, military order, chain of command, intolerance of absenteeism, and access to resources on a special basis."[52] It is critical to understand that in the Cuba of the second decade of the twenty-first century, a paradoxical process is unfolding establishing priorities between civil freedom and economic reform. Samuel Huntington notes that multiparty systems which promote freedom and social mobility lose the concentration of power necessary for undertaking reforms: "Since the prerequisite of reform is the consolidation of power, first attention is given to the creation of an efficient, loyal, rationalized, and centralized army: military power must be unified."[53] Klepak himself concludes his solid analysis with a broad assessment of the future role of the FAC: "They alone can hold the ring while that transition is sorted out and while popular expectations for rapid change (and improvement) are growing and even more demanding. They alone have the legitimacy to fulfill this potentially historic role in the eyes of the U.S. military (with whom they could more easily deal than anyone else in the Cuban State apparatus)."[54]

It is difficult to believe that even absent the charismatic hero, any of this will change fundamentally; thus there is no threat to the regime's survival. Klepak's study provides the necessary context for another study which most assuredly was not authorized by Raúl Castro but which arrives at similar conclusions. Brian Latell, for years the senior analyst on Cuba for the U.S. Central Intelligence Agency (CIA), compares and contrasts Fidel Castro's personality and charismatic qualities with those of his younger brother. His profile of Raúl Castro shows him to be the more stable and dependable of the two. In fact, Latell maintains that Raúl Castro is "the linchpin" of Fidel's succession strategy and the "guarantor" of political stability in Cuba. "It is highly unlikely," says Latell, "that Fidel could have held power so long without Raúl's steady control of the armed forces."[55] Given this analysis of the situation, it is not surprising that Latell believes that it will be Raúl who will have the opportunity and the capacity to set the revolution on a more rational and conciliatory course. This, he believes, might very well include some form of reconciliation with the United States.

It is inherently revealing that no such books on the history of the single, vanguard or "leadership" party of the revolution, the PCC, have appeared. In fact, while revealing a Fidel Castro–driven rollback of many of the liberal reforms of the 1990s, the October 1997 Fifth Congress of the PCC praised Raúl Castro. The latter was confirmed as the successor to Fidel Castro. Of special significance to the thesis of the rise of a modernizing military bureaucracy was the fifth Congress's special mention of the economic performance of the military-managed industries. Hal Klepak's thorough analysis of the depth and breadth of the military's involvement in all sectors of the economy shows why such praise was warranted.[56] It is understood in the social sciences that when we can identify one cohesive group which exercises decision-making power over several key areas of the society, we can properly speak of it as "the elite."[57] When we note that 25 percent of the Central Committee of the CCP's Political Bureau were military men,[58] we have to conclude that the military institution, with 50,000 members, not the party, with 800,000 members, is now the leadership institution of the society managing an estimated 75 percent of the economy. This is truly Cuba's new elite, a veritable military-economic oligarchy.

As unique—and successful—as the combat experience of the Cuban military has been, that institution fits into a category, the "modernizing oligarchy," well known in the sociology of development as defined by Edward Shils decades ago: political systems controlled by bureaucratic and/

or military officer cliques in which democratic constitutions have been suspended and where the modernizing impulse takes the form of a concern for efficiency and rationality. Another major goal is to eliminate corruption and traditional "familiaristic" politics. "Modernizing oligarchies," says Shils, "are usually strongly motivated toward economic development."[59] If there is strong backing for the reforms announced in 2014, it will surely come from the military.

Dealing with the new emerging Cuban elite will require a different paradigm and level of analysis than that used in dealing with what was the purely charismatic leadership of Fidel Castro. It will require a more sociological insight into the steadiness, rationality, and predictability of military-bureaucratic authority in general, plus the special revolutionary credentials of the Cuban officer corps in particular. We also have to understand how and why the "uncharismatic" Raúl Castro appears to have excelled in shaping and leading this institution. Keep in mind, however, that precisely because this military is a modernizing bureaucracy, in fact an oligarchy, it will not depend on any single leader, charismatic or otherwise.

Critical to U.S. policy, so caught up in strategizing an endgame of regime change, is that all the evidence indicates that outside attempts to split this elite will probably be futile. There is no getting around the empirical fact that the top Cuban military command has remained loyal to both brothers since the revolutionary 1950s. As two RAND analysts concluded over two decades ago, "Of all the state institutions, the military and security organs remain most critical to the present and future survival of the regime." This is why—twenty-two years ago—they made a recommendation which flew in the face of the "gambler's fallacy" that has governed U.S. policy since the beginning of this conflict: "Policymakers should be prepared to shift policy tracks or possibly recombine different elements from two or more options as problems *and opportunities* emerge. Ideally, no option should foreclose the adoption of another, nor should any option be irreversible." One of the options they recommended was to explore "informational exchanges and confidence building measures" between the U.S. and Cuban armed forces.[60]

What was sound advice in 1992 appears even more so in the first quarter of the twenty-first century. U.S. policy makers can either come to grips with the transition that is occurring in Cuba or they can, once again, place hope over experience and keep tossing the dice, trusting that the biological clock—this time Raúl's—will bring them the lucky seven.

The Battle of Ideas in Cuba is now a matter of using "soft power" to break the island's isolation. It was important enough to put a member of the Cuban Council of Ministers in charge of this initiative. And, certainly, the initiative has had some real successes: in medicine abroad,[61] in cordial diplomatic relations with virtually all the nations of the world (perhaps especially in the Greater Caribbean), and with repeated UN General Assembly condemnations by solid majorities of the U.S. embargo against Cuba. This necessarily calls for a review of U.S. policy, including a willingness to talk.

It is not as if there have not been various attempts at dialogue. Perhaps the most telling aspect of this, however, is that the most serious efforts have been in secret for reasons not difficult to discern: the tenacious and skillful opposition of the Cuban exile community. In their revealing book on secret negotiations with Cuba, William M. LeoGrande and Peter Kornbluh note that Henry Kissinger, then secretary of state, was convinced as early as 1973 that the costs of keeping existing U.S. policy toward Cuba were rising without any corresponding benefits. Important domestic forces and international allies were calling for a normalization of relations. So, indeed, Kissinger began secret talks. These foundered on the Cuba intervention in Angola.[62] Others have tried their hand at negotiation, including Presidents Jimmy Carter and Bill Clinton. Fidel Castro, it appears, has had little interest in normalization.

There are no grounds to doubt the sincerity of President Barack Obama's statement made at the Summit of the Americas meeting in 2009 that "the United States seeks a new beginning with Cuba." No one should be sanguine about the difficulties involved. It is true that two of the most intractable areas in past U.S.-Cuba relations—ties with the USSR and military interventions in Angola and elsewhere—are no longer present. As far as Cuban "internationalism" is concerned, it has been transformed from military to civilian involvements. Cuban medical, teaching, and sports missions are widely popular in the Caribbean and elsewhere.

More delicate is the question of human rights in Cuba. Cuba's record on this has not been exemplary. This just might be the stumbling block to a full-fledged process of normalization as Secretary of State Hillary Clinton discovered. She understood the complexities of the Cuban case and was under no illusions about dealing with the Castros. She had learned, she wrote, "to keep my eyes wide open" when dealing with them.[63] Yet in the final analysis she agreed with President Obama not to continue the "stale debates" of the past. Her final recommendation, while commendable regarding lifting the embargo, remains open-ended and inconclusive:

> Near the end of my tenure, I recommended to President Obama that he take another look at our embargo. It wasn't achieving its goals, and it was holding back our broader agenda across Latin America. After twenty years of observing and dealing with the U.S.-Cuba relationship, I thought we should shift the onus onto the Castros to explain why they remained undemocratic and abusive.[64]

This is all well and good as far as it goes, but it does not go far enough. The fact that such an issue is made of human rights in the Cuban case has much to do with domestic U.S. politics, "the domestic scene," as Kissinger put it. Human rights issues have never completely stalled U.S. relations with other nations—viz. China, Vietnam, Saudi Arabia, Egypt, or indeed, the brutal dictatorship of Chile's Augusto Pinochet—with whom the United States has carried on commercial and even diplomatic relations.

It is only logical to expect that people who lost everything to a revolution will resist any opening to that revolution. Logically, the most resistant to an *apertura* is the so-called *exilio histórico*, the early exiles in Miami, Florida. In the United States they also dominate Cuban politics at the state and national levels. It has, of course, been over five decades, and just as the *históricos* of the struggle in the Sierra Maestra in Cuba are aging, so are their opponents in Miami. In many ways—and beyond state-to-state relations—there is already a Miami-Cuba transnational community in place, and it is invariably the people of these communities, much more than any formal, institutional city or country administrations, that shape transnational relations.[65] All this transcends formal geographical definitions of "the city" to become a virtual or post-city phenomenon. Even without the lifting of the futile fifty-year-plus embargo and its evident revanchist tendencies, Miami and Havana, from whence 70 percent of the Cuban refugees come, have moved slowly but surely closer together. All the measures of the Cuban American politicians in Miami and the hardliners in Cuba attempting to stop this movement have been in vain.

By 2009 Miami had already been supplying Cuba with much of what it needs for its expanding tourist industry: fancy beef from Florida, Bertram yachts for its tourist industry, and even Daiquiri cocktail mix for both its legendary and newer drinking holes. Having destroyed its peasant (*guajiro*) agriculture, in 2013 Cuba imported 70 percent of its food. There is a real need to revive private initiatives. A survey by the Brookings Institution reveals that Cuban recipients of remittances sent from Miami planned to use the money to open small businesses, that is, to become *cuentapropistas*, small capitalists.[66] Given that the five-a-day chartered flights from Miami to Havana are frightfully expensive, shipping by sea began because the demand continued. Crowley Maritime, operating out of Port Everglades in Fort Lauderdale, has sent a weekly ship carrying humanitarian and other products allowed by law, and in August 2012 a once-a-week ship began ferrying similar goods to Cuba from Miami. Since no trade is allowed under the U.S. embargo legislation (the Helms-Burton law), the ship returns empty. This will eventually change.

It is evident that one of the most difficult accommodations any diaspora immigrant will have to make in Cuba will be to avoid making odious comparisons between his or her privileged economic status and the modest lifestyle and political values of the host society, especially its military elites. To the extent that there are conflicts of accommodation, they will probably have little to do with ideology and international alignments and more to do with the demands for legal guarantees for any investments the returnee makes in property (including copyrights) and heeding the deference demanded by the Cuban authorities. Consequently, while there will be relatively little cultural and psychological trauma, it will make an enormous difference whether Cuban officials as hosts will be open to meeting the returnees' expectations as to security of investments and the returnees' willingness to grant deference to those in power.

In a fine book on the relations between Miami and the island, Maria de los Angeles Torres argues that neither government can much longer impede the tremendous human desire to belong as Cubans because, no matter how hard they try, governments cannot legislate identities nor can they erase the historical memories that remain in people's hearts.[67]

Cuba's organic intellectuals have already put Marxism-Leninism behind them. This means that, as in much of the rest of the Caribbean, this radical ideology is rapidly ceding to a new realization that its time has passed and that it now contributes little if anything to the modernization process they are all pursuing. The reforms in Cuba are painfully slow to come, but come they will, first, in the economic arena. The failures of the Cuban socialist model are too severe and generalized to delay reforms much longer in this, the last Marxist holdout in the region. The United States and other Cuban friends in the Caribbean have to stand ready to assist when Cubans themselves decide to abandon the failed policies of the past fifty-five years and adopt what their organic intellectuals have been recommending for the past two decades. Then, and only then, will Cuba be a full member of a Caribbean community that has fought its own battles and moved on.

Conclusion

Confronting the Perilous Threats
of Organized Crime and Energy Dependence

Elites in the postcolonial independent Caribbean have been generally shining examples of democratic governance and strict adherence to universally recognized legal standards of human rights. There have been some stark exceptions to this. The attempt by the Stalinist clique in Grenada to establish "strict socialist manners" and their execution of the popular leaders is a case so deviant that it merits the separate discussion provided in this book. Similarly, the assassinations during the dictatorship of Suriname's Desi Bouterse have yet to be fully assigned responsibility. The Forbes Burnham dictatorship in Guyana was another aberration. The death of historian and politician Walter Rodney in 1980, never fully investigated, is only lately being revisited.[1] Human rights violations in Cuba remain of concern.

These blemishes on the record do not negate the fundamental point that the "terrified consciousness" of what independence led by black elites would bring never materialized. There was no collective sense of revenge, no settling of scores; simply honest elections, peaceful rotation of elites, and sincere and intelligent debates in academia, parliament, and the mass media. It is this steady adherence to the inherited parliamentary systems—British, French, Dutch, and American—which has allowed these small states to withstand some formidable challenges of racial and ideological conflict. An integral part of this colonial legacy has been the principle and tradition of a loyal opposition adhering to the rules of the game. So far, so good, in domestic politics. Also commendable has been their handling of international relations (see the complex Territorial Sea divisions in map 1). On that score there can be little doubt that the countries of the Caribbean have learned how to play their geopolitical cards. It is not far-fetched to say that generally they have punched above their weight.

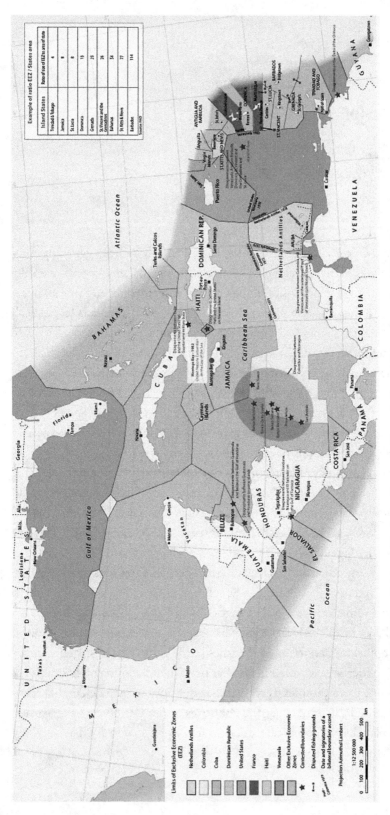

Map 1. Complex Territorial Sea divisions. "Exclusive Economic Zones in the Caribbean," courtesy of Monique Bégot, Pascal Buléon, and Patrice Roth, *Emerging Caribbean: A Political Geography* (Fort-de-France, Martinique: Association de recherche et d'études caraïbes [AREC]; Kingston, Jamaica: Ian Randle, 2009).

Their political relations, though not their trade, are as good with Cuba as they are with the United States. Many have diplomatic relations with Taiwan, but also substantial commercial ties to the Republic of China.[2] Haiti and the Dominican Republic have tense relations, but these are nothing compared with what existed when dictators François Duvalier and Leonidas Trujillo ruled their respective countries. Other than that, the claim of Guatemala to Belize is a matter of the past, and the more serious claim of Venezuela on Guyana has been put on the backburner. This is as the rest of the region wants it.

Despite this sterling record, however, Caribbean elites are keenly aware of two new and potentially perilous threats to their well-being which call for another round of regional discussions. Certainly the most immediate threat comes from the levels of crime and corruption that threaten the whole Caribbean. From one end of the region to the other, political and economic well-being is threatened by the reality and the perception of rampant crime. Criminal threats have kept Caribbean sovereignties at bay. Economies highly dependent on tourism and foreign investments struggle to maintain—and be seen to be maintaining—law and order. Domestic criminal activity and international organized crime prey on the small, vulnerable countries. The critical question is whether the accumulated democratic traditions and collective good sense of these societies, plus international conventions and cooperation, can contribute to defending this region from the threats that flow from the complex relationship between corruption and violence, much of it engendered by the drug trade and drug culture in the hemisphere.[3]

The Caribbean appears especially vulnerable to this pernicious trade. It is increasingly a route to the United States, Europe, and Puerto Rico. But it is more than that. No territory has escaped the effects of what the minister of national security in Trinidad and Tobago called "a war."[4] Never have these democratic, conservative, yet modern states faced anything as menacing to their good governance as international organized crime and the corruption it spawns. Profitable local markets for drugs have been proliferating in the region. This tends to give rise to domestic gangs at the service of international organized crime. The local gangs are no longer willing to serve only as conduits. They would rather fight to gain the value added from direct sales locally and from control of markets overseas.[5] The result has been murder rates among the highest in the world.

New studies reveal three serious weaknesses in the national security postures of modern-conservative societies. First, they are susceptible to outside influences, not just ideology and race-based ideas but also money-making opportunities, licit or illicit. Second, they exhibit a tendency to react to perfidious deeds with much-delayed moral indignation rather than being proactive with proven operational safeguards. Often it is too late to reverse dangerous activities that are first revealed in the foreign press or by foreign intelligence agencies. Third, they tend to lean too heavily on an exaggerated definition of national sovereignty. Regarding this last point, it was prominent St. Lucian scholar and statesman Vaughan Lewis who, with admirable candor and clarity, first posed the issue as a dilemma. First, he asked, what level of capabilities should be sought from outside the region "if this was deemed to be necessary?" And then the problem of policy: "If recourse to extra regional sources for technical assistance was deemed necessary, how was this to be undertaken so as to maintain both the reality and the appearance of individual and collective sovereignty?"[6]

Lewis was addressing one of the thorniest issues that have existed since the international system has involved nation-states. The fundamental idea of having a nation-state is to control its borders and to exercise power within those borders. In other words, the idea is to have sovereignty. The idea that this could be done with hermetic security, however, has always been an illusion. Tom Farer emphasizes the fact that from its beginning in the seventeenth century, "the claim of territorial sovereigns to a plenary, unreviewable discretion collided with the reality of interaction and interdependence."[7]

No greater collision with reality exists today than the breaching of virtually all sovereign controls over borders, from the monetary systems to agencies of law and order, by organized crime. Even a country such as Cuba, whose isolation has been imposed from both the outside and the inside, is not immune. Jorge Domínguez accurately points out that after fifty years in power, Fidel Castro "had only one remaining achievement: the construction of Cuba's sovereignty."[8] Yet this did not prevent an organized drug cartel from penetrating the highest levels of the regime, resulting in the execution of a much-decorated general and a key member of the Cuban international services.[9] Few of the states in the Caribbean have Cuba's capacity to defend sovereignty. This, along with their trust in the guarantees provided by sovereignty, makes them extremely vulnerable.

Moisés Naím presents with crystal clarity the multiple cases where organized crime of one sort or another has breached sovereignty. Organized crime, he says, is borderless, but states are confined by those very borders. Naím argues that for criminals, frontiers create business opportunities and convenient shields. But for the government officials chasing the criminal, "borders are often insurmountable obstacles. The privileges of national sovereignty are turning into burdens and constraints on government."[10] The idea of sovereignty is hallowed to academics and upright citizens but a hollowed idea to criminals. Recognition that the hallowed idea might have gaping holes has led to a new skepticism in intellectual circles.[11]

By the second decade of the twenty-first century, the Caribbean needed to take up another Great Debate regarding the limits of state sovereignty and the need for foreign assistance in the face of the most perilous threats they ever faced. They will notice that many of the threats to their sovereignty were neutralized by outside intervention (table 16). To the uninformed, the odds appear overwhelmingly stacked against the region; not so to the informed. Those who have studied how their elites have debated key issues of nationhood, navigated through the years of decolonization and the Cold War, and dealt with the geopolitical challenges of the post-hegemonic age are more optimistic. These nation-states have resisted and overcome the totalitarian temptations of Marxism-Leninism and the psychologically pleasing but ultimately destructive effects of racial *revanchisme*. They have accomplished this without conducting witch hunts or abandoning their traditions of constitutional democratic governance and respect for civil rights. They will continue these traditions even as they set aside many unrealistic concerns about state sovereignty and gird their loins to confront the most perilous challenges of their young history.

The second challenge stems from the fact that the entire Caribbean (with the exception of Trinidad and Tobago) is dependent on energy. Given that renewable sources of energy remain untapped, energy is derived from imported fossil fuels, and other than what it buys from the United States, this comes heavily subsidized from Venezuela's Petro-Caribe program.[12] There is no evidence of any Venezuelan or Cuban effort to compel membership in either Petro-Caribe or the Alianza Bolivariana de América (ALBA). That virtually all have joined Petro-Caribe is evidence of the generalized awareness that energy dependence makes them extremely vulnerable. All—and especially Cuba—share a vital dependence on Venezuelan largesse through its petro-diplomacy. In 2005, President Hugo Chávez launched both Petro-

Table 16. Specific events leading to a Caribbean sense of threat

Year	Event
1969	Massive urban riots in Curaçao.
1970	Black Power movement and mutiny of the army in Trinidad.
1975	Transshipment of Cuban troops (to Angola) through Barbados.
1976	Bombing (by Cuban exile terrorist group) of Cuban Airlines plane out of Barbados.
	Barbados PM Tom Adams reveals that mercenaries under Sidney Burnett-Alleyne (and supported by South Africa) were preparing to invade. French in Martinique intercept Burnett-Alleyne, and he is convicted of arms smuggling out of Martinique.
1978	The SRC corporation operating out of Barbados and Antigua is found to have links with Israel and shipping arms to South Africa through Antigua.
	British intelligence reveals a second Burnett-Alleyne attempt at invading Barbados.
1979	Marxist coup in Grenada.
	St. Vincent's prime minister, Milton Cato, requests (and receives) Barbadian military assistance with an invasion of Union Island by a group called Movement for National Liberation.
1980	Coup d'état in Suriname by sixteen NCOs.
	Cuban air force MIGs sink Bahamian Coast Guard cutter.
1981	Two separate coup attempts are made against the government of Eugenia Charles in Dominica. The recruitment of mercenaries in the United States is revealed by French intelligence in Martinique.
1982	The Regional Security System is created in the OECS.
1983	The OECS requests and receives U.S., Jamaican, and Barbadian military intervention in Grenada.
1989	Israeli arms meant for Antiguan army are transferred to Colombian mafia.
1990	Jamaat al-Muslimeen attempts a coup d'état in Trinidad. Guns are bought in Florida with Middle Eastern money, men trained in Libya.
2001	A group linked to Jamaat al-Muslimeen attempts to buy an arsenal in Florida.
2010	Jamaican combined army and police force assaults the garrison of Philip "Dudas" Coke of the Shower Posse; seventy-three are killed. Strong criminal links to the United States.

Caribe and the ALBA-Caribe Fund. The Caribbean would be in serious trouble should this Venezuelan program end. Cuba in particular has to consider what the end of the delivery of 100,000 barrels per day of Venezuelan oil would mean to its economy.

The case of Jamaica illustrates the energy need and Venezuela's assistance.

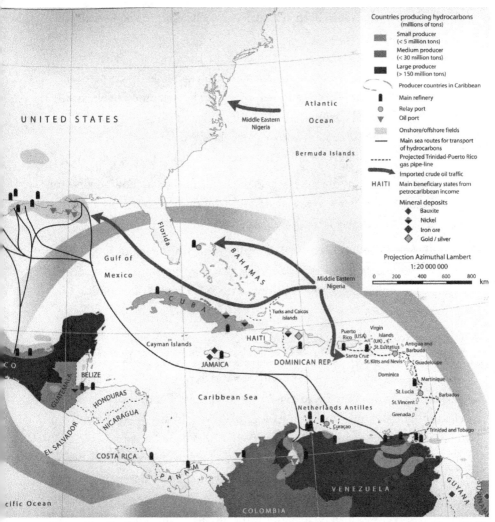

Map 2. The Caribbean is dependent on Venezuelan and Middle Eastern oil. "The Age of Oil: Crude Oil Traffic," courtesy of Monique Bégot, Pascal Buléon, and Patrice Roth, *Emerging Caribbean: A Political Geography* (Fort-de-France, Martinique: Association de recherche et d'etudes caraïbes [AREC]; Kingston, Jamaica: Ian Randle, 2009).

Jamaica imports 90 percent or more of its energy needs. This fact helps explain the compulsion it felt to secure the steady flow of oil promised by Petro-Caribe. Consider the following:

- In 2004, the year before signing the Petro-Caribe agreement, Jamaica spent over 60 percent of its export earnings on petroleum products. A barrel of crude oil cost U.S. $34, bringing the cost to double what it had been in 2001. By 2012, the price of a barrel ranged around U.S. $100.

- Using 1987 as a base year, the GDP of Jamaica had grown by 20 percent by 2010, but energy consumption increased by 112 percent. Sixty percent of petroleum imports went to generation of electricity, mining (bauxite, alumina), and manufacturing.
- Part of the agreement with Venezuela was to upgrade the island's PetroJam refinery by about 42 percent to 50,000 barrels per day.

The prime minister at the time, P. J. Patterson, summed up how adverse the global context has been to his island and why the 23,500 barrels a day imported from Venezuela were so welcome:

> A new corridor has been created for us in the Caribbean to supply to Venezuela certain goods and services that may be affected by emerging trade policy including decisions of the WTO which are inimical to member states.[13]

Patterson was referring to the World Trade Organization's decision to remove British subsidies from West Indies bananas. Faced with significant losses, Jamaica and the other islands certainly benefited from the Petro-Caribe deal and especially from the Petro-Caribe Development Fund. Venezuela's policies brought gratitude but little ideological impact. In no way did Venezuelan assistance change the dynamics and orientation of Jamaican politics. In 2007 the Jamaican people voted out the People's National Party (PNP), which had signed Petro-Caribe, and replaced it with the more conservative Jamaican Labour Party (JLP). However, Petro-Caribe was not an issue during the campaign. Nor was it an issue in the 2011 campaign, which brought the PNP back into power. The agreement had bipartisan support and was seen as a purely business arrangement, proving that whatever geopolitical and ideological intentions President Chávez and later President Maduro might have had did not materialize.

As we saw in chapter 8, Jamaica learned some painful domestic and geopolitical lessons during the 1970s when Michael Manley made a sharp turn to the left to become part of a "correlation" of leftist forces in the region, only to see the island's economy and his political base collapse. By 2013, Jamaica's politics and its foreign policies were geared toward a pragmatic search for solutions to its many domestic problems, which made the no-strings-attached Cuban and Venezuelan aid widely popular but hardly dominant.[14]

Having decided to join Petro-Caribe and to accept the Cuban-staffed and Venezuelan-financed medical assistance, most of the independent Caribbean states must have asked the pragmatic question: Is there anything more to be gained or, to the contrary, to be lost by joining ALBA, the more political-ideological component of Venezuela's policy initiatives? The answer reveals the fact that precisely because they have benefited from Petro-Caribe and Cuban medical assistance, two programs that were not explicitly ideological, they saw little to be gained and perhaps much to lose from joining the clearly ideological ALBA. A key reason is that even left-leaning leaders are hesitant to adhere to the overarching and overreaching anti-Americanism of Presidents Chávez and Maduro. Given Caribbeans' cultural preferences (often translated into voting preferences), they are not willing to recklessly bite the U.S. hand.

ALBA's modest gains in the Caribbean support the idea of a paradoxical inverse relationship between successful soft power initiatives and more explicitly ideological involvements that carry a potential heavy cost domestically and internationally. Beyond economic need, past experience leads one to deduce four major reasons why these small nations will welcome Venezuelan largesse but will hardly change their systems to suit it. First, ALBA's relative failure to advance ideologically also tends to confirm an established principle of geopolitics: small countries prefer to stick with the devil they know rather than switch to one they don't. This is especially true when—as occurs in the Caribbean—democratic pluralism allows them to voice their opinions every four years to reward or punish with their vote.

Second, while virtually all West Indian parties had their origins in a trade union movement, and many adhered to Fabian-type socialism, dramatic events in the 1970s and 1980s changed the perception of the word *socialism*.[15] It still has an ominous ring in the Caribbean. Even the case of Cuba, which engenders much sympathy and friendship throughout the region, is seen more as a case of courageous nationalistic fortitude in the face of the American onslaught than as a shining example of economic development.

Third, contemporary Caribbean politicians, whether it be West Indian Fabians, French West Indian communists and socialists, or Dutch Caribbean liberals, Social Democrats, and Christian Democrats, find Chávez and Maduro's "Socialism of the XXI Century" frankly confusing and ultimately unconvincing.

This ideology has at its pragmatic core the idea of creating through ALBA an alternative to U.S. imperialism, to capitalism (in its neoliberal free trade and privatization dimensions), and to traditional oligarchies (often defined in racial terms).[16] Its basic tenets were formulated by the German Mexican Marxist Heinz Dieterich, whose book *Socialism of the XXI Century* was adopted by Chávez as an ideological guide. After a period of ideological euphoria, Dieterich himself confessed that a series of Chávez missteps had put his revolution in danger.[17] The *caudillo*-style leadership of Venezuela and some of the ALBA countries, says Dieterich, contradicts the fundamental tenet of his model: that socialism has to grow from the bottom up and never from the top down and never become so centralized.[18]

Caribbean elites are conscious of the fact that despite the close relationship between Venezuela and Cuba, contradictory processes are operating. While Cuba is decentralizing its economy, as recommended by its organic intellectuals, Venezuela appears determined to address its deteriorating economic situation by deepening its socialist centralization. By 2014, the Maduro administration had 33 ministries and 111 vice ministries. And, as if to demonstrate the closeness of the Venezuelan-Cuban connection, President Maduro made a highly symbolic appointment of an octogenarian friend of Che Guevara's, Orlando Borrego, as a major economic advisor.[19] Given the acute problems of inflation, declining production, widespread corruption, and a critical shortage of hard currency, it is difficult to see in this appointment anything more than a gesture of Venezuela-Cuba ideological solidarity.

Finally, beyond oil and medical attention, it is also true that Bolivarianismo, Venezuela's general soft power program of material and ideological inducements, cannot compete with the attractions and "pull" of U.S. society. While in the Greater Caribbean there has long been a dislike and distrust of U.S. power (so often abused in the past), there are no clashes in areas that are the real sources of U.S. soft power:

- popular culture, including sports;
- technological modernity (the United States is first in Nobel Prizes in medicine and in hard sciences, and this pulls foreign students to U.S. universities; 28 percent of all students studying outside their countries study in the United States);
- admiration for its democratic politics in general (with the exception of the eight years of the Bush-Cheney administration, among the most unpopular in recent U.S. history); and the fact that

- since 12 percent of the Caribbean labor force and 70 percent of university graduates migrate every year, the largest numbers go to the United States. It is the easiest country in which to acculturate and assimilate as well as to secure citizenship for English-speaking West Indians and those who adopt English as a second language.

The United States is the destination of most of the Caribbean islands' exports and their migrants. It is also the country from whence come the bulk of the remittances and the majority of the tourists, and—finally and critically—it is identified as a democratic, nonmilitarized state, in other words, a state perceived as similar to theirs. In this regard, a shared English language and common law tradition allow civil society in all the West Indian islands to identify much more readily with the United States than with Venezuela or Cuba. In states such as the Dominican Republic and Haiti, recipients of much Venezuelan assistance, their long history of relations with the United States (not all benign to be sure) plus the large diasporas settled in the United States make relations with the United States logical. Additionally, to the extent that ALBA portends to be an alternative, not just to the U.S.-promoted Free Trade Area of the Americas (FTAA) but also to CARICOM, it meets resistance.

If there is a lesson to be learned from the Caribbean's skillful navigation of this new geopolitical reality, it is this: countries will seldom turn down economic assistance when there is a need; how they respond politically and domestically to that assistance will depend on the particular political culture existent in each country. The attachment of Caribbean people to their more conservative parliamentary traditions are a barrier to the ideological inroads of Venezuelan "Bolivarianism," Cuban socialism, or attempts by local politicians to radically modify the existing parliamentary system of colonial origin. When Prime Minister Ralph Gonsalves of St. Vincent and the Grenadines attempted to radically change what he termed the colonial parliamentary system in order to assert his island's "Caribbeanness," his reform bill was rejected by 55.64 percent of the electorate who voted. Matthew Louis Bishop studied the process and concluded that "there is some irony" that a significant explanation of the no vote "is that many Vincentians are actually somewhat fond of their remaining links to Britain and, in particular, Queen Elizabeth II." Evidently, Barbados is not alone in adhering to traditions that have worked well for them.[20]

A Caribbean that faces the challenges of a democracy-threatening crime wave and the dangers of a sudden cut in subsidized energy sources will have to draw strength from its best traditions of responsible and transparent government. It will also have to rein in excessive sensibilities about national sovereignty as it appeals to international assistance for help in facing threats of a global nature. Might one hope that confronting these dramatic trends will finally draw the Caribbean into a more unified region?

Notes

Prologue: The Modern-Conservative Society Framework

1. Anthony Maingot, "The Structure of Modern Conservative Societies," published in all five editions of Jan Knippers Black, ed., *Latin America: Its Problems and Its Promise* (Boulder, Colo.: Westview Press, 1984–2012).

2. Robert Nisbet, "Conservativism and Sociology," *American Journal of Sociology* 58, no. 2 (September 1952): 167–175. Quote on 75.

3. Edward Shils, *Tradition* (Chicago: University of Chicago Press, 1981), 3.

4. Karl Mannheim, "Conservative Thought," in Paul Kecskemeti, ed., *Essays on Sociology and Social Psychology* (New York: Oxford University Press, 1953), 77–164.

5. Robert Nisbet, *The Sociological Tradition* (New York: Basic Books, 1966), 17–18.

6. Michael Oakeshott, *Rationalism in Politics* (London: Methuen, 1962), 172, 191.

7. Richard M. Morse, "The Caribbean: Geopolitics and Geohistory," in Sybil Lewis and Thomas G. Mathews, eds., *Caribbean Integration:* Papers on Social, Political, and Economic Integration (Rio Piedras, Puerto Rico: Institute of Caribbean Studies, 1967); David Ronfeldt, *Geopolitics, Security, and U.S. Strategy in the Caribbean Basin* (Santa Monica, Calif.: RAND, 1983).

8. Sidney Mintz, "The Caribbean as a Socio-Cultural Area," in Michael M. Horowitz, ed., *Peoples and Cultures of the Caribbean* (New York: Natural History Press, 1971), 17–46. Quote on 18.

9. Ibid., 18.

10. Melville J. Herskovits, *Man and His Works* (New York: Alfred A. Knopf, 1952), 198.

11. For an example of such a traditional society, see Ali A. Mazrui, "Edmund Burke and Reflections on the Revolution in the Congo," *Comparative Studies in Society and History* 5, no. 2 (January 1963): 121–33.

12. Russell Kirk, *Edmund Burke: A Genius Reconsidered* (New Rochelle, N.Y.: Intercollegiate Studies Institute, 1967), 84.

13. Karl Marx, *Capital* (New York: Modern Library, 1906), 354.

14. Edmund Burke, *Reflections on the Revolution in France* (1790; New York: Penguin English Library, 1969), 90.

15. I recognize the speculative nature of this formulation limited as it is to Cuba's foreign relations. It is doubtful whether Cuba's domestic politics over the past five decades could meet Burke's definition of "practical liberty" as "social freedom."

16. Barbara W. Tuchman, *The First Salute* (New York: Ballantine Books, 1988), 102. Tuchman argues that Burke's peroration to Parliament condemning Rodney's mistreatment of the Jews was the first declaration that since the Jews were defenseless because they were stateless, they deserved to have their own country.

17. Quoted in Ian Harris, ed., *Burke: Pre-revolutionary Writings* (Cambridge: Cambridge University Press, 1993), 202.

18. Carl B. Cone, *Burke and the Nature of Politics: The Age of the American Revolution* (Lexington: University Press of Kentucky, 1957).

19. Edmund Burke, Speech on Moving his Resolutions for Conciliation with the Colonies, March 22, 1775, cited in Ian Harris, ed., *Burke: Pre-Revolutionary Writings* (Cambridge: Cambridge University Press, 1993), 236.

20. Conor Cruise O'Brien, introduction to Edmund Burke, *Reflections on the Revolution in France* (New York: Penguin English Library, 1969), 21.

21. See Friedrich Engels's "Defense of Progressive Imperialism in Algeria," in *Marx and Engels: Basic Writings*, ed. Lewis S. Feuer (Garden City, N.Y.: Doubleday Anchor Books, 1959), 450–51; also see Karl Marx's "The British Rule in India" in *The Marx-Engels Reader*, ed. Robert C. Tucker (New York: W. W. Norton, 1972), 577–88.

22. A good summary of this sad history is Stephen Kinzer, *Overthrown: America's Century of Regime Change from Hawaii to Iraq* (New York: Times Books, 2006). On the Cuban case, see Don Bohning, *The Castro Obsession: U.S. Covert Operations against Cuba (1959–1965)* (Washington, D.C.: Potomac Books, 2005).

23. Alexis de Tocqueville, *The Old Regime and the French Revolution* (New York: Doubleday, 1955), 16–17.

24. Ibid., 57–60.

25. Tocqueville, *Democracy in America*, 2 vols. (New York: Vintage Books, 1969), 2:372.

26. Ibid., 2:394.

27. Ibid., 2:397.

28. Ibid., 2:391.

29. Oakeshott, *Rationalism in Politics*, 172.

30. Georges Balandier, "Les mythes politiques de colonisation ét de decolonisation en Afrique," *Cahiers Internationaux de Sociólogie* 33 (July–December 1962): 85–96. Quote on 95.

31. C. Wright Mills, *The Sociological Imagination* (New York: Grove Press, 1959), 96–97.

32. Oakeshott, *Rationalism in Politics*, 195.

33. S. N. Eisenstadt, *Modernization: Protest and Change* (Englewood Cliffs, N.J.: Prentice-Hall, 1966).35.

34. Ibid., 119.

35. S. N. Eisenstadt, "Intellectuals and Tradition," *Daedalus* 101, no. 2 (Spring 1972): 1–19.

36. Kalman H. Silvert, "National Values, Development, and Leaders and Followers,"

in *International Social Science Journal* 15, no. 4 (1963): 650–70. See also Harry Hoetink, *Het nieuwe evolutioname* (Assen, Netherlands: Van Gorcum, 1965), 129–38.

37. Charles Wagley, "The Brazilian Revolution: Social Change since 1930," in Richard N. Adams and John P. Gillin, eds., *Social Change in Latin America Today: Its Implications for United States Policy* (New York: Vintage Books, 1960), 220–241. Quote on 221. See also Hoetink, *Het nieuwe evolutioname*; and W. F. Wertheim, *East-West Parallels: Sociological Approaches to Modern Asia* (The Hague: W. Van Hoeve, 1964), 142ff.

38. Richard Newbold Adams, *The Second Sowing: Power and Secondary Development in Latin America* (San Francisco: Chandler, 1967), 48.

39. Rupert Emerson, "Reflections on Leadership in the Third World," in A. R. Desai, ed., *Essays on Modernization of Underdeveloped Societies,* 2 vols. (Atlantic Highlands, N.J.: Humanities Press, 1976), 1:548. On this same case, also see Lloyd I. and Susanne Hoeber Rudolph, *The Modernity of Tradition: Political Development in India* (Chicago: University of Chicago Press, 1967), 199–200.

40. Émile Durkheim, *The Rules of Sociological Method* (Glencoe, Ill.: Free Press, 1950), 65–70.

41. Robert K. Merton, *Social Theory and Social Structure* (Glencoe, Ill.: Free Press, 1949).

42. George Balandier, *The Sociology of Black Africa*, trans. Douglas Garman (New York: Praeger, 1970), 274–75.

Chapter 1. Eric Williams vs. Juan Bosch: On Caribbean Historical Fundamentals

1. Fritz Stern, ed., *The Varieties of History* (New York: Meridian, 1956), 18–19.

2. Arthur Schlesinger Jr., *The Bitter Heritage: Vietnam and American Democracy, 1941–1966* (Boston: Houghton Mifflin, 1967). Also on this issue see Schlesinger, "The Historian and History," *Foreign Affairs* 41 (April 1963): 491–97, and "On the Writing of Contemporary History," *Atlantic* (March 1967): 69–74.

3. Works that show similar relationships between political needs and the uses of history across ideological lines include Cyril E. Black, ed., *Rewriting Russian History* (1962); C. Vann Woodward, *American Attitudes towards History* (1955); and Cushing Stout, *The Pragmatic Revolt in American History: Carl Becker and Charles Beard* (1958; Westport, Conn.: Greenwood Press, 1980).

4. Cf. Stuart Chase, *Guides to Straight Thinking* (New York: Harper and Row, 1956), 81–88.

5. Compare with F. A. Hayek: "The influence which the writers of history thus exercise on public opinion is probably more immediate and extensive than that of the political theorists who launch new ideas. . . . The historian is in this respect at least one step nearer to direct power over public opinion than is the theorist." See "History and Politics," in F. A. Hayek, ed., *Capitalism and the Historians* (Chicago: University of Chicago Press, 1963), 1–11. Quote on 4.

6. Cf. Herbert Butterfield, *King George III and the Historians* (New York: Macmillan, 1959), 8: "The tendency to look for an historian who will serve as an 'authority' is one which seems to have increased during my lifetime."

7. J. Ki Zerbo, "Histoire et Conscience Nègre," *Présence Africaine* 16 (October/November 1957): 45–61. Quote on 53.

8. Cf. Rupert Emerson, *From Empire to Nation* (Boston: Beacon Press, 1960), 152–56. The rewriting of history in former colonial countries is dealt with extensively in Immanuel Wallerstein, ed., *Social Change: The Colonial Situation* (New York: John Wiley, 1966), 583–658.

9. Eric Williams, *Inward Hunger: The Education of a Prime Minister* (London: André Deutsch, 1969), 25. Williams's dissertation was published as *Capitalism and Slavery* (1944; New York: Russell and Russell, 1961).

10. Williams, *Inward Hunger*, 343.

11. Eric Williams, editorial, *PNM Weekly*, June 18, 1956. This paper would later come to be called the *Nation* and was edited by C.L.R. James.

12. Eric Williams, *Massa Day Done* (Port-of-Spain, Trinidad and Tobago: PNM, 1961), 1.

13. Keith O. Lawrence, "Colonialism in Trinidad and Tobago," *Caribbean Quarterly* 9, no. 3 (September 1963): 44–56. Quote on 53.

14. Eric Williams, *British Historians and the West Indies* (Port-of-Spain, Trinidad and Tobago: PNM, 1964), 164.

15. Elsa V. Goveia, "New Shibboleths for Old," in John La Rose, ed., *New Beacon Reviews, Collection No. 1* (London: New Beacon Books, 1968), 30–41. Quote on 36.

16. Gordon Rohlehr, "History as Absurdity: A Literary Critic's Approach to *From Columbus to Castro*," in Orde Coombs, ed., *Is Massa Day Dead?* (New York: Anchor Books, 1974), 69–108.

17. Ibid., 80.

18. Ibid., 90. See also V. S. Naipaul in his *House for Mr. Biswas* (London: André Deutsch, 1961).

19. Ibid., 90–91.

20. Eric Williams, *From Columbus to Castro* (London: André Deutsch, 1970), 497.

21. Ibid., 511.

22. Ibid., 512.

23. In his *Reflections on Violence* (1908; New York: Collier Books, 1961), Georges Sorel argued that creating a generalized myth of inevitable proletarian millenarian (or messianic) violence was "sublime work" because it was terrifying to the bourgeoisie and "psychologically liberating" to the oppressed.

24. Williams, *From Columbus to Castro*, 157.

25. Ibid., 159.

26. Salvador de Madariaga, *Bolívar* (New York: Schocken Books, 1963), 215. John Lynch cites approvingly O'Leary's description of Boves as a monster, "the most bloodthirsty and ferocious" of all combatants. See John Lynch, *Simón Bolívar* (New Haven: Yale University Press, 2006), 82; Robert F. McNery Jr., ed. and trans., *Bolívar and the*

War of Independence: Memoirs of General Daniel Florencio O'Leary (Austin: University of Texas Press, 1970). Gérard Masur calls Boves, "Cold, bloodthirsty . . . and treacherous." See Gérard Masur, *Simón Bolívar* (Albuquerque: University of New Mexico Press, 1948), 147.

27. Juan Bosch, *Bolívar y la guerra social* (Buenos Aires: 1966), 87–88.

28. Ibid., 15.

29. Ibid., 85.

30. Germán Carrera Damas, "Estudio preliminary: Sobre el significado socio-económico de la acción histórica de Boves," in *Materiales para el estudio de la cuestión agraria en Venezuela 1800–1830*, vol. 1 (Caracas: Universidad Central de Venezuela, 1964).

31. Germán Carrera Damas, *Historiografía marxista venezolana* (Caracas: Universidad Central de Venezuela, 1967), 31–32.

32. Ibid., 32n.

33. Bosch, *Bolívar y la guerra social*, 122–23.

34. Leslie Manigat, *La politique agraire du gouvernement d'Alexandre Petion, 1807–1818* (Port-au-Prince, 1962), 73.

35. Cf. Carline J. Legerman, "Haitian Peasant, Plantation, and Urban-Lower-Class Family and Kinship Organization: Observations and Comments," in Richard Schaedel, ed., *Papers of the Conference on Research and Resources of Haiti* (New York: Research Institute for the Study of Man, 1969), 71–84.

36. Bosch, *Bolívar y la guerra social*, 400.

37. Ibid., 411.

38. Ibid., 20.

39. Ibid., 593–94.

40. Ibid., 32.

41. Ibid., 417.

42. Ibid., 486.

43. Paul K. Sutton, comp., *Forged from the Love of Liberty: Selected Speeches of Dr. Eric Williams* (Port-of-Spain, Trinidad and Tobago: Longman Caribbean, 1981), 420.

44. Ibid., 446, 448.

45. Ibid., 441.

46. Ibid., 449.

47. Winston Mahabir, *In and Out of Politics* (Port-of-Spain, Trinidad and Tobago: Inprint Caribbean, 1978), 55.

48. Patrick Solomon, *Solomon: An Autobiography* (Port-of-Spain, Trinidad and Tobago: Inprint Caribbean, 1981), 250.

49. Selwyn Ryan, "Doctorphobia and Decision-Making," *Sunday Express*, March 28, 1982, 23, 25.

50. Selwyn Ryan, *Eric Williams: The Myth and the Man* (Kingston, Jamaica: University of the West Indies Press, 2009), 715–37.

51. Juan Bosch, *Crisis de la Democracia de América en la República Dominicana* (México, D.F.: *Revista Panoramas*, no. 14 [suplemento], 1964), 130, 132–38.

52. Juan Bosch, *El Pentagonismo: sustituido del Imperialismo* (Buenos Aires, 1967).

53. Juan Bosch, *Viaje a los antípodas* (Santo Domingo, República Dominicana: Editora Alfa y Omega, 1978), 39.

54. Ibid., 44.

55. Ibid., 41.

56. Juan Bosch, *Capitalismo, Democracia y Liberación Nacional* (República Dominicana: Editora Alfa y Omega, 1983), 109, 124–25.

57. Bosch, *El Partido concepción, organización y desarrollo*, 152–208.

58. Juan Bosch, *La pequeña burguesía en la historia de la Republica Dominicana* (República Dominicana: Editora Alfa y Omega, 1986), 25.

59. See the excellent analysis in Jonathan Hartlyn, *The Struggle for Democratic Politics in the Dominican Republic* (Chapel Hill: University of North Carolina Press, 1998), 258–79.

60. Juan Bosch, *El Estado: Sus Origines y Desarrollo* (República Dominicana: Editora Alfa y Omega, 1988), 22.

Chapter 2. Eric Williams vs. Frank Tannenbaum: On Slave Laws, Slavery Systems, and Subsequent Race Relations

1. Published in Vera Rubin, ed., *Caribbean Studies: A Symposium* (Seattle: University of Washington Press, 1960).

2. Lewis Hanke, *The Spanish Struggle for Justice in the Conquest of America* (Philadelphia: University of Pennsylvania Press, 1949).

3. Frank Tannenbaum, *Slave and Citizen: The Negro in the Americas* (New York: Vintage Books, 1946), 56, 107–8. See also Eric Williams, *Capitalism and Slavery* (1944; New York: Russell and Russell, 1961).

4. Franklin W. Knight, *Slave Society in Cuba during the Nineteenth Century* (Madison: University of Wisconsin Press, 1970), xvi.

5. Ibid., xviii.

6. Ibid., 194.

7. Rebecca J. Scott, *Slave Emancipation in Cuba: The Transition to Free Labor, 1860–1899* (Princeton, N.J.: Princeton University Press, 1985), 319.

8. Ibid., 254.

9. David Brion Davis, *Slavery and Human Progress* (New York: Oxford University Press, 1984), 169.

10. Scott, *Slave Emancipation in Cuba*, 258.

11. Rebecca J. Scott, "Comparing Emancipations: A Review Essay." *Journal of Social History* 20, no. 3 (1987): 565–83. Quote on 578.

12. Walter Rodney, *A History of the Guyanese Working People, 1881–1905* (Baltimore: Johns Hopkins University Press, 1981); Douglas Hall, *Free Jamaica, 1838–1865: An Economic History* (New Haven, Conn.: Yale University Press, 1959); Raúl Cepero Bonilla, *Azucar y abolición* (Habana: Editorial Crítica, 1976).

13. Erna Brodber, *The Second Generation of Freemen in Jamaica, 1907–1944* (Gainesville: University Press of Florida, 2004), 130.

14. Alejandro de la Fuente, *A Nation for All: Race, Inequality and Politics in Twentieth-Century Cuba* (Chapel Hill: University of North Carolina Press, 2001), 106.

15. University of Havana Survey (Havana, 1992), 57.

16. For a rate and instructive study of the role of New York-based German capital, Louisiana management skills and Barbadian sugar biological technology in Puerto Rico, see Humberto García Muñiz, *Sugar and Power in the Caribbean* (Rio Piedras: La Editorial, Universidad de Puerto Rico, 2010), 145–200. He considers this combination "a resounding success story" (198).

17. Frank Tannenbaum, *Ten Keys to Latin America* (New York: Vintage Book, 1966), 52.

18. Stanley Stein and Barbara Stein, *The Colonial Heritage of Latin America: Essays on Economic Dependence in Perspective* (New York: Oxford University Press, 1971), 580.

19. Jean Descola, *Daily Life in Colonial Peru, 1710–1820*, trans. Michael Heron (London: Allen and Unwin, 1962), 26.

20. Knight, *Slave Society in Cuba*, xix.

21. See the report by Jorge Juan and Antonio Ulloa, *A Voyage to South America*, abridged ed., translated by John Adams (New York: Knopf, 1964), 27.

22. See the account by J. N. Brierley, *Trinidad: Then and Now* (Port-of-Spain, Trinidad and Tobago: n.p., 1912).

23. For a fuller account of this case and its consequences, see Anthony Maingot, "Civil-Military Conflict in Urban Colombia," in Stephan Thernstrom and Richard Sennett, eds., *Nineteenth-Century Cities: Essays in the New Urban History* (New Haven, Conn.: Yale University Press, 1969), 297–356.

24. José Manuel Groot, *Historia de la Gran Colombia* (Caracas: Academía Nacional de la Historia de Venezuela, 1941), 327.

25. Maingot, "Civil-Military Conflict in Urban Colombia," 318.

26. Ibid., 319.

27. Max Weber, *The Theory of Social and Economic Organization*, ed. Talcott Parsons (Glencoe, Ill., 1964), 424–29.

28. C. H. Haring, *The Spanish Empire in America* (New York: Harcourt, Brace and World, 1963), 198.

29. Eugene A. Havens, Eduardo Montero, and Michael Romieux, *Cereté, un área de latifundio. Estudio económico y social* (Bogotá: Universidad Nacional de Colombia, 1965). For similar findings, see Orlando Fals-Borda, *Peasant Society in the Colombian Andes* (Gainesville: University of Florida Press, 1955).

30. The best sources on this are the relevant documents in Robert S. Leiken and Barry Rubin, eds., *Central America Crisis Reader* (New York: Summit Books, 1987), 242–83.

31. *Censo Nacional de Población* (Managua, Nicaragua 2005).

32. Róger Almanza G., "El orgullo negro de Managua," *La Prensa*, 21 March 2014, http://www.laprensa.com.ni.

33. Quince Duncan and Carlos Meléndez, *El Negro en Costa Rica* (San José: Editorial Costa Rica, 2005), 52–53.

34. Ivan Molina and Steven Palmer, *The History of Costa Rica* (San José: Editorial de la Universidad de Costa Rica, 2004), 45.

35. Duncan and Meléndez, *El Negro en Costa Rica*, 98.

36. Ibid., 146.

37. Molina and Palmer, *The History of Costa Rica*, 72.

38. Quince Duncan, *Los cuatro espejos* (San Jose, Costa Rica: Editorial Costa Rica, 1973), 75.

39. Quince Duncan, *Hombres curtidos* (San José: Editorial Costa Rica, 1971).

40. Duncan and Meléndez, *El Negro en Costa Rica*, 146.

41. Michael David Olsin, *The Negro in Costa Rica* (Oregon: University of Oregon Press, 1967), 2.

42. Quince Duncan, ed., *El negro en la literatura costarricense* (San José: Editorial Costa Rica, 1975).

43. Carlos Luís Fallás, *Mamíta Yunai* (San José, Costa Rica: Soley y Valverde, 1947. See Victor Manuel Arroyo's prologue to the 1966 edition at http://expreso.co.cr/myunai/prologo.htm.

44. Jean Muteba Rahier, *Kings for Three Days: The Play of Race and Gender in an Afro-Ecuadorean Festival* (Urbana: University of Illinois Press, 2013), 2.

45. Yvonne Zúñiga, *Petita Palma: Al Son del "agua larga"* (Quito: Banco Central del Ecuador, 2008), 72.

46. Julio Estupiñan Tello, *El negro en Esmeraldas*. 2nd ed. (Quito: Formularios y Sistemas, 1996), 158.

47. *Ecuador*, 9th ed. (Oakland, Calif.: Lonely Planet Guides, 2012), 240.

48. Scott Dalton, "Cocaine Wars Make Port Colombia's Most Dangerous City," *New York Times,* May 22, 2007.

49. See the report on "ofensas racistas" in sport in *El Tiempo*, April 29, 2014,) www.eltiempo.com/mundo/racismo-en-el-deporte.

50. Daniel Samper Pizano, *El Tiempo*, March 22, 2014, citing a report from the U.S.-based *Human Rights Watch*.

Chapter 3. Arturo Morales Carrión vs. Gordon K. Lewis: On United States Colonialism in Puerto Rico

1. Arturo Morales Carrión, *Puerto Rico: A Political and Cultural History* (New York: W. W. Norton, 1983), ix.

2. Eugenio Fernández Méndez, *Crónicas de Puerto Rico, 1809–1995* (San Juan: Ediciones del Gobierno, 1957), 2:284.

3. Antonio S. Pedreira, *Insularismo: ensayos de interpretación puertorriqueña* (San Juan: Biblioteca de Autores Puertorriqueños, 1957), 104.

4. Ibid., 111.

5. Morales Carrión, *Puerto Rico*, 221.

6. Luís E. Agrait Betancourt, "Visión de Puerto Rico en la Obra de Arturo Morales Carrión," 1993 presentation reprinted in Hector Luis Acevedo, ed., *Arturo Morales Car-*

rión: Dimensiones del gran diplomático puertorriqueño (San Juan: Universidad Interamericana de Puerto Rico, 2012), 505–15.

7. Pedreira, *Insularismo*.

8. Morales Carrión, *Puerto Rico*, 25.

9. Ibid. It must not be believed that Morales and the Generación del 40 were completely successful in this enterprise. In his admirable *Réquiem por una cultura* (San Juan: Editorial Edil, 1970), E. Seda Bonilla argues that anomie still characterizes Puerto Rican interpersonal relations.

10. Georgie Anne Geyer, *Guerrilla Prince: The Untold Story of Fidel Castro* (Boston: Little, Brown, 1991), 281–82.

11. Arturo Morales Carrión, *Auge y decadencia de la trata negra en Puerto Rico, 1820–1860* (San Juan: Instituto de Cultura Puertorriqueña, 1978), 235.

12. Ibid., 94.

13. Luís González Vales notes that even by the end of the nineteenth century only 14.3 percent of Puerto Rico's land was under cultivation, and the slave population was 15 percent at its peak. Luís González Vales, "Towards a Plantation Society," in Arturo Morales Carrión, *Puerto Rico*, 79–125. Quote on 105.

14. Morales Carrión, *Auge y decadencia de la trata negra*, 116.

15. Morales Carrión, *Puerto Rico*, 140.

16. Ibid., 163.

17. Ibid., 153.

18. Ibid., 149.

19. Ibid., 149.

20. Ibid., 232.

21. Rexford Guy Tugwell, *The Stricken Land: The Story of Puerto Rico* (New York: Doubleday, 1947), 42–43.

22. See Arturo Morales Carrión, *Puerto Rico and the United States: The Quest for a New Encounter* (San Juan: Editorial Académica, 1990).

23. Gordon K. Lewis, *Puerto Rico: A Case Study in the Problems of Contemporary American Federalism* (Port-of-Spain, Trinidad and Tobago: Office of the Prime Minister, 1960), 75.

24. Ibid., 9.

25. This was related by Lewis in a touching eulogy to Muñoz upon his death. See "Requiem for a Lost Leader," *San Juan Star*, Sunday magazine, May 11, 1980, 7.

26. Arturo Morales Carrion, "Review," *San Juan Star*, Sunday magazine, February 11, 1979, 1.

27. Gordon K. Lewis, *Puerto Rico: Freedom and Power in the Caribbean* (New York: Monthly Review Press, 1963), 55, 288.

28. Ibid., 114, 375.

29. Ibid., 109, 113.

30. Ibid., 122.

31. Tugwell, *Stricken Land*. New Dealer Tugwell was a loyal supporter of Muñoz

Marín in the transformation of the island. Lewis was both laudatory and critical of his decisions.

32. Lewis, *Puerto Rico: Freedom and Power in the Caribbean*, 432.

33. Ibid., 420.

34. Ibid., 435.

35. Ibid., 436, 569.

36. Ibid., 565.

37. See the more than 1,000 pages of analysis in U.S. Department of Commerce, *Economic Study of Puerto Rico*, 2 vols. (Washington D.C.: U.S. Government Printing Office, 1979). This publication is the largest official U.S. study ever done on the Puerto Rican economy.

38. See the interesting essay by Jorge Rodríguez Beruff, "Luís Muñoz Marín y Rafael Leónidas Trujillo: Una pugna caribeña," in Fernando Pico, ed., *Luis Muñoz Marín: Perfiles de su gobernación, 1948–1964* (San Juan: Fundación Luis Muñoz Marín, 2003), 21–61.

39. Kwame Nkrumah, *Ghana: The Autobiography of Kwame Nkrumah* (New York: Thomas Nelson and Sons, 1957), 162–63.

40. Rupert Emerson, *From Empire to Nation* (Boston: Beacon Press, 1960), 83.

41. Lewis, *Puerto Rico: Freedom and Power in the Caribbean*, 527.

42. Ibid., 398, 431.

43. Ibid., 431.

44. Ibid., 403.

45. Lewis, *Puerto Rico: Freedom and Power in the Caribbean*, 202.

46. Ibid., 203.

47. Ibid., 411.

48. The audio of this presentation resides in the Gordon K. Lewis Collection of the Institute of Caribbean Studies, University of Puerto Rico, Río Piedras. My thanks to the director of the institute for providing me with access to the collection.

49. Albizu justified every one of these violent acts as a response to imperialist oppression. See Marisa Rosado, *Albizu Campos: La Llamas de la Aurora* (San Juan: Editora Corripio, 1992).

50. Lewis, *Puerto Rico: Freedom and Power in the Caribbean*, 135.

51. Ibid., 136.

52. Gordon K. Lewis, *Notes on the Puerto Rican Revolution: An Essay on American Dominance and Caribbean Persistence* New York: Monthly Review Press, 1974), 151.

53. Partido Socialista Puertorriqueño, *La Alternativa Socialista: Tesis Política, 1974* (Rio Piedras: Ediciones Puerto Rico, 1974). This is not to be confused with the Partido Independentista Puertorriqueño, which is a social democratic party.

54. Ibid., 203.

55. Ibid., 174.

56. Lewis, *Notes on the Puerto Rican Revolution*, 217, 281.

57. Ibid., 225.

58. See Harold J. Laski, *The Communist Manifesto: An Introduction* (New York: New American Library, 1982), 63–82.

59. Edmund Burke, opening speech of impeachment of Warren Hastings, February 16, 1788, in E. A Bond, ed., *Speeches of the Managers and Counsel in the Trial of Warren Hastings* (London: Longman, 1859), 2:8.

59. *Sunday Gleaner* (Jamaica), March 2, 1958, 10.

60. Karl Marx, *Capital*, 591n2.

61. Lewis, *Puerto Rico: Freedom and Power in the Caribbean*, 510.

62. Gordon K. Lewis, *Grenada: The Jewel Despoiled* (Baltimore: Johns Hopkins University Press, 1987), 187

63. See Puerto Rican Department of Agriculture section in U.S. Department of Commerce, Economic Study of Puerto Rico, 2:294.

64. See José Trias Monge's prologue to Luís Muñoz Marín, *Diario: 1972–1974* (San Juan de Puerto Rico: Fundacion Luís Muñoz Marín, 1999), i–x.

65. Richard Weisskoff, *Factories and Foodstamps: The Puerto Rican Model of Development* (Baltimore: Johns Hopkins University Press, 1985), 158.

66. Ibid., 121.

67. Ibid., 92.

68. James L. Dietz, *Economic History of Puerto Rico: Institutional Change and Capitalist Development* (Princeton, N.J.: Princeton University Press, 1986), 300. Dietz claims, immodestly, that his book is the only scholarly book which covers the entire period since the eighteenth century. Dietz does acknowledge that since 1940 Puerto Rico "has left underdevelopment behind and entered the ranks of the developing and industrialized nations, at least as measured by the level of *per capita* income and the size of the manufacturing sector" (307). Improvement also in social indicators, 1974: 79.1 percent families own home: "There can be no question, then, that the Puerto Rican model of development has provided real material gains to the great majority of Puerto Ricans" (308).

69. Ibid., 304–5.

70. By 2012 there were more Puerto Ricans living in the United States (4.6 million) than on the island (3.7 million). They were, by then, the second largest Hispanic group after Cubans in Florida.

71. Dietz, *Economic History of Puerto Rico*, 305.

72. Manuel Maldonado Denis, *Puerto Rico: A Socio-Historic Interpretation* (New York: Random House, 1972).

Chapter 4. Haiti: The Origins of the Caribbean's "Terrified Consciousness" about Race

1. Alejo Carpentier, *Explosion in a Cathedral* (Minneapolis: University of Minnesota Press, 2001), 248.

2. Lowell Joseph Ragatz, *The Fall of the Planter Class in the British Caribbean, 1763–1833* (New York: Carnegie Corporation, 1928), 237.

3. *Dominican Journal*, April 26, 1800, cited in Ragatz, *Fall of the Planter Class*, 285.

4. Ragatz, *Fall of the Planter Class*, 258.

5. Gerard Masur, *Simón Bolívar* (Albuquerque: University of New Mexico Press, 1948), 102.

6. Robert F. McNery Jr., ed. and trans., *Bolívar and the War of Independence: Memoirs of General Daniel Florencio O'Leary* (Austin: University of Texas Press, 1970).

7. Harold A. Bierck Jr., "The Struggle for Abolition in Gran Colombia," *Hispanic American Historical Review* 33 (August 1953): 379–85. As Bierck notes, Bolívar's efforts were sincere but ineffective because they were confronted with "a bulwark of legal technicalities and widespread silent public resistance to emancipation."

8. Salvador de Madariaga, *Bolívar* (New York: Schocken Books, 1969).

9. John V. Lombardi, *Decadencia y abolición de la esclavitud en Venezuela, 1820–1854* (Caracas: Imprenta Universitaria, 1974), 73.

10. Letter to the editor of the *Royal Jamaican Gazette*, September 28, 1815, analyzing the racial situation in the Americas. Quoted in Manuel Pérez Vila, *Simón Bolívar: Doctrina del Libertador* (Caracas: Biblioteca Ayacucho, 1976), 75–79.

11. See "En el Cuartel General de Guayama, Manifiesto del Jefe Supremo a los Pueblos de Venezuela, Agosto 5, 1817," in Pérez Vila, *Simón Bolívar*, 80–81.

12. John Lynch, *Simón Bolívar: A Life* (New Haven, Conn.: Yale University Press, 2006), 12.

13. Ibid., 106.

14. McNery, *Bolívar and the War of Independence*, 105.

15. Ibid., 114.

16. Martha Hildebrandt, *La Lengua de Bolívar* (Caracas: Universidad Central de Venezuela, 1961).

17. Bolívar to Santander, April 20, 1820, cited in Vicente Lecuna, ed., *Cartas del Libertador*, 2 vols. (Caracas, 1929), 2:149.

18. See G. W. Allport, *The Nature of Prejudice* (Cambridge, UK: Addison-Wesley, 1954), 343–59.

19. Bernard Berelson and Gary A. Steiner, *Human Behavior: An Inventory of Scientific Findings* (New York: Harcourt, Brace and World, 1964), 267.

20. The interpretations in this section draw heavily from Anthony Maingot, "Haiti and the Terrified Consciousness of the Caribbean," in Gert Oostindie, ed., *Ethnicity in the Caribbean* (London: Macmillan Caribbean, 1996), 53–80. See also Seymour Drescher, "The Limits of Example," in David Geggus, ed., *The Impact of the Haitian Revolution in the Atlantic World* (Columbia: University of South Carolina Press, 2001), 10–14.

21. Madariaga, *Bolívar*, 537.

22. Lynch, *Simón Bolívar*, 109.

23. Quoted in Williams, *British Historians and the West Indies*, 56.

24. For citations from Bolívar's letters, see H. A. Bierck Jr., ed., *Selected Writings of Bolívar*, 2 vols. (New York: Colonial Press, 1951), 1:50ff.

25. Cited in Bierck, *Selected Writings of Bolívar*, 1:140.

26. For a full discussion, see Paul Verna, *Pétion y Bolívar* (Caracas: Ministerio de Educación, 1970), including appendix.

27. Eduardo Caballero Calderón, *Historia privada de los colombianos* (Bogotá: Talleres Antares, 1960), 67.

28. José María Samper, *Ensayo sobre las Revoluciones Políticas y la condición social de las Repúblicas colombianas* (Bogotá: Universidad Nacional, 1969), 186.

29. Alexander von Humboldt, *The Island of Cuba: A Political Essay* (Kingston, Jamaica: Ian Randle, 2001), 258, 262.

30. Madariaga, *Bolívar*, 534.

31. See Aline Helg, *Our Rightful Share: The Afro-Cuban Struggle for Equality, 1886–1912* (Chapel Hill: University of North Carolina Press, 1995), 51.

32. Hugh Thomas, *Cuba: The Pursuit of Freedom* (New York: Harper and Row, 1971), 105n47.

33. Charles Chapman, *A History of the Cuban Republic* (New York: Macmillan, 1927), 31. See also Jorge I. Domínguez, *Insurrection or Loyalty: The Breakdown of the Spanish American Empire* (Cambridge, Mass.: Harvard University Press, 1980), 250.

34. Levi Marrero, *Cuba: Economía y Sociedad*, 13 vols. (Río Piedras: Editorial San Juan, 1972–87), 9:34.

35. Jorge Castellanos and Isabel Castellanos, *Cultura Afrocubana*, 2 vols. (Miami: Ediciones Universal, 1988–92), 1:251.

36. José Antonio Saco, cited in Raúl Cepero Bonilla, *Azucar y abolición* (La Habana: Editorial Ciencias Sociales, 1971), 133.

37. Leopoldo Zea, *The Latin American Mind* (Norman: University of Oklahoma Press, 1963), 260.

38. José Luciano Franco, *Antonio Maceo* (La Habana: Editorial de Ciencias Sociales, 1975), 10–11.

39. Ibid., 13.

40. Ibid., 192–93.

41. During the period when Cubans were struggling to achieve independence, Haiti was in a virtually continuous state of political chaos. As James Leyburn put it, "The era from 1883 to 1915 was Haiti's worst, politically. Revolution succeeded revolution; the country sank deep into graft and scandal; foreign powers made Haiti debase herself before them." James Leyburn, *The Haitian People* (New Haven, Conn.: Yale University Press, 1941), 223.

42. Victor Schoelcher, *Esclavage et colonisation*, introduction by Aimé Césaire (Paris: Presses Universitaires de France, 1948), 197–98.

43. Cited in Rafael Fermoselle, *Política y color en Cuba* (Montevideo: Ediciones Géminis, 1974), 30.

44. De la Fuente, *A Nation for All*, 57.

45. Helg, *Our Rightful Share*, 17–18.

46. Chapman, *A History of the Cuban Republic*, 311–13.

47. Louis A. Pérez Jr., *On Becoming Cuban: Identity, Nationality, and Culture* (New York: Ecco Press, 1999), 91.

48. Ibid., 90.

49. Alejandro de la Fuente, "Race, National Discourse, and Politics in Cuba," *Latin American Perspectives* 25, no. 3 (1998): 43–69. Quote on 44. For a fuller discussion, see de la Fuente, *A Nation for All*.

50. Martí's many references to the racism he so detested and his complaints about "the constant references to the color of men" testify to the ingrained nature of color prejudice in Cuba. For discussion of Martí's many writings on the topic, see Manuel Pedro Gonzalez and Ivan A. Schulman, eds., *José Martí: Esquema ideológico* (Mexico: Editorial Cultura, 1961), 357–68.

51. For a serious discussion, see Mark Q. Sawyer, *Racial Politics in Post-Revolutionary Cuba* (Cambridge: Cambridge University Press, 2006).

52. Ashli White, *Encountering Revolution: Haiti and the Making of the Early Republic* (Baltimore: Johns Hopkins University Press, 2010), 133.

53. Daniel Rasmussen, *American Uprising: The Untold Story of America's Largest Slave Revolt* (New York: HarperCollins, 2011), 91.

54. Mitch Kachun, "Antebellum African Americans, Public Commemoration, and the Haitian Revolution: A Problem of Historical Mythmaking," in Maurice Jackson and Jacqueline Bacon, eds., *African Americans and the Haitian Revolution* (New York: Routledge, 2010), 94, 103.

55. David Brion Davis, *Slavery and Human Progress* (New York: Oxford University Press, 1984), 169.

56. Frank Moya Pons, *The Dominican Republic: A National History* (New Rochelle, N.Y.: Hispaniola Books, 1995), 139.

57. Ibid., 123.

58. Franklyn J. Franco, *Los negros, los mulatos y la nación Dominicana*, 7th ed. (Santo Domingo, República Dominicana: Alfa y Omega, 1984), 139–43.

59. Ernesto Sagás, *Race and Politics in the Dominican Republic* (Gainesville: University Press of Florida, 2000), ix.

60. Ibid., 76.

61. Ibid., 6.

62. Victor Schoelcher, *Polémique Coloniale*, preface by René Achéen, 2 vols. (Paris: Desormeaux, 1882), 1:7, 2:51.

Chapter 5. Haitian Realities and Scholarly Myths: A Counterintuitive Analysis

1. Garry Wills, *Negro President: Jefferson and the Slave Power* (Boston: Houghton Mifflin, 2003), 44–45.

2. In Michel S. Laguerre's monumental *The Complete Haitiana: A Bibliographic Guide to the Scholarly Literature, 1900–1980* (Millwood, N.Y.: Kraus International, 1982), there are 650 entries under "U.S. Occupation." If it does nothing else, such a bibliographic reference reminds us that Haiti was under U.S. military occupation longer than any other country in the Caribbean.

3. David Geggus, ed., *The Impact of the Haitian Revolution in the Atlantic World* (Columbia: University of South Carolina Press, 2001), ix.

4. Seymour Drescher, "The Limits of Example," in Geggus, *Impact of the Haitian Revolution in the Atlantic World*, 10–14, quotation on 13.

5. Wills, *Negro President*, 40–41.

6. For this author's analysis of each of these explanations, see Anthony Maingot, "Haiti: Four Old and Two New Hypotheses," in Jorge I. Domínguez and Abraham F. Lowenthal, eds., *Constructing Democratic Governance: Mexico, Central America, and the Caribbean in the 1990s* (Baltimore: Johns Hopkins University Press, 1996), 135–58.

7. Paul Farmer, *Haiti after the Earthquake* (New York: Public Affairs, 2011).

8. Joia S. Mukherjee, "Nèg Mawon," foreword to Farmer, *Haiti after the Earthquake*, xi–xii.

9. Paul Farmer, *AIDS and Accusation: Haiti and the Geography of Blame* (Berkeley: University of California Press, 1992); Paul Farmer, *The Uses of Haiti* (Monroe, Maine: Common Courage Press, 2006).

10. Farmer, *Haiti after the Earthquake*, 160.

11. Ibid., 206.

12. Ibid., 3.

13. Ibid., 369n21.

14. Ibid., xii.

15. Ibid., 305.

16. Robert Fatton Jr., "Haiti's Unending Crisis of Governance: Food, the Constitution, and the Struggle for Power," in Jorge Heine and Andrew S. Thompson, eds., *Fixing Haiti: MINUSTAH and Beyond* (New York: United Nations University Press, 2011), 47. See also Robert Fatton Jr., *Haiti's Predatory Republic* (Boulder, Colo.: Lynne Rienner, 2002), and Robert Fatton Jr., *The Roots of Haitian Despotism* (Boulder, Colo.: Lynne Rienner, 2007).

17. Fatton, "Haiti's Unending Crisis of Governance," 56.

18. Ibid., 54.

19. Ibid., 47.

20. Laurent Dubois, *Avengers of the New World: The Story of the Haitian Revolution* (Cambridge, Mass.: Belknap Press of Harvard University, 2004).

21. C.L.R. James, *The Black Jacobins: Toussaint L'Ouverture and the San Domingo Revolution* (1938; New York: Vintage Books, 1963); David Nicholls, *From Dessalines to Duvalier: Race, Colour, and National Independence in Haiti* (Cambridge, UK: Cambridge University Press, 1979).

22. Dubois, *Avengers of the New World*, 87.

23. Ibid., 10–11.

24. Ibid., 6.

25. Ibid., 114.

26. Ibid., 115.

27. Arthur C. Millspaugh, *Haiti under American Control, 1915–1930* (Boston: World Peace Foundation, 1931), 20.

28. Eric Williams, *The Negro in the Caribbean* (Westport, Conn.: Negro Universities Press, 1942), 54–55.

29. A. Edward Stuntz, *To Make the People Strong* (New York: Macmillan, 1948), 193–94.

30. See Anthony P. Maingot, "Emigration Dynamics in the Caribbean: The Cases of Haiti and the Dominican Republic," in Reginald Appleyard, ed., *Emigration Dynamics in Developing Countries,* 3 vols. (Brookfield, Vt.: Ashgate, 1999), 3:178–231.

31. Jean-Bertrand Aristide, with Christopher Wargny, *Aristide: An Autobiography,* trans. Linda M. Maloney (Maryknoll, N.Y.: Orbis Books, 1993), 168.

32. USDA Foreign Agricultural Service, *Rice Production and Trade Report* (Washington, D.C.: Global Information Network, 2010).

33. For a more complete description of this ecological crisis, see Anthony Maingot, "Emigration Dynamics in the Caribbean: The Cases of Haiti and the Dominican Republic," in Reginald Appleyard, ed., *Emigration Dynamics in Developing Countries* (Brookfield, Vt.: Ashgate, 1999), 3:178–231.

34. Jacques Roumain, *The Masters of the Dew* (1944; Oxford: Heineman, 1978), 123.

35. Frank Tannenbaum, *Ten Keys to Latin America* (New York: Vintage Books, 1959), 205.

36. Melville J. Herskovits, *Life in a Haitian Valley* (1937; New York: Alfred A. Knopf, 1968), 297.

37. George Anglade, *L'Espace Haïtien* (1972; Montreal: Editions des Alizes, 1981).

38. Paul Moral, *Le paysan haïtien: Etude sur la vie rurale en Haiti* (Paris: Maisonneuve et Larose, 1961).

39. Anglade, *L'Espace Haïtien.*

40. Boulos A. Malik, "Food Crops," in *Haiti: A Country Study: Haiti,* ed. Richard A. Haggerty (Washington, D.C.: Government Printing Office for the Library of Congress, 1989) at http://countrystudies.us/haiti/.

41. See Oficina Nacional de Estadísticas, "Panorama del Uso de la Tierra 2013," cited by the Agence France Presse, June 17, 2014.

42. This information comes from the diary I kept during much of this period, when I served as an electoral observer for the Carter Center in Haiti.

43. During the 1970s, Manigat was director of the Institute of International Relations at the University of the West Indies, St. Augustine, Trinidad, where I held a professorship. After Trinidad, Manigat held a professorship at the Universidad Simón Bolívar in Venezuela.

44. Leslie Manigat, *Haiti of the Sixties, Object of International Concern: A Tentative Global Analysis of the Potentially Explosive Situation of a Crisis Country in the Caribbean* (Washington, D.C.: Washington Center of Foreign Policy Research, 1964), 92.

45. Anthony Maingot, "Leslie Manigat on Haitian Modernization and the Pursuit of Happiness," *Hemisphere* 1, no. 1 (Fall 1988): 19–23.

46. Anthony Maingot, interview with Gerard Latortue, Miami, August 2, 1992.

47. Jean-Bertrand Aristide, quoted in Gregorio Selser, "Haiti: El drama permanente

de su pueblo: Entrevista al sacerdote Jean-Bertrand Aristide," *El Caribe Contemporáneo* (México) 22 (January–July 1991): 50.

48. Jean-Bertrand Aristide, *In the Parish of the Poor: Writings from Haiti*, ed. and trans. Amy Wilentz (New York: Orbis, 1990), 15.

49. Amy Wilentz, *Rainy Season: Haiti since Duvalier* (New York: Simon and Schuster, 1989).

50. *Newsday*, May 14, 1990, 16. Also see similar accounts in Wilentz, *Rainy Season*.

51. Alex Dupuy, *Haiti in the New World Order: The Limits of the Democratic Revolution* (Boulder, Colo.: Westview Press, 1997), 134.

52. Conversation with the author, Miami, July 24, 1993.

53. Jean-Bertrand Aristide, *New York Times*, October 16, 1994, E-15.

54. Tom Farer, introduction to *Beyond Sovereignty: Collectively Defending Democracy in the Americas*, ed. Tom Farer (Baltimore: Johns Hopkins University Press, 1996), 15–16.

55. Catherine S. Manegold, "Innocent Abroad: Jean-Bertrand Aristide," *New York Times Magazine*, May 1, 1994, 38.

56. Ibid., 40.

57. *El Siglo*, November 28, 2000, 18.

58. Manegold, "Innocent Abroad," 41.

59. Aristide and Wargny, *Aristide: An Autobiography*, 181.

60. Dupuy, *Haiti in the New World Order*, 134.

61. David Nicholls, *Haiti in the Caribbean Context* (New York: St. Martin's Press, 1985), 220.

62. Paul Farmer, "Who Removed Aristide?" *London Review of Books*, April 15, 2004. Aristide also accused the United States of organizing the coup against him with the support of Jamaica's prime minister, J. Patterson. See "Aristide says U.S. deposed him in 'coup d'etat,'" CNN.com, March 1, 2004, http://www.cnn.com/2004/WORLD/americas/03/01/aristide.claim/index.html?iref=allsearch.

63. Alex Dupuy, *The Prophet and Power: Jean-Bertrand Aristide, the International Community, and Haiti* (Lanham, Md.: Rowman and Littlefield, 2007), 2.

Chapter 6. Two Popular Theories of Caribbean Ideology and Race Relations: Frantz Fanon's Theory of Liberating Violence and the Theory of Plantation Societies

1. George Sorel, *Reflections on Violence* (New York: Collier Books, 1961).

2. See Jean-Paul Sartre's famous preface to Frantz Fanon, *The Wretched of the Earth*, trans. Constance Farrington (New York: Grove Press, 1963), 7–34.

3. Fanon, *Wretched of the Earth*, 94.

4. Fanon analyzed this self-hatred and self-mutilation in his 1952 doctoral thesis.

5. Fanon, *Wretched of the Earth*, 39.

6. Dominique O. Mannoni, *Próspero and Caliban: The Psychology of Colonization*, trans. Pamela Powesland (1950; New York: Praeger, 1965), 8.

7. Mannoni, *Próspero and Caliban*, 17; Fanon, *Wretched of the Earth*, 40.

8. This explains why the liberation movement in Algeria could not recognize publicly those whites who contributed to their cause. See Frantz Fanon, *Sociologie d'une révolution* (Paris: Maspero, 1968), 36–54.

9. Shlomo Avinieri, *The Social and Political Thought of Karl Marx* (Cambridge: Cambridge University Press, 1968), 187.

10. Sartre, preface to Fanon's *Wretched of the Earth*, 17.

11. Frantz Fanon, *Peau Noire, Masques Blancs* (Paris: Editions de Seuil, 1952), 7–9.

12. Frantz Fanon, "Antillais et Africains," *Esprit* (February 1955), reprinted in *Pour la révolution africaines: Ecrits politiqués* (Paris: Librairie François Maspero, 1964), 35.

13. Fanon, *Wretched of the Earth*, 51.

14. Jean Franco, *Historia de la literatura hispanoamericana: a partir de la Independencia* (Barcelona: Editorial Planeta S.A., 1973), 243.

15. Kenneth Ramchand, *The West Indian Novel and Its Background* (London: Faber and Faber, 1970).

16. Gabriel R. Coulthard, *Race and Colour in Caribbean Literature* (London: Oxford University Press, 1962), 61.

17. It is telling that in a long interview with the *Trinidad Guardian* (October 12, 1971, 8–9), Aimé Césaire could not mention a single English-speaking West Indian author.

18. Lloyd Best and Kari Polanyi Levitt, *Essays on the Theory of Plantation Economy* (Mona, Jamaica: University of the West Indies Press, 2009).

19. Dominant among Caribbean decision makers at the time was W. Arthur Lewis's "Industrialization by Invitation" model, which duplicated what was being applied in Puerto Rico.

20. Juan Beneyto, *Historia social de España y de Hispanoamérica* (Madrid: Aguilar, 1961).

21. The essential work on this theme is Richard M. Morse, "Toward a Theory of Spanish American Government," *Journal of the History of Ideas* 15 (January 1954): 71–93.

22. Salvador de Madariaga, *Spain: A Modern History* (New York: Praeger, 1958), 17–18. The Spanish historian Salvador de Madariaga dates the changed attitude of the Spanish people toward the Jews and Moors as occurring in the late eleventh century.

23. J. H. Parry, *The Age of Reconnaissance* (New York: Mentor, 1964), 45.

24. Descola, *Daily Life in Colonial Peru*, 105

25. François Chevalier, "'Caudillos' et 'caciques' en Amérique," *Bulletin Hispanique* 64 (1962): 30–40. Quote on 34.

26. Verena Martínez-Alier, *Marriage, Class, and Colour in Nineteenth-Century Cuba* (Cambridge: Cambridge University Press, 1974), 15, 63.

27. A. M. Elegio de la Puente, introduction to Fernando Ortiz, ed., *Poesías Selectas de Placido* (La Habana: Colección de Libros Cubanos, 1930).

28. M. García Garofalo Mesa and Eduardo Machado y Gómez, *Plácido: Poeta y mártir* (México: Ediciones Botas, 1938).

29. Juan José Arrom, *Estudios de la Literatura hispanoamericana* (La Habana, 1950), 121.

30. Cirilo Villaverde, *La peineta calada* (La Habana: Faro Industrial, 1843).

31. García Garofalo Mesa and Machado y Gómez, *Plácido: Poeta y mártir*, 52.

32. Manuel Pedro González y Ivan Schulman, *José Martí: Esquema ideológico* (México: Editorial Cultura, 1961), 2:361–63.

33. This letter and other documents pertinent to the criollo-peninsular conflict in Latin America are found in R. A. Humphreys and John Lynch, eds., *The Origins of the Latin American Revolutions, 1808–1826* (New York: Knopf, 1966), 243–68.

34. Harry Hoetink, *El Pueblo Dominicano, 1850–1900* (Santiago, República Dominicana: Universidad Católica Madre y Maestra, 1971).

35. Marció A. Mejía Ricart, *Las clases sociales en Santo Domingo* (Ciudad Trujillo, República Dominicana: Librería Dominicana, 1953), 27–28.

36. Joaquín Balaguer, *Memorias de un cortesano de la "era de Trujillo"* (Santo Domingo, República Dominicana: Impresora Sierra, 1988), 219–22.

37. Bernardo Vega, *Trujillo y Haití* (Santo Domingo, República Dominicana: Fundación Cultural Dominicana, 1995), 1:116.

38. Joaquín Balaguer, *La Isla al revés: Haití y el destino Dominicano*, 6th ed. (Santo Domingo, República Dominicana: Editora Corripio, 1990), 230–31.

39. José del Castillo and Manuel García, *Antologia del Merengue* (Santo Domingo, República Dominicana: Banco Antillano, 1989).

40. Cf. H. Hoetink, "Curaçao como sociedad segmentada," *Revista de Ciencias Sociales* 4, no. 1 (March 1960): 179–92.

41. Edith Kovats-Beaudoux, "A Dominant Minority: The White Creoles of Martinique," in Lambros Comitas and David Lowenthal, eds., *Slaves, Free Men, Citizens: West Indian Perspectives* (Garden City, N.Y.: Anchor Press/Doubleday, 1973), 241–75.

42. Fred Constant, *La Retraite aux Flambeaux: Politique et Société en Martinique* (Paris: Editions Caribéennes, 1988).

43. Édouard Glissant, *Caribbean Discourse*, trans. J. Michael Dash (Charlottesville: University Press of Virginia, 1989).

44. Édouard Glissant, speech at Kingston, Jamaica, CARIFESTA conference 1976, Caribbean Discourse.

45. Édouard Glissant, *Poetics of Relation*, trans. Betsy Wing (Ann Arbor: University of Michigan Press, 1997), 98.

46. Ibid., 96.

47. Ibid.

48. Richard Burton, in Alistair Hennessey, ed., *Intellectuals in the Twentieth-Century Caribbean* (London: Macmillan, 1992), 2:196.

49. Aimé Césaire, "Letter to Maurice Thorez" (1956; Paris: Éditions Présence Africaine, 1957).

50. See this line of analysis in Patrick Taylor, *The Narrative of Liberation* (Ithaca, N.Y.: Cornell University Press, 1989), 152.

51. "Africans at Algiers Denounce Négritude as Outmoded," *New York Times*, July 28, 1969, 4.

52. See Anthony Maingot, "Haitian Exceptionalism: The Caribbean's Great Morality Play," in Kate Quinn and Paul Sutton, eds., *Politics and Power in Haiti* (London: Palgrave Macmillan, 2013), 115–40.

53. Nicholls, *From Dessalines to Duvalier*, 1.

54. Jacques C. Antoine, *Jean Price-Mars and Haiti* (Washington, D.C.: Three Continents, 1981), 124. Haitian author Jacques C. Antoine claims that it was a lecture by Jean Price-Mars given to black students in Paris which "inspired" both Aimé Césaire and Léopold Senghor to look to their African heritage.

55. The fundamental book for an understanding of this color competition is still James Leyburn, *The Haitian People* (New Haven, Conn.: Yale University Press, 1941).

56. Micheline Labelle, *Idéologie de couleur et classes sociales en Haïti* (Montréal: Les Presses de l'Université de Montréal, 1987).

57. Cf. Anthony Maingot, "Haiti and Aristide: The Legacy of History," *Current History* 91, no. 562 (February 1992): 65–69.

58. This section draws heavily from Anthony Maingot, "Haiti: Sovereign Consent versus State-Centric Sovereignty," in Farer, ed., *Beyond Sovereignty*, 189–212.

59. J. Michael Dash, "Marvelous Realism—The Way Out of Negritude," *Caribbean Studies* 13, no. 4 (January 1974): 57–70. Dash added the critiques of the American James Baldwin and the Guyanese Wilson Harris to his analysis.

Chapter 7. C.L.R. James, George Padmore, and the Myth of the Revolutionary Caribbean

1. C.L.R. James, *Special Delivery: The Letters of C.L.R. James to Constance Webb, 1939–1948*, ed. Anna Grimshaw (Cambridge, Mass: Blackwell, 1996), 1.

2. Ibid., 4.

3. C.L.R. James, *Beyond a Boundary* (London: Hutchinson, 1963), 3.

4. Ibid., 30.

5. Ibid., 116.

6. C.L.R. James, *The Life of Captain Cipriani: An Account of British Government in the West Indies* (London: Coulton, 1932), later published as *The Case for West Indian Self-Government* (Hogarth Press, 1933). James published an updated version of the 1933 monograph in the "Independence Supplement" of the *Trinidad Guardian*, August 26, 1962.

7. Paul Buhle, introduction to C.L.R. James, *State Capitalism and World Revolution* (Chicago: Charles Kerr, 1986), xi–xxiii. Quote on xvi.

8. Ibid., xvii.

9. C.L.R. James, *Mariners, Renegades, and Castaways: The Story of Herman Melville and the World We Live In* (New York: privately published, 1953), 187.

10. Ibid., 189.

11. Ibid., 202.

12. Ivar Oxaal, *Black Intellectuals Come to Power* (Cambridge, Mass: Schenkman, 1968), 136.

13. Anthony Maingot, interview with Prime Minister Eric Williams, Hilton Hotel, Port-of-Spain, Trinidad and Tobago, June 5, 1971.

14. Selwyn Ryan, *Eric Williams: The Myth and the Man* (Jamaica: University of the West Indies Press, 2009), 34.

15. C.L.R. James, *Modern Politics* (Port-of-Spain, Trinidad and Tobago: PNM, 1960), 109.

16. See preface to C.L.R. James, *Nkrumah and the Ghana Revolution* (1977; London: Allison and Busby, 1982).

17. C.L.R. James, *The Rise and Fall of Nkrumah* (London: Allison and Busby, 1966).

18. Wilson Harris quoted in Paget Henry and Paul Buhle, eds., *C.L.R. James' Caribbean* (Durham, N.C.: Duke University Press, 1992), 1.

19. Anthony Bogues, *Caliban's Freedom: The Early Political Thought of C.L.R. James* (London: Pluto Press, 1997).

20. Anthony Maingot, "National Identity, Instrumental Identifications, and the Caribbean's Culture of 'Play,'" *Identity: An International Journal of Theory and Research* 2, no. 2 (2002): 115–24.

21. Walton Look Lai, "C.L.R. James and Trinidadian Nationalism," in Henry and Buhle, eds., *C.L.R. James' Caribbean*, 174–209. Quote on 206.

22. Humberto García Muñiz, "Eric Williams y C.L.R. James: Simbiosis Intelectual y Contrapunteo Ideológico," in *El negro, la esclavitud y el capitalismo en el Caribe* (Havana: Casa de Altos Estudios Don Fernando Ortiz, Universidad de la Habana, forthcoming).

23. Ralph E. Gonsalves, *The Making of a Comrade: The Political Journey of Ralph Gonsalves* (St. Vincent and the Grenadines: SFI Books, 2010), 56.

24. Bruce King, ed., *West Indian Literature*, 2nd ed. (London: Macmillan Education, 1995), 209–21.

25. *New York Times*, August 4, 2001, A-15.

26. Emily Eakin, "Embracing the Wisdom of a Castaway," *New York Times*, August 4, 2001, A-14, 17.

27. James, *Mariners, Renegades and Castaways*, 202.

28. Henry and Buhle, *C.L.R. James' Caribbean*, 1.

29. Caryl Phillips, Constance Webb obituary, *Guardian*, April 15, 2005.

30. Andrew Smith, *James and the Study of Culture* (Houndsmills, Basingstoke, UK: Palgrave Macmillan, 2010), 15.

31. Ibid., 19.

32. Ibid., 37.

33. Ibid., 8–9.

34. Ibid., 8.

35. Ken Boodhoo, *The Elusive Eric Williams* (Port-of-Spain, Trinidad and Tobago: Prospect Press, 2001), 159.

36. James, *Special Delivery*, 163 (emphasis in original).

37. James, *Black Jacobins*, 1, citing Jean Jaurès, *Histoire Socialiste de la Révolution Française*, 8 vols. (Paris: Éditions de la Librairie de l'humanité, 1922–27), 2:62–84.

38. Eric Williams, *Capitalism and Slavery* (1944; New York: Russell and Russell, 1961), 209.

39. Ryan, *Eric Williams*, 39.

40. Eric Williams, *Inward Hunger* (London: André Deutsch, 1969), 23, 53.

41. H. Stuart Hughes, *Consciousness and Society* (New York: Vintage, 1961), 75–76.

42. Charles W. Mills, *Race, Class, and Social Domination* (Kingston, Jamaica: University of the West Indies Press, 2010), 7.

43. Walter Rodney, *The Grounding of My Brothers* (Trenton, N.J.: Africa World Press, 1988), 28–29. This is a reprint of his 1969 monograph.

44. Selwyn Ryan and Taimoon Stewart, eds., *The Black Power Revolution of 1970: A Retrospective* (St. Augustine, Trinidad: ISER, 1995), 1–21, 543–78, 579–606.

45. David Austin, *You Don't Play with Revolution: The Montreal Lectures of C.L.R. James* (1962; Oakland, Calif.: A. K. Press, 2009), 230–31.

46. See Anthony Cave Brown and Charles B. MacDonald, *On a Field of Red* (New York: G. Putnam's Sons, 1981), 143.

47. Patricia Pugh, *Educate, Agitate, Organize: 100 Years of Fabian Socialism* (London: Methuen, 1984), 192.

48. George Padmore, *Pan-Africanism or Communism?* (London: Dennis Dobson, 1956), 342.

49. See Rodolfo Cerdas Cruz, *La Hoz y el Machete* (San José, Costa Rica: Universidad a la Distancia, 1986).

50. Manuel Caballero, *Entre Gómez y Stalin* (Caracas: Universidad Central de Venezuela, 1989).

51. Raymond Aron, *Memoirs: Fifty Years of Political Reflection* (New York: Holmes and Meier, 1990), 472.

52. George F. Kennan, *Russia and the West under Lenin and Stalin* (Boston: Little, Brown, 1961), 186.

53. Jane Degras, ed., *The Communist International, 1919–1943: Documents* (London: Oxford University Press, 1956), 238.

54. Brown and MacDonald, *On a Field of Red*, 353.

55. Padmore commentary quoted in James R. Hooker, *Black Revolutionary: George Padmore's Path from Communism to Pan-Africanism* (New York: Praeger, 1967), 31–32.

56. George Padmore, *How Russia Transformed Her Colonial Empire* (London: Dennis Dobson, 1946).

57. George Padmore, *Africa: Britain's Third Empire* (London: Dennis Dobson, 1948), 9.

58. Ibid., 261.

59. Richard Crossman, *The God That Failed* (New York: Harper and Row, 1950), 146.

60. Azinna Nwafor, introduction to Padmore, *Pan-Africanism*, xxv–xlii. Quote on xxxvii.

61. Padmore, *Pan-Africanism*, 21–22.

62. Ibid., 351.

63. Ibid., 349–51.

64. Fitzroy Babtiste, "The African Conferences of Governors and Indigenous Collaborators, 1947–1948," in Fitzroy Baptiste and Rupert Lewis, eds., *George Padmore: Pan-African Revolutionary* (Kingston, Jamaica: Ian Randle, 2009), 37–65. Quote on 58.

65. Rupert Lewis, "George Padmore: Towards a Political Assessment," in Baptiste and Lewis, eds., *George Padmore*, 151.

66. Hooker, *Black Revolutionary*, 132.

67. Ibid., 133.

68. Ibid., 187.

69. Georgie Anne Geyer, "Black Power: Caribbean Revolt in Search of a Leader," *Los Angeles Times*, June 28, 1970, 3–4.

70. David Millette, "Guerrilla War in Trinidad, 1970–1974," in Ryan and Stewart, eds., *The Black Power Revolution of 1970*, 59–95. Quote on 652.

71. On the 1970 Black Power movement and the reasons for its failure, the most complete assemblage of studies to date is Ryan and Stewart, eds., *The Black Power Revolution of 1970*; also see David Nicholls, *Haiti in Caribbean Context* (New York: St. Martin's Press, 1985), 61–80. The military dimension is discussed by S. Hylton Edwards, *Lengthening Shadows: Birth and Revolt of the Trinidad Army* (Port-of-Spain, Trinidad and Tobago: Imprint Caribbean, 1982).

72. I held the chair of Latin American Studies at the Institute of International Relations at the university at the time and was often on the losing side of debates about the continued viability (and wide popular acceptance) of pluralist, parliamentary democracy on the island and in the region.

73. I cited the case of the amnesty given by President Rafael Caldera in Venezuela and supported by the Roman Catholic archbishop. This had saved the lives of dozens of Venezuelan guerrillas who had already been defeated.

Chapter 8. What Type of Socialism? Marxists and Social Democrats Vie for Leadership

1. Six PhD dissertations were directed by Professor Wendell Bell at the University of California Los Angeles. They covered Jamaica, Trinidad/Tobago, Guyana, and Antigua. An additional study on Barbados was included in the literature. See Wendell Bell and Ivar Oxaal, *Decisions of Nationhood: Political and Social Development in the British Caribbean* (Denver: Social Science Foundation, University of Denver, 1964), and Wendell Bell, *Jamaican Leaders: Political Attitudes in a New Nation* (Berkeley: University of California Press, 1964).

2. Wendell Bell and Ivar Oxaal, introduction to Wendell Bell, ed., *Democratic Revolution in the West Indies* (Cambridge, Mass: Schenkman, 1967), 11.

3. Michael Kaufman, *Jamaica under Manley: Dilemmas of Socialism and Democracy* (London: ZED Books, 1985), 3.

4. Trevor Munroe, "The Marxist 'Left' in Jamaica, 1940–1950," Working Paper no. 15 (Institute of Social and Economic Studies, UWI, Mona, 1977), 1.

5. Louis Lindsay, "The Myth of Independence," Working Paper no. 6 (Mona: Institute of Social and Economic Research, UWI, 1975).

6. George E. Eaton, *Alexander Bustamante and Modern Jamaica* (Kingston, Jamaica: Kingston, 1975), 13–14.

7. Gordon K. Lewis, *The Growth of the Modern West Indies* (New York: Monthly Review Press, 1968), 179.

8. Rex Nettleford, *Manley and the Politics of Jamaica: Towards an Analysis of Political Change in Jamaica, 1938–1968* (Mona, Jamaica: Institute of Social and Economic Research, University of the West Indies, 1971), 70.

9. Quoted in Rex Nettleford, ed., *Manley and the New Jamaica: Selected Speeches and Writings, 1938–1968* (New York: Africana, 1971), 61.

10. Nettleford, *Manley and the Politics of Jamaica*, 35.

11. Quoted in Nettleford, ed., *Manley and the New Jamaica*, 89.

12. Wilmot Perkins, "The Intellectuals, the PNP and the JLP," *Sunday Gleaner*, November 27, 1977, 7.

13. Eaton, *Alexander Bustamante*, 106–7.

14. Perkins, "The Intellectuals, the PNP and the JLP."

15. Cited in Darrell E. Levi, *Michael Manley: The Making of a Leader* (Athens: University of Georgia Press, 1990), 96, 131.

16. Quoted in C.L.R. James, *The Life of Captain Cipriani*, 31.

17. See *Trinidad and Tobago Disturbances, 1937. Report of Commission* (Port-of-Spain, Trinidad and Tobago: Government Printing Office, 1938), 40.

18. Even though Mr. Cola Rienzi was general president of the OWTU and of the All-Trinidad Sugar Estates and Factory Workers' Trade Union, the colonial authorities regarded Butler as the functional leader of the workers and Rienzi as "without question Butler's accredited emissary." *Trinidad and Tobago Disturbances, 1937*, 58.

19. As early as 1947 a perceptive American liberal noted, "One reason for the lack of labor unity [in Trinidad] is that thousands of East Indians have become small proprietors, not sympathetic with the proletarian aims of the Negro majority. . . . In plain English, they were afraid of Negro and mulatto control until their high birth rate gave them the majority in the population." Paul Blanshard, *Democracy and Empire in the Caribbean* (New York: Macmillan, 1947), 114.

20. See Lennox Pierre and John La Rose, *For More and Better Democracy, for a Democratic Constitution* (Port-of-Spain, Trinidad and Tobago: West Indian Independence Party of Trinidad and Tobago, 1956). The authors were encouraged no doubt by the fact that the island's best-known radical, C.L.R. James, had returned to work with the PNM as editor of its newspaper, the *Nation*. See Lennox Pierre, *Quintin O'Connor, Labour Leader: A Personal Appreciation* (Trinidad: Granderson Brothers Printing, 1959).

An English trade unionist recalled hearing a Trinidadian Marxist refer to the *Communist Manifesto* as written by Marx and Lenin. F. W. Dalley, *General Industrial Conditions and Labour Relations in Trinidad* (Trinidad: Government Printing Office, 1954), 67.

21. In 1965 they were calculated to number only fifteen. See *Report of the Commission of Enquiry into Subversive Activities in Trinidad and Tobago* (House Paper no. 2 of 1965), 19.

22. This group was led by some well-known radical labor leaders, including Raffique Shah, Lennox Pierre, Clive Nunez, Joe Young, and George Weekes.

23. *Express* (Port-of-Spain, Trinidad and Tobago), August 11, 1977, 1.

24. Cheddi Jagan, *The West on Trial: My Fight for Guyana's Freedom* (London: Joseph, 1966), 49.

25. Forbes Burnham, *A Destiny to Mould* (New York: Africana, 1970), 5.

26. Percy C. Hintzen, *The Costs of Regime Survival* (Cambridge: Cambridge University Press, 1989), 114–15.

27. Ibid. 72, 96–97. For a detailed analysis of how this electoral fraud was perpetrated, see Edward Green, "The 1968 General Elections in Guyana and the Introduction of Proportional Representation," in Trevor Munroe and Rupert Lewis, eds., *Readings in Government and Politics of the West Indies* (Mona, Jamaica: Department of Government, 1971), 134–36.

28. Michael Manley, *The Politics of Change, A Jamaican Testament* (London: André Deutsch, 1974), 1.

29. Ibid., 109–10.

30. Ibid., 30.

31. Ibid., 29.

32. Ibid., 30.

33. Speeches were compiled and edited by Michael Manley's lifelong friend John Hearne in *The Search for Solutions* (Ontario: Maple House, 1976). Later, as we shall see, Hearne became one of Manley's main nemeses.

34. Michael Manley, *A Voice at the Workplace: Reflections on Colonialism and the Jamaican Worker* (London: André Deutsch, 1975), 70.

35. Ibid., 229.

36. Michael Manley, *Jamaica: Struggle in the Periphery* (London: Third World Media, 1982), x.

37. Levi, *Michael Manley*, 69.

38. Carl Stone, "Race and Nationalism in Urban Jamaica," *Caribbean Studies* 13, no. 4 (January 1974): 28–29.

39. Manley, *Jamaica: Struggle in the Periphery*, 209–10. Cf. I. Andreyev, *The Noncapitalist Way* (Moscow: Progress, 1974), 123. "Marx and Engels formulated the noncapitalist development concept back in the late 1840s and kept working on it for almost half a century."

40. Edward Seaga, *My Life and Leadership*, vol. 1, *Clash of Ideologies* (Oxford: Macmillan Education, 2009), 243.

41. Evelyn Huber Stephens and John D. Stephens, *Democratic Socialism in Jamaica* (Princeton, N.J.: Princeton University Press, 1986), 120, 315, 319.

42. Levi, *Michael Manley*, x, 138. Further on "evidence" of destabilization, see George Beckford and Michael Witter, *Small Garden, Bitter Weed: Struggle and Change in Jamaica* (London: Zed Press, 1982), 149–62.

43. Anthony J. Payne, *Politics in Jamaica* (New York: St. Martin's Press, 1988), 58, 59.

44. *Weekly Gleaner*, February 13, 1978, 17; January 30, 1978, 8. In 1962 Wendell Bell

found that 25 percent of his elite sample were "economic radicals" and 17 percent were "liberals." In 1974 the economic radicals had dropped to 15 percent and the liberals had risen to 49 percent. Wendell Bell and J. William Gibson Jr., "Independent Jamaica Faces the Outside World," *International Studies Quarterly* 22, no. 1 (1978): 5–48. Quote on 26.

45. See Carl Stone, *The Political Opinions of the Jamaican People, 1976–81* (Kingston: Blackett, 1982), 24–25. For a Marxist version of the changes, see Trevor Munroe, *Jamaican Politics: A Marxist Perspective in Transition* (Kingston: Heinemann, 1990), 246–49.

46. Carl Stone, *Electoral Behavior and Public Opinion in Jamaica* (Mona, Jamaica, 1974), 79; Carl Stone Poll, *Weekly Gleaner*, April 17, 1978, 7.

47. Carl Stone Poll, *Weekly Gleaner*, January 16, 1978, 1.

48. Levi, *Michael Manley*, 263.

49. Ibid., 205, 210.

50. Stone, *Electoral Behavior and Public Opinion*, 96.

51. Michael Manley, *Up the Down Escalator: Development and the International Economy, a Jamaican Case Study* (London: André Deutsch, 1987), 7.

52. Foreign Broadcast (FBIS), November 4, 1989.

53. Latin American Regional Report, *Caribbean Report*, February 22, 1989.

54. *Weekly Gleaner*, June 13, 1989.

55. Trevor Munroe, "The Workers' Liberation League," *World Marxist Review* 30 (March 1990): 1–6.

56. Arthur Lewin, "The Fall of Michael Manley: A Case Study of the Failure of Reform Socialism," *Monthly Review* 33, no. 9 (February 1982): 56–57.

57. Austin, *You Don't Play with Revolution*, 129, 232.

Chapter 9. The Failure of Socialism and "Militarism" in Grenada, 1979–83

1. Robert Dahl and Edward R. Tufte, *Size and Democracy* (Stanford, Calif.: Stanford University Press, 1973), 6. Not surprisingly, authors did not find that any size of state is optimal for democracy.

2. Ibid., 11.

3. See, for instance, M. G. Smith, *Kinship and Community in Carriacou* (New Haven: Yale University Press Caribbean Series, 1962); Elsa V. Goveia, *Slave Society in the British Leeward Islands at the End of the Eighteenth Century* (New Haven: Yale University Press Caribbean Series, 1965); Michel Rolph Trouillot, *Peasants and Capital: Dominica in the World Economy* (Baltimore: Johns Hopkins University Press, 1988).

4. Proof that "smallness" is relative is the fact that Trinidadians and Barbadians call Grenadians "small islanders" and Grenadians call men from Carriacou "small island men." Prime Minister Herbert Blaise, born on Carriacou, was often taunted with this sobriquet.

5. Archie W. Singham, *The Hero and the Crowd in a Colonial Polity* (New Haven: Yale University Press Caribbean Series, 1968), 11.

6. George Brizan, *Grenada: Island of Conflict From Amerindians to People's Revolution, 1498–1979* (London: Zed Books, 1984), 246.

7. Singham, *The Hero and the Crowd*, 198, 227.

8. Brizan, *Grenada: Island of Conflict*, 271.

9. Patrick Emmanuel, *Crown Colony Politics in Grenada, 1917–1951*, Occasional Papers no. 7 (Barbados: University of the West Indies ISER, 1978), 184–85.

10. Singham, *The Hero and the Crowd*, 188.

11. Simon Rottenberg, "Labour Relations in an Underdeveloped Economy," *Caribbean Quarterly* 4, no. 1 (1955): 56.

12. Singham, *The Hero and the Crowd*, 307. For a critique of this type of socio-psychological characterization of Caribbean societies, see Anthony Maingot, "National Identity, Instrumental Identifications and the Caribbean's Culture of 'Play,'" *Identity: An International Journal of Theory and Research* 2, no. 2 (2002): 115–24.

13. Singham, *The Hero and the Crowd*, 253, 330.

14. Ibid., 315.

15. Interview published in *Bohemia*, August 19, 1977; reprinted in Maurice Bishop, *Maurice Bishop Speaks* (New York: Pathfinder Press, 1983), 22.

16. See Anthony Maingot, *The United States and the Caribbean: Challenges of an Asymmetrical Relationship* (London: Macmillan; Boulder, Colo.: Westview, 1994), 133.

17. See George Odlum's long explanation of how this would—or should—unfold in D. Sinclair Da Breo, *Of Men and Politics: The Agony of St. Lucia* (Castries: Commonwealth Publishers International, 1981), 173–98.

18. Institute of International Relations, *Independence for Grenada: Myth or Reality?* (St. Augustine: IIR, University of the West Indies, 1974), 32, 33.

19. Ibid., 75.

20. Ibid., 77.

21. See essay by Anthony Maingot in Institute of International Relations, *Independence for Grenada: Myth or Reality?* 37, 39.

22. W. Richard Jacobs, ed., *Butler versus the King: Riots and Sedition in 1937* (Port-of-Spain, Trinidad and Tobago: Key Publications, 1976), 11, 14, 26.

23. Bishop, *Maurice Bishop Speaks*, 19.

24. Sidney E. Cherwick, Chief of Mission, *The Commonwealth Caribbean: The Integration Experience*, World Bank report (Baltimore: Johns Hopkins University Press, 1978).

25. Bishop, *Maurice Bishop Speaks*, 144.

26. Speech of April 13, 1979 in Bishop, *Maurice Bishop Speaks*, 29.

27. Tony Thorndike, *Grenada: Politics, Economics, and Society* (London: Frances Pinter, 1985), 66–67.

28. Presentation of 1982 National Plan and Budget: Comrade Bernard Coard, March 9, 1982, in Coard, *To Construct from Morning* (St. Georges: Fedon, 1982), 17.

29. Ibid., 26.

30. Jay R. Mandle, *Big Revolution, Small Country: The Rise and Fall of the Grenada Revolution* (Lanham, Md.: North-South, 1985), 23, 29.

31. Thorndike, *Grenada*, 130.

32. Bishop, *Maurice Bishop Speaks*, 144.

33. See the prologue by Jorge Rodríguez Beruff in the very comprehensive study of this "militarization" by Humberto García Muñíz, *La estrategiade los EE.UU. y la militarizacion del Caribe* (Rio Piedras, Puerto Rico: Instituto de Estudios del Caribe, 1988); Alma H. Young and Dion E. Phillips, eds., *The Militarization of the Non-Hispanic Caribbean* (Boulder: Lynne Reiner, 1986).

34. See the summaries in Samuel E. Finer, *The Man on Horseback* (New York: 1962).

35. Alfred Vagts, *A History of Militarism, Civilian and Military* (London: Hollis and Carter, 1959), 14.

36. This is drawn from the following captured documents: Document no. 25 (February 19, 1981) from Nicaraguan General Humberto Ortega; Agreement on Cooperation between the NJM and the Communist Party of the Soviet Union, July 27, 1982; "List of Special Materiel to Be Delivered to Grenada from Soviet Union in 1980–1981 / free-of-charge" (October 27, 1980); List of Special Equipment to Be Delivered to the Army of Grenada from the Soviet Union in 1983–1985 (July 27, 1982); Protocol of the Military Collaboration between the Government of the Republic of Cuba and the People's Revolutionary Government of Grenada (signed by both parties but no date attached).

37. "Line of March for the Party" of September 13, 1982. This and all other "confidential" or "secret" documents of the PRG are found in Jiri Valenta and Herbert J. Ellison, eds., *Grenada and the Soviet/Cuban Policy* (Boulder, Colo.: Westview Press, 1986), 257–485.

38. Anthony Payne, Paul Sutton, and Anthony Thorndike, eds., *Grenada: Revolution and Invasion* (New York: St. Martin's Press, 1984), 108.

39. "Line of March for the Party" of September 13, 1982.

40. See W. Richard Jacobs and Ian Jacobs, *Grenada: The Route to Revolution* (Habana: Cuadernos Casa, 1980). The Jacobs brothers were leaning on the then-popular Soviet theory of noncapitalist development.

41. See the criticism of this approach in Steve Clark, "The Second Assassination of Maurice Bishop," *New International: A Magazine of Marxist Politics and Theory*, no. 6 (1987): 1–98, 37–40.

42. Charles W. Mills, *Radical Theory, Caribbean Reality: Race, Class, and Social Domination* (Mona, Jamaica: University of the West Indies Press, 2010).

43. Tony Thorndike includes an extensive bibliography in his book *Grenada: Politics, Economics, and Society*. For an American Marxist interpretation with a good bibliography, see Clark, "Second Assassination."

44. "Extraordinary Meeting of the Central Committee of the NJM" (September 15, 1983), in Valenta and Ellison, eds., *Grenada and the Soviet/Cuban Policy*, 325–27.

45. Ibid., 480

46. In fact, these students were the safest people on the island, since the new leadership had given strict orders to keep them safe. Richard A. Gabriel did the most detailed study of Operation Urgent Fury and concluded that even with an American advantage of 10 to 1, "almost all the operations were a failure." Richard A. Gabriel, *Military Incompetence* (New York: Noonday Press, 1985), 161.

47. Brizan, *Grenada: Island of Conflict*, 350

48. Jeffrey M. Elliot and Mervyn M. Dymally, *Fidel Castro: Nothing Can Stop the Course of History* (New York: Pathfinder Press, 1986), 146, 152.

49. Ibid., 153, 157.

50. Valenta and Ellison, *Grenada and the Soviet/Cuban Policy*, 69.

51. Armando Choy, Gustavo Chui, Moisés Sío Wong, *Our History Is Still Being Written* (New York: Pathfinder Press, 2005), 97.

52. Luís Báez, *Desclasificado: Secretos de Generales* (La Habana: Editorial SI-MAR, 1996), 443. Interviews with twenty-eight Cuban generals.

53. In Jamaica, public opinion was divided by political party loyalties: Seaga's JLP supporters were 76 percent in favor, Manley's PNP, 38 percent, and the Communist Party (Workers Party of Jamaica), 0 percent. Among those unaffiliated, the support was 58 percent for and 24 percent against. See Carl Stone Poll, *Weekly Gleaner*, November 7, 1983, 23. In Trinidad the invasion was supported by 63 percent, while 56 percent felt that Trinidad should have joined the Caribbean forces. *Express,* November 6, 1983, 1.

54. Much of this was first published in Anthony Maingot, *Sunday Gleaner*, January 20, 1985, 25–26.

55. Tony Buxo was the person who photographed Bernard Coard's meeting with Trevor Munroe of Jamaica, Teelucksingh of Guyana, and Michael Alsop of Trinidad just before the tragic events of October 19, 1983. These photos were used as evidence of a conspiracy in the trial of Bishop's murderers.

56. Beverly Steele, "Social Stratification in Grenada," in Institute of International Relations, *Independence for Grenada: Myth or Reality?* (St. Augustine, Trinidad: IRR, 1974), 17.

57. See Harold Alfred Bierck, *The U.S. and Latin America, 1933–1968* (New York: Macmillan, 1969), 62. The vote was bought by the United States with the promise to build an airport.

58. See the account in Janet Higbie, *Eugenia, the Caribbean's Iron Lady* (London: Macmillan, 1993), 209–14; and in Irving W. Andre and Gabriel J. Christian, *In Search of Eden: Dominica, the Travails of a Caribbean Mini-State* (Roseau: Pond Casse Press, 1992).

Chapter 10. Transcending Race: Self-Interest and Self-Determination in the Non-Independent Territories

1. Kwame Nkrumah, *Ghana* (New York: Thomas Nelson and Sons, 1957), 162–63.

2. Luís Muñoz Marín, "A Development through Democracy," *Annals of the American Academy of Political and Social Science* 285 (January 1953): 1–8. Emphasis added.

3. Rupert Emerson, *From Empire to Nation* (Boston: Beacon Press, 1960), 83.

4. Gert Oostindie and Inge Klinkers, *Decolonizing the Caribbean: Dutch Policies in Comparative Perspective* (Amsterdam: Amsterdam University Press, 2003), 10.

5. Juan R. Torruella, *Global Intrigues* (San Juan: Editorial de la Universidad de Puerto Rico, 1987), 165.

6. See Humberto García Muñiz, *La estrategia de Estados Unidos y la militarización del Caribe* (Río Piedras: Instituto de Estudios del Caribe, 1988); Jorge Rodríguez Beruff, *Strategy as Politics: Puerto Rico on the Eve of the Second World War* (San Juan: La Editorial, Universidad de Puerto Rico, 2007).

7. The term and the general argument come from Robert O. Keohane, *After Hegemony: Cooperation and Discord in the World Political Economy* (Princeton, N.J.: Princeton University Press, 1984).

8. See UN Decolonization Committee Resolution on Puerto Rico (18 June 2012) at http://overseasreview.bloggspot.com/2013/06/un-decolonization_comm.

9. This capacity to use ethnicity strategically is evident wherever Caribbean people settle. See the analysis of Cuban and Haitian maneuvers for advancement in Miami in Anthony Maingot, "Relative Power and Strategic Ethnicity in Miami," in Ronald J. Samuda and Sandra L. Woods, eds., *Perspectives on Immigrant Education* (New York: University Press of America, 1983).

10. Ivar Oxaal, *Race and Revolutionary Consciousness* (Cambridge, Mass.: Schenkman, 1971), 40.

11. The best collection of photographs of this Curaçao uprising is contained in Edward A. de Jongh, *30 di mei, 1969, e día de mas histórico* (Curaçao: VAD, 1970).

12. The Official Commission of Inquiry report was published under the title *De Meidagen van Curaçao* (Willemstad: Algemeen Culturele Maanblad, 1970).

13. René Antonio Romer, "Un pueblo na Kaminda," PhD diss., Department of Sociology, University of Leiden, June 1977, 170–80.

14. The Official Commission of Inquiry, *De Meidagen*, 187.

15. Original statement in Paul Sutton, "Political Aspects," in Colin Clarke and Anthony Payne, eds., *Politics, Security, and Development in Small States* (London: Allen and Unwin, 1987); retraction in Paul Sutton, introduction to Peter Clegg and Emilio Pantojas-García, eds., *Governance in the Non-Independent Caribbean* (Kingston, Jamaica: Ian Randle, 2009), xxiii.

16. Sutton, introduction, xli.

17. *Financial Times*, December 8, 2005, 2.

18. Oostindie and Klinkers, *Decolonizing the Caribbean*, 10.

19. Ibid., 166.

20. Edward Dew, *The Difficult Flowering of Surinam: Ethnicity and Politics in a Plural Society* (the Hague: Nijhoff, 1978), 12. Dew reported on the several studies done on language use in Suriname and found that among Creoles, Dutch was the most used language at home, while the Sranan Tonga dialect is the language of the marketplace.

21. Albert L. Gastmann, *The Politics of Suriname and the Netherlands Antilles* (Rio Piedras: Institute of Caribbean Studies, 1968), 138.

22. Oostindie and Klinkers, *Decolonizing the Caribbean*, 114.

23. Ibid.

24. During intense seven days of research in Aruba, I was introduced to the various

intricate schemes to smuggle cigarettes (from Paraguay) as well as computers and coffee. Field research, May 9–16, 2000.

25. Gabriel Zucman, *La richesse cachée des nations. Enquête sur les paradis fiscaux* (Paris: Editions du Senil, 2013), 32, 91.

26. The story is drawn from *El País* for our purposes.

27. *El País*, January 22, 2014, 1.

28. *El País*, January 23, 2014, editorial.

29. *New York Times*, January 23, 2014, 10.

30. See articles by Lucy Komisar, "OECD Tax Havens Deal Falls Short, Critics Say" at http://thekomisarscoop.com (May 12, 2009); Scott Wilson, "Obama Details Plans to Shutter Tax Havens," *Washington Post*, May 4, 2009, 1.

31. *New York Times*, June 6, 2014, 1, 8.

32. Zucman, *La richesse cachée des nations*, 50–51.

33. Ronen Palan, *The Offshore World* (Ithaca, N.Y.: Cornell University Press, 2003), 44.

34. R. Thomas Naylor, *Wages of Crime: Black Markets, Illegal Finance, and the Underworld Economy*, rev. ed. (New York: Cornell University Press, 2004).

35. Alan A. Block and Constance A. Weaver, *All Is Clouded by Desire: Global Banking, Money Laundering, and International Organized Crime* (Westport, Conn.: Praeger, 2004).

36. L. H. Moreno Jr., *Panamá: una vocación de servicio* (Panamá: Banco Nacional de Panamá, 1991).

37. See more on this in Anthony Maingot, "Offshore Banking in the Caribbean: The Panamanian Case," in Elizabeth Joyce and Carlos Malamud, eds., *Latin America and the Multinational Drug Trade* (Basingstoke, UK: Macmillan, 1998), 149–71.

38. International Monetary Fund, "Offshore Financial Centers: Background Paper," (June 23, 2000).

39. Palan, *The Offshore World*, 44.

40. See Marcelo Justo's story at http://www.bbc.co.uk/mundo/noticias/2014/09/140923.

41. This study was summarized in Great Britain's *Guardian*, April 3, 4, 2013.

42. Edwards Report, "Financial Regulation in the Crown Dependencies," London, 1998; KPMG Report, "Financial Regulations in the Overseas Territories," London, July 2000.

43. Michael Bradley, Attorney General, Cayman Islands, September 1986 (Gilmore, 1990), 383.

44. Overseas Territories Review, Walter Brown, "Bermuda: We Are Not a Tax Haven" at http://overseasreview.blogspot.com/2013/07/bermuda (July 1, 2013).

45. See Helen Hintjens, "France in the Caribbean," in Paul Sutton, ed., *Europe and the Caribbean* (London: Macmillan Education, 1991), 53.

46. Cited in Anthony Maingot, *The United States and the Caribbean* (London: Macmillan, 1994), 175.

47. "U.S. Treasury Seeks Caribbean Help to Curtail Offshore Tax Evasion," at http://www.Caribbean360.com/index (November 12, 2012).

Chapter 11. Barbados: Tradition and Modernity in a Model Small State

1. Mia Mottley at http://www.caribbean360.com/index (December 22, 2013).

2. Owen Arthur cited at http://www.caribbean360.com/news/devaluation-of-barbados-dollar.

3. Carl Howell at http://www.jamaicagleaner.com/gleaner/20140609.

4. See the comments of Clyde Mascoll at http://www.caribbean360.com/business/barbados.

5. Sir Roy Trotman, "BWU: Few Joys," at http://www.nationnews.com/articles (January 2, 2014).

6. For more on this style of governance, see Patrick Gomes, "Social Partnerships and New Modes of Governance: The Barbados Experience," in *CARICOM Perspectives* 2, no. 69 (July 2000): 68–70.

7. Governor of the Central Bank of Barbados, Dr. DeLisle Worrell, predicted that there would be a 2 percent rise in 2015 and 2.5 percent in 2016. Cited at http://www.caribbean-council.org/barbados-bank-governor.

8. Terrence Farrell, "Denting Bajan Pride," at http://www.trinidadexpress.com (January 5, 2014).

9. Richard Ligon, *True and Exact History of the Island of Barbados* (London, 1657), 71, 162–63.

10. Otis P. Starkey, *The Economic Geography of Barbados: A Study of the Relationship Between Environmental Variation and Economic Development* (New York: Columbia University Press, 1939), 201.

11. Ibid., v, vi.

12. Mintz, "The Caribbean as a Socio-Cultural Area," 912–37.

13. Further on this in Anthony Maingot and Wilfredo Lozano, *The United States and the Caribbean* (New York: Routledge, 2005), 89–17.

14. See Michael W. Collier, *Political Corruption in the Caribbean Basin* (New York: Routledge, 2005), 91.

15. There is no need to engage here in any extended discussion of what we mean by culture. It is sufficient to accept two of the eleven characteristics cited by Clyde Kluckhon in his *Mirror of Man*: (1) the total "way of life" of a people, a result of (2) "the legacy" the individual acquires from his or her group; in other words, the inherited and internalized customs of a people.

16. See Lowell Joseph Ragatz, *Fall of the Planter Class in the British Caribbean, 1763–1833* (New York: Century Co., 1928). For an indication of how rich and plentiful the research on the topic had been up to 1931, see Lowell Joseph Ragatz, *A Guide for the Study of British Caribbean History, 1763–1834 Including the Abolitionist and Emancipation Movements* (Washington, D.C.: Government Printing Office, 1932).

17. W. Arthur Lewis, "Economic Development with Unlimited Supplies of Labour," *Manchester School* 28, no. 2 (1954).

18. W. Arthur Lewis, *Industrialization of the British West Indies* (Port-of-Spain, Trinidad and Tobago: Caribbean Commission, 1950).

19. Lloyd Best, "An Outline Model of Pure Plantation Economy," *Social and Economic Studies* 17, no. 3 (October 1968), 283–326.

20. Lloyd Best, "On the Teaching of Economics," presented to Secondary School Teachers, October 1973. Reprinted in the *Trinidad and Tobago Review*, April 18, 2005.

21. M. Eugene Sirmans, *Colonial South Carolina: A Political History, 1663–1763* (Chapel Hill: University of North Carolina Press, 1966).

22. See Richard B. Goddard, *George Washington: Visit to Barbados, 1751* (Wildey, Barbados: Cole Printery, 1997).

23. Hilary McD. Beckles, *Great House Rules* (Kingston, Jamaica: Ian Randle, 2004), 58. Beckles was recently knighted, and as Sir Hilary he is now a widely praised principal of the Cave Hill campus of the University of the West Indies.

24. National Commission of Sustainable Development, *The Barbados Sustainable Development Policy* (Bridgetown: Ministry of Housing, Lands and the Environment, January 2004), 19.

25. Beckles, *Great House Rules*, 59.

26. World Bank, *A Time to Choose: Caribbean Development in the 21st Century*. Report no. 31725-LAC (April 7, 2005), 36.

27. Niall Ferguson is correct in emphasizing the role of the insalubrious climate in the mortality rate in the Caribbean. He is wrong to include Barbados in that generalization. As the case of the Washington brothers cited above illustrates, Barbados was famous for its healing winds and lack of mosquitoes. Ferguson's assertion that it took "an immigration of 150,000 to produce a population of 20,000" on the island ignores the role of migration to the Carolinas. See Niall Ferguson, *Empire: The Rise and Demise of the British World Order and the Lesson for Global Power* (New York: Basic Books, 2002), 77.

28. David McCullough, *The Path between the Seas* (New York: Simon and Schuster, 1977), 579.

29. Cited in Matthew Parker, *Panama Fever* (New York: Doubleday, 2007), 469.

30. Ferguson, *Empire*, xxiv.

31. Letter, *Weekly Gleaner*, January 28, 1957. Cited in David Lowenthal, "The West Indies Chooses a Capital," *Geographic Review* 40 (July 1958): 358n47.

32. Gordon K. Lewis, *The Growth of the Modern West Indies* (New York: Monthly Review Press, 1968), 226, 227.

33. Anthony Trollope, *The West Indies and the Spanish Main* (London, 1859), 203, 208.

34. James Anthony Froude, *The English in the West Indies, the Bow of Ulysses* (New York: Charles Scribner's Sons, 1897), 101, 36.

35. Note the introduction to a book by two Barbadians, one white and the other black: "With its perfect climate (70–85°F year-round), stable government, beautiful

beaches, landscape and architectural heritage, is it not the most livable country in the world?" Warren Alleyne and Henry Fraser, *The Barbados-Carolina Connection* (Oxford: Macmillan Education, 1988), 69.

36. P. L. Fermor, *The Traveller's Tree: A Journey through the Caribbean Islands* (New York: Harper, 1950), 140.

37. On this case of "portraits" and "self-portraits," see David Lowenthal, "The West Indies Chooses a Capital," *Geographic Review* 40 (July 1958): 358n47.

38. Ibid., 354.

39. Hilary McD. Beckles, *A History of Barbados* (Cambridge: Cambridge University Press, 1990), 210.

40. Linden Lewis, "The Contestation of Race in Barbadian Society and the Camouflage of Conservatism," in Brian Meeks and Folke Lindahl, ed., *New Caribbean Thought: A Reader* (Mona: University of the West Indies Press, 2001), 144–45.

41. Michael Howard, *Dependence and Development in Barbados, 1945–1985* (Bridgetown: Carib Research and Publications, 1989), 6–7, 135.

42. Edward Shils, "Intellectuals, Tradition, and the Traditions of Intellectuals: Some Preliminary Considerations," *Daedalus* 101 (Spring 1972): 21–34.

43. Shils, "Tradition," in A. R. Desai, ed., *Essays on Modernization of Underdeveloped Societies,* 2 vols. (Atlantic Highland, N.J.: Humanities Press, 1976), 1:16., 38.

44. See Robert A. Nisbet, "On Authority," in his *The Sociological Tradition* (New York: Basic Books, 1966), 107–73.

45. V. S. Naipaul, *The Mimic Men* (London: Andre Deutsch, 1967). Predictably, Naipaul skipped Barbados in his now famous tour which established so many stereotypes about the Caribbean. See *The Middle Passage* (London: Andre Deutsch, 1962).

46. Alleyne and Fraser, *The Barbados-Carolina Connection,* 68–69.

47. Cited in Jean S. Holder, *The Right Excellent Errol Walton Barrow* (Barbados: Panagraphix, 2007), 56. In *The Life and Times of Errol Barrow*, Peter Morgan claims that Barrow often traced the island's independence to 1651 when its General Assembly, in protest against the Navigation Laws, issued a Declaration of Independence.

48. G. E. Cumper, ed., *The Economy of the West Indies* (Kingston, Jamaica: ISER, 1960), 19.

49. M. G. Smith, *The Plural Society in the British West Indies* (Berkeley: University of California Press, 1965), 195.

50. Singham, *The Hero and the Crowd,* 306, 323, 97–98.

51. This section is fully developed in Anthony Maingot, *The United States and the Caribbean: Challenges of an Asymmetrical Relationship* (London: Macmillan, 1994).

52. George Beckford, *Persistent Poverty* (Oxford: Oxford University Press, 1972).

53. Courtney N. Blackman, *The Practice of Persuasion* (Bridgetown: CEDAR Press, 1982), 173.

54. Holder, *The Right Excellent Errol Walton Barrow,* 20.

55. On these two geopolitical realities, see Anthony P. Maingot, "The Difficult Road to Socialism in the English-Speaking Caribbean," in Richard R. Fagen, ed., *Capital-*

ism and the State in U.S. Latin American Relations (Stanford: Stanford University Press, 1979), 254–89.

56. See DeLisle Worrell, *Small Island Economies: Structure and Performance in the English-Speaking Caribbean since 1970* (New York: Praeger, 1987), 139.

57. See Errol Barrow and J. E. Greene, *Small Business in Barbados: A Case of Survival* (Cave Hill, Barbados: ISER, 1979), 69.

58. Cited in Hilary McD. Beckles, *Corporate Power in Barbados: The Mutual Affair* (Bridgetown: Lighthouse Communications, 1989), 12. Beckles, one of the major leaders of the protest, presents his version in a very plausible and convincing way.

59. Selwyn Ryan and Lou Anne Barclay, eds., *Sharks and Sardines: Blacks in Business in Trinidad and Tobago* (St. Augustine, Trinidad: ISER, 1992), 199.

60. Henderson Carter, *Business in Bim* (Kingston, Jamaica: Ian Randle, 2008), 211. *Bim* is a localism for Barbados.

61. As evident in the *2007 Annual Report of the Fair Trading Commission*.

62. See *Protocol Five of the Social Partnership, 2005–2007* (Bridgetown: Government Printing Department, n.d.), 6. Interviews with two members of the present commission convinced me that the protocols did little more than formalize a social contract that already existed on the island. Interviews, Barbados, August 10–20, 2008.

63. Ministry of Economic Affairs and Development, *Barbados Economic and Social Report* (Bridgetown: Government Printing Department, May 2007), 45.

Chapter 12. Cuba, the Last Holdout: "Organic" Intellectuals Defend the Revolution by Abandoning Marxist-Leninism

1. Eduardo Galeano, cited in *El País* (Madrid), May 5, 2014. Galeano explained: "No sería capaz de leerlo de nuevo. Caería desmayado. . . . Para mí, esa prosa de la izquierda tradicional es aburridísima. Mi físico no aguantaría. Seria ingresado al hospital. . . . Ni Obama ni Chávez entenderían el texto."

2. See Howard Hunt, major CIA agent and advisor to the Nixon administration: "Assassinate Castro *before* or coincident with the [Bay of Pigs] invasion (a task for Cuban patriots)." *Give Us This Day: The Inside Story of the CIA and the Bay of Pigs Invasion . . . by One of Its Key Organizers* (New Rochelle: Arlington House, 1973), 38.

3. Frank Tannenbaum, "A Castro no pueden salvarlo ya ni los Estados Unidos," *Bohemia Libre*, November 19, 1961, 30–31.

4. Don Bohning, *The Castro Obsession* (Washington D.C.: Potomac Books, 2005).

5. Fulbright quoted in the *New York Times*, March 26, 1964.

6. J. William Fulbright, *The Arrogance of Power* (New York: Random House, 1966).

7. Mikhail Gorbachev, *Perestroika: New Thinking for Our Country and the World* (New York: Harper and Row, 1987), 188. Francis Fukuyama had anticipated Gorbachev's moves by two years. See Francis Fukuyama, *Moscow's Post-Brezhnev Reassessment of the Third World* (Santa Monica, Calif.: RAND, 1986).

8. It is the exception among guerrilla movements in Latin America—viz. the Colom-

bian FARC and the Peruvian Sendero Luminoso, which did not receive direct support from the Fidel Castro regime.

9. Eric Hobsbawn, *The Age of Extremes* (New York: Pantheon Books, 1994), 437, 438, 440.

10. Ibid., 440.

11. Cuban Research Institute, Cuban polls (Miami: Florida International University, 1991, 1997, 2004, 2011, 2014).

12. Letter appeared on May 19, 2014, Bloomberg News and the Associated Press. It can be accessed at http://www.as-coa.org/articles/open-letter-president-obama-support-civil-society-cuba.

13. Gary Clyde Hufbaner and Barbara Kotschwar, *Economic Normalization with Cuba: A Roadmap for U.S. Policymakers* (Washington, D.C.: Peterson Institute for International Economics, 2014).

14. See *El País* at http://internacional.elpaís.com/internacional/2014/06/29.

15. See the editorial in the *Miami Herald* opposing any further changes in U.S.-Cuban policy, May 23, 2014.

16. An excellent source for the study of not just the institutional changes but the attempts at changing the "style" of Cuban political culture is Richard R. Fagen, *The Transformation of Political Culture in Cuba* (Stanford, Calif.: Stanford University Press, 1969).

17. Carmelo Mesa-Lago, *Are Economic Reforms Propelling Cuba to the Market?* (Miami: North-South Center, 1994), 71.

18. The Havana Consulting Group at http://thehavanaconsultinggroup.com/index.php?option.

19. Cf. José Rivero Muñiz, *El primer Partido Socialista Cubano* (Santa Clara: Universidad Central de Las Villas, 1962).

20. Carlos Baliño, who in 1925 was instrumental in founding the Cuban Communist Party, resigned from *Agrupación Socialista de la Habana* in 1909 because of that group's pro-Spanish worker stance. Cf. *Pensamiento revolucionario cubano* (La Habana, 1971), 279–81.

21. Hugh Thomas, *Cuba* (New York: Harper and Row, 1971), 577.

22. Cf. "Mella y la Unión Soviética," in Raquel Tibol, *Julio Antonio Mella en El Machete* (México: Fondo de Cultural Popular 1968), 76–96.

23. Robert Alexander, *Communism in Latin America* (New Jersey: Rutgers University Press, 1957), 36–41.

24. Victor Alba, *Politics and the Labor Movement in Latin America* (Stanford: Stanford University Press, 1968), 290.

25. Alexander, *Communism*, 276.

26. Quoted in Thomas, *Cuba*, 712–13.

27. David Forgacs and Geoffrey Nowell-Smith, ed., *Antonio Gramsci: Selections from Cultural Writings* (Cambridge, Mass: Harvard University Press, 1985), 14.

28. Quintin Hoare and Geoffrey Nowell Smith, eds., *Selections from the Prison Notebooks* of *Antonio Gramsci* (London: Lawrence and Wishart, 1971), 8. Karl Mannheim called those who defended the status quo "ideologues" and those who strived to change

it to "utopians." See Karl Mannheim, *Ideology and Utopia* (New York:, Harcourt, Brace, 1936).

29. See Peter M. Haas, "Epistemic Communities and International Policy Coordination," *International Organization* 46, no. 1 (1992): 1–36.

30. Benjamin L. Whorf, "The Relation of Habitual Thought and Behavior to Language," in Leslie Spier, A. Irving Hallowell, and Stanley S. Newman, eds., *Language, Culture, and Personality* (Menasha, Wisc.: Sapir Memorial Publication Fund, 1941), 75–93.

31. See Edward Sapir, "Communication," *Encyclopedia of the Social Sciences* (New York: Macmillan, 1931), 4:78–81.

32. See the speech printed in the *Miami Herald*, January 3, 1989, 1, 12.

33. Cited in Mesa-Lago, *Are Economic Reforms Propelling Cuba to the Market?* 65.

34. See Mauricio Giuliano, *El caso CEA: Intelectuales e Inquisidores en Cuba* (Miami: Ediciones Universal, 1998); Alberto F. Alvarez García y Gerardo González Nuñez, *¿Intelectuales vs. Revolución?* (Montreal: Ediciones Arte, 2001).

35. Alfredo Muñoz-Usain poses this question but also asserts that "fermenta el panel intelectual de la isla." See "Debate cultural en la Habana," *Contrapunto de América Latina*, no. 9 (July–September 2007): 102–6.

36. Che Guevara's ideas won this debate with the support of Fidel Castro. See Bertram Silverman, ed., *Man and Socialism in Cuba: The Great Debate* (New York: Athenaeum, 1971); Roberto M. Bernardo, *The Theory of Moral Incentives in Cuba* (Tuscaloosa: University of Alabama Press, 1971).

37. Juan Triana Cordoví and Ricardo Torres Pérez, "Políticas para el crecimiento económico: Cuba ante una nueva era" (Washington, D.C.: Brookings Institution, October 2013), 23.

38. Carmelo Mesa-Lago and Jorge Pérez-López, *Cuba's Aborted Reform* (Gainesville: University Press of Florida, 2005), 61, 164.

39. Ibid., 164–67.

40. Rafael Hernández, "On Hearing the Right Questions," *Revista*, Spring–Summer 2005, 16–17.

41. Haroldo Dilla, "El fin del bloqueo, la fiesta por la Victoria y la política en Cuba: notas para un debate," in Alejandra Liriano de la Cruz, ed., *Cuba en el Caribe en el Post-Embargo* (Santo Domingo, República Dominicana: FLACSO, 2005), 226–27.

42. Tania García in Liriano, *Cuba en el Caribe en el Post-Embargo*, 231.

43. See the discussion in Paul Ransome, *Antonio Gramsci: A New Introduction* (Hertfordshire: Harvester Wheatsheaf, 1992), 198ff.

44. Pavel Vidal Alejandro and Omar Everleny Pérez Villanueva, *La Reforma Monetaria en Cuba hasta el 2016: Entre gradualidad y "Big Bang"* (Habana: Centro para el Estudio de la Economía Cubana, September 26, 2013).

45. Interview with Dr. Luís Suárez Salazar of the Instituto Superior de Relaciones Internacionales, Universidad de la Habana, Miami, June 2, 2014.

46. Lic. Oscar Espinoza Chepe, "Situación económica, política y social de Cuba," Ponencia, XXI Conferencia de la Asociación Para el Estudio de la Economía Cubana, Miami, August 2011, 2.

47. The concept was first developed by Lyford Edwards in *The Natural History of Revolution* (1927) and became central in Crane Brinton's *The Anatomy of Revolution* (1936).

48. Jean-François Fogel and Bertrand Rosenthál, *Fin de siglo en la Habana: Los secretos del derrumbe de Fidel* (Bogotá: Tercer Mundo Editores, 1994), 264.

49. On the role of new militaries in nation-building, see Morris Janowitz, *The Military in the Political Development of New Nations* (Chicago: University of Chicago Press, 1964) and Samuel Huntington, *Political Order in Changing Societies* (New Haven: Yale University Press, 1968), 205–21.

50. Mary-Alice Waters, ed., *Making History: Interviews with Four Generals of Cuba's Revolutionary Armed Forces* (New York: Pathfinder Press, 1999), 48.

51. Hal Klepak, *Cuba's Military, 1990–2005: Revolutionary Soldiers during Counter-Revolutionary Times* (New York: Palgrave Macmillan, 2005), 52–57.

52. Ibid., 63.

53. Samuel Huntington, "The Political Modernization of Traditional Monarchies," in Special Issue on Tradition and Change, *Daedalus* (Summer 1966): 774.

54. Klepak, *Cuba's Military*, 278.

55. Brian Latell, *After Fidel* (New York: Palgrave Macmillan, 2005), 21. Latell was for some twenty-five years the CIA's top analyst on Cuba.

56. Klepak, *Cuba's Military*, 80–86.

57. See Harold Lasswell, *The Comparative Study of Elites* (Stanford: Stanford University Press, 1954), 6.

58. Instituto de Relaciones Europeo-Latinoamericano, "Cuba despues del V Congreso del PCC," Madrid, November 5, 1997.

59. Edward Shils, "Political Development in New States," Unpublished Ms.1959, cited in Gabriel A. Almond and James S. Coleman, ed., *The Politics of the Developing Areas* (Princeton, N.J.: Princeton University Press, 1960), 53.

60. Edward González and David Ronfeldt, *Cuba Adrift in a Post-Communist World* (Santa Monica, Calif.: RAND, 1992), 81.

61. See Julie M. Feinsilver, "La diplomacia médica cubana," *Foreign Affairs en Español*, October–December 2006; Pedro Margolles, "La cooperación cubana presente en 155 países," *Digital Granma Internacional*, (May 22, 2007).

62. William M. LeoGrande and Peter Kornbluh, *Back Channel to Cuba* (Chapel Hill: University of North Carolina Press, 2014), 127–28.

63. Hillary Rodham Clinton, *Hard Choices* (New York: Simon and Schuster, 2014), 258.

64. Ibid., 265.

65. This section draws heavily from Anthony Maingot, *Miami: A Cultural and Literary History* (Oxford: Signal Books, 2013), 228, 229, 231.

66. See Richard Feinberg, *Soft Landing in Cuba? Emerging Entrepreneurs and Middle Classes* (Washington, D.C.: Brookings Institution, November 2013).

67. Maria de los Angeles Torres, *In the Land of Mirrors: Cuban Exile Politics in the United States* (Ann Arbor: University of Michigan Press, 2001).

Conclusion. Confronting the Perilous Threats of Organized Crime and Energy Dependence

1. In February 2014, thirty-four years after the incident, Guyana established an international commission of inquiry into Walter Rodney's death. Rodney's party, the Working People's Alliance, showed no enthusiasm for the inquiry. See stories in *Stabroek News*, February 25 through June 6, 2014.

2. As of 2014, eleven of the twenty-two countries that recognize Taiwan are in the Greater Caribbean: Dominican Republic, Haiti, El Salvador, Guatemala, Honduras, Nicaragua, Panama, Belize, St. Kitts-Nevis, St. Lucia, and St. Vincent and the Grenadines. In Latin America, only Paraguay has kept relations with Taiwan.

3. See Anthony Maingot, "Challenges of the Corruption-Violence Link," in Ivelaw Griffith, ed., *Caribbean Security in the Age of Terror* (Kingston, Jamaica: Ian Randle, 2004), 129–53.

4. Minister Gary Griffith, June 9, 2014, at http://www.trinidadexpress.com/internal.

5. See Anthony Maingot, "The Decentralization Imperative in Caribbean Criminal Enterprises," in Tom Farer, ed., *Transnational Criminal Enterprises in the Americas* (New York: Routledge, 1999), 143–70.

6. Vaughan A. Lewis, "The Eastern Caribbean States: Fledgling Sovereignties in the Global Environment," in Jorge I. Domínguez, Robert A. Pastor, and R. Delisle Worrell, eds., *Democracy in the Caribbean—Political, Economic, and Social Perspectives* (Baltimore: Johns Hopkins University Press, 1993), 113.

7. Tom Farer, "Collectively Defending Democracy in the Western Hemisphere," in Farer, ed., *Beyond Sovereignty*, 5.

8. Jorge I. Domínguez, "Cuba in the International Community in the 1990s: Sovereignty, Human Rights and Democracy," in Farer, *Beyond Sovereignty*, 297.

9. The most detailed account of the drug running through Cuba and the CIA's penetration of those involved is Jean-François Fogel and Bertrand Rosenthal, *Fin de Siglo en la Habana: Los Secretos del derrumbe de Fidel* (Bogotá: TM Editores, 1994), 25–66.

10. Moisés Naím, *Illicit* (New York: Doubleday, 2005), 13.

11. See, for instance, Stephen D. Krasner, *Sovereignty: Organized Hypocrisy* (Princeton, N.J.: Princeton University Press, 1999); and Maryann Cusimano Love, ed., *Beyond Sovereignty: Issues for a Global Agenda* (Boston: Wadsworth/Cengage Learning, 2011).

12. See Anthony Maingot, "Responses to Venezuelan Petro-Politics in the Greater Caribbean," in Anthony Maingot and Ralph S. Clem, eds., *Venezuela's Petro-Diplomacy* (Gainesville: University Press of Florida, 2011), 102–15.

13. See statement to Parliament by the Most Hon. P. J. Patterson, July 13, 2005, at www.jis.gov.jm/special_sections/CARICOM.

14. See, for instance, Norman Girvan, "Alba, Petro-Caribe, and CARICOM: Issues in a New Dynamic," in Ralph S. Clem and Anthony Maingot, eds., *Venezuela's Foreign Policy: The Role of Petro-Diplomacy* (Gainesville: University Press of Florida, 2011).

15. On this point, see Anthony Maingot, "The Difficult Road to Socialism in the Eng-

lish-Speaking Caribbean," in Richard R. Fagen, ed., *Capitalism and the State in U.S.-Latin American Relations* (Stanford: Stanford University Press, 1979), 254–89, and "Political Processes in the Caribbean, 1970s to 2000," in Bridget Brereton, ed., *UNESCO General History of the Caribbean* (London: Macmillan, 2004), 5:312–45.

16. In January 2008, I noticed that even in racially homogeneous Argentina, the "oligarchy" was described as "*los blancos*."

17. See Heinz Dieterich, "*Derrota estratégica en Venezuela: peligro mortal para Bolivia y Cuba*," December 3, 2007, at http://www.aporea.org/tiburón.

18. Further on Dieterich, see "Entrevista a Heinz Dieterich," *Diario La Tercera* (Santiago, Chile, March 29, 2007; Pedro Páramo, "Chávez y el Padre del Socialismo del Siglo XXI," *Contrapunto* (Madrid), January–March 2008, 23–25.

19. See the announcement of this appointment at http://www.eluniversal.com/economia/140704.

20. Matthew Louis Bishop, "Slaying the 'Westmonster' in the Caribbean? Constitutional Reform in St. Vincent and the Grenadines," *British Journal of Politics* 13, no. 3 (August 2011): 420–37.

Index

Page numbers in *italics* indicate illustrations. Page numbers in **bold** indicate tables.

Ferguson, Niall, 256, 337n27

Fermor, P. L., 257–58

Fermoselle, Rafael, 92

Fernández, Leonel, 33

Fernández Méndez, Eugenio, 57

Financial Action Task Force on Money Laundering (FATF), 244

Fisk University, 171

Fixing Haiti (Fatton), 101

FNDC. *See* National Front for Change and Democracy

Food stamps, 79–80

Foreign Account Tax Compliance Act (FATCA), 243, 245

Forged from the Love of Liberty (Williams), 30–31

Francisco (Suárez Romero), 130

Franco, Franklyn, 95

Franco, Jean, 126

Franco, José Luciano, 91

French West Indies, 228–29

Frente Obrero i Liberashion, 229

Friedrich, Carl, 65

From Columbus to Castro: The History of the Caribbean (Williams), 13, 18–21

From Dessalines to Duvalier (Nicholls), 102

Froude, James Anthony, 257

Fulbright, J. William, 269–70

Fund for Social Analysis, 73

Gairy, Eric, 205–7, 213, 215, 220–22

Galeano, Eduardo, 268

Gambler's fallacy, 269, 288

García Muñiz, Humberto, 165

Garvey, Marcus, 52, 184

Gastmann, Albert L., 234

Geggus, David P., 98

La Generación del 40, 57–58, 60, 65, 68, 70, 78

Geyer, Georgie Anne, 61, 179

Glissant, Edouard, 137–38

Globalization and Its Discontents (Stieglitz), 282

GNP. *See* Grenada National Party

Gonsalves, Ralph, 303

Gorbachev, Mikhail, 269–70, 278

Goveia, Elsa V., 17–18

Gramsci, Antonio, 273, 276–78, 282

Gran Colombian War of Liberation, 82–84

Great Britain: Barbados and, 35, 251, 255–57, 261, 303; democracy in, 192; democratic socialism of, 185; non-independent territories of, 226, 228, 239–42; Padmore and, 172, 176–77

Greene, J. E., 264

Grenada: airport in, 155, 209–12, 217–19, 224; Bishop and, *148*, 155, 202, 207, 209–24, 229; Coard and, 180, 202, 208–9, 211, 214–17, 222, 333n55; Cuba and, 209–13, 217–19, 224; elections in, 219–24; Marxism in, 203, 207–8, 214–16, 223–24, 293; Marxism-Leninism in, 181, 203, 215–16, 224; militarism in, 213–16, 220–21, 224; NJM in, 207–11, 214–15, 218–21, 223–24; PRG in, 208, 211, 213–17, 219–21, 223; Revolution, 2, 77, 153–54, 181, 207, 263; Singham's study of, 204–7; size of, 204–6; socialism failing in, 207–11, 214, 221; St. David's parish in, 220–23; U.S. and, 209–13, 216–20, **219**, 224; USSR and, 213; WPJ and, 202

Grenada: The Jewel Despoiled (Lewis, G.), 77

Grenada National Party (GNP), 209, 220–21

Grenada United Labour Party (GULP), 209, 220–23

Grenadian Voice, 215

Grimshaw, Anna, 159, 165

Griñan Peralta, Leonardo, 91

Groot, José Manuel, 48–49

Gual, Pedro, 88–89

Guerra, Ramiro, 44

Guevara, Che, 21, 61, 180, 272, 279

GULP. *See* Grenada United Labour Party

Guyana, 2, 218–19, 293, 343n1; political system in, 190–92, 200; slavery in, 43–44

Haiti: agriculture in, 102–6, **107**; Aristide in, 99–100, 104, 114–20, 141; Bolívar and, 82–86, 88–89; class conflict in, 140–41; Colombia and, 89; contemporary studies on, 98–99; Dominican Republic and, 94–96, 132–35; earthquake in, 99–102; elections in, 107–8, 141; foreign intervention in, 99–104, 106, 108–9, 113, 118–20; ideology triumphing over experience in, 120; Manigat in, 26–27, 107–13; military of, 108–13, 116–18; myths about, 99, 106, 113, 118; neoliberalism in, 101, 104; as pariah, 91–92; plantation societies theory and, 139–40; political system of, 106–20; race and, 81–97, 102, 131–32, **132**, 140–41; slavery and, 61–62, 81–83, 93–95, 98–99; structural problems of, 104–6, **107**; Tannenbaum on, 105; as terrifying, 81–97; urban migration in, 105–6, **107**; U.S. and, 93–94, 99–101, 113, 118–20, 140; Venezuela and, 82–86, 89; Voodoo in, 99, 109; Williams and, 103

Professor emeritus of sociology at Florida International University, Anthony Maingot is past president of the Caribbean Studies Association. He is co-author of *A Short History of the West Indies*, now in its fourth edition, and author of *The United States and the Caribbean: Challenges of an Asymmetrical Relationship* and *Miami: A Cultural History*.